The
EAGLE
and the
TRIDENT

The

EAGLE

and the

TRIDENT

*U.S.-Ukraine Relations
in Turbulent Times*

STEVEN PIFER

BROOKINGS INSTITUTION PRESS
Washington, D.C.

The Brookings Institution is a private nonprofit organization devoted to research, education, and publication on important issues of domestic and foreign policy. Its principal purpose is to bring the highest quality independent
research and analysis to bear on current and emerging policy problems. In-
terpretations or conclusions in Brookings publications should be understood
to be solely those of the authors.

Library of Congress Cataloging-in-Publication data are available.
ISBN 978-0-8157-3040-8 (cloth : alk. paper)
ISBN 978-0-8157-3062-0 (ebook)

9 8 7 6 5 4 3 2 1

Typeset in Sabon

Composition by Westchester Publishing Services

Contents

Introduction

The collapse of the Soviet Union was a seminal event in the late twentieth century. While hardly the great catastrophe bemoaned by Vladimir Putin—certainly not in the eyes of subject peoples who gained the opportunity to shape their own nations and destinies—it dramatically altered the geopolitical landscape of Europe and Asia. Fifteen states emerged from the territory that mapmakers formerly called the Soviet Union.

The collapse was especially remarkable in two aspects. First, the rapidity of the end. In the mid-1980s, the Soviet Union stood as one of two global superpowers. Approaching the fifth decade of the Cold War, it challenged the United States and the West politically, militarily, economically, and ideologically. By the end of 1991, it had ceased to exist. Second, the relatively quiet nature of the collapse. While some bloodshed occurred, mainly as long-suppressed ethnic tensions broke out, the end was far more peaceful than might have been expected. For the most part, Soviet structures simply evaporated.

The collapse saw Ukraine regain its independence from Russia as well as from the Soviet Union. Ukraine had been a part of the Russian Empire or Soviet Union since Ukraine's Cossack leaders signed the

1

Treaty of Pereyaslav in 1654, except for a brief period from 1918 to 1921, roughly between the collapse of Czarist Russia after the October Revolution in 1917 and the formal founding of the Union of Soviet Socialist Republics in late 1922. Ukrainians and Russians both claimed Kyivan Rus'—the state that from 882 to 1240 A.D. occupied much of present-day Ukraine—as central to their historical, religious, and cultural heritage.

Official Washington was slow to recognize the coming collapse and showed a significant degree of ambivalence about the Soviet Union's demise. However, it became clear to all in December 1991 that the Soviet Union and its leader, President Mikhail Gorbachev, had no future. The U.S. government then moved swiftly to establish relations with each of the twelve New Independent States, in addition to the Baltic nations of Lithuania, Latvia, and Estonia, whose incorporation into the Soviet Union the United States had never diplomatically accepted and whose independence Moscow had recognized the previous September.

Of the new states, Ukraine was bound to receive a great deal of attention—indeed, the most attention after Russia. With nearly 52 million people in 1991, it was the second most populous post-Soviet republic. The largest country entirely within borders of the European continent, it lay just to the east of the nations of Central Europe. Now freed of the Warsaw Pact, those states would soon begin to press to join the European Union and the North Atlantic Treaty Organization (NATO), which would mean that Ukraine would find itself bordering two key European institutions as well as share a lengthy border with Russia. How Ukraine developed would have a big impact on the U.S. goal, dating back to the George H. W. Bush administration, of building a Europe whole, free, and at peace. How Ukraine developed was also bound to have an impact on how Russia evolved in the post–Cold War and post-Soviet world.

Ukraine seemed well placed to prosper as an independent state and become one of the early post-Soviet success stories. It had a highly educated and talented workforce. Economically, it contained agricultural land with immense productive potential, including some 30 percent of the world's black earth—rich and productive agricultural land (whereas the black earth is a foot deep in Iowa, it is three to four feet deep in Ukraine). The country also had a good portion of the Soviet Union's industrial base, particularly in the high-tech, heavy-metal, aerospace, electronics, and chemical sectors. Many analysts saw interesting prospects for mutually beneficial trade and investment. Proximity to Central Europe was seen as an advantage, to the extent that reforms already moving forward in countries such as Poland might serve both as a model and as encouragement for Ukraine to set a reform path of its own.

These factors plus the existence at the end of 1991 of nearly 2,000 strategic nuclear weapons—warheads atop intercontinental ballistic missiles and warheads for air-launched cruise missiles—on its territory meant that Ukraine was bound to figure significantly in U.S. foreign and security policy calculations.

This book does not try to capture all that has happened in Ukraine since it regained its independence. That is a long and complex story. This book focuses instead on the U.S.-Ukraine relationship from 1991 to the end of 2004. Much of my career as a foreign service officer during those years dealt with Ukraine: as a deputy coordinator in the Office of the New Independent States at the Department of State from 1993 to 1994; director then senior director and special assistant to the president in the Directorate for Russia, Ukraine, and Eurasian Affairs at the National Security Council from 1995 to 1997; U.S. ambassador to Ukraine from 1998 to 2000; and deputy assistant secretary of state responsible for Russia and Ukraine from 2001 to 2004. With the generous assistance of the Department of State, the National Security Council, and the Clinton Presidential Library, I was able to draw on my contemporaneous notes and records from much of that period in writing this book. I should note that the content, opinions, and characterizations in this book are my own and do not necessarily represent official positions of the U.S. government.

After my retirement from government service in late 2004, I found what other American diplomats who have served in Kyiv have found: Ukraine gets in one's blood. I continued to follow developments there, first with the Center for Strategic & International Studies and, beginning in 2008, at the Brookings Institution. I have had the opportunity to visit Ukraine regularly, to engage with senior Ukrainian officials, and to consult on U.S. policy toward Ukraine with officials at the State Department, the Pentagon, and the White House. While I have tried to stay informed about what is happening in Ukraine and in U.S.-Ukraine relations, I have not had the front-row seat on U.S. policymaking that I enjoyed when in government. Hence my decision to focus on the period 1991–2004. The reader needs to be forewarned: there is a rather dramatic difference between chapters 1–6 and chapter 7. The latter describes the key developments in U.S.-Ukraine relations from 2005 to 2016 but offers much less detail than the chapters covering the previous thirteen years.

This book is not intended to be a memoir. It is a diplomatic history. Much can be learned from Washington's experience in those thirteen years about how and why U.S. policies toward Ukraine succeeded, how and why they failed, and how the United States might do better in advancing its primary objective with Ukraine. That objective has stayed remarkably consistent for the past twenty-five years: to see the country develop as a stable, independent, democratic state, with a growing market economy and increasing links to the West. That is the kind of Ukraine that is best compatible with broader American interests.

Some lessons from the early years can be applied to U.S. and Western policy toward Ukraine today, as the country struggles to cope with two daunting challenges. The first has been with Ukraine since the beginning: adopting real reforms to build a modern European state. While its difficult Russian neighbor regularly posed problems for Kyiv after 1991, the second challenge only emerged in such stark terms in 2014: dealing with armed Russian aggression in Crimea and the Donbas region in eastern Ukraine. Kyiv has to solve both of these challenges in order to succeed. If it makes genuine reforms that solidify democratic institutions and get the economy growing on a sustainable path, but conflict continues in the Donbas, that is not success. Likewise, if Kyiv reaches a genuine settlement of the conflict in eastern Ukraine and finds a way to address Crimea with Moscow, but reforms fail and the economy falls apart, that also is not success.

The first six chapters of this book describe the history of U.S.-Ukraine relations from 1991 through the end of 2004. For much of that period, the bilateral relationship was strong, seen in both capitals as contributing to their foreign policy objectives. The relationship found itself in more difficult straits in other years.

Chapter 1 briefly addresses Washington's ambivalent approach over the course of 1991 toward the Soviet Union's demise. It also describes the first steps in establishing a bilateral U.S.-Ukraine relationship as the sides set about defining an agenda for engagement in the busy and uncertain early days of Ukraine's regained independence.

Chapter 2 delves in detail into the issue that dominated the first three years of the relationship between Washington and Kyiv: what to do about the strategic nuclear weapons left in Ukraine when the Soviet Union collapsed. No goal figured higher on the U.S. agenda for Ukraine than ensuring the elimination of those weapons—and it no doubt often seemed to many in Kyiv to be the United States' only goal.

Chapter 3 covers 1995 to 1997, when the two countries filled out a broader relationship. Among other things, they declared a strategic partnership and launched a special binational commission co-chaired by Vice President Al Gore and President Leonid Kuchma. U.S. assistance to Ukraine began to grow as the two countries discussed ways to increase trade and investment. Washington encouraged the establishment of a "distinctive" NATO-Ukraine relationship in order to deepen Kyiv's links to the West and help ensure that it not be consigned to a gray zone of insecurity between institutional Europe and Russia.

Chapter 4 covers 1998 to 2000, my time in Kyiv. The relationship made progress, particularly in aligning the countries' approaches on nonproliferation. But it also began to encounter difficulties. The limits of the United States' ability to encourage and affect economic and political reforms became more apparent, and concern arose in Washington that something had begun to go awry in Ukraine's development as a democratic state. Still, the start of 2000 brought a brief burst of optimism that Kyiv might finally get things right on economic reform.

Chapter 5 addresses the years 2001 to 2004, when bilateral relations entered a particularly difficult stretch. Doubts grew about Kyiv's commitment to real democracy, and Kuchma's approval of an arms sale to Iraq badly shook Washington's confidence in the Ukrainian leadership. Meanwhile, the sides proved unable to find solutions to a growing number of irritating problems that burdened the bilateral agenda. Only Kuchma's readiness to dispatch troops to join the Iraqi stabilization coalition prevented a near-total breakdown.

Chapter 6 looks at the second half of 2004, the run-up to the presidential election, and the Orange Revolution. It describes the U.S. effort to encourage a democratic election process and, when that failed, to help secure a peaceful outcome to the ensuing political crisis.

At the end of each of the first six chapters is a section entitled "Reflections"—my thoughts on how U.S.-Ukraine relations developed in those years, written with the benefit of time and the opportunity to look back.

Chapter 7 briefly recaps how U.S.-Ukraine relations developed from 2005 through 2016, and chapter 8 sums up key lessons learned and offers recommendations for how U.S. policy might today more effectively advance the American vision for a modern Ukraine.

In the coming pages I argue that, broadly speaking, Washington succeeded in mobilizing the right carrots—and sometimes sticks—to achieve its goals with regard to Ukraine's foreign and security policies. For example, Kyiv agreed in 1994 to transfer the nuclear warheads on its territory to Russia for elimination, destroy the strategic missiles, missile silos, and bombers that it had inherited from the Soviet military, and accede to the 1968 Nonproliferation Treaty as a non-nuclear weapons state.

U.S. policy proved less successful, however, in encouraging Ukraine to adopt the difficult political, economic, and anticorruption reforms needed for it to become a modern European state. The lack of success was not for lack of effort. Promoting reform was high on the agenda when the president and other senior officials engaged their Ukrainian counterparts. It was a top priority for the U.S. embassy in Kyiv, which hosted a large U.S. Agency for International Development mission to oversee American efforts to promote reform. Washington devoted substantial resources—indeed billions of dollars—to the task. In the late 1990s, for example, the United States provided Ukraine $225 million per year in FREEDOM (Freedom for Russia and Emerging Eurasian Democracies and Open Markets) Support Act funds, as well as assistance funds from other accounts, such as those of the Department of Defense and Department of Energy, for a total of $300 million to $350 million per year. Ukraine also received assistance and low-interest credits from the international financial institutions, the European Union, and individual Western states. But the reform push often encountered resistance, which hindered achievement of the American vision for Ukraine.

One obstacle to comprehensive reform was the leadership in Kyiv, which often seemed not to share the vision or lacked the will and ability to move in the direction of realizing it. As ambassador, I regularly hosted dinners at the residence structured around a theme. One evening in mid-1998 the theme was Ukraine's national security. We had a good turnout, including officials from the ministries of foreign affairs and defense and the National Security and Defense Council, two parliamentary deputies, and representatives from Kyiv's fledgling think tank community. Partway through the dinner, I asked, "What today is the greatest single threat to Ukraine's national security?" After a pause, a voice at the end of the table replied "Ukrainians." That prompted a round of laughter, which evolved into a serious and insightful discussion. The upshot was that my Ukrainian guests saw their country's biggest national security challenge as the inability of the leadership and political elites to agree on a strategic objective, develop a sound plan to achieve that objective, and then take the necessary steps to implement that plan. Implementation, in particular, was often the major problem.

I think about that discussion when considering the biggest reason why, in 2014, when Ukraine faced the threat of Russia's military aggression, it was such a frail, fragile, and vulnerable state: weak leadership, starting at the presidential level. The weak leadership included those who eschewed pursuing needed economic reforms because they feared the political consequences of the economic dislocation that might result. It included presidents who got bogged down in political battles with the parliament or fights with their own prime minister. And it included those—the epitome of which was Viktor Yanukovych—who placed greed, corruption, and personal political power above the country's national interest. The culture of political corruption that permeates the country has posed one of the biggest obstacles to Ukraine's successful development.

These failures of leadership had real and dramatic consequences. In 1990, the year before the Soviet Union's end, gross domestic product per capita in Poland and in what was then the Ukrainian Soviet Socialist Republic were roughly equal. By 2013, however, gross domestic product per capita in Poland was three times larger than that in Ukraine. That change reflected the fact that Polish leaders had made the tough choices on reform and anticorruption measures and sustained political support for implementing those choices, while Ukraine's leaders all too often fell short. The gap only widened after 2013.

Part of the failure to achieve more dramatic reform rests with the American side. We did not fully grasp the dynamics within Ukraine and the motivations behind those resisting change, particularly those who saw the development of a modern Ukrainian state as posing a threat to their personal economic and political interests. We could have done a better job of trying to understand. That might have led to different, and perhaps more successful, strategies to advance U.S. reform objectives. The U.S. government might also have mobilized its resources earlier to assist reform efforts in Ukraine; significant reform assistance programs only began in 1994.

Americans and Ukrainians often talked past one another. This was not a big surprise, since their political cultures are so different. Ukraine emerged from the wreckage of the Soviet system. The American approach tended to be businesslike: identify the problem, fix on a solution, and implement. That direct approach was not always destined to be the most successful in Kyiv. Diplomatic subtlety also sometimes confused the issue. Ukrainian officials at times were too willing to say yes to American requests, doing so when they had no plan for getting to yes or perhaps no intention of following through. Their attitude made for a good meeting, with smiles and handshakes all around, but it also led to inevitable frustration down the road when agreements seemed to have been forgotten or ignored.

Finally, the Ukrainian elite seemed to overestimate Ukraine's geopolitical value between the West and Russia and assumed that Western support would continue—regardless of what Kyiv did or did not do—out of fear that the Ukrainians might otherwise turn back to Moscow.

Many of these problems continue to dog the bilateral relationship today. A different approach might increase the prospects for a successful American policy, and for the successful Ukraine that that policy aims to support. The final chapter outlines such an approach.

CHAPTER 1

Establishing Relations

On the evening of December 1, 1991, Larry Napper, one of the State Department's foremost Soviet experts and destined to be the last director of its Office of Soviet Union Affairs, walked the streets of Kyiv. He had accompanied Assistant Secretary of State for European affairs Thomas M. T. Niles to observe the independence referendum that the Ukrainians had held earlier that day. The results of the vote streamed in, and they sent a resounding message. In the end, with a large turnout, more than 90 percent of the voters had opted for an independent state. Independence won even in Crimea, garnering 54 percent of the vote in the only part of Ukraine where ethnic Russians constituted a majority of the population. As Napper tracked the incoming vote tally and watched the reaction of Ukrainians in the capital, he quietly admired their inspirational act of self-determination and thought to himself: "It's clear; the jig is up for the Soviet Union." Washington now had to prepare urgently for the final collapse of its Cold War rival and the emergence of the New Independent States, including Ukraine. And, after that happened, the U.S. government needed to get about the business of establishing a relationship with the new nation.

Ukraine's Long and Complex History

At its height in the early eleventh century, Kyivan Rus' was the largest state in Europe. It entered a period of decline and fragmentation in the latter part of that century, culminating in collapse after the Mongol invasion. The Golden Horde sacked Kyiv in 1240. The city would not become a major population, political, and commercial center again until the 1800s.

Parts of present-day Ukraine fell under the dominion of various other entities in the centuries after 1240: the Grand Duchy of Lithuania, the Polish-Lithuanian Commonwealth, the Ottoman Empire, Muscovy, the Crimean Khanate, Poland, the Russian Empire, the Austro-Hungarian Empire.[1] As a result, the western regions of what is present-day Ukraine were affected by the political, religious, and cultural influences that swept across Central Europe; what is now eastern Ukraine was not similarly affected. This history produced a country of regional differences. Ethnic Ukrainians and Russians constitute the largest groups today, but Crimean Tatars, Belarusians, Bulgarians, Hungarians, Jews, Poles, and Romanians also make up sizable parts of the population. The Cossacks created a Hetmanate in what is now central Ukraine in 1648, which enjoyed a brief period of independence but did not develop the institutions of a contemporary state. Following the 1654 Treaty of Pereyaslav, much of modern Ukraine became part of the Russian Empire, while parts of western Ukraine found themselves in the Polish-Lithuanian Commonwealth, then the Austro-Hungarian Empire, and later again Poland. Crimea and the south remained a part of the Crimean Khanate until conquered by the Russian Empire in the late eighteenth century. The bulk of Ukraine would remain a piece of the Russian Empire or the Soviet Union from 1654 until 1991, with the exception of the brief period from 1918 to 1921 in the chaotic aftermath of World War I and the Bolshevik Revolution.[2]

The twentieth century was not kind to Ukraine or its people. World War I and the Russian civil war between the Reds and the Whites were followed by the Great Famine under Joseph Stalin—Ukrainians called it the Holodomor (killing by starvation)—in which millions died. And few parts of the Soviet Union suffered more during World War II than the Ukrainian Soviet Socialist Republic, which lost some 15 percent of its population.[3]

One of the remarkable things about Ukraine is that the national identity stayed alive for so long—hundreds of years—absent a physical nation-state. As noted, for much of the time after the Golden Horde's sacking of Kyiv, Ukraine was a part of the Russian Empire, which further solidified the intertwined historical, religious, and cultural links between Ukrainians and Russians, links that dated back to when both claimed the Kyivan Rus' as their starting point. Those historical ties affected the views of both the Ukrainians and the Russians. Russians came to think of Ukraine as an integral part of their country, often referring to Ukrainians as "little Russians." Indeed, when Russian president Vladimir Putin visited Kyiv in 2013 to mark the 1,025th anniversary of the Kyivan Rus's acceptance of Christianity, he pointedly said that Ukrainians and Russians were all one people. Putin's comment, like the term "little Russians," infuriated Ukrainian nationalists, who liked to point out that it was a grand prince of Kyiv who founded Moscow in 1147.[4]

Views in Ukraine were more diverse. Those in the western part of the country tended to look toward Europe. The west was where Ukrainian nationalism was strongest, and those holding the memory of the Holodomor often continued to regard Moscow as an adversary. In eastern Ukraine, where a higher proportion of the population was ethnic Russian—though Crimea is the only part of modern Ukraine in which ethnic Russians constitute a majority—the population had a more positive view of Russia and of Russians, and they tended to see their identity linked more closely to Russia. Language reflected Ukraine's mix: Ukrainian was more common in the west, while Russian—the language of the Soviet Union—was heard more frequently in the east and south. The number of those who regarded Russian as their first language far exceeded the number of ethnic Russians, but most people in Ukraine, if they could not speak both languages, had a basic understanding of the other language. As will be seen, however, regional, linguistic, and ethnic differences were swamped by the scale of the vote in favor of independence in 1991.

In the early 1990s, many saw Ukraine as divided into two parts: the west and center was one region, the east and south (including Crimea) the other. This division was based partially on language, though most Ukrainians were practical when it came to bridging language differences; it was not uncommon to hear two people in conversation on the street in which one spoke Russian and the other responded in Ukrainian. The perceived east-west difference also reflected the fact that the bulk of ethnic Russians, some 17 percent of the population in 1991, resided in the east and south. The east-west divide has some value for understanding Ukraine, but it is a useful prism only up to a point. In the years after 1991 the line between east and west began to blur; for example, political parties based in the east began to make some inroads in the west and center in the 2000s, and vice versa. Although residents of the eastern areas such as Donetsk and Luhansk wanted good relations with Russia, polls in April 2014 showed that a large portion of the population in the east wished to remain part of Ukraine.

An Empire Collapses

In the run-up to its quiet end, the Soviet Union underwent dramatic changes during Mikhail Gorbachev's time in the Kremlin. Perestroyka and glasnost—restructuring and openness—were his watchwords when he became general secretary of the Communist Party of the Soviet Union in 1985. They foreshadowed his willingness to allow greater political space and a degree of democracy and autonomy internally. The external changes in Soviet policy from 1985 to early 1991 were even more striking: conclusion of a treaty banning all U.S. and Soviet land-based intermediate-range missiles; withdrawal of Soviet troops from Afghanistan; acceptance of German unification and agreement to withdraw Soviet forces from the former German Democratic Republic; allowance of greater latitude for Warsaw Pact countries to determine their own political course, including no longer insisting on a leading role for the communist parties in those states; and then the dissolution of the Warsaw Pact itself.

Gorbachev did not intend to bring down the Soviet Union, but the forces he unleashed did so. In the Caucasus, the dispute between Armenia and Azerbaijan over Nagorno-Karabakh weakened Moscow's hold. The strongest push for independence arose in the three Baltic states—Estonia, Latvia, and Lithuania—whose incorporation into the Soviet Union had never been recognized by the United States. As the Baltic states pushed for greater sovereignty and ultimate independence, so did other Soviet republics. That included Ukraine, where Volody-myr Shcherbytskiy, head of the Ukrainian Communist Party and a conservative opponent of Gorbachev's reforms, had resigned in 1989. The democracy movement, including the pro-independence Rukh Party, won an impressive 25 percent of the vote in the March 1990 election for the Verkhovna Rada (the Supreme Council of the Ukrainian Soviet Socialist Republic, which would become Ukraine's parliament; it is also referred to simply as the Rada). On July 16, 1990, the Rada adopted a declaration of state sovereignty, one month after a similar declaration had been approved by the Congress of People's Deputies of the Russian Soviet Federative Socialist Republic, under the chairmanship of Boris Yeltsin. Among other things, the Rada's declaration asserted the primacy of Ukraine's laws over those of the Soviet Union.

If anything, most of Washington was slow to pick up on the strength of the centrifugal forces gaining momentum within the Soviet Union. In the spring of 1991, however, debate began within the U.S. government on the future of the Soviet Union and the appropriate policy. Views differed in interagency discussions. It was not clear at the White House that the Soviet Union was on the verge of collapse, and it leaned toward supporting Gorbachev. President George H. W. Bush valued personal relationships with foreign leaders and had developed a close and pro-ductive relationship with Gorbachev, including on issues important to Bush, such as German reunification and reducing strategic nuclear arms. The White House view was also shaped by the unfavorable impression that Yeltsin had left in a September 1989 visit to Washing-ton. There was little enthusiasm among those closest to Bush for en-couraging the secession train. The Pentagon, in contrast, saw geostra-tegic advantages in the weakening of the Soviet center and a shift of power to the republics. Defense Department officials, including Secre-tary of Defense Dick Cheney, believed Gorbachev's authority was ebb-ing, favored engaging Yeltsin, and regarded an independent Ukraine as a positive development, one that could serve as a check on Russian power. Some even seemed open to the idea of a nuclear-armed Ukraine, the better to serve as a block on possible Russian ambitions. A breakup of the Soviet Union, moreover, could push any conventional military threat 600 miles back from NATO territory. Secretary of State James Baker and his team recognized that change was under way but worried that a Soviet collapse could follow the violent course of the Yugoslavia breakup and lead to a much messier situation; the fate of thousands of Soviet nuclear weapons was high among their concerns.[5]

The U.S. government had eyes on the ground in Kyiv. Foreign service officers Jon Gundersen and John Stepanchuk (from the State Department) and Mary Kruger (from the U.S. Information Agency) arrived in the Ukrainian capital in February 1991 to establish a consulate general. Earlier attempts to open a consulate there had been derailed, first in 1979 by the Soviet invasion of Afghanistan, and then in 1986 by the explosion at the Chornobyl nuclear power plant, just sixty miles north of Kyiv. The three arrived with a mandate to report on developments and gently encourage democracy and market economy reforms but to do nothing that would be seen as encouraging Ukrainian independence. Their reporting, however, reflected the growing popular sentiment for independence and for Ukraine's reestablishing itself as a sovereign state free of the Soviet Union. Since the consulate had no classified communications ability, Gundersen and Stepanchuk made regular trips to Moscow, where they could draft and send classified reporting at the embassy. They found the embassy skeptical about developments in Ukraine and what they might portend for the future of the Soviet Union, but they continued to believe the political trend in Ukraine was very clear. As questions regarding the Soviet Union's future grew, the consulate managed a stream of visits by congressional delegations and former senior officials, including Richard Nixon, Henry Kissinger, and Zbigniew Brzezinski.

At the State Department, Napper saw two possible policy courses. The U.S. government could conclude that Gorbachev was finished—either because he would ultimately turn out to be at heart committed to the Soviet system, or because he would be overthrown by Soviet hardliners—and turn the focus of American attention to Yeltsin and leaders of the other republics. (In Ukraine, that would be Leonid Kravchuk, then chairman, or speaker, of the Rada.) Alternatively, Washington could stick with Gorbachev and the Soviet Union while engaging the republics—with the exception of the Baltic states, which were a separate issue—in other ways, for example, by establishing consulates. By the summer, many within the U.S. government had come around to the idea of some level of engagement with the republics. The United

States' ability to shape events within the Soviet Union was limited, however. The prevailing wisdom recognized that and argued for riding things out and seeing what would happen.

Bush paid his last visit to the Soviet Union at the end of July 1991. Following a two-day stop in Moscow, he traveled to Kyiv on August 1. Hundreds of thousands lined the streets of the president's motorcade route, giving him an enthusiastic welcome. Bush met briefly at Mariinskyy Palace with Kravchuk (as Rada speaker, he was the nominal head of state of the Ukrainian Soviet Socialist Republic). Kravchuk had been born in 1934 in a Polish town that became part of Ukraine after World War II. He joined the Communist Party at an early age and rose as an apparatchik through the ranks, ultimately becoming a member of the Politburo and ideology secretary. Smart, and with good political instincts, he had a sense that things were changing, particularly after the July 1990 declaration of state sovereignty. He adapted accordingly. In the first part of 1991, he sought to be seen as the leader of a new, if not necessarily independent, Ukraine. At the same time, he showed caution, eschewing any anti-Russian lines in public.

Kravchuk told Bush that he was proceeding on the basis of Ukraine's declaration of state sovereignty, cited the difficult economic issues that Ukraine faced, and welcomed the establishment of a U.S. consulate in Kyiv. He indicated his desire to press for greater autonomy though did not raise independence. Acting prime minister Vitold Fokin asked for most-favored-nation trading status. He also sought investment, including in the privatization of Ukraine's industries. Bush said he saw a new opening for relations between the United States and Ukraine, though he added that Washington would "deal officially with the center [Moscow]." But he expected more direct dealings with Ukraine and other republics, as would be allowed by the union treaty that the Soviet republics were in the process of working out.[6] Moscow, which had become increasingly nervous about political developments in Ukraine and had tried, unsuccessfully, to persuade the White House to drop the Kyiv visit, sent Soviet vice president Gennadiy Yanayev to take part in the meeting. Consulate head Gundersen was tasked to pull Yanayev away for a few minutes so that Bush and Kravchuk could have a private word.

Following his meeting with Kravchuk, Bush stuck with a cautious approach in his speech to the Rada, reflecting White House concern that a sudden or violent breakup of the Soviet Union could adversely affect U.S. interests, in particular the security of Soviet nuclear weapons. Nearly one-quarter of the seats were empty, though Kravchuk told the president that it was a relatively large gathering for the body. While expressing support for "the struggle in this great country for democracy and economic reform," Bush dismissed as a "false choice" having to pick between "supporting President Gorbachev and supporting independence-minded leaders throughout the USSR." He warned, "Americans will not support those who seek independence in order to replace a far-off tyranny with a local despotism. They will not aid those who promote a suicidal nationalism based upon ethnic hatred."[7] His speech won polite applause in the Rada, but Ukrainian nationalists panned it, and William Safire in the *New York Times* dismissingly dubbed it the "chicken Kyiv" speech.

Less than three weeks later, on August 19, eight senior Soviet officials (including Yanayev), constituting a self-proclaimed State Committee for the State of Emergency, claimed to have assumed power after asserting that Gorbachev had taken ill in Crimea. The attempted coup lasted just four days, falling apart in almost comical fashion. Gorbachev returned to Moscow as Soviet president. But the failed coup triggered reverberations throughout the Soviet Union, weakening the center and Gorbachev's authority. On August 24, the Rada declared independence.[8]

Not yet fully convinced that Gorbachev's days were numbered, Washington waited for what would happen next. State Department officials saw Kyiv as central. If Ukraine indeed broke away, other republics would follow, and the Soviet Union would fall apart. If Ukraine stayed, the Soviet Union might have a chance to survive. The White House believed the U.S. government should not intervene in any overt way. Bush sought to carefully modulate his relationships with Gorbachev and Yeltsin, as the former's influence waned while the latter's was on the rise. Estonia, Lithuania, and Latvia were the exception. Bush quietly encouraged Gorbachev to recognize their independence. The Kremlin did so in September.

Kravchuk traveled to Washington on September 25. He told Bush at the White House that Ukraine had begun developing its own governmental institutions and expressed confidence that the public would endorse independence in a referendum set for December 1. He noted that Ukrainian structures had assumed authority as the Soviet Union was "virtually disintegrating." Ukraine intended to be a non-nuclear weapons state and wanted "direct, diplomatic relations" with the United States. Bush said America would "be on the side of democracy and reform of the economic system." On some issues, Washington had to deal with the center, "but not to the exclusion of the republics." Bush indicated that U.S. ambassador to the Soviet Union Robert Strauss would have responsibility for the consulate general in Kyiv. He welcomed Kravchuk's statement on nuclear weapons. He asked Kravchuk whether there had to be an economic union among the Soviet republics "with a center or not." Kravchuk dismissed the idea: "The center is incapable of doing anything."[9]

Washington watched as the Soviet government tried to work out an arrangement with the republics. The tea leaves became clearer over the course of the autumn. The consulate in Kyiv predicted a strong majority vote for independence.

The Ukrainian American community, which had organized to support the Rukh movement's call for independence, increased its push for diplomatic recognition of Ukraine in the fall. Three groups—Ukraine 2000, the Ukrainian National Association, and the Ukrainian National Information Service, assisted by the *Ukrainian Weekly* paper—mobilized letters and petitions from across the country targeted at building congressional interest in and support for Ukraine. Robert McConnell, a political consultant who had served in the Reagan administration, became Ukraine 2000's government relations committee chairman, drawing on his contacts in the executive branch and on Capitol Hill. The effort produced a draft congressional resolution calling on the administration to recognize Ukraine, with ninety House sponsors and nearly thirty from the Senate. Congress did not pass the resolution as a standalone measure, but it did pass it as an amendment to an appropriations bill in November.

The executive branch felt pressure as well. Bush met with a group of Ukrainian Americans at the White House on November 27, just four days before the Ukrainian referendum, and said the United States would "salute independence, and then we will start to take the steps leading to recognition." He noted that the U.S. government was engaged in a balancing act—every time he called Gorbachev, he placed a call to Yeltsin—and did not want to complicate things. With the referendum, the Ukrainian people will have spoken. "The only question now is how the Ukrainian people can peacefully get what they want."[10] (Although Bush adjusted his policy, the Ukrainian American community and other Central and Eastern European constituencies saw the president as clinging too long to Gorbachev and slow to accept the Soviet Union's demise. That would have political consequences for Bush in November 1992.)

The December 1 referendum asked voters whether they supported the August 24 declaration of independence adopted by the Rada. Coincident with the referendum, the voters would also choose among Kravchuk, whom the Rada had appointed acting president, and five other candidates for the presidency. All six made it clear that they favored independence. When Sherman Garnett and Thomas Graham from the Defense Department paid a visit to Kyiv in late November, they found broad support for independence, including among pensioners who hoped for a better economic future.

The State Department dispatched Niles and Napper to Kyiv to observe the referendum. At polling sites, they watched enthusiastic crowds voting yes. The overwhelming vote for independence—90 percent in favor, with turnout exceeding 80 percent of the electorate—surprised the consulate staff as well as many Ukrainians. A serious argument within the U.S. government for sticking with Gorbachev was no longer possible. On December 3, Bush placed a congratulatory call to Kravchuk, who had handily won the presidential election. The U.S. government, however, still held back from formal recognition. As Napper recalled, no one seemed especially enthusiastic about the turmoil that might be unleashed by "plunging a stake into the heart of the [Soviet] beast."

Kravchuk, Yeltsin, and Belarusian Supreme Soviet chairman Stanislav Shushkevich took care of that. The three met on December 7 and 8 at Belavezhskaya Pushcha in Belarus. The three announced the end of the Soviet Union as "a subject of international law" and the establishment of the Commonwealth of Independent States, an as-yet-undefined institution that would link the post-Soviet republics. U.S. officials began communicating with Ukrainian leaders and proposed key principles that would form a basis for recognition and the establishment of diplomatic relations, including democracy, respect for human rights, no use of force against political opponents, and market economy reforms.

Baker made a quick December 15–19 trip to Moscow, Kyiv, Minsk, and Central Asia. In meetings with Gorbachev, Yeltsin, and Kravchuk, Baker focused on the fate of the large Soviet nuclear arsenal, stressing that it should remain under a single authority and that the post-Soviet states other than Russia should be non-nuclear and accede to the 1968 Nonproliferation Treaty as non-nuclear weapons states. This approach tracked with Washington's decision to back Russia as the "continuation state" in legal terms, which meant, for example, that Russia would assume the Soviet Union's permanent seat on the UN Security Council. Baker also described a slightly amended set of principles that would serve as guidelines for U.S. recognition: "self-determination, respect for borders, support for democracy, safeguarding of human rights, and respect for international law."[11]

Meeting in Almaty, Kazakhstan, on December 21, leaders of eleven of the Soviet republics endorsed the establishment of the Commonwealth of Independent States. Four days later the Soviet Union formally ceased to exist. Yeltsin's military advisers took charge of the briefcase with the nuclear codes, and the hammer and sickle came down over the Kremlin, replaced immediately by the Russian tricolor. Later that day, on Christmas evening, Bush gave a short televised address to the American people. He announced recognition of Russia, Ukraine, and ten other now independent republics. He noted that Ukraine and several of the other republics had given the United States assurances of their commitment to responsible nuclear security policies and to democratic principles.

Relations Get Started

Baker turned to the Office of Soviet Union Affairs (about to be renamed the Office of Independent State and Commonwealth Affairs) with an urgent tasking. The secretary believed treating the post-Soviet republics as independent states required establishing embassies in each, and he wanted missions on the ground within ninety days. The State Department began assembling small teams of five to seven personnel, who were sent to the capitals of the post-Soviet states with a satellite radio and thin stacks of $100 bills (credit cards were useless where there were no real banks, and no one knew if Soviet rubles would have any value). The teams set up working areas in hotel rooms while searching for appropriate office space. U.S. military aircraft delivered pallets with startup kits, including office furniture, office equipment, and—given uncertainties about what awaited in some cities—meals-ready-to-eat and other emergency rations. If an unassigned foreign service officer spoke Russian, he or she could not be slotted into a new job unless Napper confirmed the officer was not needed in one of the new embassies.

The American presence in Kyiv had a head start, given the consulate team already on the ground. Things moved quickly. On January 23, 1992, Gundersen met with Foreign Minister Anatoliy Zlenko and conducted an exchange of diplomatic notes that formally established diplomatic relations. As acting head of what had now become an embassy, Gundersen became the chargé d'affaires. Shortly thereafter, the White House announced the president's nomination of Roman Popadiuk to serve as the first U.S. ambassador to Ukraine. A Ukrainian team arrived in Washington in February to set up its embassy. In April, Oleh Bilorus, Ukraine's first ambassador to the United States, took up his post.

Among other tasks, Gundersen and Bilorus set about finding permanent offices for their missions. Gundersen's team worked out of a small office in a run-down apartment building across the Dnipro River from downtown Kyiv until the Ukrainian government made available a former local Communist Party headquarters building located a short drive from the foreign ministry and downtown. An administrative team from Washington agreed to lease the building because it could comfortably accommodate between sixty and seventy-five American and Ukrainian employees, which the State Department envisaged as the maximum size of the official U.S. presence, an estimate that turned out to be wildly off the mark. Gundersen moved into his office, which still contained propaganda posters and multiple direct phone lines to party functionaries. One thing that had to go immediately: the large wall bust of Vladimir Lenin that dominated the building's meeting room, which would later house the embassy's political section (the bust ended up in the bar at the quarters of the embassy's Marine Security Guard detachment). The Ukrainians gave the Russians an identical former local party headquarters building for use as their embassy. But while the U.S. building was centrally located, the Russians found themselves much farther out, on the road to Zhulyany airport. Ukrainian diplomats in Washington spent a year in temporary facilities before relocating to what became their permanent embassy in Georgetown, near the Key Bridge. It was purchased largely with funds raised by the Ukrainian American community.

The single-minded American focus in the first years of U.S.-Ukraine relations centered on eliminating the nuclear weapons that were located on Ukrainian territory when the Soviet Union collapsed. At the beginning of 1992 almost 2,000 strategic nuclear warheads for intercontinental ballistic missiles and air-launched cruise missiles were in Ukraine, on top of the 2,500 tactical nuclear weapons that were already in the process of being withdrawn by Russia. Early on, Ukraine had stated its intention to denuclearize and become a nuclear-weapon-free state. Washington wanted to make that a reality as soon as possible. The nuclear weapons issue dominated Baker's mid-December 1991 stop in Kyiv as well as visits in early 1992 by Under Secretary of State for International Security Affairs Reginald Bartholomew.

Kyiv understood the importance of the nuclear arms question but had many more items on its wish list for the bilateral relationship—not surprisingly, since the Ukrainians were in the process of founding a state with a full foreign policy agenda. Facing a daunting set of reform needs, Ukrainian officials sought economic assistance and support at the International Monetary Fund and World Bank for low-interest credits. They wanted to expand trade and investment, so they asked for most-favored-nation trading status to increase export possibilities to the United States as well as for a program with the Overseas Private Investment Corporation (OPIC), which might encourage U.S. investment in Ukraine. Kyiv also wanted U.S. political support in general, which it viewed as an important counterweight to what the Ukrainians anticipated would be a difficult relationship with Russia.

Washington feared that crippling food shortages could lead to hunger and even political unrest in the post-Soviet states in early 1992. The Bush administration organized an international conference of donors to provide humanitarian and other assistance, pledged to provide $500 million, and put Pentagon veteran Richard Armitage in charge of the U.S. assistance program. As part of this effort, U.S. military aircraft flew food and medical supplies into Kyiv, generating a fair amount of positive local publicity.

Dennis Ross, director of the State Department's Policy Planning Staff, led a senior interagency team to Kyiv in April 1992. The delegation included Under Secretary of Defense for Policy Paul Wolfowitz and National Security Council senior director Ed Hewett (Hewett's Directorate for Soviet Affairs had become the Directorate for Russia and Eurasian Affairs; it would later be renamed again, this time the Directorate for Russia, Ukraine, and Eurasian Affairs). Whereas Bartholomew's visits focused on the disposition of nuclear weapons, the Ross team had a broad mandate to discuss the overall relationship. In meetings with Kravchuk and other senior officials, Ross and the others conveyed a message of U.S. interest in an independent Ukraine and said the United States was prepared to aid the country's development. They talked about how the bilateral relationship could grow, noting that it could proceed in a way that was not anti-Russia. They described certain principles for Ukraine's development, such as democratic norms, a strong civil society, a market economy, and good civil-military relations; and they encouraged the Ukrainians to move away from a statist model and undertake economic and political reform.

Kravchuk made an official working visit to Washington in early May, the first trip by the president of independent Ukraine to America. The timing was important, as Bush had received Yeltsin for a summit visit in early February, and the administration wanted to balance that with a meeting with Kravchuk. The Ukrainians sought, and Ukrainian American groups lobbied for, a state visit, which would have added some diplomatic bells and whistles, such as a state dinner at the White House. They did not get that, but Bush invited Kravchuk to Camp David. The Ukrainian president also met with Vice President Dan Quayle, Baker, and other Cabinet secretaries, as well as members of Congress and the business community. As expected, nuclear weapons dominated the discussions with executive branch officials. Baker, Kravchuk, and Zlenko discussed the terms for a protocol that would be signed shortly thereafter in Lisbon, in which the Soviet Union's commitments under the 1991 U.S.-Soviet Strategic Arms Reduction Treaty (START) would be undertaken by Russia, Ukraine, Belarus, and Kazakhstan.

Kravchuk spent considerable time discussing his concern about Russia and Russian readiness to accept Ukraine as an independent state. He singled out the status of Crimea, whose parliament had just declared independence from Ukraine, subject to a referendum to be held in the summer. Kravchuk called the referendum unconstitutional and accused Russia of stirring up problems, citing Russian vice president Aleksandr

Rutskoy as having made "aggressive statements" when visiting the Crimean Peninsula, where ethnic Russians—many of them retired military—constituted about 60 percent of the population. Bush asked about the status of the Black Sea Fleet, most of which was based in Crimea, including at its main port, Sevastopol. Kravchuk said Kyiv did not want the entire fleet, but Russian negotiators insisted that all the ships belonged to Russia. Kravchuk agreed with Bush on the importance of the United States staying engaged with Russia and said Ukraine also wanted relations with Russia, but "equal" relations.[12] Russian behavior regarding Crimea and the Black Sea Fleet clearly raised deep concern in Kyiv.

U.S. officials also raised the need for economic reform in order to attract trade and investment. Kravchuk and his team seemed uncertain about what types of reform to undertake, which left their American interlocutors uncertain about how hard they should push.

The two presidents issued a joint declaration, "U.S.-Ukrainian Relations and the Building of a Democratic Partnership." It noted the two countries' commitment to democratic values and advancing economic freedom. The declaration asserted U.S. readiness to use technical assistance programs "in areas like defense conversion and food distribution" to assist reform and recovery, and noted the conclusion of a trade agreement conferring most-favored-nation trading status. (Kyiv, however, remained subject to the Cold War–era Jackson-Vanik amendment to the Trade Act of 1974 and would have to wait until 2006 for Congress to grant it permanent most-favored-nation status.) The presidents stated that their two countries could work together to promote a more secure and democratic Europe, and would regularize a bilateral dialogue on such questions. The declaration attached priority to nonproliferation and reaffirmed Kyiv's previously stated decision to eliminate all nuclear weapons on its territory, with assistance from the United States. The presidents concluded by noting that "the United States and independent Ukraine have laid the foundation for a strong and special partnership."[13]

The joint declaration captured the nascent nature of the relationship less than four months after the formal establishment of diplomatic relations. It recorded Ukraine's specific commitment on denuclearization—the key issue for Washington—while laying out a framework for issues that could fill out the U.S.-Ukrainian agenda. The reference to U.S.

assistance in defense conversion and food distribution reflected the fact that Congress had just begun to consider legislation for broader assistance. The FREEDOM Support Act would not be enacted until October 1992. Likewise, the declaration noted the Conference on Security and Cooperation in Europe and the North Atlantic Cooperation Council as the multilateral venues for discussing questions of security and democracy in Europe. NATO had not yet begun to think seriously about how it would engage Central European countries, let alone former Soviet states.

In addition to the joint declaration and trade agreement, Kravchuk's visit produced other minor agreements that began to add some limited substance to the framework of the U.S.-Ukraine relationship. It was agreed that OPIC would open its programs for Ukraine and that the Peace Corps would begin sending volunteers. The sides also agreed on extending agricultural credits under guarantee by the Commodity Credit Corporation for use in purchasing American foodstuffs.

While the embassies in Washington and Kyiv went about the day-to-day business of bilateral relations, the Bush-Kravchuk summit in May was the last high-level engagement of 1992. Kravchuk faced a host of problems at home: the basic tasks of nation building and creating the institutions of an independent state; dealing with a faltering economy on the verge of freefall; and sorting out what was becoming an increasingly messy divorce from the Soviet Union. He would have welcomed more high-level American attention in the second half of 1992, but Bush focused on his campaign for a second term, a campaign in which domestic economic questions constituted the dominant issue. Baker, who had driven U.S. policy on denuclearization, left the State Department for the White House in August to assist in Bush's reelection effort.

In June, Popadiuk arrived in Kyiv, presented his credentials, and took up his post. He and the small embassy staff spent considerable time reporting on political and economic developments. Popadiuk discussed economic reform with a variety of senior Ukrainian officials. They saw the need for reforming the economy but had little idea how to move forward or how to overcome the communist economic legacy. In one meeting with a visiting U.S. official, Fokin said he was pushing the cabinet of ministers on building a market economy but that the government still had to determine the correct market prices for commodities—a statement that hardly reflected an understanding of how markets worked. Embassy interlocutors continued to express concern about Russia and the political, military, and economic threat it could pose to newly independent Ukraine.

Popadiuk also set about building a full-service embassy. By the end of the summer, the consular section began issuing visas, so Ukrainians no longer had to apply at the embassy in Moscow. The first contingent of Peace Corps volunteers—slated to do small-business training—arrived in November. (By the end of the 1990s, Ukraine would host one of the largest contingents of Peace Corps volunteers in the world.) The U.S. Agency for International Development established a mission at the embassy, although in its first months it could provide only limited technical and humanitarian assistance, since Congress did not appropriate significant funds for the FREEDOM Support Act until the second half of 1993. Working with the International Finance Corporation, it was able to launch the first small-scale privatization effort in Lviv at the beginning of 1993.

The Clinton Administration

Bill Clinton took office as the forty-second president of the United States in January 1993. He spoke by phone to Kravchuk almost immediately, addressing not just nuclear weapons but also the economic and political elements of the bilateral relationship. However, while the Ukrainians might have hoped for a different approach (on both nuclear arms and the overall relationship), the new administration quickly made clear that it shared the Bush administration's priority: for Ukraine to eliminate the nuclear weapons on its territory and accede to the Non-Proliferation Treaty (NPT) as a non-nuclear weapons state. Ukraine had committed to these objectives, but by the end of Bush's term in office not a single strategic nuclear warhead had actually moved out of Ukraine, nor had Kyiv begun the internal legislative process of accession to the NPT. Secretary of State Warren Christopher wrote Zlenko about this in February, and the issue topped the agenda when Zlenko visited Washington in March. During Zlenko's meeting with Clinton at the White House, the president stressed the need for Ukraine to ratify START as part of its denuclearization commitment, calling the treaty a "precondition" for a "successful" bilateral relationship. As if to underscore the point, the White House let it be known that, if Prime Minister Leonid Kuchma came to Washington in April, a meeting with Clinton would not be possible. Kuchma should instead defer the visit until after Ukraine had delivered on denuclearization by ratifying START and acceding to the NPT. (Kuchma ended up canceling his trip.)[14]

In the spring, ambassador at large for the New Independent States Strobe Talbott oversaw an administration review of policy toward Ukraine. Talbott, who had once shared a house with Clinton when both were students at Oxford University, had a long and passionate interest in the Soviet Union. He translated and edited Nikita Khrushchev's memoirs, published as *Khrushchev Remembers* in the 1970s, and had a lengthy career as a reporter at *Time* magazine, where he covered Europe and U.S. foreign policy. He wrote extensively about arms control, publishing several books documenting U.S.-Soviet negotiations on nuclear weapons. While the National Security Council chaired most interagency groups in the Clinton administration, Talbott ran the group managing policy toward the New Independent States. In addition to Talbott, Napper from State, Under Secretary of the Treasury Lawrence Summers, deputy assistant secretaries of defense Ashton Carter and Graham Allison, and Nicholas Burns and Rose Gottemoeller from the National Security Council took part in the review. No one in the U.S. government questioned the basic nuclear approach. Ukraine could not keep nuclear weapons; it had to deliver on its commitment to denuclearization. Washington would continue to push Kyiv on this. But Defense Department officials and others pressed for more, making the case that a broader relationship could be leveraged on the nuclear question. In the end, the review concluded that the U.S. government should hold out the prospect of a broader relationship that would include political, economic, and (non-nuclear) security links. That kind of relationship would become possible as the nuclear arms issue was resolved.[15]

With the policy review complete, Talbott previewed the basic conclusion to Deputy Foreign Minister Borys Tarasyuk in early May. Tarasyuk was an intelligent and experienced diplomat who had served at the Ukrainian mission to the United Nations in the early 1980s. A nationalist who held a deep skepticism about Russia and its intentions toward his country, he robustly defended Ukraine's positions and prerogatives—sometimes overplaying his hand, to the annoyance of U.S. officials. Their positions at times annoyed Tarasyuk as well. He nevertheless became a key shaper of Ukraine's policy toward the United States and later of its effort to draw closer to the European Union and NATO, which won him few fans in Moscow. For most of the 1990s (and later in the 2000s), he would be an important interlocutor for senior U.S. officials.

Talbott set off for Kyiv to share the review's conclusions there. The embassy succeeded in arranging a meeting with Kravchuk, which took some effort, as the Ukrainians were still smarting over Kuchma's inability to get a meeting at the White House. Talbott handed over a letter from Clinton, in which the U.S. president described his desire to expand the U.S.-Ukraine relationship and stated that Talbott could talk about the full range of issues that would constitute such a relationship. Talbott made clear that the U.S. government was ready to discuss political, economic, and security questions. He also told Kravchuk that Washington was prepared to help Kyiv and Moscow find solutions to some of the problems between them.[16]

As Washington began to consider how it would allocate FREEDOM Support Act assistance, one question was how much would go to Ukraine, to Russia, and to the other New Independent States. The Ukrainians understandably argued that, as the largest of the states (other than Russia), they should receive an appropriate share of the assistance. The administration was sympathetic to that view but mindful that the other states also had dire needs. U.S. officials viewed the allocation of the new funding for Cooperative Threat Reduction assistance, launched by senators Sam Nunn and Richard Lugar to provide funds to help reduce the former Soviet nuclear arsenal, as a useful card in getting Ukraine to move on the nuclear agenda. Those funds became available before FREEDOM Support Act assistance.

In late June, Talbott testified before the Senate Foreign Relations Subcommittee on European Affairs. He said the U.S. government sought to broaden its relationship with Kyiv and laid out five themes underlying the American approach: Ukraine had a crucial geopolitical role to play in Central and Eastern Europe, and developments there would affect the security of the region; an independent, sovereign, and prosperous Ukraine was important to U.S. interests; the United States would conduct its relationship with Ukraine independent of its relationship with Russia; Ukraine had legitimate security concerns that could be addressed by a series of bilateral and multilateral links; and implementation of the May 1992 Lisbon Protocol, in which Ukraine agreed to implement START and accede to the NPT, would advance Ukraine's security.[17]

Denuclearization as soon as possible remained the major issue for Washington. From the summer of 1993 onward, however, nuclear weapons no longer figured as the only big question for discussion between the two governments. Another such question was the Ukraine-Russia relationship. It was not going well.

The Challenge of Russia

Most could see from the beginning that there would be tensions between Kyiv and Moscow. Many in Moscow seemed to believe that they could simply bluff and pressure Ukraine. Given that and Kyiv's desire to build stronger links to the United States and the West, it came as no surprise that Russia would consistently find a place in the U.S.-Ukrainian dialogue. Ukrainian presidents regularly and openly described to their American counterparts the ups and downs in Ukraine-Russia relations, as Kyiv sought to manage tensions in Crimea, regularize the status of the Black Sea Fleet, secure Russian acknowledgment of Ukraine's sovereignty and territorial integrity, and enlist U.S. support for its positions on these issues. Popadiuk found Russia a regular subject of his conversations around Kyiv.

Above and beyond the nuclear weapons issue, the Ukrainian government faced a series of challenges in dealing with its large neighbor. The links between Kyiv and Moscow were not only historical and cultural. Much of the Soviet leadership came from or spent significant time in Ukraine, which made a vital economic contribution to the Soviet gross domestic product. Despite the devastation caused by forced collectivization and World War II, Ukraine's fertile black earth made up the Soviet bread basket. Until the discovery of the gas fields in western Siberia, Poltava in central Ukraine was the prime production area for Soviet natural gas. Ukrainian cities such as Kharkiv, Donetsk, and Luhansk became centers of heavy industry production, with the Donetsk-

Luhansk region becoming the most economically prosperous in the Soviet Union after Moscow and Leningrad (now St. Petersburg). Ukrainian industry made a special contribution to Soviet military production, accounting for some 30 percent of arms and arms-related manufacturing, including missiles and rockets, aircraft, and aircraft engines.

The breakup was difficult for many Russians to accept. As a senior Russian foreign ministry official remarked to me in 1994, "In my head, I understand that Ukraine is an independent country; in my heart, it will take time." For some, it plainly would take a lot of time. Many Russians, particularly those who aspired to retain, or regain, great power status for Moscow, felt the loss of Ukraine far more painfully than the loss of the other republics. Ukraine figured prominently in Russian domestic politics in the early 1990s, as nationalists came to view the outcome of the December 1991 referendum as an enormous loss for Russian state interests. (Years later, President Vladimir Putin would describe the collapse of the Soviet Union as the greatest geopolitical catastrophe of the twentieth century.)

All this only served to feed fears in Kyiv that Russia did not accept Ukraine's independence. As the smaller party, Ukrainians lacked confidence in dealing with Moscow and showed great suspicion of almost any Russian proposal, particularly Moscow's efforts to build the Commonwealth of Independent States (CIS) as a transnational institution in the post-Soviet space. Ukrainian diplomacy strived to keep the CIS a weak mechanism, concerned that Russia would dominate it in ways that would undermine Ukraine's interests. When the Rada ratified the agreement on the CIS, it did so with multiple reservations, and Ukraine never ratified the subsequent, more formal charter. This reflected in part the importance that Ukraine attached to its sovereignty, independence, and territorial integrity. Ukrainian officials preferred to deal with Moscow bilaterally rather than within the context of the CIS and sought early negotiation of a bilateral treaty of friendship and cooperation that would include a reaffirmation of those three key points.

Kyiv showed a tendency early on, which continued through most of the 1990s, to worry that the United States would shape its policy toward Ukraine as a component of its Russia policy. To be sure, Washington had major interests in dealing with Moscow. Among other things, Russia still held most of the Soviet Union's nuclear weapons, had to complete withdrawal of Russian military forces from Germany and the Baltic states, had assumed the Soviet Union's permanent seat on the UN Security Council, and maintained remnants of the Soviet global role. On big questions, such as German reunification, START, and the 1991 Gulf War, the Kremlin had proven a helpful partner. U.S. officials, however, sought to deal with Ukraine and Russia on their own merits, while recognizing the many issues that connected the two. On a number of issues regarding Ukraine, Washington took positions that left Moscow unhappy.

A second big question between Kyiv and Moscow concerned Crimea and Sevastopol, the largest city in Crimea and homeport of the Soviet Black Sea Fleet. Ethnic Russians, including a large number of retired military, constituted about 60 percent of the population on the Crimean Peninsula and nearly 70 percent of the population in Sevastopol. Crimea had been part of the Russian Soviet Federative Socialist Republic until 1954, when First Secretary of the Communist Party Nikita Khrushchev had the peninsula transferred to the Ukrainian Soviet Socialist Republic to mark the three hundredth anniversary of the Treaty of Pereyaslav. When the Soviet Union collapsed and the United States recognized the New Independent States on December 25, 1991, Washington's recognition of each republic in its existing borders reflected the belief that any attempt to redraw borders could lead to an unraveling of many lines on the map and cause geopolitical chaos. It is difficult to overestimate the importance of this aspect of U.S. policy toward the post-Soviet states. Both the Bush and Clinton administrations worried that territorial, ethnic, and even confessional tensions could plunge the region into conflict. In the American view, Crimea unquestionably belonged to Ukraine. Although Yeltsin usually quietly accepted that view—indeed, he had already recognized the other republics in their existing borders—there was no coherent line in the Russian capital because the government itself was in some disarray. Others supported separatist elements on the peninsula, and the Supreme Soviet (later, the Duma) raised questions about Crimea's status almost from the beginning.

U.S. officials closely followed the situation in Crimea, recognizing its potential as a tinderbox between Kyiv and Moscow. They had a lot to follow. In January 1992, Yevgeniy Ambartsumov, chair of the Supreme Soviet's Committee on Foreign Affairs, questioned the legality of Crimea's transfer in 1954, and other parliamentarians proposed a draft resolution to nullify the decision. In April, Rutskoy traveled to Crimea and said the peninsula should be part of Russia. In May, the Supreme Soviet declared the transfer had been made "without juridical force" and several months later asserted that Sevastopol had not been part of Crimea because a 1948 decree had given it the status of an "independent administrative-economic center," though the 1954 transfer clearly superseded the 1948 decree in practice. On regular visits to Sevastopol, Moscow's mayor Yuriy Luzhkov continually claimed it to be a Russian city.

Yeltsin wished to avoid a domestic political dispute over the question but periodically reaffirmed, as did his foreign ministry, that Sevastopol and Crimea belonged to Ukraine. The issue flared up again in mid-1993. On July 9, the Supreme Soviet voted unanimously to assert Russian ownership of Sevastopol, as well as to call for the preservation of "a single, united, glorious Black Sea Fleet."[18] Yeltsin distanced himself from the Supreme Soviet's action the next day, saying, "There is no better way to make war with Ukraine. It is not a responsible decision. We must return to a cautious policy and negotiations with Ukraine."[19] The dispute between Yeltsin and his nationalist and communist critics over Ukraine represented a subset of the broader tensions that would erupt into violence in October 1993, leading to the infamous Russian army shelling of the parliament building where Yeltsin's opponents held out.

The Ukrainian government immediately denounced the Supreme Soviet vote. The American embassy in Kyiv prepared a statement that referred to Sevastopol and Crimea as "integral parts" of Ukraine, which became the U.S. government line. That stance won appreciation from Ukrainian officials, and it encouraged supportive statements for Ukraine by Britain and other European countries. The Ukrainian government appealed to the UN Security Council, which on July 20 produced—with tacit support from the Russian delegation—a statement by the president of the Security Council reaffirming the Security Council's support for Ukraine's territorial integrity.

A third major issue, closely related to the question of Sevastopol and Crimea, was the disposition of the Black Sea Fleet. In 1992 the fleet comprised some 240 major warships and submarines, small combatant vessels and support ships, as well as shore-based supporting air units and naval infantry. Although some extremists in the Supreme

Soviet proposed that Russia assert full control of the fleet—and of the entire Soviet military structure—the Russians offered to negotiate. Kyiv and Moscow reached a tentative agreement in summer 1992 on a fifty-fifty split of the Black Sea Fleet's vessels. Since the Ukrainian navy did not need its full allotment, Kyiv agreed to transfer almost two-thirds of its ships back to Russia in exchange for a debt write-off, an arrangement that some in Kyiv challenged but which ultimately held.

The more vexing problem proved to be finding agreement on the terms for continuing to base the Russian portion of the fleet in Sevastopol and other Crimean ports. Sevastopol possessed the finest harbor on the Black Sea and had been founded by the Tsarist military in 1783 specifically to serve as home port for the Black Sea Fleet. The post-Soviet Russian navy lacked facilities at Novorossysk and other Russian ports to accommodate all its ships. Russian negotiators sought a long-term lease that, in effect, would give Russia sovereignty over the entire city of Sevastopol. That was absolutely unacceptable to Ukrainian negotiators, who instead proposed to lease specific facilities and made clear that Kyiv intended to maintain full sovereignty over the city.

A fourth issue concerned economics. Despite the collapse of the Soviet Union, the Ukrainian and Russian economies were closely intertwined and would remain so for years to come. Ukraine remained in a common ruble zone with Russia until 1993, which had an impact. As Russia liberalized its prices, prices rose in Ukraine, contributing to the country's hyperinflation in 1993. Ukraine also amassed large ruble debts to Russia.[20] Russia in the 1990s provided Ukraine its largest export market. The two economies were particularly linked by Ukraine's energy needs. Ninety percent of the oil for Ukraine's six large refineries came from Russia, as did all of the fuel rods for its nuclear power reactors, a Russian monopoly that would take almost twenty years to break. As for natural gas, Ukraine's largest energy source, more than 75 percent was imported from Russia or from Central Asia on pipelines that transited through Russia. Given the economic dislocation in Ukraine at the beginning of the decade, Kyiv often had trouble paying for its energy imports. Kyiv also disputed Moscow's claim to all of the Soviet international debts and assets.

All of these issues combined to make a full and problematic agenda between Ukraine and Russia. Wanting good relations with both countries, and hoping that a serious contretemps between the two might be avoided, Washington paid close attention. Later, it would actively involve itself in an attempt to resolve some of the problems.

Reflections

Washington was slow to recognize the Soviet Union's demise. Moreover, once they realized its likelihood, many senior officials, including in the White House, became apprehensive at the prospect. Some even seemed to look for ways to slow the processes under way inside the Soviet Union, which the United States could hardly affect. An earlier understanding and acceptance in the U.S. government of the coming end might have affected U.S. policy somewhat. It could have positioned U.S. policymakers to begin dealing earlier with the aftermath of the collapse. But an earlier understanding would not have affected the dynamics of the process that led to the end of the Soviet Union and to Ukraine regaining its independence.

Once Washington saw that the collapse was inevitable, it moved quickly to establish relations with Ukraine and the other New Independent States. The State Department moved with uncommon speed to get embassies in place in each of the new capitals. Still, putting in place the tools to engage the new states took time. For example, the FREEDOM Support Act, which would become the primary channel for moving U.S. assistance to the post-Soviet states, was not enacted until October 1992, and initial funding was not approved by Congress until autumn 1993, almost two years after the end of the Soviet Union. Thus the kinds of assistance that Washington could offer the new Ukrainian state were limited.

Kravchuk eagerly worked to develop relations with the West, and the United States in particular, as he sought a counterweight to Russia. He recognized that Ukraine faced a difficult set of issues with its eastern neighbor, including what to do about former Soviet nuclear weapons and military forces such as the Black Sea Fleet; how to divide up Soviet assets and liabilities; and how to structure the myriad post-Soviet economic and energy relationships between Ukraine and Russia. And he had to deal with these issues while facing a Russian political elite, including many in the leadership, that did not fully accept the idea of Ukraine as an independent state.

The U.S. government focused its attention primarily on the nuclear arms issue and ensuring the elimination of the nuclear weapons and strategic delivery vehicles in Ukraine. This topic, which I discuss in detail in chapter 2, dominated the Bush administration's approach to Kyiv. It provided the focus for the first months of the Clinton administration's approach as well until May 1993, when the interagency process moved to begin expanding Washington's engagement with Ukraine and developed a strategy designed to support a broader relationship.

In retrospect, the U.S. government erred during the first two years of its engagement with Ukraine in focusing so heavily on the nuclear weapons issue. While it was certainly a critical issue on the U.S. agenda, the overly narrow focus failed to create confidence in Kyiv that, once the nuclear weapons question was resolved, there would be a robust bilateral relationship or, for that matter, any significant U.S. interest in Kyiv. The alternative would have been to signal more clearly from the outset that Washington intended to engage Kyiv on a wide set of issues. In reality, and as became apparent, many factors argued for pursuing a broad relationship: Ukraine's key geopolitical position and potential contribution to a more stable and secure Europe; the prospect of mutually beneficial commercial relations with a country of some 50 million people; and possible Ukrainian support in addressing other proliferation challenges, such as the control of ballistic missile technology. However, in the aftermath of the Soviet collapse and with fears that "loose nukes" might fall into the hands of third countries or even nonstate terrorist organizations, Washington's attention centered on nuclear weapons, and U.S. officials conditioned steps toward a broader relationship on Ukraine's actions in the nuclear area.

The dominant focus on nuclear arms may have had the unintended consequence of inflating the value of those weapons in the minds of Ukrainian officials. That likely made the nuclear negotiation more difficult. If Kyiv thought that all Washington cared about was the nuclear weapons, it had every incentive to drive a hard bargain for their elimination. In any event, Strobe Talbott's visit to Kyiv in May 1993, followed by Warren Christopher's trip in October, began to outline Washington's vision for a broad and robust relationship and to allay concern among

Ukrainian officials that all they would hear about from their American interlocutors was the nuclear issue.

Many in Washington saw Ukraine as one of the post-Soviet states best positioned to succeed, but the new country faced difficult challenges. First, it had to develop the political institutions, ideally democratic, of an independent state. Second, it had to build a market economy from the crumbling remains of the Soviet command economy. Third, it had to devise an independent foreign and security policy appropriate for a country of Ukraine's size and geopolitical circumstances. Any one of these challenges would have been tough to tackle. Kyiv had to face all three, at a time of great uncertainty and with its economy—like virtually every other post-Soviet economy—about to go into a severe contraction. Washington might not have fully appreciated the depth of these challenges. It looked to help Kyiv move forward on all three challenges but did not define priorities among them; doing so, in any case, would have been a hard call. How could one compare the importance of building working political institutions with building the institutions of a functioning market economy?

Moreover, Ukraine had to tackle these tasks without undergoing a revolution of the kind that brought new leaders to positions of power in Central European countries such as Poland and the Czech Republic. For the most part, the "new" Ukrainian political elite—including the presidents, prime ministers, and many cabinet ministers during the decade of the 1990s—emerged from the nomenclature that had occupied positions of power in Soviet times. Indeed, had one been asked to project in 1989 who would be running the Ukrainian Soviet Socialist Republic in 1999 (had it lasted that long), many of the names would have been the same as those who ran independent Ukraine in the 1990s. It should not have been a surprise that Vitold Fokin, who had headed the Ukrainian Soviet Socialist Republic's government planning agency before becoming prime minister of an independent Ukraine, would note that the state—not supply and demand—still had to determine the correct market prices for commodities. Like many of the others assuming key positions in the Ukrainian government, his background hardly prepared him to shape a modern, democratic, market-oriented European state. A clearer understanding of this might have tempered American expectations for early progress.

At the same time, the U.S. government's machinery and funding to promote and assist reform in Ukraine and other post-Soviet states needed time to develop. Had Washington had the tools in place to press Kyiv on economic reform immediately after Ukraine regained independence and before the economic decline accelerated and new patterns of corruption took hold, could it have succeeded in encouraging Ukraine's leadership to move more rapidly to implement real change?

In the first months and first years after Ukraine regained independence, the country's domestic politics and economic policy were marked by a fair degree of chaos, perhaps understandably. Kravchuk focused his attention on state building. Absent a skilled elite familiar with the workings of a market economy and a democratic political system, and with limited policy capacity, Kyiv's ability to make dramatic reforms had constraints. At the same time, unfortunately for the country, a number of the elite saw opportunity in the chaos and the weakened rule of law. Oligarchs who would come to dominate so much of economic and political life in the country began to build their power.

CHAPTER 2

Dealing with Nuclear Weapons

A principal theme of Bill Clinton's presidential campaign in 1992 was "It's the economy, stupid." The following year, Jim Steiner, the intelligence adviser in the State Department's Office of the New Independent States, kept a small sign on his desk: "It's the nukes, stupid." That reminder accurately captured the focus of the George H. W. Bush and Clinton administrations' policy toward Ukraine in 1992 and 1993: eliminate the nuclear weapons on Ukraine's territory as part of a broader effort to ensure that the collapse of the Soviet Union did not result in an increase in the number of nuclear weapons states. When it became clear in summer 1993 that negotiations between Kyiv and Moscow were making little headway, American diplomacy engaged and successfully brokered a trilateral arrangement that removed the nuclear weapons while meeting Kyiv's conditions for doing so. But the process of finding an agreement took longer than expected and at times frustrated both Washington and Kyiv.

Ukraine's Views and Interests

In the aftermath of the Soviet Union's collapse, Ukraine held on its territory the world's third largest nuclear arsenal. Forty-six SS-24 intercontinental ballistic missiles (ICBMs), each armed with ten nuclear warheads, sat in underground silos in the wheat and sunflower fields of southern Ukraine around the city of Pervomaysk. Forty SS-19 ICBMs, older and less powerful than the SS-24s, but nevertheless each armed with six nuclear warheads, also rested underground near Pervomaysk. Ninety more SS-19s were deployed in silos to the west around Khmelnytskyy.[1] The 176 ICBMs, capable of carrying 1,240 strategic nuclear warheads, targeted (or could target) all of the United States.

Ukraine also inherited nineteen Tu-160 Blackjack and twenty-five Tu-95 Bear-H strategic bombers at air bases at Uzhyn and Pryluky. These aircraft could carry six to twelve nuclear-armed, long-range cruise missiles and, like the SS-24 and SS-19 ICBMs, could strike targets throughout the United States. All told, Ukraine had 1,900 strategic nuclear warheads—more than the total nuclear arsenals of Britain, France, and China combined. In addition, Ukraine had some 2,500 tactical nuclear warheads.[2] Dealing with these warheads, and the strategic missiles and bombers that carried them, posed the first major challenge for U.S.-Ukraine relations.

Early Ukrainian political pronouncements—even preceding the Soviet Union's breakup—suggested that achieving the goal of a non-nuclear Ukraine might be relatively simple. The still raw experience of the 1986 Chornobyl nuclear disaster, which had resulted in a 1,000-square-mile closed zone around the nuclear power plant, sharply colored thinking on things nuclear. Many in the pro-independence Rukh movement had their roots in the protests against state secrecy about Chornobyl, and the movement itself had something of a nuclear neuralgia. Section IX of the Declaration of State Sovereignty, passed by the Rada (parliament) on July 16, 1990, effectively committed Ukraine to the status of a non-nuclear weapons state, declaring, "The Ukrainian SSR [Soviet Socialist Republic] . . . adheres to three nuclear-free principles: to accept, to produce and to purchase no nuclear weapons."[3] The Rada reaffirmed this position on October 24, 1991, in a statement on the non-nuclear status of Ukraine. That statement, however, envisaged a two-step approach to nuclear disarmament. Ukraine would first implement reductions in accordance with the Strategic Arms Reduction Treaty (START), signed the previous July, followed by a second phase in which the remaining nuclear weapons would be eliminated. While some saw this as a possible step back from the 1990 declaration, the U.S. consulate in Kyiv did not attach undue concern when reporting the statement.

Not everyone in Ukraine agreed on becoming a non-nuclear weapons state. Nationalists in the Rada, some officials in the executive branch, and other "hotheads," as described by one former Ukrainian official, opposed denuclearization. They regarded an independent nuclear deterrent as desirable, given fears about Russian encroachment on the new Ukrainian state's sovereignty—in particular, the questioning of the status of Crimea. Others in Kyiv, however, felt that Ukraine had no choice but to give up the weapons.

Ukrainian officials did weigh the technical feasibility of retaining nuclear arms. Shortly after regaining independence, senior officers of the 43rd Rocket Army, responsible for all ICBMs deployed in Ukraine, met with foreign and defense ministry officials to explore what maintaining an independent nuclear force would entail. The officers outlined the technical questions: Could Ukraine develop an independent system to control and launch the ICBMs? Could Ukraine maintain the nuclear warheads, which required delicate handling and had a service life of no more than ten years, possibly less? How would Ukraine manage issues such as the production of tritium, which boosts the power of a nuclear detonation but decays over time? How would Ukraine dispose of old warheads and their fissile material? Could Ukraine have confidence—lacking its own test site and data from Soviet nuclear tests—in the reliability of the warheads over time?[4]

Participants concluded that the technical challenges of retaining an independent nuclear force would be daunting, particularly as many of the warheads and ICBMs would reach the end of their service life in the second half of the 1990s. Ukraine had the technical expertise to maintain an ICBM force (the Pivdenmash rocket plant in Dnipropetrovsk had produced the SS-18 and SS-24 ICBMs), but maintaining and possibly building new nuclear warheads was a very different undertaking. An independent nuclear force would have required developing a nuclear infrastructure at an unknown cost that was certain to run into the billions of dollars.

Finally, officials weighed the broader political considerations: It was unclear how retaining a nuclear force would help Kyiv deal with the political challenges expected from Moscow, while doing so would definitely raise hurdles in Ukraine's relations with the United States and Europe. They recognized that a positive relationship with the United States—which they regarded as essential for balancing Russia—would not be possible if Ukraine tried to retain nuclear arms.

The Ukrainian government thus accepted that it should give up the nuclear arms on its territory, but several questions had to be addressed. First, possession of nuclear weapons conferred—or was seen to confer—certain security benefits. What guarantees or assurances would there be for Ukraine's sovereignty and territorial integrity after it gave up strategic nuclear arms?

Second, the nuclear warheads had commercial value in the form of the highly enriched uranium (HEU) that they contained. HEU could be blended down into low enriched uranium (LEU) and used to produce fuel rods for nuclear power reactors. How would Ukraine ensure that it received the value of the HEU from the nuclear warheads on its territory?

Third, eliminating the ICBMs, ICBM silos, strategic bombers, and nuclear infrastructure would be an expensive proposition, particularly at a time when the new Ukrainian economy was sharply contracting. Who would cover the costs?

And fourth, how, where, and under what conditions would the strategic nuclear warheads, ICBMs, and bombers be eliminated?

Government officials and Rada members were also concerned that, as a successor state to the Soviet Union, Ukraine had certain rights, including the right to ownership of the nuclear weapons on its territory. How would these rights be respected? Finally, President Leonid Kravchuk—and his successor, Leonid Kuchma—sought to manage this question in a manner that would not provoke discord with the Rada or the public.

Early U.S. Engagement and the Lisbon Protocol

U.S. officials began thinking about the fate of Soviet nuclear weapons even before the end of the Soviet Union. Some in the Bush administration saw value in an independent Ukraine retaining nuclear weapons.

Such a force could serve as a hedge to protect Kyiv's sovereignty against a possibly resurgent Russia; moreover, the fewer the number of nuclear weapons in Moscow's hands, the better. Secretary of State James Baker took a sharply different view. He believed it to be in America's interest that only a single nuclear power remain in the post-Soviet space and saw no value to potential nuclear rivalries between Moscow and its neighbors. A crisis between a nuclear-armed Russia and a nuclear-armed Ukraine would hardly be in the U.S. interest. Baker argued for moving quickly to ensure the elimination of all nuclear weapons from the post-Soviet republics aside from Russia. In the end, no one challenged Baker on this. Ukraine's denuclearization became the central plank of the George H. W. Bush administration's policy toward Kyiv.[5]

The point people for Baker—Under Secretary of State for International Security Affairs Reginald Bartholomew and his senior adviser, James Timbie—believed Ukraine would give up the nuclear weapons. They did not see how Ukraine could be an independent nuclear power when it lacked the resources to maintain a nuclear capability and when the command-and-control arrangements for the ICBMs were so closely tied to Russia.

U.S. pursuit of a denuclearized Ukraine stemmed from the fact that Washington did not want the breakup of the Soviet Union to lead to a net increase in the number of nuclear-armed states, particularly states armed with strategic weapons that could target the U.S. homeland. The existence of a larger number of nuclear-armed states would undermine the U.S. effort to secure indefinite extension of the 1968 Nonproliferation Treaty (NPT) at its 1995 review conference. Washington also was eager to get on with implementation of the START treaty signed by presidents George H. W. Bush and Mikhail Gorbachev. It provided for significant reductions in U.S. and Soviet strategic forces. The bilateral U.S.-Soviet treaty would have to be made a multilateral agreement to take account of the fact that the Soviet missiles, bombers, and warheads were now located in four independent countries—Russia, Belarus, Kazakhstan, and Ukraine. The United States sought to make sure that the START reductions process eliminated all the strategic nuclear weapons in Ukraine and wanted to get Ukraine to accede to the NPT as a non-nuclear weapons state.

Early indications looked positive. In late December 1991, as the Commonwealth of Independent States (CIS) began to sort out what the Soviet Union's demise meant in practical terms, arrangements for managing Soviet nuclear arms topped the list. CIS leaders at first aimed to maintain joint command of the strategic forces. A December 30 agreement on strategic forces signed by eleven of the twelve CIS leaders stated that nuclear weapons in Ukraine "shall be under the control of the Combined Strategic Forces Command, with the aim that they shall not be used and be dismantled by the end of 1994, including tactical weapons by 1 July 1992." They further agreed that any decision to use nuclear weapons would be taken by the Russian president in agreement with the leaders of Belarus, Kazakhstan, and Ukraine and in consultation with other CIS leaders.[6]

When Baker stopped in Kyiv shortly after the December 1991 Belavezhskaya Pushcha agreement announcing the end of the Soviet Union, the nuclear weapons issue was a central focus of his discussions. Kravchuk assured him that Ukraine would destroy all nuclear weapons on its territory.

Bartholomew led an interagency team to Moscow and Kyiv in January 1992 to discuss how to handle START. He suggested two options: First, the United States could conclude a bilateral protocol with Russia regarding the START treaty and leave it to the Russians to deal with Belarus, Kazakhstan, and Ukraine. Alternatively, the United States could negotiate with the four post-Soviet states on a protocol, by which Russia, Belarus, Kazakhstan, and Ukraine would take on the Soviets' START obligations.

Russian officials preferred the first option; their Ukrainian counterparts strongly favored the second. Kostyantyn Hryshchenko, then director of the arms control and disarmament directorate in Ukraine's foreign ministry, observed, "For us, from the very start, what was important was the establishment of our role as a country which would be responsible for the implementation of the START treaty, thus establishing our equal rights with other parties."[7] Washington nevertheless decided to give Moscow time to see if it could make the first option work. It soon became apparent that the Russians could not. Bartholomew and U.S. officials then begin to pursue the negotiation of a multilateral protocol under which Russia, Belarus, Kazakhstan, and Ukraine would assume the Soviet Union's START obligations, and the latter three states would adhere to the NPT as non-nuclear weapons states.

The first hiccup between Ukraine and Russia occurred early in 1992 and concerned the tactical, or nonstrategic, nuclear warheads located in Ukraine. These numbered in the thousands (the U.S. government used the figure of 2,500, but other estimates ranged from 2,000 to 4,200). Kravchuk had stated in February that half of the tactical nuclear warheads had been transferred to Russia, which put Ukraine well on the road to meeting the July 1 deadline agreed in December. But the Ukrainian president announced at a March 12 press conference that Kyiv had decided to halt the transfer, asserting that Ukraine had no guarantee that the weapons transferred were actually being dismantled.[8] His decision also reflected frustration in Kyiv that the Russians treated the transfers as a unilateral withdrawal and did not adequately consult with Ukrainian officials. His actions concerned Washington, particularly as Kravchuk had assured Bush in a telephone conversation two weeks before that Ukraine would meet the July 1 deadline.

Within a month, the Ukrainians and Russians had worked out arrangements allowing the resumption of the tactical nuclear warhead transfer, which came just in time for Kravchuk's visit to Washington. Kravchuk met with Bush on May 6 and reiterated Ukraine's commitment to remove all tactical nuclear weapons from its territory by July 1 and the strategic nuclear weapons within seven years in accordance with START (which had an implementation period of seven years). Baker and Kravchuk hammered out language for the protocol that would multilateralize the Soviet START obligations. They also agreed on the text for a letter from Kravchuk to Bush affirming Ukraine's commitment to join the NPT as a non-nuclear weapons state and to eliminate all strategic offensive arms—missiles, missile silos, and bombers—on its territory within seven years.

On May 7, Kravchuk publicly stated that all tactical nuclear weapons, except for those belonging to the Black Sea Fleet (whose ownership remained disputed between Moscow and Kyiv) had been removed from Ukraine. This claim reversed an answer he had given at the White House press conference the previous day, when he contradicted a statement by Russian officials that all tactical nuclear weapons had already been transferred out of Ukraine. Whatever the confusion—whether it reflected a disconnect between the Ukrainian president and his ministry of defense or Russian removal of the weapons without keeping Ukrainian officials fully informed—Ukraine had fulfilled its commitment regarding tactical nuclear weapons with almost two months to spare.

The Washington discussions set the stage for a meeting of U.S., Russian, Belarusian, Kazakhstani, and Ukrainian negotiators in Lisbon to finalize language for what became known as the Lisbon Protocol to START. U.S. negotiator Thomas Graham easily closed issues with the Belarusian and Kazakhstani sides but found his Ukrainian counterparts difficult. The Ukrainians indicated uncertainty as to whether Foreign Minister Anatoliy Zlenko could sign the protocol. They resisted the "inequality" of the protocol, which treated Russia differently from the other post-Soviet states. The U.S. side had thought this was understood, particularly following Kravchuk's discussions in Washington. Graham phoned the secretary's party, which was in London and due to arrive in the Portuguese capital the next day. An angry Baker called Zlenko directly. The call was difficult, but American officials believed it did the trick.[9]

On May 23, Baker and Zlenko joined Russian foreign minister Andrey Kozyrev, Belarusian foreign minister Pyotr Krauchanka, and Kazakhstani state counselor for strategic affairs Tulegen Zhukeyev to sign the "Lisbon Protocol to the Treaty between the United States of America and the Union of Soviet Socialist Republics on the Reduction and Limitation of Strategic Offensive Arms." The protocol provided that Belarus, Kazakhstan, Russia, and Ukraine, as successor states to the Soviet Union, would assume the Soviet Union's START obligations. It required Belarus, Kazakhstan, and Ukraine to accede to the NPT as non-nuclear weapons states "in the shortest possible time" and begin "immediately" to pursue the internal constitutional steps necessary to accomplish that.

The protocol was accompanied by the letter from Kravchuk to Bush that had been worked out earlier in Washington. It stated that Ukraine would "have a non-nuclear status" and would eliminate "all nuclear weapons, including strategic offensive arms located in its territory" within START's seven-year period for implementation of reductions. Finally, Kravchuk's letter noted the importance of international monitoring to confirm that the nuclear explosive packages removed from the nuclear weapons were not reused.[10] The protocol recognized Ukraine as a successor to the Soviet Union for purposes of START, a key point for Kyiv. (The Lisbon Protocol remains the only legal document in which Moscow recognized Ukraine's claim to successor state status.)

Following Lisbon, Ukraine had committed to a path of giving up all of the nuclear weapons on its territory. Future discussions would deal with the terms.

With the Lisbon Protocol done, the U.S. Senate gave its consent to ratification of the START treaty in October. Two months later, the Russian Supreme Soviet approved the treaty. The Supreme Soviet's ratification, however, required that the exchange of the instruments of ratification for START—the necessary step to bring the treaty into force—could occur only once Belarus, Kazakhstan, and Ukraine had acceded to the NPT as non-nuclear weapons states.

U.S. officials were pleased with the completion of the Lisbon Protocol but felt some unease. While Ukraine had agreed in CIS documents at the end of 1991 to the withdrawal of all nuclear weapons from its territory by the end of 1994, Kravchuk's May 7, 1992, letter committed to elimination of all strategic nuclear weapons only within seven years of START's entry into force. Ukrainian officials, moreover, had begun to talk of holding on to some of the more modern SS-24 missiles.[11]

Ukrainian-Russian Negotiations

U.S. officials hoped that Kyiv and Moscow could work out arrangements for the disposition of strategic nuclear arms on Ukrainian territory. The Ukrainian-Russian discussions were complicated by debates in the Rada, where some deputies suggested Ukraine keep the SS-24 ICBMs and arm them with conventional warheads. Others suggested that Ukraine implement the Lisbon Protocol over fourteen years and only then accede to the NPT. Rada deputy Dmytro Pavlychko asserted that Ukraine should eliminate the SS-19 ICBMs over the first seven years, eliminate the SS-24 ICBMs over the following seven years, and only then join the NPT.[12] A number of deputies argued, moreover, that Ukraine could not accede to the NPT as a non-nuclear weapons state because it "owned" nuclear weapons as a successor to the Soviet Union.

Early in the bilateral discussions, Yuriy Dubinin, the head Russian negotiator, indicated Moscow's readiness to consider a number of issues of interest to Kyiv, including providing security guarantees. Russia was also prepared to provide fuel for Ukrainian nuclear reactors as compensation for the HEU in the strategic nuclear warheads that Ukraine transferred to Russia for elimination, provided that Kyiv agree to transfer all warheads. Dubinin's opposite number, Environment Minister Yuriy Kostenko, asserted that Ukraine had a "right to own nuclear munitions" and had yet to decide where the nuclear warheads should be dismantled. This followed a December 1992 memorandum circulated by the Ukrainian foreign ministry that raised Ukraine's "right to own all components of nuclear warheads . . . deployed on its territory."[13]

Moscow adamantly opposed any claim by Kyiv to "ownership." Russian diplomats argued that, if Ukraine "owned" the weapons, it could not accede to the NPT as a non-nuclear weapons state. Russian concerns were fueled when Ukrainian defense minister Kostyantyn Morozov asserted that Ukraine should have the status of a state that temporarily had nuclear weapons (a status not provided for by the NPT), and Prime Minister Leonid Kuchma stated that Ukraine should "confirm itself temporarily as a nuclear state."[14]

The Russians argued that they could not participate in any way in a change of Ukraine's status from a non-nuclear weapons state. U.S. officials tended to agree but took a less dogmatic approach. They tried to sidestep the ownership issue, regarding it as nothing but trouble. Washington firmly believed, however, that Ukraine had ownership rights to the economic value of the HEU contained in the warheads and made that point to both the Russians and the Ukrainians.

Ukrainian-Russian discussions over the first months of 1993 proceeded in three working groups, addressing the schedule for transferring nuclear warheads from Ukraine to Russia, the amount of the compensation that Ukraine should receive, and arrangements for servicing and maintaining ICBMs. Russian negotiators offered proposals to begin reducing the alert status of the strategic nuclear systems on Ukrainian territory. These included removing the targeting data from all ICBMs, removing the warheads from all ICBMs and transferring them to Russia, and removing the nuclear air-launched cruise missiles to Russia.[15]

Negotiations were not helped when 162 Rada deputies issued a statement in April calling Ukraine a nuclear power, both legally and de facto. The deputies argued, among other things, that Kyiv could not ratify START and the Lisbon Protocol and assume the obligations under those documents if Ukraine did not own the missiles, bombers, and warheads it was to eliminate. In early July, the Rada went a step further, adopting by a vote of 226 to 15 a foreign policy doctrine embodying Ukraine's claim to ownership. The doctrine stated that the country had "acquired its own nuclear weapons for historical reasons" but went on to say that Ukraine would not employ them. Many, in both Russia and the United States, read this doctrine as close to a declaration by Ukraine of its status as a nuclear weapons state.[16] Some U.S. officials believed Kravchuk had a significant degree of control over the Rada and coordinated behind the scenes with the parliamentary body. He may have thought that Rada adoption of the foreign policy doctrine would give him extra leverage in dealing with Russia and the United States.

An August meeting between Russian prime minister Viktor Chernomyrdin and Kuchma resulted in a new Dubinin visit to Kyiv. Dubinin later wrote that his talks in Kyiv had led to agreement on virtually all of the nuclear issues. Ukraine would transfer strategic nuclear warheads to Russia, where they would be disassembled, and Ukraine would receive compensation for the warheads. Russia would remove HEU from the weapons and return to Ukraine fuel rods with an equivalent amount of LEU, less the cost of converting the HEU into LEU. The only open issue was the exact schedule for the transfer of the warheads. Dubinin regarded this as a major breakthrough.[17]

Yeltsin and Kravchuk met in Masandra in Crimea at the beginning of September. They announced agreement on the nuclear weapons and other issues. They confirmed the draft agreements reached in August and further agreed that the transfer of all nuclear weapons to Russia would be completed within two years of Rada ratification of START and the Lisbon Protocol.

The Masandra summit results, however, fell apart almost immediately. They were met with sharp disapproval in the Rada and other quarters in Kyiv—as much over the overall nature of the agreements as over the specific resolution of the nuclear weapons question. A flurry of charges and countercharges ensued between Kyiv and Moscow, including Russian claims that Ukraine had sought to alter the agreement on the transfer of nuclear weapons and no longer agreed to transfer all weapons. Kravchuk's foreign policy adviser, Anton Buteyko, reportedly deleted "all" from the agreement on transferring the weapons to Russia, although Ukrainian and Russian officials disputed when the change was made—before or after the document was initialed.[18]

Despite the collapse of the Masandra agreements, the Ukrainian-Russian discussions succeeded in defining several elements of the ultimate resolution. Dubinin believed, as did other Russian officials, that the bilateral channel had come close to success and, left on its own, would eventually produce an agreement. Ukrainian officials, however, strongly disagreed. They saw little future in the bilateral channel and turned instead to a negotiation involving the United States.

Security Assurances, Compensation, and Other Issues

Something resembling a trilateral process had in fact been working since early 1992. In parallel with the bilateral negotiations between Kyiv and Moscow, Washington discussed issues such as security assurances and compensation separately with Russian and Ukrainian officials, even if the three did not sit down together until 1993.

The Ukrainians raised security guarantees with Bush administration officials in 1992, suggesting that Ukraine receive a NATO Article 5–type guarantee. (Article 5 of the 1949 Washington Treaty, which established NATO, states, "The Parties agree that an armed attack against one or more of them in Europe or North America shall be considered an attack against them all, and consequently they agree that, if such an armed attack occurs, each of them . . . will assist the Party or Parties so attacked.")[19] Such a guarantee would have committed U.S. military forces to Ukraine's defense. The suggestion went nowhere.

Secretary of State Baker initially showed little enthusiasm even for lesser security assurances, fearing that extending them to Ukraine would trigger a flood of requests from other post-Soviet states. Adviser Timbie pointed out, however, that, once Kyiv acceded to the NPT as a non-nuclear weapons state, it would automatically receive a "negative security assurance" from Washington; the United States had stated that it would not use nuclear weapons against any non-nuclear weapons state that was a party to the NPT unless that state was attacking the United States or a U.S. ally in conjunction with a state armed with nuclear weapons. Baker proved amenable to packaging such an assurance in a Ukraine-specific document, provided that the U.S. government would be reiterating existing commitments. Timbie later suggested adding other assurances that the United States had already provided to all signatories of the 1975 Final Act of the Helsinki Conference on Security and Cooperation in Europe. Baker agreed since these were not new. They included commitments to respect Ukraine's independence, sovereignty, and existing borders, to refrain from the threat or use of force, and to refrain from economic coercion. As discussions proceeded with the Ukrainians, Timbie held parallel conversations with Russian and British embassy officers in Washington. Washington saw it as essential that the Russians also provide Kyiv security assurances. The logic for including the British stemmed from the fact that Britain, like the United States and Russia, was a depositary state for the NPT.

American officials decided the assurances would have to be packaged in a document that was not legally binding. Neither the Bush nor the Clinton administration wanted a legal treaty that would require Senate consent to ratification. State Department lawyers took careful interest in the actual language, in order to keep the commitments of a political nature.

Mindful of the legal distinction, U.S. officials used the term "assurance" instead of "guarantee." To American ears, "guarantees" suggested commitments of the nature that the United States had extended to its NATO allies and could require Senate approval. "Assurances," on the other hand, suggested a lesser commitment. In particular, they did not imply the commitment of American military force. The problem was made more complicated by the fact that the Ukrainian and Russian languages used "guarantee" for both English words, "guarantee" and "assurance."

Drawing from documents such as the Helsinki Final Act, U.S. officials began drafting a set of security assurances. Ambassador Roman Popadiuk discussed the text of possible assurances with Deputy Foreign Minister Borys Tarasyuk in fall 1992.

The Clinton administration in early 1993 began to consider more closely the compensation issue as well as security assurances. Given the large energy debt owed by Ukraine to Russia, primarily for natural gas, U.S. officials suggested that Russia compensate Ukraine for the economic value of the HEU in the strategic nuclear warheads by writing off part or all of Ukraine's energy debt. Russian officials did not like that idea and instead favored providing LEU in the form of fuel rods for Ukraine's nuclear reactors as compensation. American officials pressed the Russians to make this part of the package for getting the strategic weapons out of Ukraine.

U.S. and Russian negotiators in February 1993 concluded an agreement—sometimes referred to as "megatons to megawatts"—under which Russia would convert 500 metric tons of HEU extracted from dismantled Soviet nuclear warheads, blend it down to LEU, and sell the LEU to the United States for fuel for nuclear reactors. U.S. officials soon thereafter informed their Russian counterparts that implementation of the agreement would require arrangements to ensure that Kyiv was fairly compensated for HEU from weapons that had been deployed in Ukraine.

U.S. officials also began to consider how the United States might assist Ukraine in eliminating the nuclear legacy it had inherited from the Soviet Union. The Cooperative Threat Reduction program, also referred to as the Nunn-Lugar program, provided funds to help reduce the former Soviet nuclear arsenal. While the administration and Congress assumed that the bulk of the money would go to Russia, American officials suggested that Ukraine could receive a portion. Ukrainian officials expressed interest, and Kravchuk raised this idea directly with Senator Richard Lugar. By the end of 1992, Bush had told Kravchuk in a letter that the United States was ready to provide Nunn-Lugar funding to assist with the costs of Ukraine's nuclear disarmament.[20] Kravchuk thanked Bush in a December 24 telephone conversation, and Bush told him that he expected the incoming Clinton administration also to agree on Nunn-Lugar funding.[21] Clinton reiterated that commitment in a phone call to Kravchuk shortly after taking office in January 1993.

American officials also began to press Ukraine to commit to deactivate the SS-24 ICBMs. The older and less sophisticated SS-19s were rapidly approaching the end of their service life, while the SS-24s carried more warheads and could remain in service longer. Moreover, there had been suggestions in Kyiv about retaining SS-24s, perhaps armed with conventional warheads. Since the SS-24s had been built in Ukraine, the Ukrainians were better positioned to maintain them. Secretary of Defense Les Aspin visited Kyiv in June 1993 and suggested that Ukraine deactivate the SS-24s by removing the warheads, even if the warheads would be stored for a time in Ukraine before being sent to

Russia. Aspin told Rada deputies that the nuclear weapons were problem number one for Washington.

Tarasyuk visited Washington in July to discuss, among other things, the draft of a charter on U.S.-Ukraine relations. U.S. officials had previously taken the position that the charter—ultimately to be signed by the presidents—had to reflect the Lisbon Protocol in the past tense; that is, the charter could only be signed after the Rada had ratified START and the protocol, and after Ukraine had joined the NPT as a non-nuclear weapons state. Ambassador-at-Large Strobe Talbott and National Security Council (NSC) senior director Nicholas Burns told Tarasyuk that a Kravchuk visit would be possible provided that Ukraine committed to and had begun substantial deactivation of its ICBMs. The deputy foreign minister responded positively, noting that the Ukrainian government accepted the deactivation plan. He also, however, handed over the draft of a treaty on security guarantees. U.S. officials pushed back hard against the idea of a treaty.

Morozov came to Washington shortly thereafter. The defense minister several times referred to a "temporary deterrent," which caused unease on the American side. They pressed him to include SS-24s in the deactivation process. Aspin told him that excluding SS-24s would alarm the Russians as well as pose a problem in securing Senate support for Nunn-Lugar assistance for Ukraine. Morozov responded that deactivating SS-24s would be politically difficult in Kyiv. He suggested that Ukraine could ask the Russians to remove the targeting tapes from the missiles; Chairman of the Joint Chiefs of Staff Colin Powell pointed out that they could be quickly replaced. Deputy Secretary of Defense Bill Perry suggested a working group to discuss deactivation, an idea that Morozov found interesting, but he insisted that the Russians could not know about it. That stipulation posed a dilemma for the Americans; they had been transparent with the Russians and worried that any secret working group would, once discovered by Moscow, be very damaging—and they believed Russian penetration of the Ukrainian government was such that the Russians would inevitably find out. The Americans did not pursue the idea. Morozov's visit nevertheless cemented a good working relationship with the Pentagon, which arranged side visits to the naval base at Norfolk, Virginia, and to an aircraft carrier. In discussions with Department of Defense officials, it became clear that he had begun thinking about Ukraine's non-nuclear future and how Kyiv might then manage its relations with Russia.

Meanwhile, the Ukrainians began to remove warheads from twenty of the older SS-19 missiles. Ambassador James Goodby, head of the U.S. delegation for the Safe and Secure Dismantlement of Nuclear Weapons, traveled to Kyiv to begin negotiation of agreements for providing Nunn-Lugar assistance.

In early July, Clinton and Yeltsin met on the margins of the Group of Seven (G-7) summit in Tokyo and discussed the question of nuclear weapons in Ukraine. (The G-7, consisting of the United States, Britain, Canada, France, Germany, Italy, and Japan, had begun including the Russian leader in some of their meetings.) Yeltsin suggested an idea that had begun to be considered at lower levels in the U.S., Ukrainian, and Russian governments: a trilateral process. Clinton quickly agreed.[22]

The first trilateral meeting took place in London in August, with Talbott joined by Tarasyuk and Dubinin. In addition, Russian deputy foreign minister Georgiy Mamedov participated. He and Talbott had begun to develop a close and productive working relationship. Mamedov, relatively young for his rank, was smart and had a sardonic wit. He had a more creative mind than most Russian diplomats, understood the often byzantine workings in Moscow, and could tell what would and would not sell at home. He was, moreover, prepared to take chances to solve problems. The four reviewed the issues that were being addressed in the Ukrainian-Russian channel and discussed the way forward. The Ukrainians continued to insist on compensation not just for the HEU in the strategic nuclear warheads they would be returning, but also for the HEU in the tactical nuclear warheads transferred in 1992. The Russians were not prepared to agree to provide nuclear fuel to compensate for the tactical warheads. Talbott subsequently suggested to Mamedov that Moscow consider writing off a portion of Ukraine's energy debt as compensation for the HEU in the tactical warheads. Ukraine owed Russia an estimated $1.5–2 billion for natural gas. Given the dire state of the Ukrainian economy, Russia had little real prospect of collecting this money, so it might instead write off the debt to satisfy the Ukrainian demand for compensation.

Moving from Bilateral to Trilateral Talks

Following the London meeting, U.S. officials believed the tentative agreements reached by the Ukrainians and Russians during the August Kuchma-Chernomyrdin meeting in Kyiv were sound. They remained prepared to see a solution worked out in the bilateral channel, but the collapse of the Masandra summit's outcome in early September convinced Washington that the Ukrainian-Russian channel would not deliver.

Washington concluded that it needed to become more directly involved. Ukrainian officials clearly wanted U.S. engagement. Although the Russians showed less enthusiasm, Yeltsin had opened the door in July. The U.S. embassies in Moscow and Kyiv, including ambassadors Thomas Pickering and William Miller (who had taken up his position as the second American ambassador to Ukraine in October 1993), began regular dialogues on what a trilateral solution might look like with host country officials, in particular Mamedov and Tarasyuk, who had become the point officials on the Russian and Ukrainian sides. While both Kyiv and Moscow accepted more active U.S. engagement, Mamedov cautioned Talbott that there would be unhappiness in both capitals: "Those people that you're dealing with in Kyiv will resent your taking away the strongest card in their hand, and many on our side will resent your meddling in something that they believe is none of your business. Remember, anything between us and the Ukrainians is a family affair, and any disagreement we have is a family feud."[23]

Washington's sense of urgency climbed a notch in the autumn when it became apparent that at least some nuclear weapons were solely under Ukrainian physical control. U.S. officials had been told that any launch of an ICBM from Ukraine would require orders by both the Russian and the Ukrainian president. Quite apart from the question of launch authority was the issue of spare ICBM warheads and the nuclear warheads for the air-launched cruise missiles, which were kept in storage bunkers. American officials assumed these bunkers were manned by Russian guards with Ukrainian guards providing an outer layer of security. When Timbie and I suggested this was how nuclear weapons in Ukraine were stored, Ukrainian officials essentially responded, "Why would you think that?" The only Russian military personnel in Ukraine were those in the Black Sea Fleet, and they had no responsibility for strategic nuclear weapons. All other military personnel, including those of the 43rd Rocket Army, had taken loyalty oaths to Ukraine.

American officials subsequently confirmed with Russian officials that only Ukrainian military forces were guarding—and thus physically controlling—the nuclear weapons at storage sites as well as manning the ICBM launch control posts and strategic bombers. They did not believe Kyiv could launch the missiles by themselves, though Russian officials from time to time suggested that the Ukrainian military had sought to crack the launch codes. Surprisingly for U.S. officials, their Russian counterparts did not seem particularly concerned about the stored weapons. Whatever the political tensions between Kyiv and Moscow, Russian military commanders—having served side by side in the Soviet Strategic Rocket Forces with the Ukrainian officers now running the 43rd Rocket Army—had confidence that their Ukrainian counterparts would act responsibly. The Russian military saw no threat and trusted the Ukrainian military's ability to secure the warheads.[24] U.S. officials had not considered the lingering effect of these kinds of professional and personal relationships. Despite their assurances, however, the Russians seemed to lack total confidence in the Ukrainians: I was later told that they had removed the firing devices from the warheads in the storage bunkers.[25]

Secretary of State Warren Christopher visited Kyiv in late October. The issue of nuclear weapons figured prominently in his talks, particularly as just a week earlier the Rada had approved a military doctrine calling Ukraine an "owner" of the nuclear arms as a result of "historical circumstances" and stating that the SS-24s would not be covered by START. Kravchuk assured Christopher of Ukraine's intention to fulfill its commitments under the Lisbon Protocol, a message reiterated by Zlenko in a separate meeting. Both Kravchuk and Zlenko said Ukraine was prepared to take certain steps regarding the SS-24s. Rada speaker Ivan Plyushch told Christopher that there was "no question" that Ukraine would adhere to the Lisbon Protocol. Over dinner, the Ukrainian president appeared close to agreeing to deactivation of the SS-24s, but Zlenko and Buteyko pulled him back.

The secretary also devoted time to the message that Talbott had carried to Kyiv in May regarding the U.S. view of a broader bilateral relationship. He discussed the daunting economic problems facing the

Ukrainian economy, which had begun rapidly contracting following the collapse of the Soviet Union. That discussion followed up on earlier talks in Kyiv conducted by an interagency team led by Burns on the importance of economic reform, possible U.S. assistance, and Ukraine's relations with the International Monetary Fund and World Bank. These conversations began giving Ukrainian officials greater confidence that Washington intended to shape an active bilateral relationship above and beyond the nuclear weapons question. By the end of the Christopher visit, the sides had concluded the umbrella agreement needed for Ukraine to begin receiving Nunn-Lugar assistance for the elimination of strategic arms, with an initial allocation of $175 million.

On November 18, the Rada took action on the START treaty and the Lisbon Protocol, approving a resolution of ratification. The resolution, however, incorporated numerous conditions that raised worries in Washington and Moscow. One condition effectively renounced the Lisbon Protocol's commitment to accede to the NPT "in the shortest possible time." Another suggested that Ukraine was required to eliminate only 36 percent of the strategic launchers and 42 percent of the warheads on its territory rather than all warheads, missiles, bombers, and silos. Still other conditions asserted Ukrainian ownership of the nuclear weapons, conditioned their elimination on receipt of security guarantees and financial assistance, and demanded compensation for the HEU in the tactical nuclear weapons removed to Russia in 1992.

The Rada's conditions called into question Ukraine's readiness to become a non-nuclear weapons state. Although the embassy in Kyiv believed the Rada action could nevertheless move the process forward, Washington found the resolution's language unacceptable: how could the Rada ratify START and the Lisbon Protocol while rejecting key provisions of those documents and the associated Kravchuk letter? A flurry of unhappy communications ensued between Washington and Kyiv, including a phone call from Clinton to Kravchuk, to express concern that Ukraine appeared to be backing away from its commitments. Ukrainian officials tried to reassure their American contacts. Kravchuk stated on November 19, "We must get rid of [these nuclear weapons]. This is my viewpoint from which I have not and will not deviate." He added, "I shall try to bring before a new parliament a proposal concerning START and joining the NPT."[26] The Ukrainians also informed Washington that they had begun the deactivation process for SS-24s by removing warheads from some missiles, a welcome step.

Clinton was scheduled to travel to Moscow to meet with Yeltsin on January 13 and 14, 1994. Although unhappy about the latest twist in the Rada, U.S. officials saw the Moscow visit as offering a target. If the trilateral process could be brought to a successful conclusion, the three presidents—Clinton, Yeltsin, and Kravchuk—could meet there to sign documents recording their agreement.

Vice President Al Gore visited the Russian capital in mid-December for a previously planned meeting of the U.S.-Russia Binational Commission, which he co-chaired with Chernomyrdin. Over lunch, Kozyrev blasted the Ukrainians' stance on denuclearization. He asserted that the Americans were being played by Kyiv and suggested a tough approach. Chernomyrdin complained that Kyiv told Moscow and Washington different things. Talbott, a member of the vice president's party, suggested that he and Mamedov travel to Kyiv to ensure that the Ukrainians were giving the Americans and Russians the same line. Gore and Chernomyrdin agreed. Perry, who was part of the Gore team and who had his own military aircraft, set off for Kyiv with Talbott, Assistant Secretary of Defense Ashton Carter, and NSC director Rose Gottemoeller (Perry and Carter were somewhat distracted, as at home Clinton had just announced that Aspin would step down as defense secretary). Mamedov went along, composing a Russian delegation of one. In Kyiv, Deputy Prime Minister Valeriy Shmarov led the Ukrainian delegation, which included Tarasyuk. Shmarov came out of the military industrial sector and had served as deputy director general of the National Space Agency of Ukraine. He added weight to the Ukrainian delegation.

The Kyiv discussions went well and covered all the major pieces necessary for a trilateral agreement—including security assurances, U.S. assistance for dismantling the strategic nuclear systems, and compensation for the HEU in the nuclear warheads. U.S. officials returned to Washington believing they had the outline of a settlement and saw a strong possibility to bring the deal to closure. Shmarov impressed U.S. officials with his straightforward and practical approach, as well as his readiness to make decisions. Talbott extended invitations to Mamedov, Shmarov, and Tarasyuk to visit Washington in early January to finalize the agreement.

Closing the Trilateral Deal

When the Russian and Ukrainian delegations arrived in Washington, the U.S. side had prepared drafts of both the Trilateral Statement and an accompanying annex. The annex addressed secondary issues and details; U.S. officials thought that either the Russians or the Ukrainians might wish to keep the annex confidential, in contrast to the statement, which was intended for signature and release as a public document.

Talbott, Mamedov, Shmarov, Tarasyuk and their aides discussed the draft texts on January 3 and 4. They agreed that Ukraine would confirm its commitment to eliminate all strategic nuclear weapons on its territory and to accede to the NPT as a non-nuclear weapons state "in the shortest possible time." The statement, taking account of discussions among Ukrainian, Russian, and American officials over the previous year, described the specific security assurances that Ukraine would receive once Ukraine acceded to the NPT, including the commitments of the United States, Britain, and Russia to respect Ukraine's independence, sovereignty, and existing borders and to refrain from the use of force or threat of force against Ukraine. Russia would agree to compensate Ukraine for the HEU in the strategic warheads by providing an equivalent amount of LEU in the form of nuclear fuel rods. The United States would commit to provide Nunn-Lugar Cooperative Threat Reduction assistance to help Ukraine defray the costs of eliminating the missiles, bombers, silos, and nuclear infrastructure on its territory. The statement also recorded the sides' agreement that the transfer of nuclear weapons to Russia and Russian delivery to Ukraine of the compensating nuclear fuel rods would take place simultaneously.

The annex set out early actions to be taken by the sides. It noted that warheads would be removed from all SS-24s within ten months. It also specified that, within ten months, Russia would provide nuclear fuel rods containing 100 tons of LEU, and Ukraine would in the same period transfer at least 200 ICBM warheads to Russia for dismantling, in order to get the warhead and fuel rod flows moving. One issue concerned timing: the Russian ministry of atomic energy would have to incur expenses almost immediately in order to prepare and ship fuel rods to Ukraine, but the ministry was financially stretched. The U.S. government arranged to advance Russia $60 million to "jump start" the process. The statement also recorded the U.S. commitment to provide

Ukraine a minimum of $175 million in Cooperative Threat Reduction funds and to seek to expand that assistance.

By the afternoon of January 4, the sides had reached agreement on the two texts and concluded that the annex as well as the statement could be public documents. But two substantive questions held up overall agreement. First, the agreed language in the annex said Ukraine would transfer the warheads to Russia "in the shortest possible time" but left that time undefined. Shmarov indicated that Ukraine was prepared to commit to transfer all warheads by June 1, 1996. However, given domestic political sensitivities, Kyiv wished, at least for the time being, to keep confidential the fact that it would transfer the nuclear warheads in considerably less time than the seven-year elimination period specified in START.

Second, the Ukrainians continued to insist on compensation for the HEU in the tactical nuclear weapons. The Russians indicated a readiness to write off a portion of Ukraine's energy debt as compensation, but Mamedov said Moscow could not state that publicly. The Russian government feared disclosing this arrangement would trigger demands for compensation from other post-Soviet states.

The negotiations concluded on January 4 without a resolution on the two points, and Mamedov departed for previously scheduled meetings in New York. Following his departure, U.S. officials came up with a possible solution: Ukraine would commit to the June 1, 1996, end date for transfer of all nuclear warheads, and Russia would commit to compensate Ukraine for the HEU in the tactical nuclear weapons in documents that would not be made public. The three presidents could record this in an exchange of confidential letters. The letters would note agreement to the end date for removal of all nuclear warheads from Ukraine (twenty-eight and one-half months after the planned mid-January meeting in Moscow, which equated to June 1, 1996) and Russia's agreement to provide Ukraine compensation for the HEU in the tactical weapons and to work out the exact figure within four months.[27] In a hastily arranged meeting at the Ukrainian embassy on January 5, Shmarov and Tarasyuk agreed to this approach and the U.S. draft texts. Talbott reached Mamedov by phone in New York, and he agreed as well.

American officials moved quickly to lock in agreement and sent instructions to the embassies in Kyiv and Moscow. On January 6, U.S.

embassy officials in each capital handed over the text of the statement, annex, and letters that had been worked out in Washington, noting that Clinton had personally approved them and would be prepared to sign the statement at a meeting of the three presidents in Moscow on January 14.

Shmarov and the Ukrainian delegation, which had met with Christopher the afternoon of January 5, went to the White House on January 6 to meet with National Security Adviser Anthony Lake. Lake informed Shmarov that, if convenient for the Ukrainian side, Clinton wanted to make a short stop in Kyiv the evening of January 12 on his way to Moscow—something U.S. officials understood that the Ukrainians very much desired.

Washington believed the deal was close but not yet fully in the bag. I traveled with a small team of U.S. officials to Moscow on January 10 to conform the texts of the statement and annex ("conforming" refers to ensuring that texts in different languages say essentially the same thing; it is particularly important for documents that are being signed at the presidential level). The process of conforming the English and Russian texts went smoothly and took just a few hours. Conforming the English and Ukrainian texts proved more difficult, as the Ukrainian delegation, led by Hryshchenko, apparently had instructions to revise certain aspects of the statement. The U.S. team made clear it had no authority to reopen the texts; ensuring the Ukrainian and Russian language texts matched the agreed English texts was the remaining task.

One key detail took place in a joint meeting of the three delegations, given that "guarantee" and "assurance" both translate as "guarantee" in Ukrainian and Russian. I read for the negotiating record a statement to the effect that, whenever "guarantee" appeared in the Ukrainian and Russian language texts of the Trilateral Statement, it was to be understood in the sense of the English word "assurance." The Ukrainian and Russian delegations confirmed that understanding.

Meanwhile, Clinton arrived in Kyiv the evening of January 12 for a three-hour stop and meeting with Kravchuk in a hastily constructed VIP room at Borispil Airport. He found Kravchuk having second thoughts about the trilateral arrangement (this likely explained the recalcitrant approach of the Ukrainian delegation in Moscow). With the press already reporting expectations of a deal, a breakdown would have been seen as a failure for all three presidents and would have badly, perhaps irreparably, damaged the trilateral process. In a one-on-one meeting, Clinton stressed to Kravchuk that giving way to second thoughts would jeopardize his welcome in Moscow, set back—perhaps even destroy—the trilateral process, and risk major damage to U.S.-Ukraine relations. Kravchuk set aside his doubts and told Clinton he would agree.

Late the next evening, January 13, all three delegations gathered at the Ukrainian embassy, where the Ukrainians and Russians still struggled to finish conforming their texts. The antipathy between the two delegations was palpable, and disputes over language dragged on. Just before midnight, Buteyko, who had come from Kyiv with Kravchuk, arrived. He gave firm instructions to the Ukrainian delegation, undoubtedly reflecting the Kravchuk-Clinton conversation. The sides finished conforming the texts early in the morning on January 14, just hours before the Kremlin signing ceremony.

As it turned out, not only the Ukrainians were having second thoughts. Just before the bilateral Yeltsin-Clinton dinner on the evening of January 13, Mamedov cautioned Talbott that the Russian president wanted to reopen some issues. Forewarned, Clinton recounted to Yeltsin how in Kyiv he had dissuaded Kravchuk from trying to renegotiate the agreed language. Were the trilateral process to fall apart now, it would be a huge setback; the January 14 meeting of the three presidents could not degenerate into a negotiating session. Yeltsin seemed to get the message. He did not propose any changes.

The Ukrainians and Russians preferred to put the statement and annex on treaty paper. This was not normal American practice, but the U.S. team agreed. It turned out that the Ukrainians' portable printer could not handle treaty paper, which was much thicker than regular bond. The U.S. delegation agreed to take the Ukrainian treaty paper to the American embassy and copy the Ukrainian-provided texts of the statement and annex onto the treaty paper. The embassy's copy machine could handle the Ukrainian treaty paper . . . barely. For every page successfully printed, another page or two would jam and burn through. With no more Ukrainian treaty paper within 450 miles of Moscow, the Americans finished printing the Ukrainian texts with one page of treaty paper to spare.

The morning of January 14, Clinton, Kravchuk, and Yeltsin met briefly in the Kremlin and then appeared before the press to sign the Trilateral Statement. U.S. officials left Moscow regarding the trilateral signing as a major achievement but recognizing that significant work remained. Ukraine still had to accede to the NPT, and a number of details to implement the Trilateral Statement and annex had yet to be settled: a schedule for transferring all warheads, a schedule for provision of compensatory fuel rods, and an agreement on how much debt Russia would write off to provide compensation for the HEU in the tactical nuclear warheads transferred in 1992. U.S. officials expected to have to engage intensely to broker agreement on those details.

Returning to Kyiv, Kravchuk faced criticism in the Rada for the Trilateral Statement. Some deputies complained that it was a political document rather than a legally binding agreement. Kravchuk and other senior officials argued that they had negotiated the best possible agreement and that Ukraine lacked both technical expertise and funds to sustain an independent nuclear deterrent.[28]

On February 3, 1994, the Rada held a second vote on ratifying the START treaty and Lisbon Protocol. This time, it approved ratification by a vote of 260 to 3 without the troublesome conditions that it had attached the previous November. The Rada failed, however, to pass a bill regarding accession to the NPT. The White House welcomed this "unconditional" ratification of START and the Lisbon Protocol and noted that, under the terms of the protocol, Kyiv had committed to accede to the NPT in the shortest possible time. Washington decided to take the bird in the hand and keep working on Ukraine's NPT accession.

Ukrainian and Russian officials met in early February to discuss the key implementing questions left over from January and succeeded in reaching agreement, to the happy surprise of their American counterparts. They agreed on monthly schedules for warhead transfers from Ukraine to Russia and shipment of fuel rods in the opposite direction, and both sides shared the schedules with American officials. The Ukrainians and Russians agreed to a debt write-off in the range of $400–520 million to compensate Ukraine for the HEU in the tactical nuclear weapons. They also agreed on provisions that would allow Ukrainian experts to monitor the elimination of strategic warheads transferred to Russia.

Broadening U.S. Appreciation for Ukraine

At the beginning of 1994, with the Trilateral Statement done, U.S. officials continued to think about a broader relationship with Kyiv. With Clinton's visit to Kyiv, however short, having followed Christopher's, and Kravchuk due to come to Washington in March, the high-level political dialogue began to gain momentum. Perry launched a program of military-to-military contacts, and the sides had begun talking about U.S. assistance for economic reforms in Ukraine. U.S. officials had committed $155 million in assistance and suggested that more would be possible if Kyiv energetically pursued reforms. Washington began to see the "old" business of nuclear weapons moving into the past— though it would take the rest of the year to wrap up the loose ends— and anticipated that the bilateral agenda could increasingly focus on political and economic questions, which could form the basis for the Clinton-Kravchuk meeting.

U.S. officials saw two primary challenges facing Ukraine. The first was the economy. If Kyiv shied away from tough reform decisions, things would only get worse. The economy would continue to underperform, while international assistance providers would become less and less willing to help. Second, Kyiv had to find a modus vivendi with Moscow. Neither needed the distraction of further arguments over questions such as the arrangements for basing the Black Sea Fleet, which remained an open question despite agreement on the division of the fleet's warships.

Defense Department officials suggested that Washington might play a role in helping the Ukrainians and Russians resolve the basing question and replicate the success of the trilateral process regarding nuclear weapons. No one, not even in Kyiv, expected the Russian navy to pull up stakes overnight. Novorossiysk and other facilities on the Russian Black Sea coast lacked the infrastructure to support the Russian ships then based in Sevastopol and elsewhere in Crimea. Washington could offer Kyiv and Moscow experience. With bases all around the world, the U.S. Navy had become adept at negotiating agreements that respected host-nation sovereignty while preserving the operational flexibility that its warships required.

The Ukraine desk at the Defense Department worked with U.S. Navy officials to prepare translations of a number of basing agreements, the terms of which might offer Ukrainian and Russian negotiators models for resolution of their differences over basing the Black Sea Fleet. Ukrainian officials at the ministries of defense and foreign affairs eagerly embraced the idea of a second trilateral discussion. Russian officials, however, made clear they regarded the trilateral process on nuclear weapons as a unique case. They showed no interest in U.S. assistance in resolving the Black Sea Fleet basing question or other problems on the Ukraine-Russia agenda.

In early March 1994, Clinton again hosted Kravchuk in Washington. They noted "a new era" in bilateral relations and agreed to broaden the relationship, including in the areas of democracy, rule of law, free trade, and economic cooperation. Although the nuclear issue was discussed, the main headlines from the summit concerned U.S. assistance for Ukraine. As noted in the presidents' joint statement, the United States intended to provide Ukraine with $700 million in assistance, counting $350 million in Nunn-Lugar funds for denuclearization in fiscal years 1994–96 and up to $350 million in FREEDOM Support Act funds for fiscal year 1994 to support economic reform and the development of a democratic society. The presidents agreed that the signing of a bilateral investment treaty and an agreement on the avoidance of double taxation could encourage U.S. investment in Ukraine while noting that Ukrainian actions to improve the investment climate remained critical.[29] Kravchuk's visit concluded with a dinner hosted by Vice President Gore in the ornate Benjamin Franklin Room at the State Department (thus began a tradition of the vice president hosting meals at the State Department for presidential visitors).

Following up on Secretary of State Christopher's visit to Kyiv five months earlier, Washington had begun to fill out a broader bilateral U.S.-Ukrainian relationship. Shortly after the Clinton-Kravchuk meeting, Perry traveled to Ukraine. While he focused on denuclearization, visiting an ICBM site at Pervomaysk, he also discussed broader military cooperation with his Ukrainian hosts. He offered Cooperative Threat Reduction assistance to provide housing for retired Ukrainian missile officers. He also discussed the possibilities for defense conversion and helping Ukraine's large military-industrial complex reorient itself toward production for civilian needs. There was intense interest in defense conversion, as in the United States, but converting defense plants in Ukraine to efficient and economic nondefense production proved difficult.

Perry's visit was followed weeks later by an economic delegation headed by the NSC's Nicholas Burns, with officials from the U.S. Agency for International Development, the Treasury Department, and the Overseas Private Investment Corporation. They discussed reform assistance and the establishment of a U.S.-Ukraine enterprise fund to support the growth of private business, including American investment. Privatization was one particular theme, especially in view of the European Bank for Reconstruction and Development's estimate that only 15 percent of Ukraine's GDP in 1993 had come from the private sector.

Economic reform, however, was making little progress, in part owing to focus on the Rada elections held in March and April. The election law in 1994 required that a candidate for a constituency seat win 50 percent of the vote plus one, and that at least 50 percent of eligible voters vote, or there would be a runoff election. Any runoff again required 50 percent participation for the vote to be valid. As a result of these requirements, when the new Rada met in July, only 338 of the 450 seats had been filled. Fifteen parties were represented, with the Communists being the largest, but many deputies took their seats as independents. It was hardly a parliamentary configuration to drive tough economic reforms.

On the nuclear front, good news began to arrive from both Moscow and Kyiv in the spring. Russian officials confirmed to the U.S. embassy that warheads were being transferred in accordance with the agreed schedule; the first sixty warheads arrived in March. In April, Ukrainian officials advised that Ukraine had begun to receive fuel rods. The warhead and fuel rod flows continued, albeit with some minor delays and finger-pointing. Despite these bumps, both Russia and Ukraine appeared to be abiding by the Trilateral Statement and the subsequent implementing arrangements.

Positive news on a related subject came in May. Shmarov visited Washington and signed with Gore a bilateral memorandum of understanding on the transfer of missile equipment and technology. Ukraine, still possessing a sizable rocket- and missile-building industry, agreed to observe the requirements and limitations of the multilateral 1987 Missile Technology Control Regime, while the United States agreed to work with Ukraine to make it a member of the regime.

A Presidential Election, and a Plan Forms

In the summer of 1994, U.S. officials began to consider how to complete the trilateral process, which meant achieving Ukraine's accession to the NPT, formal extension of the security assurances set out in the Trilateral Statement, and bringing START into force. The December summit of the Conference on Security and Cooperation in Europe (CSCE) in Budapest offered a venue where the relevant leaders—including the U.S., Russian, and Ukrainian presidents—could be present. Budapest became the target.

Meanwhile, Ukrainians prepared to go to the polls for a preterm presidential ballot in June, four months after they had voted in a new Rada. Kravchuk faced off against Kuchma, who had resigned as prime minister in the fall of 1993 in order to contest the presidency. Rightly or wrongly, the election was viewed by many in stark regional terms. Kravchuk was seen as the stronger nationalist favoring an independent Ukraine, while Kuchma was viewed as more interested in stronger links to Russia rather than in developing ties to the West. In the June 26 election, the electorate split largely on regional lines—the west and center for Kravchuk, the east and south for Kuchma. Although Kravchuk came in first, because he failed to secure 50 percent of the vote, a runoff was required. Kuchma won the second ballot on July 10, in an election that was judged largely free and fair. Kuchma's victory was seen as significant in the post-Soviet space in that it produced a peaceful transfer of presidential power. Kuchma became president on July 19. Many interpreted his win as a rejection of the more ideological views of western Ukraine and a rebalancing toward the interests of the eastern part of the country.

During the election campaign, both Kravchuk and Kuchma had sought to portray themselves as having links to senior U.S. leaders. Washington took no public position between the candidates, but U.S. officials quietly hoped for Kravchuk's reelection. He presented a known quantity who had delivered on the nuclear question. U.S. officials had had less contact with Kuchma and were less certain of his views. Washington pondered how to engage the newly elected president and ensure fulfillment of the Trilateral Statement.

Kuchma had a background in aerospace engineering. He had long worked in the Soviet space and rocket industry, rising to become general director of the large Pivdenmash missile and rocket factory in Dnipro-petrovsk in eastern Ukraine. Pivdenmash (also known by its Russian name, Yuzhmash) produced space launch vehicles, as well as many of the Soviet ICBMs that had concerned the U.S. military. A self-described pragmatist, Kuchma was not as overtly nationalistic as Kravchuk or other Ukrainian politicians, but nevertheless sought to preserve and strengthen the country's independence and sovereignty. A native Russian-speaker, he made an effort to use Ukrainian as he assumed national office. He could show good humor but also demonstrated a thin skin, reacting badly to criticism. He had a quick temper and could be pro-fane in private. He was detail oriented, sometimes distractingly so in meetings. Kuchma appeared almost obsessed with balance, both in Ukraine's position between Russia and the West and in domestic poli-tics, playing off against one another the various political forces and oligarchs around him. Uncomfortably for Washington, as it came to bet-ter understand the new president's network of associates, it included a number of people who were deeply corrupt. As would become clear later, Kuchma's commitment to democratic practices was weak, and his government would regularly abuse administrative tools in dealing with his political opponents.

By happenstance, Gore was scheduled to visit Warsaw from July 30 to August 1 for meetings with the Polish leadership. At the White House, Burns and Gottemoeller discussed with Leon Fuerth, the vice president's national security adviser, the possibility that the vice presi-dent could make a brief stop in Kyiv on August 2. Gore agreed and became the first senior foreign official to pay a call on Kuchma follow-ing his assumption of the presidency. In the context of a broad discus-sion of the U.S.-Ukraine relationship, Gore noted the opportunity to complete the trilateral process in Budapest during the upcoming CSCE summit and extend security assurances to Ukraine. Kuchma expressed interest. The two also discussed the possibility of an early Kuchma visit to Washington to meet Clinton, which was subsequently scheduled for November.

U.S. officials followed up by pressing their Ukrainian counterparts to move forward with Rada ratification of Ukraine's accession to the NPT in order to enable closure in Budapest. They finalized the lan-guage of the security assurances that had been promised in the Janu-ary Trilateral Statement, secured Russian and British agreement to the text, and shared the text with Kyiv. The Ukrainians indicated the text was acceptable, particularly as it now included a provision that the parties would "consult in the event of a situation arising which raises a question" concerning the statement's commitments. As Kuchma's November 21–23 visit to Washington neared, U.S. officials made clear that a prior Rada vote on NPT accession would create a positive atmosphere during his visit.

With Washington urging closure, Kuchma pressed the Rada to move forward on NPT accession. He addressed the body directly on the need to act, and the Rada on November 16 passed a resolution of accession by a vote of 301 to 8. Like the Rada's first attempt at ratifying START, however, the wording of the resolution contained a twist: instead of affirming Ukraine's accession as a non-nuclear weapons state, the resolution was, at best, ambiguous. At worst, it suggested that the country was an owner of nuclear arms. This interpretation would have reaffirmed a position Kyiv had taken since 1991, that Ukraine owned the weapons by right of being a successor state to the Soviet Union even if it intended to become a non-nuclear weapons state. The resolution raised serious questions.

When reviewing the text in Washington, State Department lawyers noted that, as a depositary state for NPT instruments of accession, the United States (as well as Russia and the United Kingdom) had some leeway under international law to interpret ambiguous documents. In their view, the U.S. government could accept the language of the Rada resolution as meaning that Ukraine acceded as a non-nuclear weapons state.

Washington consulted with Moscow and London. British lawyers concurred with the State Department's legal view, but the Russians took a less flexible position. They said the Rada resolution did not meet their requirement that Ukraine accede to the NPT as a non-nuclear weapons state. It thus would not suffice to allow START entry into force or extension of security assurances to Ukraine. On November 17, the Russian foreign ministry issued a statement addressing the Rada vote:

Moscow appreciates the Ukrainian leadership's efforts to resolve the issue of Ukraine's accession to the Non-Proliferation Treaty of July 1, 1968. In this connection, we were satisfied to hear the news that the Supreme Soviet of Ukraine [the Rada] yesterday passed a law on accession to this treaty. At the same time, we cannot ignore the fact that the adopted law stipulated some conditions. The content of these terms makes unclear the status—nuclear or non-nuclear—in which Ukraine is planning to join the NPT. . . . These questions must be answered because the NPT depositaries are now completing the drafting of a document on security guarantees [assurances] for Ukraine, which are planned to be given to it as a state not possessing nuclear weapons. The importance of clarifying these issues is quite understandable.[30]

The White House took a more positive line, issuing a press statement welcoming the Rada vote, noting that it cleared the way for Ukraine to accede to the NPT as a non-nuclear weapons state, and concluding that Ukraine's accession to the NPT opened a new period of expanded U.S.-Ukrainian cooperation. State Department officials meanwhile weighed how to deal with the Rada language and the Russian rejection. Asking the Rada to vote on a new resolution, as Russian officials suggested, appeared to be a nonstarter. No one in the American embassy in Kyiv or the State Department saw any chance that the Rada would take up the question again. The problem boiled down to finding a way to "clarify" the Rada's ambiguous language so that it satisfied the Russian demand for a clear statement that Ukraine acceded to the NPT as a non-nuclear weapons state. The problem became more complicated when Ukrainian officials advised that the Rada's resolution of ratification would have to be transmitted to the U.S., Russian, and British governments as Ukraine's instrument of accession to the NPT.

Despite these complications, Kuchma's November 1994 state visit to Washington proved successful and covered a growing range of issues on the bilateral agenda. Kuchma and Clinton signed the "Charter on American-Ukrainian Partnership, Friendship and Cooperation," which outlined a framework for further developing the bilateral relationship, and reached a number of other agreements. The presidents discussed the evolving security situation in Europe. Clinton announced funding to support Ukraine's participation in NATO's Partnership for Peace, which Kyiv had joined at the beginning of the year. The two presidents agreed to begin an international military training and education program to help the professional development of Ukraine's military.

On economic questions, Clinton and Kuchma stressed the importance of market-oriented economic reforms for Ukraine. (In fact, U.S. officials had been favorably impressed by Kuchma's initial moves on economics, including his October reform package and his reliance on reformers such as Viktor Yushchenko and Viktor Pynzenyk.) The presidents welcomed the first meeting of the joint commission on trade and investment, established to address ways to increase bilateral trade and steps that Kyiv might take to improve the investment climate. Clinton announced $200 million in economic assistance for Ukraine in fiscal year 1995, on top of the $350 million in reform assistance announced during the Clinton-Kravchuk meeting the previous March. The presidents agreed to cooperate to close Chornobyl. Earlier in the year, at the July G-7 summit in Naples, the United States had helped to secure agreement on an action plan to close the nuclear plant with substantial international assistance. As for the remaining nuclear arms questions, the joint statement noted that the two presidents looked "forward to early entry into force of the START treaty and agreed that the Lisbon Protocol signatories should exchange instruments of ratification on the margins of the Budapest CSCE summit."[31]

Facing a tight deadline, U.S. officials hit on a possible solution to the problem posed by the ambiguity of the Rada's resolution: have the Ukrainian government clarify the language of its legislative branch's document. U.S. officials suggested to the Ukrainians that, when Kuchma transferred the resolution of ratification to Clinton, Yeltsin, and British prime minister John Major in Budapest, he hand it over under cover of a diplomatic note stating that Ukraine acceded to the NPT as a nonnuclear weapons state.

This proposal satisfied the Russians in principle, and the Ukrainians were amenable to the approach, though working out the precise language went down to the wire. With leaders set to gather in Budapest on December 5, discussions between the U.S. embassy and Ukrainian officials failed to come to terms on an acceptable text of a cover note on December 3. The discussions moved to Budapest the next day. Christopher met with Kozyrev late the evening of December 4; the Russian foreign minister essentially gave the Americans his proxy to work out the final language with the Ukrainian side, and he retired for the night.

James Collins, coordinator in the Office of the New Independent States, led a small group of officials to follow up with Ukrainian foreign minister Hennadiy Udovenko, Hryshchenko, and the Ukrainian team—with no Russian officials present. The meeting ran into the early hours of December 5, interrupted by periodic phone calls from Air Force One asking whether the language had been settled. At several points Udovenko seemed ready to accept the language, but Hryshchenko raised legal or technical objections over what seemed to be minor points. Finally, Timbie and I engaged Hryshchenko, while Collins took Udovenko to another room, where they reached agreement on the language for the Ukrainian diplomatic note—as in January in Moscow, just a few hours before the signing ceremony.

In a carefully orchestrated ceremony later that morning, Kuchma passed to Clinton, Yeltsin, and Major the Rada's instrument of accession to the NPT, covered by a diplomatic note making clear that Ukraine joined the treaty as a non-nuclear weapons state. The four leaders then signed the Budapest Memorandum of Security Assurances for Ukraine, following which Clinton, Kuchma, Yeltsin, Kazakh president Nursultan Nazarbayev, and Belarusian president Alyaksandr Lukashenka exchanged the documents to bring the START treaty into force. For Clinton, the ceremony was the highlight of an otherwise difficult visit that featured a very public blast by Yeltsin against the prospect of NATO enlargement.

The Budapest Memorandum, as it came to be called, reaffirmed the commitments of the United States, Britain, and Russia "to respect the independence and sovereignty and the existing borders of Ukraine"; "to refrain from the threat or use of force against the territorial integrity or political independence of Ukraine"; "to refrain from economic coercion designed to subordinate to their own interest the exercise by Ukraine of the rights inherent in its sovereignty"; and "to seek immediate United Nations Security Council action to provide assistance to Ukraine, as a non-nuclear-weapon state party to the Treaty on the Non-Proliferation of Nuclear Weapons, if Ukraine should become a victim of an act of aggression or an object of a threat of aggression in which nuclear weapons are used." The memorandum also reflected U.S., British, and Russian commitments "not to use nuclear weapons against any non-nuclear-weapon state party to the Treaty on the Non-Proliferation of Nuclear Weapons" and "to consult in the event a situation arises which raises a question concerning these commitments."[32]

France and China separately extended parallel security assurances to Ukraine, important gestures for Kyiv, because they meant that the newly independent state had assurances from all five permanent members of the UN Security Council. The political importance that Ukraine attached to the memorandum and assurances was evidenced by the fact that Kyiv treated the memorandum as, in effect, an international treaty, including by publishing the document in a compendium of Ukraine's treaties.

For all the challenges of completing the Trilateral Statement and Budapest Memorandum, implementation proceeded in a remarkably smooth fashion. Trains carrying warheads removed from SS-19 and SS-24 ICBMs and Kh-55 air-launched cruise missiles regularly departed Ukraine for Russia, where the weapons were delivered to a dismantlement facility. In return, the Russians made regular shipments of assembled fuel rods for use in Ukrainian nuclear power plants. The Ukrainian and Russian governments kept Washington informed on the progress. There were brief delays, but no major hitches.

On May 31, 1996, two trains carrying the last strategic nuclear warheads departed Ukraine, so that all nuclear warheads were transferred by the June 1, 1996, deadline, an achievement that was welcomed by Washington. With significant Cooperative Threat Reduction assistance from the United States (in the hundreds of millions of dollars), Ukraine removed the SS-19s and SS-24s from their silos and destroyed the silos. The SS-19 missiles were defueled and destroyed, though some were sold to Russia (such transfer was permitted under START). Most of the Blackjack and Bear-H bombers were eliminated in accordance with START's terms—the wings were cut off, and the fuselages were cut into three pieces—though Ukraine agreed in 1999 to transfer some Blackjack bombers to Russia (also permitted). The SS-24 missiles were broken down into stages; their final elimination was delayed as Ukraine and the United States worked out a process for removing the solid fuel from the missile stages. In October 2001, the last SS-24 silo was destroyed, eliminating the final START-accountable item on Ukraine's territory.

Reflections

By the end of 1994, the U.S. government had put in place arrangements to achieve its goal of getting the nuclear weapons out of Ukraine. Although the process was painful at times, Washington in the end succeeded in assembling a package of measures that met the fundamental requirements of all three countries. Russia and the United States wanted the nuclear weapons out of Ukraine. Kyiv sought four outcomes: security assurances; compensation for the value of the HEU in the nuclear warheads; assistance in eliminating the nuclear legacy inherited from the Soviet Union; and satisfactory conditions for elimination of the missiles, bombers, and nuclear warheads. From Ukraine's perspective, the trilateral process produced acceptable, if not ideal, outcomes on each issue.

Other events no doubt influenced the process and timing of success. In late 1993, Ukrainian authorities seemed to grow concerned that dragging out the process could alienate the United States at a difficult time. The strong showing by Vladimir Zhirinovskiy's ultranationalist Liberal Democratic Party in the December 1993 Russian parliamentary elections worried Kyiv (as well as U.S. officials). That unwelcome event came when the Ukrainian government faced an uneasy situation in Crimea and a relationship with Russia already burdened with difficult issues. The Ukrainians concluded that it was time to cash in the nuclear bargaining chip; the costs of holding on to nuclear weapons were too high, especially when the weapons seemed to provide little real benefit.

U.S. engagement, while not preordained, proved necessary to bring the denuclearization process to a conclusion. American officials recognized that Ukraine, still struggling to establish state institutions and find its way in international relations, had a hard time dealing one-on-one with Russia. They could look for ways to advise, support, and sometimes even console the Ukrainians on the difficult choices they faced.

The process also succeeded because the sides were prepared to look for practical solutions and "do what worked," as one American participant described it. Thus, while Baker strongly resisted new commitments to Ukraine, State Department officials deftly repackaged existing assurances from documents such as the UN Charter and Helsinki Final Act. Although the assurances themselves were not new, their packaging

in a Ukraine-specific document was symbolically and politically important to Kyiv as it sought to bolster its sovereignty. The January 1994
exchange of private letters among the three presidents conveyed commitments that at the time were problematic for Kyiv and Moscow to
make publicly. Doing what worked did not require that they make those
commitments public. When the Rada resolution of accession to the NPT
contained ambiguous language regarding Ukraine's status as a non-
nuclear weapons state, the three sides agreed that the Ukrainian government would "clarify" it in a cover note. Such practical solutions
successfully overcame thorny questions.

The U.S. government's ability to mobilize funds also proved important to the success of the trilateral process. The early commitment of
substantial Nunn-Lugar Cooperative Threat Reduction assistance as-
suaged Ukrainian concerns that they might have to foot the bill for
implementing the reductions required by START. Likewise, the advance of $60 million to Russia enabled the production of fuel rods for
Ukrainian reactors well before Russia could generate revenues by selling to the United States low enriched uranium that had been blended
down from highly enriched uranium extracted from dismantled weapons. There was a subsequent $100 million advance, and the $160 million was later repaid from revenues generated by the delivery of low
enriched uranium.

U.S. officials used events and presidential engagement to drive
the process. In January 1994, the possibility of a trilateral Clinton-
Kravchuk-Yeltsin meeting, preceded by President Clinton's visit to
Kyiv, even if just for a few hours, helped the push to conclude the Trilateral Statement. At the end of the year, the Budapest summit became
the target for completing the remaining steps so that the assurances
could be formally conveyed in conjunction with Ukraine's accession to
the NPT and START's entry into force.

Kyiv was sometimes frustrated with Washington, believing U.S.
officials joined with their Russian counterparts to push Ukraine too
hard. In retrospect, Washington might not have fully understood
or appreciated the pressures on Kravchuk and Kuchma. They faced
questioning at home regarding the wisdom of giving up nuclear weapons. They needed to be able to show that their diplomacy yielded real
benefits in return. That said, some Rada resolutions and statements
might have been quietly encouraged by the Presidential Administration

in order to strengthen the Ukrainian hand in dealing with Washington and Moscow. Overtly hardball tactics, particularly from the Russian side, did not go down well in Kyiv. A more nuanced approach by the United States and Russia might have led to a smoother negotiating process. And, as I noted in chapter 1, the U.S. government's single-minded focus on nuclear weapons likely provoked worry in Kyiv about what relationship, if any, it would have with Washington once it had disposed of the nuclear arms.

The conclusion of the Budapest Memorandum largely cleared the nuclear question from the U.S.-Ukraine agenda. The relationship subsequently turned to other issues, and the years 1995–97 witnessed a major expansion of U.S.-Ukraine relations, in ways that put to rest any lingering concerns in Kyiv that the U.S. government cared only about the nuclear arms question. It likewise opened the door to an expansion of Ukraine's relations with Europe.

When he decided to sign the Trilateral Statement, Kravchuk undoubtedly had a sense of the political and other costs that Ukraine would incur if it tried to keep even some nuclear weapons. The country could not have an independent nuclear weapons capability if it was dependent on the Russian nuclear complex for technical support and maintenance of the nuclear weapons. While Ukraine likely had the scientific and engineering expertise to develop its own nuclear infrastructure, the cost would have been prohibitive. By all appearances, Kravchuk recognized that there was no realistic option for an independent nuclear force.

In 2014, in the aftermath of Russia's military seizure of Crimea and its support—in the form of leadership, funding, weapons, and in some cases regular units of the Russian army—for armed separatism in eastern Ukraine, many in Kyiv questioned the wisdom of giving up nuclear arms. Their skepticism was understandable, given how Russia's actions blatantly violated the assurances it gave Ukraine in 1994 in the Budapest Memorandum as well as commitments it undertook elsewhere to respect its neighbor's sovereignty, independence, and territorial integrity. Many Ukrainians felt that, had their country retained a nuclear arsenal, Russia would never have dared to occupy Crimea or foster separatism in the Donbas region, and they saw the Budapest Memorandum as responsible for their vulnerability to Russian aggression. As one of the U.S. negotiators of the memorandum, I hear about this just about every time I return to Ukraine.

Alternative histories are always speculative. Had Ukraine chosen to keep nuclear weapons, as many Ukrainians now wish it had, that decision would have carried significant political and economic consequences for the country. Kyiv might not have ended up with the pariah status that North Korea has attained, but a nuclear-armed Ukraine would have found itself very much an outsider in relations with the West. Such a Ukraine would not have developed the kinds of relationships that I discuss in subsequent chapters: a strategic partnership with the United States and establishment of a binational commission co-chaired by Gore and Kuchma; a distinctive partnership with NATO supported by a standing NATO-Ukraine commission; and a partnership and cooperation agreement (and, years later, an association agreement) with the European Union. None of these developments would have occurred had Kyiv chosen to retain nuclear arms.

Moreover, if Ukraine had kept nuclear weapons, neither the United States nor the European Union would have launched major assistance programs to help it reform and modernize. One can debate the effectiveness of that assistance, but a nuclear-armed Ukrainian state would have received nothing. It would have had to finance reform itself, as well as deal alone with the costs of such programs as construction of a new sarcophagus to cover the remains of reactor number four at Chornobyl. U.S. and European executive directors at the International Monetary Fund, World Bank, and European Bank for Reconstruction and Development undoubtedly would have blocked low-interest credits for Ukraine, and the country might have faced Western economic sanctions. All of this would have come at a time when the economy was contracting at a painfully high rate. The economy also would have been burdened with the costs of building the infrastructure to support an independent nuclear weapons capability.

Kyiv would likely have found that, in any dispute that it had with Moscow, the United States and Europe would have been neutral at best. In some cases, the West, or at least some countries in the West, might have been inclined to support Russia.

Some in retrospect now ask why Ukraine did not demand that the United States and United Kingdom provide more robust assurances—

for example, a NATO Article 5–type security guarantee that would have committed U.S. and British military forces to Ukraine's territorial defense. That question also is understandable, but Kyiv would not have succeeded. Washington wanted nuclear weapons out of Ukraine, but neither the Bush nor the Clinton administration was prepared to offer that kind of guarantee.

The Ukrainian government thus had no alternative to the security assurances, which seemed to many in Kyiv and elsewhere so painfully thin in 2014. For its part, Washington supported Ukraine and moved to sanction Russia, with the first sanctions leveled in March 2014. The U.S. government, however, could and should have done more. First, the Obama administration should have more frequently cited the Budapest Memorandum to put its actions in context. The memorandum answered the question of why Americans should care about a country nearly 5,000 miles away: the U.S. government in 1994 made a commitment in order to achieve a goal that was very important to American security interests, the elimination of nearly 2,000 nuclear warheads built to strike the United States.

Second, the administration should have provided additional assistance. With the European Union, it could have offered greater economic assistance—tied closely to the implementation of specific reforms by Kyiv. And it could have provided greater military assistance, including some lethal military equipment, to strengthen Ukraine's ability to defend itself and deter further Russian aggression.

CHAPTER 3

The Relationship Blossoms

When Air Force One touched down at Kyiv's Borispil Airport on May 11, 1995, the briefing book for President Bill Clinton's meetings with President Leonid Kuchma contained just a single talking point on nuclear weapons: praise for Ukraine's denuclearization effort and for the positive example it set for the Nonproliferation Treaty review conference, which was just concluding in New York. For the first time, a meeting between the American and Ukrainian presidents could focus on issues other than nuclear weapons. The bilateral relationship, the outlines of which had been laid down in the second half of 1993 and 1994, blossomed in the years 1995–97. The two countries announced a strategic partnership, began an even broader exchange of views, including on Ukraine's place in the American vision for an evolving Europe, and saw their cooperation expand into new areas. It was a period of ambitious and positive development of the relationship.

Clinton to Kyiv

The second half of 1994 laid a solid basis for relations between Clinton and Kuchma, as well as between Vice President Al Gore and the Ukrainian president. The vice president indicated his readiness to take a leading role in managing the relationship with Ukraine, as he already was doing with Russia. While Clinton continued to take a strong interest, having the vice president engage personally meant that Washington had two interlocutors who could share the dialogue with Kuchma. Kuchma wanted face and phone time with Clinton, but he never insisted that he should deal solely with the president.

On January 25, 1995, Gore phoned Kuchma in what became a routine series of calls to discuss developments in the bilateral relationship and other issues of concern to Kyiv. Typical of those phone conversations, this one covered issues ranging from economic reform to the difficulties Kuchma faced in dealing with Moscow to how the NATO-Ukraine relationship might develop. Gore assured Kuchma that he was available whenever the Ukrainian president might want to call or write. In March, the two met briefly on the margins of the United Nations Summit on Social Development in Copenhagen.

Ukrainian officials made clear their desire to host Clinton, and the White House in early 1995 put a Kyiv stop on its agenda for the spring. When Clinton decided to travel to Moscow to commemorate the fortieth anniversary of the end of World War II in Europe, Kyiv was tentatively added to the trip. By that time I had joined the National Security Council (NSC) staff, and I asked the U.S. embassy in Kyiv to explore whether a May visit would be convenient for Kuchma's schedule. The Ukrainians agreed immediately and in their eagerness announced the visit without waiting for the customary coordinated announcement by Washington.

White House schedule-minders, always keen to minimize the president's time outside of the country, originally suggested that the president make a day stop. Ambassador William Miller reported that the Ukrainians very much wanted an overnight stay. Kyiv attached value to symbols, and an overnight and state dinner would allow Kuchma to emphasize the special nature of the U.S.-Ukraine relationship. The White House schedulers relented, and the Ukrainians got their first glimpse of what a presidential overnight visit entailed. Among other things, Deputy Chief of Mission James Schumaker conveyed the White House request for 700 hotel rooms to accommodate the president's party, White House staff, Secret Service, the advance and support teams, and the large number of accompanying press. Ukrainian protocol officers gasped but told the embassy that they would find the rooms.

With dates set (the president would arrive from Moscow on May 11 and depart for Washington the afternoon of May 12), U.S. and Ukrainian officials began discussing the substance and possible summit deliverables. The presidents the previous November had signed the "Charter on American-Ukrainian Partnership, Friendship and Cooperation" and announced $200 million in new assistance for Ukraine. American officials regarded the Kyiv summit more as an opportunity for discussion between the presidents than as a venue for announcing major initiatives or achievements. They saw the visit as an opportunity to signal U.S. support for macroeconomic reform and privatization in Ukraine. Postnuclear cooperation and the question of European security were logical additional topics. Miller suggested time also be included for a one-on-one meeting between the presidents, where Kuchma would be interested in an exchange of views on Russia and Russian president Boris Yeltsin—no surprise given the difficulties that continued to plague relations between Kyiv and Moscow.

Deputy Secretary of State Strobe Talbott led a U.S. team to Kyiv in early April to advance the substance of the president's visit. Foreign Minister Hennadiy Udovenko underscored the "exceptional" importance the Ukrainian side attached to Clinton's visit and proposed the signing of an ambitious set of agreements, including a mutual legal assistance treaty and a commercial space launch agreement. Talbott cautioned that the agreements would not be ready in time. They also discussed the upcoming May review conference for the nuclear Nonproliferation Treaty (NPT). Talbott noted that Ukraine's decision to give up nuclear weapons should be recognized at the conference as an important step in the effort to reduce nuclear arms.

In a separate discussion, Deputy Prime Minister (and Defense Minister) Valeriy Shmarov dwelled mainly on Russia, particularly the ongoing haggling over terms for the Russian Black Sea Fleet's continued presence in Sevastopol and Crimea. Ukrainian and Russian negotiators had previously worked out a division of the Black Sea Fleet's ships but remained far apart on basing terms. Talbott assured Shmarov that, during his discussions in Moscow before coming to Kyiv, he had made clear the U.S. position that any arrangement for the Black Sea Fleet's basing had to respect Ukrainian sovereignty.

Kuchma expressed gratitude for U.S. reform assistance and for support for Kyiv's requests for low-interest credits from the International Monetary Fund (IMF) and World Bank. The president reviewed the complex relationship with Russia, including the Black Sea Fleet basing question, and the complicated politics he faced at home. He said Ukrainian leftists—who formed the largest grouping in the Rada (parliament)—wanted to return to the Soviet Union, while the "radical right" asserted that Ukraine did not need Russia at all. Kuchma regarded both courses as impossible; he said he needed to pursue a middle course. Talbott indicated that Clinton would be interested in discussing European security and the role that Ukraine could play as institutions such as NATO evolved.

Volodymyr Horbulin, Kuchma's National Security and Defense Council secretary, visited Washington on May 1 to review preparations for the Clinton visit. His meeting with National Security Adviser Anthony Lake showed that the sides held similar views regarding the agenda: reform developments in Ukraine, European security, and relations with Russia. Horbulin raised the possibility of inviting Kuchma to attend the June 1995 Group of Seven (G-7) summit to be hosted by the Canadians in Halifax. President Leonid Kravchuk had attended the 1994 G-7 summit in Naples, where assistance for Ukraine and the closure of Chornobyl had been major topics. U.S. officials were not enthusiastic about the Ukrainian president attending back-to-back G-7 summits, fearing Kyiv might then seek to join the annual G-7 meetings on a regular basis. They gently poured cold water on the idea.

The Clinton state visit to Kyiv came off well. Presidential discussions addressed the economic reform steps that Kuchma had announced in late 1994 and early 1995. Among other things, those reforms had liberalized prices and freed the exchange rate. In parallel, the National Bank of Ukraine halted credit emissions, which rapidly reduced the inflation rate.[1] These measures sufficed to secure a $1.5 billion standby program from the IMF, as well as assistance from other international donors. The presidents announced that the U.S. government would provide a $250 million credit facility to support Ukraine's import needs. They also discussed space cooperation and steps to close the Chornobyl power plant.

Clinton and Kuchma dealt with more sensitive topics in a small group discussion. Kuchma described the difficulties that Kyiv faced with Moscow. Clinton, who personally liked Yeltsin and believed he could work with him, reiterated that the United States hoped to be helpful in smoothing relations between Ukraine and Russia. The presidents also discussed NATO's pending enlargement. Clinton underscored that the U.S. government would seek to manage enlargement in a manner that would not undercut the security of any European country. He expressed understanding of Ukraine's position, situated between a soon-to-enlarge NATO and Russia.

With Ukraine and Russia implementing the understandings that had been reached in the Trilateral Statement and nuclear warheads flowing back to Russia for dismantlement, the presidents had little to discuss on nuclear arms. Clinton simply praised Kuchma for the very positive nonproliferation example Ukraine had set. Clinton's visit coincided with the conclusion of the NPT review conference in New York, which agreed to extend the term of the treaty indefinitely. Clinton publicly credited Ukraine's decision to give up nuclear arms as having been a major factor in that decision.

The joint statement issued by the two presidents on May 12 reflected the broadening nature of the bilateral relationship. Like most joint statements, the language had been worked out between the capitals in advance. In contrast to earlier U.S.-Ukrainian documents, which often required a final negotiation into the early hours just before signing, Jon Purnell of the Department of State's Ukraine desk and embassy officers had met with the foreign ministry and finished the joint statement the day before Clinton touched down. The only outstanding issue was the Ukrainian government's desire to have the joint statement signed by the presidents. This was not normal U.S. practice, but on board Air Force One en route from Moscow to Kyiv, Lake approved signing the statement. There was, however, one glitch. The U.S. translator, believing his work done, had departed Kyiv that morning. He had not certified that the English and Ukrainian texts were substantively identical, as that was not necessary for joint statements that would be issued without signatures. Lacking that, NSC staff informed the Ukrainians that Clinton could sign only the English text. (Kuchma went ahead and signed both.)

The joint statement highlighted the increased attention to economics and economic reform. It began by addressing economic reform and Ukraine's potential to access $2.7 billion in financing from the IMF and other international financial institutions. It noted the important role that trade and investment would play in strengthening Ukraine's economy and stressed both countries' commitment to restructure and reform the Ukrainian energy sector. The presidents expressed pleasure that commercial space launch negotiations had begun and announced that a Ukrainian astronaut would fly on space shuttle mission STS-87, scheduled for 1997. The statement briefly noted Kyiv's accession to the NPT and Ukraine's receipt of security assurances in Budapest the previous December before describing increasing cooperation between the two sides' militaries and their intent to consult on issues regarding Europe's security architecture in light of NATO's prospective enlargement.[2]

In addition to his meetings and state dinner with Kuchma, Clinton's schedule included a speech on the steps of the Taras Shevchenko University in the center of Kyiv. On a rather cold morning before the red façade of the university's main building, the president told the crowd, "your efforts [at reform] will be repaid, for your independent country has a better chance to create freedom and prosperity than it has had in centuries, and to do it in a way that is uniquely your own as one of Europe's oldest peoples forging one of its newest democracies." He added that "as you build your future, the United States will stand by you" and closed with "God bless America. Slava Ukrayini [Glory to Ukraine]."[3]

During the speech, the White House staff were in a holding area behind and below the president's podium; they could only see the street cleared for security reasons directly in front of the president, not the tens of thousands of students and other citizens of Kyiv gathered in the park opposite the university. (Mindful of the unfortunate experience of the previous American president's address in Ukraine—President George H. W. Bush's "chicken Kyiv" speech—I had invited a prominent Ukrainian American to privately preview a draft of the speech to make sure that it had no similar problems.) Judging by the applause, the speech turned out well. Clinton traveled to Babyn Yar (Babiy Yar), a ravine where Nazi troops had slaughtered more than

33,000 Jews in September 1941. Given the sensitivities of the government and the local Jewish community, the president visited and laid wreaths at both the official memorial and at the menorah erected by the Jewish community at the edge of the ravine.

In January 1994, Clinton's three-hour stop had allowed no time to leave the airport. The May visit thus was his first real time in the Ukrainian capital. The White House advance team had prepared suggestions for sites to visit, including St. Sofia's Cathedral and the Pechersk Lavra monastery, should the president desire to do some sightseeing at the conclusion of his official schedule. The city clearly charmed Clinton. He enjoyed the sights, and Air Force One lifted off for Washington more than two hours later than planned.

The visit cemented a positive trajectory for U.S.-Ukraine relations. The one missed stop was the Rada, which the advance team had cut from the schedule. That decision unfortunately left Rada speaker Oleksandr Moroz feeling snubbed. The other negative note discussed on the flight back to Washington had taken place at the hotel housing the bulk of the American party. White House and State Department staffers arriving at their floor found the usual warning signs posted that rooms were not secure for classified conversations. Several signs, however, had the warning that rooms "may be bugged" scratched out, with "are bugged" scrawled in by hand. Security officers sweeping Secretary of State Warren Christopher's suite before he arrived had found and removed several listening devices. Some things apparently were slow to change.

Moving to a Strategic Partnership

From 1995, the pace of high-level U.S.-Ukrainian contacts increased markedly. The vice president met with Prime Minister Yevhen Marchuk in the fall. Secretary of Defense Bill Perry made several visits to Ukraine, including in January 1996, when he joined Shmarov and Russian defense minister Pavel Grachev on a visit to Pervomaysk. The three witnessed the destruction of an intercontinental ballistic missile silo after narrowly avoiding disaster when their aircraft overshot an icy runway and ploughed into a snowfield. Christopher met with Kuchma in Helsinki on February 8, 1996, and they announced that Kuchma would make a working visit to Washington on February 21–22. Carlos Pascual, who had taken over as the NSC director for Ukraine, put together a full schedule for Kuchma, including meetings with the president, vice president, and secretaries of state, defense, and treasury—a program that went way beyond what a working visit normally entailed.

It was a good visit overall for the Ukrainian president. He and Gore signed a commercial space launch agreement. But it was far from Kuchma's best meeting with Clinton. He opened the meeting in the Oval Office with a twenty-five minute monologue on Chornobyl and the technical issues involved in shutting the plant down, leaving virtually no time for any other topic or for the American president to say much. Clinton finished the session a bit bemused and more knowledgeable about the intricacies of nuclear reactor cooling pipes. For Kuchma, just the fact of the meeting—and the public message that it broadcast of a growing U.S.-Ukrainian closeness—appeared as important as the substance. (NSC staff later took to cautioning the Ukrainians that their president should leave time for Clinton to speak, as he might well have things to say of interest to them.)

Christopher paid a visit to Kyiv in mid-March. It turned out to be well timed, as the Russian Duma (parliament) had just passed another of its periodic resolutions that questioned Ukraine's sovereignty and territorial integrity. The secretary used his visit to reassure his hosts, including Kuchma, of U.S. support as well as to discuss assistance for closing Chornobyl and Ukraine's relationship with NATO.

Kyiv remained interested in establishing a more formal mechanism to oversee bilateral relations, with Kuchma and Gore as co-chairs. U.S. officials suggested alternatives, such as a "non-" commission: the established trade and investment committee and an economic reform committee just being formed could meet in parallel, following which the U.S. and Ukrainian co-chairs could meet jointly with Gore. The Ukrainians continued to press for more.

In mid-July, the Ukrainians advised that Prime Minister Pavlo Lazarenko and Udovenko would visit Washington just a week later—despite the fact that the vice president would be traveling outside of the capital. As a result, Lazarenko had relatively low-level meetings, which focused on the economic situation in Ukraine. Lazarenko's main conversations took place at the IMF and World Bank, where Kyiv hoped to keep the assistance flowing even as the pace of the government's economic reforms had slowed.

Over the summer, discussion continued between the NSC and vice president's staff about creating a bilateral commission with Gore as a co-chair. The idea originally horrified Leon Fuerth, the vice president's national security adviser, and his deputy, Bill Wise. The vice president already chaired bilateral commissions with the Russian prime minister and South African vice president, and he was heavily engaged on Balkans issues in the aftermath of the breakup of Yugoslavia. They did not see how the vice president's schedule would allow the time. But Gore, who had become an instrumental player in both shaping and implementing the Clinton administration's foreign policy, agreed to take it on. It was decided that the State and Defense Departments would set up two new committees to cover foreign policy and security issues. These would complement the two established committees on trade and investment, and sustainable economic development, with all four reporting to Gore and Kuchma.

Horbulin visited Washington in early September. U.S. officials by then had come to recognize him as a serious and high-value interlocutor. A rocket engineer by training, he had been a chief designer for the large, multiple warhead SS-18 intercontinental ballistic missiles that had caused so much concern in the Pentagon during the Cold War. Horbulin was close and loyal to Kuchma, with whom he had worked at the Pivdenmash rocket plant. He showed no independent political ambitions. In addition to being perhaps Ukraine's best strategic thinker, Horbulin knew how to get results within the bureaucracy in Kyiv, the workings of which still mystified Washington, and he proved adept at practical problem solving. Many regarded him as the fourth most powerful official after Kuchma, the prime minister, and the speaker of the Rada. An ardent basketball fan, he headed the Ukrainian national basketball association and adored Michael Jordan. Horbulin became a "go-to" person when difficult questions arose on the U.S.-Ukrainian agenda. The weight that U.S. officials attached to Horbulin showed in the program prepared for his visit. It included meetings with Lake, Perry, Talbott, Fuerth, and CIA director John Deutsch.

Horbulin and Fuerth finalized the details for the U.S.-Ukraine Binational Commission, which came to be more commonly called the Gore-Kuchma Commission, for which Horbulin and Fuerth would serve as the executive secretaries. The four committees would meet periodically on their own, and once a year or so, they would come together and meet under the chairmanship of Gore and Kuchma. If the committees had differences that they could not resolve, they could refer those questions to the two principals for guidance.

On September 19, Washington and Kyiv announced the creation of the Gore-Kuchma Commission, which would "build even closer ties between Ukraine and the United States and deepen our strategic partnership." The joint statement said Kuchma and Gore had instructed the committees "to begin their work immediately."[4] The announcement contained the first reference to a "strategic partnership," a phrase with political value for Kyiv. (Washington saw this in less momentous terms, as the United States had many strategic partners—by one count, more than thirty.) The first working committee, on sustainable economic development, took place in Kyiv in October. The other committees aimed to meet later in the year or in early 1997.

Gore and Kuchma had a brief bilateral meeting in early December, on the margins of the 1996 Organization for Security and Cooperation in Europe summit meeting in Lisbon. They devoted most of their time to discussion of adaptation of the Conventional Armed Forces in Europe (CFE) Treaty, specifically the provisions that applied special limits to military equipment in the treaty's flank zones, which covered much of Ukraine.

One sensitive question emerged in late 1996. It dealt with corruption, which permeated most sectors of the economy and virtually all levels of business, government, and society, in part a legacy of Soviet times. Indeed, party members had seized Communist Party assets and cash, and many went on to become "red entrepreneurs," setting themselves up as businessmen. Anyone who could work out a deal in which he or she could buy commodities at artificially low domestic prices and then arrange their export for sale overseas at global market prices could realize huge profits. The Rada was far from immune. U.S. officials regularly heard rumors of large payments, either to secure a Rada member's vote on a particular bill or to draw a member into another faction. The same was true with the judicial system, leading to a practice in which litigants shopped for particular courts—often located far from their residence, place of business, or location of the dispute—in which they could buy a legal ruling in their favor. Customs was such a lucrative area for graft that those wanting to be customs officers reportedly had to pay sizable dollar bribes to get and then keep their jobs. There was also corruption on a micro scale. Traffic cops needing lunch money flagged over cars for imagined offenses. University students seeking entry to courses or good grades often had to pay.

Polls regularly showed that frequent encounters with corruption were one of the most frustrating aspects of daily life in Ukraine. Graft led to poor governance decisions. It discouraged foreign business and investors from coming into the country. U.S. companies, in particular, had to take this into account. Under the Foreign Corrupt Practices Act, they could be held criminally liable in American courts if they engaged in corruption in Ukraine. One of the challenges for U.S. assistance was how best to help those Ukrainians who wanted to push back against graft.

At the end of 1996, reports about Lazarenko's involvement in corrupt activities had begun flowing more frequently and alarmingly to the U.S. embassy in Kyiv. Lazarenko was seen as embodying big-time corruption, in contrast to post-Soviet bureaucrats who seemed less interested in pillaging the country's assets. Trained as an agronomist, Lazarenko rose quickly through government ranks following Ukraine's independence. He was appointed governor of Dnipropetrovsk oblast (region) in 1992 and selected in 1995 as first deputy prime minister with responsibility for energy questions—when the energy sector was the most corrupt part of the economy. As deputy prime minister and, from May 1996, as prime minister, Lazarenko reportedly used his office to engage in a variety of shady business dealings, including with Yuliya Tymoshenko, then head of United Energy Systems, a gas trading company. By the end of the year, the reports reached a critical mass. No one in Washington regretted that the vice president had been out of town during Lazarenko's visit the previous July. The question that White House and State Department officials began to consider quietly was what they could ask the Ukrainians to do about the problem.

Concern regarding Lazarenko grew as preparations got under way for the first full-scale Gore-Kuchma Commission meeting, to be held in May 1997. U.S. officials envisaged an agenda drawing on issues from each of the four working groups. In the foreign policy and security area, the principals would want to touch on formalizing a NATO-Ukraine relationship, steps to resolve differences between Washington and Kyiv with regard to a modification of the CFE Treaty, and Ukraine-Russia relations. In the economic cooperation and trade areas, U.S. officials planned to discuss the slow pace of reform, which was complicating relations with the international financial institutions, the energy sector, and progress on closing Chornobyl.

Carlos Pascual and Assistance Coordinator for the New Independent States Richard Morningstar traveled to Kyiv at the end of April, where they joined Miller in making the rounds to prepare for Kuchma's visit. They met with Kuchma and Lazarenko, focusing on the need for movement on economic reform. They also raised the question, which had begun to attract attention in Congress, of business dispute cases in which American investors appeared to have been taken advantage of by Ukrainian partners or had encountered problems dealing with government agencies. Pascual flagged for Horbulin concerns in Washington on proliferation issues, particularly the involvement of the Turboatom plant in Kharkiv in the Russian-led construction of a nuclear power plant at Bushehr, Iran.

As the visit neared, the vice president's staff began to question whether unresolved problems—lack of progress on fighting corruption, the business dispute cases, and questions about Ukraine's commitment to reform—would cast a shadow over the first commission meeting. At the beginning of May there were many unresolved issues. Washington felt that Kuchma was now doing little on reform. When Ukraine fell short on meeting the conditions needed to secure assistance from the IMF and World Bank, it became more difficult for the United States to support Ukraine with the international financial institutions. U.S. officials at times quietly urged them to cut Kyiv some slack in meeting the reform conditionalities, but that was difficult when Kyiv failed to meet a large number of the conditionalities. World Bank officials told the vice president's office that they saw a deteriorating economic situation. They attributed much of the problem to Lazarenko, who did not inspire confidence as an honest interlocutor and whose administrative interventions interfered with needed reforms. They questioned whether Kuchma could manage Lazarenko.

The Gore-Kuchma Commission meeting opened with a discussion of foreign policy issues. Kuchma attached importance to the developing NATO-Ukraine relationship. He said Yeltsin had agreed to sign a treaty on friendship and cooperation, something the Ukrainians had long sought. The vice president described U.S. concerns about Ukraine's relations with pariah states. In particular, a bilateral "123 agreement" on civil nuclear cooperation, named after section 123 of the Atomic Energy Act, would not be possible absent a categorical assurance from Kyiv that there would be no nuclear cooperation with rogue states, especially Iran. The security committee reported a productive agenda. The one open question had been the method for eliminating the SS-24 intercontinental ballistic missiles, and the sides had found agreement on this question.

On economic issues, Kuchma asked U.S. support for $3.5 billion in financing from the IMF and World Bank. Assistant Secretary of the Treasury for International Affairs David Lipton and Morningstar explained the reform steps that Ukraine needed to take in order to get IMF financing. Kuchma and his team listened to the presentations, though it was not clear how much impact they had. Over lunch, Kuchma expressed frustration at the difficulties in dealing with his fractious Rada, noting that he intended to use "everything except tanks" against the parliament.

Gore raised the sensitive Lazarenko issue in a one-on-one meeting with Kuchma. He noted reports of the prime minister's involvement in corrupt activities and said these were negatively affecting Ukraine's image. This question required Kuchma's attention. (Two months later, Lazarenko resigned amid rumors that Kuchma was about to sack him. Kuchma later would assert that the vice president had asked him to fire Lazarenko. In fact, Gore had taken care only to voice U.S. concerns, leaving it to Kuchma to draw the appropriate conclusion.)

Kuchma and Gore met with Clinton in the Oval Office following the commission meeting. Clinton sought to bolster Kuchma's commitment to needed reform steps. He also expressed hope that NATO and Ukraine could agree on a relationship before the July NATO summit in Madrid; doing so would allow a NATO-Ukraine summit to be held then. Kuchma made clear his interest in a meeting with NATO leaders. He described his domestic challenges and conceded that securing a new constitution and monetary problems had diverted his focus from fighting corruption and crime. Kuchma thought Yeltsin wanted to close disputes over the Black Sea Fleet and Crimea, but he wished that Yeltsin and senior Russian government officials would react more vigorously when the Duma challenged Ukrainian sovereignty over Sevastopol.

Ukrainian officials expressed pleasure with the visit, despite the difficult issues. U.S. officials felt the meeting had gone better than it might have, but much depended on follow-up. They began preparing for two more high-level meetings: Gore would hold a short bilateral with Kuchma in New York on June 23 on the margins of the UN Earth Day Summit, and Clinton would meet with Kuchma on the margins of the July NATO summit in Madrid.

The Gore-Kuchma discussion in New York focused on economic problems. The vice president again expressed concern about the lack of movement on reform, which continued to hold up financing from the IMF and World Bank. Moreover, the absence of action on business dispute cases had hurt Ukraine's reputation in Congress. Kuchma expressed frustration with the IMF and World Bank, asserting that Ukraine had met most of the conditionalities but received no financing. He rhetorically asked what he could do if the Rada did not pass a budget, a key IMF conditionality. He felt the IMF had applied harsher conditions on Ukraine than it had on Russia, and Moscow in any event benefited from French, German, and Italian bilateral credits.

Just over two weeks later, on July 9, Clinton met with Kuchma in Madrid immediately after the inaugural NATO-Ukraine summit. Both came to the bilateral in a celebratory mood. Clinton stressed the importance of Ukraine moving to build a substantive relationship with the alliance; it would be good for NATO and Ukraine and could also create a climate in which Russian attitudes toward both might change in a positive way. Kuchma agreed. He noted the value of the NATO-Russia relationship that had been established in May (which made it easier for Kyiv to establish its own relationship with the alliance). Kuchma also described the problems he continued to face in dealing with the Rada; because it still had not passed a budget, the IMF financing was blocked.

Kuchma paid his fourth 1997 visit to the United States in November to take part in a conference for countries pledging assistance to Chornobyl; he served as an honorary co-chairman along with Gore. The conference drew new pledges of funding for the shelter (or sarcophagus) project to encase reactor number four, which had exploded in 1986, and highlighted continued international interest. Kuchma also traveled to Cape Canaveral to watch the November 19 launch of the space shuttle Columbia. Columbia carried into orbit an international crew, including Colonel Leonid Kadenyuk of the Ukrainian air force.

First Lady Hillary Clinton closed out the high-level contacts in 1997 with a November 16–17 visit to Lviv. Although hospital and church visits—traditional fare for such trips—constituted a big part of the agenda, Clinton also made a stop at the Monument to the Victims of Soviet Repression, which endeared her to western Ukrainians as well as to the Ukrainian American community at home. She used the occasion of a speech in the Lviv Opera House to announce a program to combat trafficking in women, a problem that plagued Ukraine.

Ukraine's Relationship with NATO

As part of its outreach to former Warsaw Pact members and the New Independent States of the former Soviet Union, NATO launched the "Partnership for Peace" program in January 1994. The program aimed to establish bilateral partnerships between the alliance and interested countries, offering activities related to defense reform, defense policy and planning, military-to-military cooperation, disaster response, and civil-military relations. NATO hoped to use the partnerships not only to build relations with countries to its east but also to help underpin democratic reforms and civilian control of the military. Ukraine signed a partnership agreement within weeks of the program's announcement, becoming the fourth country to do so. Kyiv regarded a relationship with NATO as a means to gain greater of freedom of maneuver vis-à-vis Russia, not unlike how the Ukrainian government had come to see its relationship with the United States.

Thinking in Washington about NATO's future evolved over the first half of 1994. By the summer, the White House had quietly moved beyond the question of whether the alliance should enlarge to consider when and how rapidly the process should proceed. This decision occurred somewhat stealthily within the U.S. government. Although the White House, NSC staff, and State Department by the end of the summer had oriented themselves to how to manage an alliance enlargement process, the fact that enlargement had become a matter of when, not whether, only became clear to the Pentagon late in the fall.

In October 1994, Deputy Foreign Minister Borys Tarasyuk visited Washington and raised with Talbott the future European security architecture. Tarasyuk expected alliance enlargement in the not-too-distant future, potentially bringing NATO to the western border of Ukraine. Meanwhile, Moscow seemed increasingly unhappy about the prospect. What, Tarasyuk asked, was the U.S. vision for Ukraine, caught between the two? Would Ukraine be consigned to a no-man's land or a gray zone of insecurity? Tarasyuk made clear that the notion of being a buffer state had no appeal for Kyiv.

Talbott answered that he did not have a good answer at the time, but he thought the United States and NATO could find ways to respond adequately. Talbott assured Tarasyuk that the U.S. government would devote attention to the question, which became a regular topic at high-level bilateral meetings for the next three years.

U.S. officials subsequently concluded that the answer lay in part in expanding bilateral links between the West and Ukraine. This became a prime motivator for deepening the U.S.-Ukraine relationship, and American diplomats encouraged NATO partners to deepen their bilateral relationships with Kyiv. Another part of the answer appeared to be building ties between NATO and Ukraine. The Partnership for Peace, available to all former Warsaw Pact and post-Soviet states, would not suffice.

Kyiv appeared nervous that the enlargement process would proceed rapidly. It lacked, however, a clear picture of how far it wanted a NATO-Ukraine relationship to go. In a January 1995 telephone conversation, Kuchma agreed with Gore that no third country should have a right to veto a NATO invitation to a country to join, but he hoped that the NATO-Ukraine process would "be evolutionary, without a precise timeframe." U.S. officials believed Ukraine wanted enlargement to proceed at a slow pace, which would relieve pressure on Kyiv to make a hard decision about what it wanted with the alliance.

Shortly thereafter, Ambassador Yuriy Shcherbak confided to me that Ukraine's leadership worried that NATO enlargement could increase pressure from Moscow on Kyiv to join a Russian sphere of influence. Ukraine did not oppose enlargement and did not seek to join NATO, but it did not want the door closed on the future possibility. Kyiv was interested in some kind of special relationship with NATO.

Udovenko made the same points when Talbott visited Kyiv in April 1995. Talbott acknowledged the Ukrainian concerns and noted Clinton's desire to manage the enlargement process in a way that did not produce two competing spheres of influence. Kuchma told Talbott that Ukraine did not want to hang between NATO and Russia, but he thought there was time to work out this question.

At the Rada, Moroz had a different proposition for Talbott. He suggested that Ukraine announce that it would take on permanent neutral status with guarantees, much in the same way that the United States, Britain, France, and the Soviet Union had guaranteed Austrian neutrality in 1955. That idea had little appeal to Washington—or, it appeared, to many in Kuchma's government. Talbott replied that Ukraine would have a robust (if as yet undefined) relationship with NATO, and the alliance would seek to evolve in a way that could avoid creating new blocs in Europe.

Shmarov told Talbott that Kyiv did not want to see new blocs or spheres of influence develop and thus hoped that NATO enlargement would proceed at a moderate pace. He noted that, while Ukraine was an associate member of the Commonwealth of Independent States (CIS), it did not take part in the military component.

By the summer, U.S. officials could share with Ukrainian diplomats the timeline for NATO's enlargement. The alliance planned to devote the remainder of 1995 and first half of 1996 to discussing the how and why of enlargement—that is, its process and rationale. In the second half of 1996, NATO would begin to consider which countries would be eligible for membership (this timing not coincidentally pushed the discussion of who would join NATO back until after the summer 1996 presidential election in Russia). The initial focus would be on the Visegrad Four countries—Poland, Hungary, the Czech Republic, and Slovakia. American officials made clear to their Ukrainian counterparts that they did not want to leave Ukraine in a gray zone. The starting point was the Partnership for Peace, and U.S. officials urged Ukraine to use its individual partnership program to develop closer relations with NATO. In addition, the U.S. government decided to support a special relationship between NATO and Ukraine, which would parallel a special relationship to be established between NATO and Russia. Kyiv needed to identify the issues that should make up the substance, and it needed to ask the alliance for such a relationship.

From the U.S. perspective, these developments filled out the answer to Tarasyuk's October 1994 question about Ukraine's place in the U.S. vision for Europe. By September 1996, Ukraine and the United States had declared a strategic partnership and established the Gore-Kuchma

Commission. Over the following nine months, U.S. officials intended to work with NATO and Kyiv to develop a special relationship between the alliance and Ukraine. A web of connections between the West and Ukraine had begun to take form, including Ukraine's expanding bilateral ties with countries such as Poland and the United Kingdom, and its link with the European Union, with which Ukraine had concluded a partnership and cooperation agreement. Washington hoped that this growing set of links would give Kyiv confidence that it had a strong anchor in the West.

During his September 1996 visit to Washington, Horbulin devoted considerable time to the NATO question. He cautioned that enlargement would raise anxiety in Moscow and could have negative blowback for Ukraine. Horbulin noted Kyiv's worry that the first tranche of NATO enlargement could leave Ukraine isolated, as it would separate Ukraine from countries such as Poland and the Czech Republic if they joined. Although Kyiv did not seek to join NATO at present, he did not exclude the possibility that the position on no bloc membership could change. His American interlocutors reiterated their readiness to work with Kyiv to develop a NATO-Ukraine relationship, but they noted that in 1997 the alliance almost certainly would invite some countries to join.

When Udovenko visited Washington the following month, Deputy National Security Adviser Sandy Berger told him that, as the enlargement process went forward and NATO developed its relationship with Russia, it was equally important to develop the NATO-Ukraine relationship. Udovenko expressed concern, as he had in an earlier meeting at the Department of Defense, that NATO enlargement not lead to the deployment of American nuclear weapons on the territory of new NATO members, some of which might be Ukraine's neighbors. He proposed a nuclear-weapon-free zone in Central Europe.

The Ukrainian government's position was understandable, particularly as Kyiv had just a few months earlier shipped the last strategic nuclear warheads to Russia for dismantlement. However, there was no enthusiasm in NATO or among prospective new members for a nuclear-weapon-free zone. Since U.S. nuclear weapons provided the ultimate guarantor of NATO security, such a zone might be seen to undercut the alliance's security commitment to new members in Central Europe. Berger explained to Udovenko that Washington understood Kyiv's concern, particularly after Ukraine's denuclearization, but NATO had to protect its rights. NATO had no plans to deploy nuclear weapons on the territory of new member states, though the alliance needed time to work out how it would articulate that position publicly.

The Ukrainians provided a paper outlining their thinking on a NATO-Ukraine relationship. It offered a good basis for beginning work, though it still left open how far Kyiv wanted to go with the alliance. In early 1997, as he was beginning to engage Russian deputy foreign minister Georgiy Mamedov on the basic elements of a document establishing a NATO-Russia relationship and a standing NATO-Russia body, Talbott asked Andrew Weiss of the State Department's Policy Planning Staff to draft a memo outlining the basic elements that might go into a parallel NATO-Ukraine document. Not all at the State Department were enthusiastic, but Talbott brought the interagency group on board. Weiss and Debra Cagan, senior adviser for nuclear and security policy in the State Department's Bureau of European Affairs, made two trips to Kyiv, where they met with Ihor Kharchenko, director of the foreign ministry's policy planning department, to discuss the main elements of a NATO-Ukraine relationship. The discussions went smoothly, the only bump being that Weiss and Cagan had to fend off Ukrainian suggestions for what would have amounted to a backdoor security guarantee. As with the draft NATO-Russia document developed by Talbott and Mamedov, U.S. officials turned the draft elements for a NATO-Ukraine document over to NATO secretary general Javier Solana, who took over the lead on concluding both in his discussions with Russian and Ukrainian officials.

With Solana, Ukrainian officials expressed their interest in having a standing NATO-Ukraine consultative body and in receiving an Article 5–like security guarantee. Although the idea of a standing body appeared workable, neither Washington nor other NATO members were prepared to extend an Article 5 guarantee to Kyiv, a commitment that the alliance had provided to no non-NATO member state.

Ukrainian officials hoped to conclude a document establishing a NATO-Ukraine relationship in time for signing at the planned NATO summit in Madrid in July. That schedule tracked with Washington's thinking. In fact, U.S. officials wanted to see the document finished even sooner, if possible before the NATO-Russia document was done and made public. They believed each document should reflect the substance of its respective relationship and anticipated a wider range of interactions between the alliance and Russia than would exist between NATO and Ukraine. They did not want Kyiv to seek to replicate in its charter every point that might be contained in what became known as the NATO-Russia Founding Act. U.S. officials encouraged Solana to bring the NATO-Ukraine document to closure before May 20, the date set for the NATO-Russia summit meeting in Paris, where NATO leaders and Yeltsin would sign the Founding Act.

By the end of April, work at NATO headquarters was well along. Solana had a text describing the principles and subjects for the NATO-Ukraine relationship to take to Kyiv on May 7. The Ukrainians accepted it as the basis for finalizing the drafting work. They understood that Ukraine would not receive an Article 5 security guarantee, but they indicated strong interest in having the NATO-Ukraine document reflect NATO support for the security assurances that Ukraine had received in the 1994 Budapest Memorandum (which the document ultimately did include).

Ukrainian officials desired to rapidly complete the NATO-Ukraine document. During the May 16 Gore-Kuchma meeting, the Ukrainian president expressed interest in having it finished by May 30, when Udovenko and other NATO partner foreign ministers would meet with their alliance counterparts in Sintra, Portugal. Gore thought that was a good idea: Sintra would provide an opportunity to initial the document, with the formal signing saved for the NATO-Ukraine summit meeting in July.

Negotiation of the text progressed quickly during the last two weeks of May. With other NATO foreign ministers witnessing, Solana and Udovenko initialed the "Charter on a Distinctive Partnership between the North Atlantic Treaty Organization and Ukraine" on May 30 on the margins of other meetings in Sintra. (As it turned out, Washington's worry that the Ukrainians would try to capture in their document many of the points in the NATO-Russia Founding Act proved groundless. Kyiv had its own ideas about the substance for its cooperation with the alliance.)

Talbott and Shcherbak met in mid-June to discuss U.S.-Ukraine and NATO issues. In response to Shcherbak's question, Talbott said NATO was serious about its "open-door" policy, under which any

European state that met the standards of the alliance and could contribute to trans-Atlantic security was eligible to apply for membership. If a democratic, reformed Ukraine wanted that option in the future, the U.S. government intended that it would be available.

As preparations were finalized for the July 8–9 NATO meetings in Madrid, one minor sticking point arose over scheduling. NATO's plan called for a NATO summit, followed by a NATO meeting with the heads of Poland, the Czech Republic, and Hungary—the three countries that NATO would invite to join the alliance—on July 8. The Euro-Atlantic Partnership Council and NATO-Ukraine summit would take place on July 9. Shcherbak and his counterpart in Brussels lobbied hard to move the NATO-Ukraine meeting to July 8. They seemed suspicious that meeting on the second day would somehow diminish the NATO-Ukraine summit's importance. U.S. and NATO officials pushed back; there simply was no time on July 8. Moreover, the headline on July 8 would be the invitations to Poland, the Czech Republic, and Hungary to join NATO; anything else would get lost in the noise. (Kyiv remained dubious about this until July 9. Immediately after the NATO-Ukraine summit, Tarasyuk and Shcherbak joined me to watch CNN top its hourly news report with pictures of Kuchma and Solana signing the charter while Clinton and other NATO leaders watched.)

The Charter on a Distinctive Partnership provided the basis for an ongoing relationship between NATO and Ukraine. It outlined the principles for developing relations and noted the right of states "to be free to choose or change their security, including treaties of alliance," an important point for Kyiv, even if it had not yet decided how far it might take its relationship with the alliance. The charter specified a lengthy list of areas for consultation and/or cooperation and outlined the arrangements for consultation, including the NATO-Ukraine Commission. The final section of the charter noted that the alliance would "continue to support Ukrainian sovereignty and independence, territorial integrity, democratic development, economic prosperity and its status as a non-nuclear weapons state, and the principle of inviolability of frontiers." It went on to state that NATO "welcomes and supports the fact that Ukraine received security assurances from all five nuclear weapons states parties to the Treaty on the Non-Proliferation of Nuclear Weapons" and praised Ukraine's decision to give up nuclear arms. On one last nuclear note, the charter reflected Kyiv's welcome of the fact that NATO had stated that it had "no intention, no plan and no reason to deploy nuclear weapons on the territory of new members nor any need to change any aspect of NATO's nuclear posture or policy."[5]

Continuing Problems with Russia

Ukrainian-Russian relations remained tense in the mid-1990s. Washington continued to pay close attention, particularly to Crimea in 1994. The election of Yuriy Meshkov as Crimean "president" that January, followed by efforts in the Crimean parliament to assert a degree of independence, provoked new tensions between authorities on the peninsula and Kyiv.

By the end of 1994, however, tensions between Kyiv and Crimea had subsided, in part because the economic situation had improved somewhat, with hyperinflation coming to an end. Political strains between Meshkov and the Crimean parliament had emerged, and the peninsula's sputtering economy drew attention away from separatist ideas. Kyiv played a smart strategy, avoiding provocations while putting out subtle hints about a possible economic embargo and cutoff of water supplies (the arid peninsula drew much of its fresh water from the mainland). Moreover, at the beginning of 1995, the dispute between Moscow and a rebellious Chechnya flared into open military conflict. Russian officials became more particular about respect for Russia's territorial integrity and less inclined to raise questions about Ukraine's.

In his April 1995 meetings in Kyiv before the Clinton visit, Talbott told his Ukrainian interlocutors that, during his prior stop in Moscow, he had made clear to senior Russian officials Washington's position on Crimea's status. He discussed with Shmarov the need to resolve questions regarding the Russian Black Sea Fleet and reiterated that the United States was ready to help if both Kyiv and Moscow desired it. Shmarov indicated that the Ukrainians understood that Russian ports could not accommodate all of the ships of the Black Sea Fleet. The problem centered on defining the conditions for leasing port facilities in Crimea to the Russian navy.

When Horbulin visited Washington three weeks later, he again expressed interest in a trilateral discussion on Crimea and the Black Sea

Fleet to Lake. Lake noted the U.S. readiness to be helpful but added that it should do so in a way that would preserve Washington's credibility as a neutral interlocutor. (In any event, the Russians never showed interest in a trilateral discussion of these questions.)

In June, Kuchma's chief of staff, Dmytro Tabachnyk, visited Washington. He told NSC senior director Coit "Chip" Blacker that Kyiv believed it had found a formula to settle the basing issue and, if that was resolved, it would open the path to signing the treaty of friendship and cooperation with Russia. The Ukrainian formulation would identify specific basing areas within Sevastopol to be leased by the Russian Black Sea Fleet, rather than treating the entire city of Sevastopol as the base.

By August, Washington had received reports that the Russian military was handing over many of the facilities that it had used in Crimea except for those in Sevastopol. The atmospherics seemed to improve. The Russians backed off of their demand to lease all of Sevastopol and instead proposed specific facilities that they desired. Moreover, the sides had begun to work on the text of a lease agreement. It still had a number of open issues: Would the Black Sea Fleet remain in Sevastopol for ten or twenty-five years? What would be the payment terms? What arrangements would be made for Ukrainian navy access to facilities in Sevastopol?

As Ukrainian-Russian negotiations proceeded, Marchuk told Pascual and me in October that Kyiv feared that differences within the Russian government over these questions would complicate finding a resolution. That seemed more than plausible, given the continuing display of differences between Yeltsin and his parliament on the question. Marchuk suggested that Kuchma had a narrow path to walk. On the one hand, the president faced Russian demands for broad access to facilities in Sevastopol, and the Russians were reluctant to allow the Ukrainian navy use of even some facilities in the harbor. On the other hand, certain elements in the Rada worried that Kuchma might concede too much.

At the end of October, Horbulin told Miller that Ukrainian and Russian officials had reached agreement on Black Sea Fleet issues, but it then collapsed. The Russians backed away from the deal following a protest demonstration by pro-Russia Black Sea Fleet pensioners in Sevastopol. The Ukrainians believed the Russian government had orchestrated the demonstration as well as a vote in the Duma in which

Russian deputies overwhelmingly approved a law barring any division of the Black Sea Fleet.

Reporting from the embassy in Kyiv over the remainder of 1996 and first part of 1997 gave pessimistic assessments of the negotiations. Miller advised in February 1997 that the Ukrainians had received two Russian offers regarding Sevastopol: Yeltsin had offered to lease port facilities within the city, something Kyiv could work with, but his foreign minister, Yevgeniy Primakov, subsequently again proposed to lease the entire city, which the Ukrainians regarded as a total nonstarter.

In early spring 1997, however, Ukrainian officials told their U.S. colleagues that progress had begun to pick up, both regarding the Black Sea Fleet basing question and signing of the long-negotiated treaty of friendship and cooperation. Kuchma informed Gore at the May 16 Gore-Kuchma Commission meeting that he had agreement with Yeltsin on signing the treaty in Kyiv, though, he ruefully added, this would be "the seventh time" he had had such an agreement with the Russian president. When Kuchma saw Clinton, he opined that Yeltsin wanted to close out these issues. Kuchma seemed to have confidence in Yeltsin as someone with whom he could deal, but he expressed concern that the future Russia could be different. This led him to attach importance to the prospective NATO-Ukraine relationship.

Ten days later, on May 27, Clinton met briefly with Yeltsin on the margins of the NATO-Russia summit in Paris, following the signing of the NATO-Russia Founding Act. Clinton recalled his discussion with Kuchma in Washington and told Yeltsin that Kuchma wanted to work with him to resolve difficult issues on the Kyiv-Moscow agenda. Clinton urged Yeltsin to take advantage of his upcoming visit to Kyiv to improve relations.

Three days later, Yeltsin made his oft-postponed visit. He and Kuchma signed the "Treaty of Friendship, Cooperation, and Partnership between the Russian Federation and Ukraine" and announced that they had also reached agreement to lease basing facilities in Crimea, principally in Sevastopol, to the Russians for a period of twenty years, until 2017. Miller reported from Kyiv that the Ukrainians were delighted with the Yeltsin visit and the results, a message that Shcherbak conveyed to Talbott as well. Washington breathed a sigh of relief—another potential Ukrainian-Russian bullet dodged.

Yeltsin's decision to sign the treaty on friendship and cooperation and to finally resolve the Black Sea Fleet basing question appeared to U.S. officials to indicate a change in Moscow's overall approach. Their assessment was that developments in Ukraine's relations with the United States and NATO over the previous year had had an effect in Moscow. The hardline approach that the Kremlin had taken toward Kyiv had had the unintended consequence of pushing Ukraine toward the West. U.S. officials speculated that Moscow had reviewed its Ukraine policy, concluded it was not working, and decided to take a new tack, moving to resolve two longstanding problems with Ukraine. By the summer of 1997, the Ukrainian-Russian relationship appeared to have achieved a degree of stability. Summer 1997 represented the high point for relations between Kyiv and Moscow.

New Opportunities

As U.S.-Ukraine relations broadened, new opportunities for cooperation emerged. Commercial space launches offered one such prospect. Kuchma took particular interest in this, given his background as a former director of the Pivdenmash plant, at one time the largest rocket and missile production facility in the world.

The commercial space launch market of the 1990s was not a normal market. U.S. companies produced a large percentage of the world's commercial satellites. Because they incorporated high-technology components, the satellites required export licenses, approved by the U.S. government, if they were to be shipped overseas for launch on another country's space launch vehicle. The U.S. government thus had a virtual veto over who could launch American-built satellites.

In early 1995, Washington began to consider whether Ukraine could enter that market. That consideration became possible because Kyiv in May 1994 had agreed in a bilateral U.S.-Ukrainian memorandum of understanding to observe the conditions of the Missile Technology Control Regime (MTCR), even though it was not a member. The U.S. government had launched the MTCR with other G-7 states with the objective of controlling the proliferation of missile technology. The regime applied limits to "Category I" systems, which were rockets or major subsystems for rockets capable of carrying a 500-kilogram payload more than 300 kilometers. MTCR partners—by 1994, twenty-five countries had joined the regime—agreed to exercise special care in exporting Category I systems.

Kyiv's desire to gain access to the U.S. commercial space launch market provided a major motivation for observing the MTCR guidelines. During Kuchma's November 1994 visit to Washington, the sides agreed to "work together to open prospects for Ukrainian access to international aerospace markets."

In 1994 and 1995, major American aerospace companies reciprocated the Ukrainian interest. Rockwell International developed a proposal based on Ukrainian-Russian cooperation that envisaged using Pivdenmash's Zenit space launch vehicles to put commercial payloads into orbit from the Russian-operated launch site at Baykonur, Kazakhstan. The Boeing Company came forward with a more radical proposition. Its "Sea Launch" project would combine a Zenit booster with a fourth rocket stage produced in Russia, mating the booster and fourth stage with a satellite at a facility in Long Beach, California. Boeing then intended to transport the assembled rocket and satellite by ship to a location near the equator in the Pacific Ocean, where the rocket would launch a satellite to geosynchronous earth orbit from a converted Norwegian oil-drilling platform. Launching from the middle of the ocean reduced safety issues, and launching from the equator took advantage of the earth's spin so that a given booster could loft a larger payload into orbit. The concept struck many in the U.S. government as complicated and borderline fantasy, but Boeing had concluded an agreement with Pivdenmash regarding use of the Zenit rockets and let it be known that it was prepared to invest $420 million in the project.

What Rockwell and Boeing needed to know, however, was whether the U.S. government would allow Ukraine to launch American-built satellites. If not, neither company's plan made commercial sense. Hughes Satellite Systems Corporation, the main American satellite producer, also took an interest. From its perspective, the more commercial space launch providers, the better, as greater competition could mean lower costs to put satellites into orbit. That mattered to Hughes; for some payloads, the launch services could amount to nearly half of the total cost of a commercial satellite.

I chaired an interagency working group in early 1995 to decide how the U.S. government should fulfill the president's commitment to open access for Ukraine to the space launch market. The group had to weigh the commercial, space, and missile proliferation aspects of this issue and included representatives from the Departments of State, Defense, Commerce, and Transportation, the Joint Chiefs of Staff (JCS), the Arms Control and Disarmament Agency, the U.S. Trade Representative's Office, and the National Aeronautics and Space Administration. Within the White House, the vice president's office, the National Economic Council, and the Office of Science and Technology took an interest.

Most agency representatives agreed that, if Ukraine maintained a good record of observing the MTCR requirements and strictly controlled the export of its missile and rocket technologies, it deserved access to the U.S. market. The Department of Transportation was virtually the only agency opposed, fearing the negative impact on U.S. commercial space launch providers and believing that someone should take a position supporting them. The JCS representative did not oppose access for Ukraine but did express concern about preserving a strong domestic rocket industry to support launches of military satellites. While other agencies were mindful of the interests of U.S. space launch providers, the interagency group was told that the contribution of satellite makers to the gross domestic product was some ten times that of the contribution of commercial space launch providers. Lower launch costs, moreover, could increase the demand for commercial satellites. That clinched the economic argument.

In March 1995, an NSC decision memorandum went forward to Sandy Berger, who approved granting Ukraine access. The matter then became the purview of the U.S. Trade Representative's Office, which had to negotiate with Ukraine how much access—that is, the number of Ukrainian launches per year. Ukrainian officials originally hoped to sign the agreement during Clinton's visit in May, which was unrealistic, as only the first round of negotiations could be held before then. In the fall, the interagency working group agreed that Ukraine should receive a quota of sixteen guaranteed launches and perhaps more to geosynchronous earth orbit in the period 1997–2001, after which the U.S. government planned to transition to a system without quotas.

The agreement was ultimately signed in February 1996. Boeing immediately moved forward with the Sea Launch project. Two years later, after taking up my position in Kyiv, I had my first opportunity to visit Pivdenmash. The tour of the facility concluded in a large assembly hall, where the plant previously had completed assembly of Soviet intercontinental ballistic missiles (ICBMs) designed to target the United States; the hall this time held six Zenit rockets, each nearing completion and marked for Sea Launch. (While a promising concept, Sea Launch never attained the volume of launches that Boeing and Pivdenmash hoped for. Weak demand pushed the project into bankruptcy in 2009. Energia, a Russian company, acquired a 95 percent majority interest in 2010, though the project remained tangled in lawsuits among the former partners.)

A Growing Defense Relationship

The relationship between the Pentagon and the Ukrainian military also took off in 1995. Defense Secretary Perry had a strong interest in using Cooperative Threat Reduction funds to assist Ukraine in denuclearizing, consistent with its commitments under the START treaty and Lisbon Protocol. He paid regular visits to observe progress in this regard, including the elimination of ICBMs and ICBM silos.[6] Perry also directed the Defense Department to broaden other areas of engagement, an effort led by Assistant Secretary of Defense Ashton Carter.

In May 1995, U.S. Army troops took part in the first joint U.S.-Ukrainian peacekeeping exercise, "Peace Shield-95," conducted at the Ukrainian training site at Yavoriv in western Ukraine. Perry joined Shmarov to observe the exercise. Perry returned in early 1996 to witness the destruction of an empty SS-19 ICBM silo near Pervomaysk, which essentially entailed filling the hardened concrete headworks of the silo with conventional explosives and setting it off. He also inspected housing built under the Cooperative Threat Reduction program for retired Ukrainian missile personnel, though Congress soon thereafter cut funding for such housing projects.

"Peace Shield-96" was conducted at Yavoriv in June, this time with the participation of troops from seven countries in addition to the

United States and Ukraine, including Russia and Poland. Making his last trip to Ukraine as secretary, Perry observed the exercise and then made one more trek to Pervomaysk, this time to view acres of sunflowers that had been planted in a field that had once housed an underground ICBM silo. (In restoring former Soviet ICBM silos to fields, the Cooperative Threat Reduction program applied the same standards that were applied to the restoration of former U.S. Minuteman ICBM silos to fields. When I visited Pervomaysk in September 1999, the only indication that a field of sunflowers had once housed a silo containing an SS-19 missile with its six nuclear warheads was a flag that the Ukrainian military had placed to mark the spot.) In September, the Ukrainian navy sent its flagship, the *Hetman Sahaydachny*, accompanied by a second naval vessel, to pay a port call at Norfolk, Virginia, the largest U.S. naval base, and to conduct joint training with the U.S. Navy.

U.S. forces took part in two major exercises in Ukraine in 1997: "Cooperative Neighbor-97," a multilateral exercise at Yavoriv, which the new secretary of defense, William Cohen, observed, and "Sea Breeze-97," the first of what became a series of U.S.-Ukrainian exercises, usually with the participation of other countries. Planning for Sea Breeze-97, however, encountered a bump. In addition to U.S. and Ukrainian naval and land forces, the exercise was planned to include soldiers and sailors from other NATO countries, Russia, and other Black Sea littoral states. As planning progressed in the spring—at the same time that discussions regarding the NATO-Ukraine and NATO-Russia relationships were proceeding—Moscow vigorously objected to the Ukrainians' proposed exercise scenario. Russian officials even raised their concerns on the margins of the Clinton-Yeltsin summit in Helsinki in March. It turned out that the Ukrainian military had proposed a scenario centered on a multilateral military effort to assist Ukrainian military forces in suppressing an armed uprising that was receiving support from a neighboring state. The proposed site for the exercise was Crimea. Given past tensions between Moscow and Kyiv over Crimea, this hit way too close to home for the Russians—and for the Americans as well. One U.S. official wondered what role the Ukrainians had in mind for the participating Russian troops: the opposing force?

U.S. military officers counseled their Ukrainian counterparts on a more neutral scenario, one involving humanitarian assistance. Kyiv agreed to change the plan and to move the land portion of the exercise from Crimea to a training facility northeast of Odesa, which would become a regular host for Sea Breeze exercises. In the end, the Russians nevertheless declined to participate.[7] (Interestingly, the Russians did agree to participate in Sea Breeze-98 the following year, contributing both warships and aircraft. The scenario for that exercise, the land portion of which was conducted near Odesa, centered on a multilateral humanitarian mission to assist an area struck by an earthquake, including protecting food and other supplies from small rampaging armed groups. Although the exercise scenario was humanitarian in nature, it was nonetheless quite robust. In the Black Sea, participating warships, including ships from the Russian Black Sea Fleet, practiced antisubmarine operations together.)

In addition to regular exercises, the U.S. military began inviting Ukraine to send officers to training programs in the United States. As the Pentagon paired each post-Soviet state's military with a state national guard, the California National Guard took on responsibility for certain military contacts with Ukraine.

Reform and Assistance

Reforming the country's economic and political systems was bound to pose a severe test for the newly independent Ukrainian state. Both had been badly warped by more than seventy years under the Soviet command economy system. Unlike some of its neighbors to its immediate west in Central Europe, Ukraine did not have the experience or memory of a capitalist economic system or of a fledgling democracy during the years between World War I and World War II. Reform thus was going to prove a more difficult proposition than in Central Europe; just how difficult was probably not fully appreciated in the West.

The Ukrainian economy in the early 1990s was in desperate need of reform to move from a Soviet-style command economy to a more efficient market economy. In the aftermath of Ukraine's regaining its independence, the economy remained largely state owned while the supply of money went out of control. That led to hyperinflation that peaked at over 10,000 percent in 1993 and a prolonged period of economic contraction. (Only in 1994 did Ukraine start fighting inflation seriously, but it took until 2000 to put in place sufficient structural reforms to reverse the decade of decline and restart growth.)

The agricultural sector—which had been the Soviet Union's bread basket—was dominated in the early 1990s by large collective and state farms. They continued to operate largely as they had under the Soviet system. The farm staff worked only normal hours, even at harvest time. (At one farm, I saw a nearly new John Deere harvester. The American agricultural adviser noted that U.S. farms work round-the-clock to bring in the wheat crop when it is ready and lamented that the harvester had never used its headlights.)

The government controlled the sale of inputs such as seeds and fertilizers and bought much of the produce, restraining the development of functioning agricultural markets. In 2000, when farms were divided and workers given title to specific tracts of land, they could not freely sell their land or mortgage it. They thus could not use their most valuable asset to raise capital to buy better inputs and equipment. This made it difficult for the country to realize its potential to become an agricultural powerhouse on par with Canada or Australia. (The fact that farm workers were allowed to lease land did contribute to some agricultural growth after 2000.)

Heavy industry and the steel and coal sectors had problems adapting, as demand for their products in other post-Soviet states fell dramatically. They now faced a more competitive world (in some cases in Soviet times, factories simply responded to production orders from Moscow). Overwhelmingly still state owned and run, they usually found that they could not compete in quality with European goods. The government looked for ways to keep the plants operating, however, offering large budget subsidies in order to avoid massive unemployment. In some cases, that was the only reason to keep industrial concerns going. The coal mines in the Donbas region in eastern Ukraine produced coal at a cost higher than the cost of coal imported from neighboring Poland or Russia, to say nothing of the cost in lives from the all-too-frequent mine accidents. The state, however, kept the mines running in order to provide jobs. As the state slowly moved to privatize large industrial concerns, the arrangements were often fixed and opaque. A number of oligarchs, drawing on insider connections, profited and came to dominate certain sectors of the economy.

Small and medium-sized enterprises, which typically generate more than 50 percent of employment in established market economies, were slow to develop in Ukraine, inhibited in part by a tangled morass of regulations and taxes. U.S. embassy officials heard tales of some businesses having to obtain as many as 100 permits or licenses in order to operate legally, with many requiring bribes. The slow development of small and medium-sized enterprises meant that they could not quickly absorb much excess labor from large industrial concerns.

Setting up a functioning market economy also required creating some institutions from scratch in an environment where few Ukrainians had experience in how markets functioned. For example, the country needed independent banks to provide domestic finance and an asset registry system if it was going to have a working stock market.

In the early 1990s, the Ukrainian political system was preoccupied with nation building and failed to devote sufficient attention to the need for economic reform. The president, elected by popular vote, headed the executive branch and appointed the prime minister and cabinet, subject to approval by the Rada. While the prime minister was subservient to the president, the dual executive structures—the Presidential Administration and National Security and Defense Council, on the one hand, and the cabinet of ministers and individual ministries on the other—sometimes fell into conflict. The president also appointed the oblast governors. As a result, they owed their political loyalty to Kyiv, not to regional bodies or the local population. That political structure made for inefficient governance and weak accountability to the governed.

The legislative branch had important authorities but was generally less powerful than the executive branch. Part of the problem was the large number of political parties that held the Rada's 450 seats. In 1995, the Rada counted twelve factions, with a number of unaffiliated deputies. Some of those factions or parties represented particular business groups, and the immunity that came with a seat in the Rada was attractive to oligarchs. All too often, those factions sought to protect narrow interests rather than embrace broad reform that would have promoted a more open and competitive economy. Moreover, with so many factions, building sustainable political coalitions posed a challenge. That was a problem for the president, who needed to win 226 votes to get legislation passed.[8]

As the bilateral relationship deepened, the U.S. government began to expand its assistance programs aimed at promoting both economic and political change. In October 1992, Congress passed the FREEDOM (Freedom for Russia and Emerging Eurasian Democracies and Open Markets) Support Act, which provided technical assistance for reforms in the post-Soviet states. FREEDOM Support Act funds began to be allocated in significant amounts to Ukraine in 1994, as the focus of the nonmilitary U.S. assistance effort shifted from humanitarian aid to support for reform. In fiscal years 1992–96, the U.S. government budgeted some $717 million in FREEDOM Support Act grants for Ukraine, though actual obligation and expenditure of the funds took time to complete.[9]

Following his election to the presidency in July 1994, Kuchma had embarked on a series of significant economic reforms in the fall. He appointed a team that the U.S. government and international financial institutions such as the IMF and World Bank regarded as proreform. Kuchma announced a comprehensive series of steps, including financial stabilization, unification and liberalization of the currency exchange rate, deregulation, and price liberalization.[10]

These reforms were all essential, but the conditions for implementing them were hardly favorable. Ukraine's economy had declined dramatically in the early 1990s. This was not unique to Ukraine. The economies of virtually every post-Soviet state, like those of every former communist state in Central Europe, had plunged into recession and contraction as they began the process of moving away from a command economy toward one based on market principles.

While developing and preparing to announce the reform program, Kuchma's economic team worked closely with the IMF and in September 1994 reached agreement on a systematic transformation facility. Under its terms, the IMF would provide credits to Ukraine so long as Kyiv met the agreed reform conditionalities. Just two months before the agreement between the IMF and Ukraine, in July at the G-7 summit in Naples, Clinton and other G-7 leaders had agreed that "with a renewed commitment to comprehensive market reform, Ukraine could gain access to international financing of over $4 billion in the course of a two-year period following the commencement of genuine reforms."[11] The systematic transformation facility represented a major piece of this, and Ukraine in 1995 began negotiation with the IMF of a follow-on standby agreement worth $1.5 billion in credits, which was approved in April. Ukraine also received significant assistance from the World Bank. The U.S. executive directors at those international financial institutions, as well as at the European Bank for Reconstruction and Development, generally took supportive positions.

U.S. officials lobbied their European and Japanese counterparts to support a generous IMF program for Ukraine and to make bilateral assistance and financing available. When Clinton visited Kyiv in May 1995, the summit's joint statement tallied significant international assistance for Ukraine: the $1.5 billion IMF standby agreement, $1 billion in direct bilateral financial support from the G-7 countries, and $3 billion in rescheduling of debts for natural gas owed to Russia and Turkmenistan.

The burst of reform in 1994 registered some success in taming hyperinflation and beginning to stabilize the country's finances, but progress on other reform priorities faltered. Meanwhile, the economy plummeted, contracting by 9.7 percent in 1992, 14.2 percent in 1993, and 22.9 percent in 1994.[12]

The Ukrainian government had problems fulfilling the conditionalities of its agreed IMF and World Bank reform programs. Among other things, the organized left in the Rada began pushing back against promarket reforms. By the end of 1995, U.S. officials had grown concerned that Ukraine had not met its performance criteria and was in danger of going off track with the IMF, which could put at risk as much as $900 million in IMF disbursements planned for the first part of 1996. A big part of the U.S.-Ukraine dialogue began to focus on the need for Kyiv to stay on course so as to avoid delayed disbursements or, even worse, termination of the program. Unfortunately, this would become an all too familiar pattern: Ukraine signed an agreement with the IMF, received one or two tranches of credits, and then fell off track in meeting the agreement's conditionalities, which led the IMF to suspend the program and further credits.

On the bilateral side, by the second half of the 1990s, FREEDOM Support Act grants for Ukraine broke down into four categories. The first was economic restructuring, which included programs for privatizing state-owned assets and stimulating the development of private sector enterprises; creating the legal and regulatory framework conducive to a vibrant private sector; and building a more economically sound and environmentally sustainable energy sector. Of the budgeted fiscal year 1997 FREEDOM Support Act funds, over half went to economic restructuring projects.

The second assistance category covered democracy programs. These included projects to promote citizen participation in political decision-making, independent media development, a legal system that would support democratic and economic reforms, and more effective and responsive local governments. The third category covered quality-of-life issues, such as developing a sustainable system for providing social benefits and services and reducing the environmental risks to public health (many in a post-Soviet country).

The fourth category comprised special initiatives, the second largest FREEDOM Support Act category after economic restructuring. This funded a wide range of U.S. government programs, including support for exchange programs (students and professional development), the Peace Corps, law enforcement training, and environmental activities. It also funded programs to close Chornobyl and to enhance safety at other nuclear power plants, which met about half of Ukraine's electricity needs.

On top of the FREEDOM Support Act grants, the U.S. government in fiscal years 1992–96 budgeted for Ukraine an additional $586 million in grant assistance. More than $400 million came from the Pentagon (primarily Cooperative Threat Reduction money but also funds for other military-to-military programs); Department of Agriculture assistance had a value of $123 million, primarily in the form of excess food commodities for Ukraine. These contributions brought total U.S. grant assistance budgeted to Ukraine in fiscal years 1992–96 to $1.3 billion, with an additional $790 million provided in the form of credits from the Export-Import Bank, the Overseas Private Investment Corporation, and the Department of Agriculture.

By 1997, Ukraine had become one of the largest recipients of U.S. assistance, by one count ranking fourth after Israel, Egypt, and Russia. U.S. assistance budgeted for Ukraine in fiscal year 1997 included $225 million in FREEDOM Support Act funds and an additional $131 million from the Departments of Defense, Agriculture, and Energy, as well as more than $300 million in credits. The expansion of the assistance program meant that, by the end of 1997, the U.S. Agency for International Development (USAID) had more than 100 line items in its Ukraine program—a very broad-based effort, though the breadth made it difficult to succinctly describe the program's focus.

In designing American assistance programs for Ukraine, U.S. officials, headed by the assistance coordinator for the New Independent States (first Tom Simons, then Richard Morningstar), the Treasury Department, and USAID, agreed that the IMF should lead in developing a program of macroeconomic reform. U.S. bilateral assistance would aim at specific measures to advance that program, as Washington desired to avoid giving Kyiv competing policy prescriptions. On the ground in Kyiv, USAID held regular meetings with representatives from the European Union, the IMF, the World Bank, and others to discuss what each was doing. Ideally, such coordination would help avoid duplication of effort and ensure that assistance was flowing to the most critical reform needs.

Most U.S. assistance took the form of programs (for example, USAID and the Treasury Department provided technical advisers who could help the National Bank of Ukraine set up a modern central bank), and Congress usually ensured that a good portion of the money was spent on consultants and institutions in congressional districts. On rare occasions, the U.S. government was prepared to provide an open credit that the Ukrainian government could use to close budget financing or balance-of-payments gaps.

One focus of U.S. and international assistance centered on reform in the energy sector, in particular, promoting energy conservation. Ukraine had one of the most energy-intensive economies in the world, with some estimates showing that it used twice as much energy per unit of gross domestic product as neighboring Poland and five to six times as much as Germany. As a result, the country had enormous energy demands. It consumed 75 to 80 billion cubic meters of natural gas per year, but produced less than 20 billion cubic meters domestically. It thus had a large gas import bill and a potentially dangerous vulnerability in that the remainder of the gas came from Russia or from Turkmenistan in pipelines that ran through Russia. Ukraine's energy needs gave Moscow a potential stranglehold over a critical Ukrainian energy resource (which the Russians would later employ).

One USAID program aimed to encourage the installation of meters in individual apartments so that occupants could be charged for their actual electric or gas usage, rather than simply paying a flat fee. The flat fee created no economic incentive to conserve energy. For example, on a typical winter night in Kyiv and other large cities one saw apartment buildings with windows wide open, venting hot air into the chilly night. Ukrainian municipal utilities charged households a fraction of the cost of producing the heat, which compounded the government's precarious fiscal situation. The U.S. government, along with the European Union and international financial institutions, thus urged Kyiv to raise the energy tariff to cover the full cost and put in place a program of targeted subsidies for those households for whom the higher tariffs would pose a true hardship. Western advisers recommended other steps to make the energy sector, the gas sector in particular, more competitive and transparent, which would reduce the possibilities for corruption.

The refusal to raise tariffs, and the fact that virtually all energy consumed by households and for municipal purposes was highly subsidized, had major negative implications for the Ukrainian budget. The World Bank argued that Ukraine did not need more energy production capacity but, with perhaps $3 billion in investment in conservation and the right policy choices, could cut its energy consumption by 40 percent. However, proposals for price increases to promote conservation rarely received a positive reception from the Ukrainian government.

Endemic corruption also undermined efficient energy markets. Murky middlemen took part in energy sales, both within Ukraine and between Ukraine and Russia. Analysts assessed the complex and nontransparent arrangements as mechanisms designed to skim money out of the energy sector, which was believed to then flow into both Ukrainian and Russian hands. Lazarenko prospered greatly from such opaque dealings in the gas market. Government policy created opportunities for corruption in the energy sector. Kyiv held down the price that it would pay for domestically produced natural gas, in order to be able to also hold down the tariffs charged to households. Individuals who had connections to the right officials could buy such gas at the artificially low price and then sell it at the higher industrial price or even export it. Many analysts regarded the energy sector as the most corrupt in the country.

Getting assistance to Ukraine was a cumbersome process. Once the U.S. government decided how to budget funds, it had to notify Congress; then contracts were negotiated and funds actually obligated, a process the might take a year or even longer.

Chornobyl

The international community directed a large part of its assistance to promote the closure of Chornobyl. The Chornobyl nuclear power plant grabbed global headlines in April 1986, when a poorly planned test in reactor number four (of four at the plant) triggered a series of explosions that led to a catastrophic near-meltdown. The explosions destroyed much of the roof over the reactor, and the ensuing fire vented radioactive particles into the open air, where winds carried the plume to the northwest over Belarus and toward Scandinavia. The first indication that the West received of any problem was when a radiation alarm went off at a nuclear power plant in Sweden; the Swedes quickly ascertained that the radiation had come from the direction of the Soviet Union.

Heroic efforts in the initial hours by local firefighters, many of whom died of acute radiation sickness, supplemented by help in the following days from tens of thousands of firefighters and military troops from around the Soviet Union, extinguished the fire on May 10. But the damage to the plant and surrounding environment was severe. The local town of Pripyat, which had housed most of the Chornobyl workforce, was evacuated the day after the explosion. Some 100 villages around the plant were also emptied as authorities established an exclusion zone with a radius of thirty kilometers around the stricken nuclear facility.

By 1994, Chornobyl had begun to figure heavily in Kyiv's discussions with the United States and European countries. The sarcophagus that had quickly been erected to encase destroyed reactor number four had begun to weaken. Experts expressed concern about its structural integrity, fearing that a collapse would result in more venting of radioactive particles into the air. They recommended stabilizing the old sarcophagus and constructing a new shelter over the old one. Ukraine had no way to fund this itself.

European countries also began to press Kyiv to close permanently the other reactors at Chornobyl. Like reactor number four, they were of the RBMK-1000 design. Western nuclear experts had serious doubts about the RBMK-1000's safety features. Reactor number two had ceased operation in 1991 following a fire in its turbine hall, but reactor numbers one and three continued to operate in the mid-1990s.

During the summer of 1995, Pascual worked with Bob Ichord from USAID and Carol Kessler, a civil servant at the State Department, to develop the draft of a memorandum of understanding to close down Chornobyl. They won Canadian support (Canada chaired the G-7 in 1995), and other G-7 members subsequently bought on. That December, G-7 countries and the European Union concluded a memorandum of understanding with Ukraine offering some $2.3 billion in grants and loans that would, among other things, help to close Chornobyl and build a more stable shelter over reactor number four. The package also included loans that would help Ukraine complete construction of two VVER-type nuclear reactors at Rivne and Khmelnytskyy, with safety systems upgraded to Western standards, in order to make up for the electrical production that would be lost as the two remaining operating reactors at Chornobyl shut down.

Mobilizing concrete assistance for closing Chornobyl and financing the replacement reactors took longer than expected. Kyiv regularly expressed frustration at the slow pace, though its reluctance to promote more vigorous reforms in the energy sector was part of the problem. There was little enthusiasm in Europe for financing the completion of two new reactors until their commercial viability was established. That turned in large measure on their ability to receive a fair price for the electricity they generated. Absent the financing for the two reactors, Kyiv was reluctant to commit to a date for closing Chornobyl.

Chornobyl was a subject for the June 1997 meeting in Denver of the G-8 (Russia had joined the other G-7 members). They discussed a shelter implementation plan to complete the sarcophagus for reactor number four, estimated to cost just over $700 million. The State Department set up a special office to oversee the plan. Managed by Kessler, the paper printout of the plan covered several walls, from floor to ceiling, of a large office. (The costs for the shelter escalated dramatically in succeeding years. The new shelter was moved into place over the destroyed reactor number four in November 2016.)

And New Problems—CFE

One of the unexpectedly difficult issues that arose between Washington and Kyiv in 1996–97 turned out to be adjusting the Conventional Armed Forces in Europe (CFE) Treaty. The treaty, signed by NATO and Warsaw Pact member states in November 1990, placed limits on military equipment, such as main battle tanks, held by NATO and Warsaw Pact members in Europe. Special limits applied in the flank zones, one of which covered southern Ukraine and Crimea.

Following the Soviet Union's collapse, a May 1992 CIS agreement allocated the Soviet Union's CFE equipment entitlements among those post-Soviet states with territory in the treaty's zone of application—that is, states with territory west of the Ural Mountains. After Russia, Ukraine emerged with the second largest allocation of military equipment, far more than the rapidly shrinking Ukrainian military could possibly utilize.

In 1993, Russia began lobbying to suspend the flank limits, which fell most heavily on Russian territory, arguing that abolishing the limits was appropriate given the changing strategic circumstances. Moscow in particular sought the ability to deploy more equipment in the North Caucasus region, where it was concerned about growing unrest (the Chechnya conflict would explode into a full-scale war in 1995). Ukraine also asked for relief from the flank limits. While not accepting the Russian or Ukrainian positions in their entirety, the United States and other NATO members felt that Moscow and Kyiv had a reasonable point. Turkey and Norway—the two allies most directly protected by the flank limits regime—originally showed reluctance but ultimately agreed to accept a modification of the flank constraints.

U.S. diplomats intensely shepherded the process of adjusting the flank limits. They had to apply pressure on Azerbaijan and Georgia but, when consulting with other post-Soviet states that might be affected, heard no objections from Ukrainian officials. With U.S. guidance, the parties reached an agreement to retain the limits on military equipment permitted in the flanks but to reduce the size of the flank zones. Thus the amount of Russian and Ukrainian territory subject to the flank limits would be smaller than under the treaty's original terms. In May 1996, CFE signatories approved the flank agreement at the treaty's first review conference.

Hints of Ukrainian unhappiness emerged toward the end of 1996. Ukraine, along with Moldova and Azerbaijan, worried that the agreement might legitimize the presence of Russian troops and military equipment on their territory. For Ukraine, that meant the armored vehicles and other equipment belonging to the Black Sea Fleet's naval infantry in Crimea. U.S. officials thought those concerns were overstated. Moreover, if the flank agreement collapsed and caused Russia to withdraw from the CFE Treaty, there would be no constraints whatsoever on Russian military equipment in the flank region.

With Gore scheduled to meet Kuchma briefly on December 2, 1996, on the margins of the Organization for Security and Cooperation summit in Lisbon, the CFE question topped the U.S. agenda. John Herbst, deputy coordinator in the State Department's Office of the New Independent States, had led the U.S. effort to find a solution to the flank limits issue with Russia and, in the process, had visited other post-Soviet states, including Ukraine, to discuss the question. He met with Ukrainian officials in Lisbon before the vice president's arrival to urge Kyiv not to back away from the flank agreement.

During their meeting, Gore told Kuchma that the flank agreement was key to the viability of the CFE Treaty. If the treaty fell apart, Russia could deploy much more equipment near Ukraine. Kuchma worried that the agreement still gave Russia the ability to deploy military units on the territory of other CFE countries. He added that he was working with Russia on this question, which was intertwined with the broader issue of the terms for continuing the Black Sea Fleet's presence in Crimea (which would only be resolved in spring 1997). He hoped the United States would be supportive. Gore expressed understanding for Kuchma's concern but pointed out that the flank agreement provided some regulation of Russian forces while Kyiv and Moscow worked further on the Black Sea Fleet question.

The issue jumped to the top of the U.S.-Ukrainian agenda on April 8, 1997. With no warning to U.S. officials, Ukraine, Azerbaijan, and Moldova issued a statement to the effect that they would not ratify the May 1996 flank agreement. Washington felt blindsided and saw Kyiv as the organizer. Talbott phoned Horbulin, Secretary of State Madeleine Albright wrote to Udovenko, and American officials in Vienna, where CFE Treaty matters were handled, vigorously engaged their Ukrainian (and Azerbaijani and Moldovan) counterparts. Although U.S. officials were not unsympathetic to the position of the three governments, they made clear to Kyiv that this kind of surprise was not what Washington expected from a strategic partner.

Ukrainian officials in Vienna said they would "clarify" the April 8 statement, and the Ukrainian embassy in Washington advised that there would be a breakthrough on the question, but none emerged.

Gore called Kuchma on May 6 to ask that Kyiv not hold up the flank agreement. Kuchma said the Ukrainians wanted to solve the problem, but they remained worried about the presence of the Black Sea Fleet's naval infantry. The Ukrainians also worried that Russian equipment in Crimea could count against Ukraine's limit. Kuchma wanted language in the NATO-Ukraine charter making clear that the alliance concurred with Kyiv that foreign troops could be deployed on the territory of another CFE state only with the host state's consent. Georgia, Moldova, and Azerbaijan shared Kyiv's concern.

On May 7, NATO secretary general Solana handed over the draft text of the NATO-Ukraine charter. He discussed with Kuchma how the foreign troops question might be handled in that document. When Kuchma met with Gore on May 16, he told the vice president that he could accept compromise language in the NATO-Ukraine charter. NATO and Ukrainian foreign ministers on May 30 initialed the Charter on a Distinctive Partnership, which stated that NATO and Ukraine "share the view that the presence of foreign troops on the territory of a [CFE] participating state must be in conformity with international law, the freely expressed consent of the host state or a relevant decision of the United Nations Security Council."[13]

Missiles and Relations with Pariahs

In early 1996, Ukrainian officials indicated that they wished to go beyond the bilateral memorandum of understanding on Ukraine's observance of MTCR guidelines and join the regime. At that point, Ukraine had built a good record in controlling its exports of missiles and related technologies, but the U.S. government had asked countries desiring to join the regime to first eliminate any missiles in their inventories with ranges in excess of 300 kilometers. The only still existing Ukrainian missiles with a range of 300 to 500 kilometers were several hundred aging SCUD missiles.

In the fall of 1996, U.S. officials informed their Ukrainian counterparts that they would have to give up the SCUDs in order to secure U.S. support for entry into the MTCR. Horbulin told Miller in November that, given the negative climate of Ukrainian-Russian relations, Ukraine was unable to commit not to develop missiles in the 300 to 500 kilometer range band. The U.S. approach sounded acceptable, but the timing and politics were not favorable.

The subject remained open when the Gore-Kuchma Commission met in May 1997. Horbulin noted Kyiv's interest in joining the MTCR, but the U.S. government had blocked consensus. Ukraine was prepared to commit not to transfer any missiles in the 300 to 500 kilometer range band. Kuchma added that Ukraine could even halt production of such missiles, but it needed to retain the existing force with conventional warheads. The sides could not come to closure and agreed to discuss the issue further at the working level.

Other troublesome issues arose on the proliferation agenda. The Russian government in the early 1990s had negotiated a contract to build a nuclear power reactor at Bushehr in Iran. This issue had become a problem for U.S.-Russian relations, as Washington sought to dissuade Russia from going forward with the project owing to concerns about Iran's nuclear ambitions. The type of reactor the Russians were building at Bushehr typically used a turbine generator provided by the Turboatom plant in Kharkiv, and the Russians had placed an order for such a turbine with Turboatom. As part of its effort to stop Bushehr, the U.S. government began to lobby Kyiv to cancel the turbine contract and agree not to participate in the construction at Bushehr or in any nuclear cooperation with Iran.

U.S. officials had a carrot to offer. The Ukrainians had expressed interest in concluding a section 123 agreement that would authorize civil nuclear cooperation between American companies and Ukraine, something that Kyiv very much wished to pursue. Washington made clear that a 123 agreement was out of the question so long as Ukraine continued any nuclear-related cooperation with Iran.

American officials had other concerns regarding Kyiv's relations with what they considered "pariah" states. In June 1996, Ukraine and Libya had announced a "strategic" relationship to be managed by a ministerial-level oversight group, at a time when Libya remained on the American list of state sponsors of terrorism. U.S. officials did not like the idea of a strategic relationship between Kyiv and Tripoli. Washington communicated its concern and asked the Ukrainian government to explain what it would and would not do with Libya.

When Udovenko visited Washington that October, Berger suggested that the Gore-Kuchma channel take up the activities of some Ukrainian companies in Libya. Given strong congressional concerns about Libya, those activities could prove problematic with Congress and might even trigger U.S. sanctions. Udovenko responded that Kuchma had taken account of the U.S. concerns; any Ukrainian contracts with Libya, Iraq, or Iran would have to be approved by the foreign ministry. While this might have put in place a system for government review of such contracts, U.S. officials were unsure what standards the foreign ministry would apply in reviewing contracts and worried that, given the possible commercial benefits, the ministry would find itself under great pressure to approve contracts.

In early December, the issue became public when the *Washington Times* published a story alleging that Kyiv planned to sell ballistic missiles to Libya. The Ukrainian embassy and foreign ministry vigorously denied the report, but U.S. officials privately shared with Kyiv information about troublesome contacts with Libya.[14] Kyiv agreed to investigate the reports and issued a public statement at the beginning of January saying that it would not support military cooperation with Libya.

U.S. officials debated how to raise these issues in the run-up to the May 1997 Gore-Kuchma meeting in Washington. Kuchma's visit could provide the opportunity to announce U.S. readiness to negotiate a 123 agreement, but Ukraine's responses to U.S. démarches regarding withdrawal of Turboatom from the Bushehr project had not been fully reassuring. It seemed that Kyiv sought to maintain a degree of ambiguity, where Washington wanted a categorical assurance of no nuclear cooperation with Iran.

At the Gore-Kuchma meeting, Horbulin explained that Ukraine adhered to all UN Security Council resolutions and to its bilateral agreements with the United States; Ukraine was not leaking sensitive technology to pariah states. Gore stressed that the United States was ready to negotiate a 123 agreement but first needed a strong assurance that there would be no nuclear cooperation with pariahs, especially Iran. Kuchma said Ukraine would do its best but added that this sometimes led to "expensive" decisions for Kyiv, a reference to lost contracts. The Gore-Kuchma discussions closed with each side having laid down its position, but a considerable gap remained as 1997 came to a close.

Reflections

No longer burdened by the nuclear weapons issue, the bilateral relationship between Washington and Kyiv made substantial progress in the period 1995–97, as the U.S. government's strategy aimed to fill out a broad agenda and increase Ukraine's links with the West. A key driver on the American side was the desire to find a response to the question that Tarasyuk posed to Talbott in autumn 1994: how to keep Ukraine out of a gray zone between institutional Europe (the European Union and NATO) and Russia. U.S. diplomacy produced good answers to that question, both in supporting more robust bilateral relations with Kyiv and in linking Ukraine more closely to NATO.

Over the three years, Kuchma had a regular series of high-level meetings with Clinton and Gore, making four trips to the United States in 1997 alone. The announcement of a strategic partnership and establishment of the Gore-Kuchma Commission in 1996 further solidified ties between the two countries, providing the level, intensity, and visibility of engagement with the White House that Kyiv wanted. For their part, U.S. officials were pleased that the president and, in particular, the vice president took a strong personal interest in Ukraine, even if it meant the occasional extended lecture on Chornobyl piping. The vice president's readiness to engage gave Washington an additional channel to use in reaching out to Kuchma. Building personal relationships at the highest level, along with the strategic partnership and Gore-Kuchma Commission, helped shape the kind of bilateral links that it was hoped would ease concerns in Kyiv that it might end up in a gray zone. A budding bilateral defense relationship, pushed by Perry, added more meat to the bilateral framework. It moved beyond Cooperative Threat Reduction assistance to help Ukraine fulfill its START reduction obligations to include funding for joint exercises, reform of the ministry of defense, and even provision of some military equipment.

Another strand in the web of links that Washington sought to encourage between the West and Ukraine was Kyiv's relationship with NATO. In some ways, the European Union connection might have been more logical, given the urgency of Ukraine's political and economic reform needs. However, that institution in the early 1990s seemed slow to recognize the role it might play in engaging countries on its eastern flank, beginning with countries such as Poland and the

Czech Republic. The European Union had a difficult time achieving consensus between those member states who favored a "deeper" and more integrated European Union and those who favored a "wider" union. EU enlargement into Central Europe trailed NATO's by several years, and the European Union appeared to lack a strategic vision for how to deal with Ukraine. In any event, the United States was not a member of the European Union. American and EU officials consulted regularly, but U.S. influence with that body was limited.

U.S. diplomats encouraged Kyiv to join NATO's Partnership for Peace early on. Soon after Washington decided to pursue NATO enlargement and an accompanying attempt to build a cooperative NATO-Russia partnership, it decided to add a third parallel track: a NATO-Ukraine relationship. That decision reflected Washington's desire to build connections between Kyiv and the West as well as the sense that, owing to its size and location, Ukraine could play a special role in developing a more stable and secure Europe. U.S. officials discussed a NATO-Ukraine relationship with their Ukrainian counterparts, then shifted the dialogue to NATO, encouraging other NATO member states to support such a relationship. In doing so, U.S. diplomats found a willing partner in the alliance's secretary general, who saw the value of anchoring Ukraine to the West.

Kyiv eagerly took up the opportunity and came to quick agreement with NATO on the particulars of what became the Distinctive Partnership. More problematic for Ukraine, however, was the looming enlargement of the alliance. Senior Ukrainian officials made no secret of their desire for enlargement to proceed slowly. It was clear that Ukrainian leaders had not decided how far they wished to take their country's relationship with NATO. They worried that, as Ukraine's western neighbors received invitations to join the alliance, the spotlight might turn to Kyiv, which could appear increasingly separated from the Central European countries. Indecision about how far to proceed with NATO also reflected Kuchma's desire to find a geopolitical balance between the West and Russia, what he would refer to as a "multi-vector" foreign policy of engaging the United States, Europe, and Russia. He sometimes appeared more interested in managing the tactics of balance rather than in adopting a bold strategic course. That could have been due in part to his understanding of the ambivalence with which most Ukrainians viewed NATO.

Kuchma understandably remained concerned about Russia and Russian policy. Although the trilateral process had resolved the nuclear weapons question, Kyiv still had a problematic relationship with Moscow. Russia's handling of the Black Sea Fleet basing question, and the manner in which it delayed signing of the treaty of friendship and cooperation, had the unintended consequence of fueling Kyiv's desire for a relationship with NATO, even if Kuchma personally had confidence in Yeltsin. The resolution of the basing issue and the signing of the treaty came only after Kyiv had begun negotiating with the alliance on establishing a special relationship—leading U.S. analysts to wonder whether that might have been prompted by the NATO-Ukraine discussions.

An alternative security construct for Ukraine could have taken as a model the 1955 Austrian State Treaty, which enabled Austria's reestablishment as a sovereign state and provided for the withdrawal of U.S., Russian, British, and French occupation forces. Following the treaty's signing, Austria declared permanent neutrality. Few pushed this idea in the 1990s. Kuchma and the Ukrainian leadership did not appear to have a firm idea about where and how Ukraine would fit into the transforming European political landscape. Years later, following Russia's seizure of Crimea in 2014, some suggested an Austrian State Treaty–like solution for Ukraine, but the idea had little appeal for most Ukrainians. Moreover, the Austrian model (like the Finnish model also sometimes proposed for Ukraine) allowed for membership in the European Union. From 2010 on, it became increasingly clear that Moscow opposed EU as well as NATO membership for Kyiv.

In retrospect, a couple of problems could be seen in the mid-1990s that foreshadowed later difficulties between the United States and Ukraine. First, senior Ukrainian officials, especially Kuchma, focused in discussions with Americans on status issues (the strategic partnership) and institutional questions (establishing the Gore-Kuchma Commission and a relationship with NATO). Kyiv saw these as important achievements, which they were. They demonstrated to the public that Ukraine mattered in the West, and to Moscow that Kyiv had a counterbalance to Russia. But senior Ukrainian leaders did not devote sufficient attention to practical actions and the need for internal reform, steps that would underpin the country's foreign relationships and build a more effective state. After an initial spate of reform decisions at the beginning of his presidency, Kuchma's attention seemed to turn elsewhere. Ukraine soon fell off-program with the International Monetary Fund. Questions about Kuchma's commitment to reform, among other problems, even led White House officials to revamp how the vice president would approach the first full meeting of the Gore-Kuchma Commission. The meeting went ahead, but it lost some of the celebratory nature that it might have had.

All too often, discussions between U.S. and Ukrainian officials on reform took the form of the Americans urging and pressing their Ukrainian counterparts to do more—and to do it faster—but hearing instead explanations why Kyiv could not move more rapidly and why IMF conditions should be relaxed. The Ukrainian government conveyed little sense of urgency when it came to implementing reforms. True, U.S. officials may not have fully appreciated the pressures that the Ukrainian leadership was under, but that leadership often did not convey an impression that it knew what it had to do and that it was prepared to do it. Americans saw internal reform as critical to Ukraine's development as a stable, economically growing, and stronger state. It often seemed, however, that their Ukrainian counterparts failed to make the connection between the country's progress on reform and the country's ability to deal with its external challenges, particularly the difficult neighbor to its east. U.S. officials tried different approaches, including the use of carrots and sticks, to encourage Kyiv to press forward on reform but only rarely saw the kind of change that they believed was necessary. Americans did not always fully understand the competing pressures—political, economic, and sometimes corruption—that prevented adoption of reforms whose value seemed self-evident.

These pressures were particularly strong with regard to reform of the energy sector. Kuchma refused to raise energy tariffs, which meant that the state budget had to continue to provide huge subsidies to the energy sector so that every household, no matter how wealthy the owner, could enjoy inexpensive energy. The reason for Kuchma's reluctance was clear: hitting every household with a tariff increase would carry political consequences, even if the government put in place a program to subsidize those households at lower income levels. Another big factor: the unreformed energy sector created large opportunities for corrupt activities by gas traders who had ties to the government.

The refusal to reform the energy sector had reverberations that badly distorted Ukraine's economy. Low prices created lesser incentives to conserve. In order to provide cheap gas for households and communal services, the Ukrainian government held down the price that it paid for domestically produced gas, which lowered incentives for greater production in Ukraine, leaving the country more dependent on gas imported from Russia or from Central Asia via Russia.

More broadly, U.S. assistance to Ukraine was just gearing up in 1994 as Kuchma launched a wave of reforms. Looking back today, one can ask whether, if Washington had had the FREEDOM Support Act in place and funded earlier, and if it had pressed Kuchma harder on reform, that initial wave might have been sustained. Doing so could have required more explicit links between the provision of assistance and Kyiv's adoption of specific reforms and a stricter approach by Clinton and Gore with Kuchma; but such an approach is not always easy at the highest level with a leader of a friendly country.

A related question is whether there should have been a more regular and candid discussion with Kuchma of the problems posed by corruption. To be sure, Gore's expression of concern about Lazarenko had an impact. Would a more extended conversation with Kuchma have done more? One cannot be certain, but Washington might have devoted more high-level attention to pressing senior Ukrainian officials to combat corruption. Part of the problem was that the U.S. government in the mid-1990s was only beginning to recognize how much corruption permeated the Ukrainian system, distorting economic decisions and warping the political process.

Ultimately, the CFE flank issue was resolved to the satisfaction of all parties, but its handling in Kyiv did not go down well in Washington. U.S. officials understood Ukraine's concerns and believed they could address them. But the surprise April 1997 announcement by Ukraine, Azerbaijan, and Moldova, apparently organized by Kyiv, that they would not ratify the flank agreement concluded the previous year showed that Ukrainian officials were still learning how to deal with their American counterparts. The surprise went down so badly that Washington briefly instructed the U.S. mission to NATO to withhold agreement on the draft NATO-Ukraine charter that the secretary general intended to take to Kyiv. A better course for Kyiv would have been to make clear the Ukrainian concerns earlier. The conversations could have been difficult, but they would have avoided the surprise that struck American officials as inconsistent with the notion of a strategic partnership.

Another question that foreshadowed later problems was Kyiv's relationships with states that were regarded as pariahs in Washington, including Iran and Libya. The fact that these involved nuclear and missile proliferation greatly magnified the problems in American eyes. U.S. officials tried to craft carrots and held out the prospect of sticks, but coming to a common view on these issues with their Ukrainian counterparts proved tougher than expected. In retrospect, it seems that Washington did not fully appreciate the economic importance of these deals for Kyiv. Although the dollar amounts involved were not huge, they mattered for struggling Ukrainian industries that faced the specter of bankruptcy. The terms of the U.S. assistance program, however, did not allow Washington to buy out those contracts—and doing so would have been unwise, as it could have created incentives for Ukrainian firms to conclude more such contracts. On the other side, Ukrainian officials did not seem to appreciate the level of concern in Washington, both in the executive branch and on Capitol Hill, about pariah states gaining access to weapons of mass destruction and systems for their delivery.

CHAPTER 4

The Relationship Matures . . . but Problems Appear

So I am pleased and encouraged by the outcome of today's discussions. They have deepened a strategic partnership that is strong today and will grow stronger in the years to come." With those words, Secretary of State Madeleine Albright concluded her opening statement at a Kyiv press conference on March 6, 1998. The first months of 1998 carried over much of the momentum that had developed over the previous four years in U.S.-Ukraine relations. The secretary's visit aligned U.S. and Ukrainian policies on nuclear nonproliferation. Vice President Al Gore visited in July, for the first Gore-Kuchma Commission meeting to be held in Ukraine, as the relationship deepened further on a range of issues. But it also encountered problems, ranging from lack of follow-through on economic reforms and business issues to complications for Ukraine's relationship with NATO to a problematic presidential election campaign in 1999.

Clearing Up the Proliferation Agenda

I arrived in Kyiv on January 8, 1998, and took up my position as the third American ambassador to Ukraine. James Schumacher, a talented foreign service officer with long expertise in Soviet and post-Soviet affairs, had already served as deputy chief of mission for more than two years. He quickly brought me up to speed on the embassy and its perspective on key U.S.-Ukraine issues. I became fully "official" upon presenting my credentials to President Leonid Kuchma in the Mariinskyy Palace on January 20.

I brought a one-page mission statement that I had worked out with the Ukraine desk at the State Department. It proceeded from the starting point that Ukraine's development as a stable, independent, democratic, market-oriented, and prosperous state was in the U.S. national interest. Such a Ukraine would be a key partner in tackling international challenges in the post–Cold War world, such as proliferation, as well as in expanding trade and investment relations and shaping a more secure Europe. Three items topped the embassy's agenda for the first few months of 1998: settling differences on proliferation issues; resolving business dispute cases that disadvantaged American investors and threatened to disrupt U.S. assistance; and monitoring the spring Rada (parliament) election.

The proliferation issues commanded the most urgent action. Washington wanted Kyiv to fully disengage from the nuclear power plant project at Bushehr, Iran. The Ukrainian government sought to conclude a 123 agreement that would enable American firms to engage in civil nuclear cooperation with Ukraine, and allow Kyiv to consider importing fuel rods for its nuclear power plants—which generated 50 percent of the country's electricity—from American companies as an alternative to its Russian supplier. The Ukrainian government also wished to join the Missile Technology Control Regime (MTCR) as a full member. Ukrainian officials regularly pointed out that they had assumed all of the obligations of MTCR membership but received none of the benefits.

Ambassador-at-Large for the New Independent States Stephen Sestanovich visited Kyiv in mid-February for a meeting of the Gore-Kuchma Commission's foreign policy committee. Deputy Foreign Minister

Kostyantyn Hryshchenko headed the Ukrainian side. Sestanovich also had side meetings with other officials, including Deputy Foreign Minister Anton Buteyko and National Security and Defense Council secretary Volodymyr Horbulin. The discussions focused on nuclear cooperation with Iran and Ukraine's aspirations to join the MTCR. Sestanovich proposed setting Albright's March visit as the target for resolving these issues.

Albright was due to visit on March 6. On March 2, Deputy Assistant Secretary of State for Nonproliferation Robert Einhorn and Debra Cagan, senior adviser for nuclear and security policy in the State Department's Bureau of European Affairs, arrived in Kyiv. U.S. and Ukrainian negotiators had all but finished the text of a civil nuclear cooperation agreement, but Einhorn and Cagan reiterated that the U.S. government would sign only with a clear understanding that Ukraine would not cooperate in the nuclear area with Iran.

Einhorn, Cagan, and I met primarily with Horbulin and Hryshchenko. Hryshchenko had originally served in the Soviet foreign ministry and was one of a few who resigned and returned to Kyiv to become a Ukrainian diplomat. A lawyer by training, he had a sharp mind and was a good debater. He could show a temper when defending Ukrainian positions, sometimes scowling theatrically, but he also knew how to break into a broad grin when squabbles reached a silly point. He clearly was valued in Kyiv, serving in senior positions under four presidents: Kravchuk, Kuchma, Yushchenko, and Yanukovych. U.S. officials at first found Hryshchenko difficult to work with, including in a nearly all-night session before the signature of the Budapest Memorandum, but that view changed as they increased their interactions with him.

Horbulin and Hryshchenko agreed that there would be no nuclear cooperation with Iran and confirmed that the government would block contracts by Ukrainian companies in the nuclear field. That would be difficult politically; Turboatom was a major employer in Kharkiv. Einhorn and Cagan outlined sweeteners to balance that loss. In addition to assistance to qualify an alternate provider of fuel rods for Ukraine's nuclear plants, Washington intended to boost funding for the Science and Technology Center of Ukraine, which supported civilian research projects by former weapons scientists, and target special assistance to Kharkiv, in what later became known as the "Kharkiv initiative."

As for Ukraine's accession to the MTCR, the U.S. government still wanted Ukraine to destroy its existing inventory of aging SCUD missiles. Horbulin and Hryshchenko indicated that Kyiv planned to keep some SCUDs in service for another fifteen years. We agreed that half of the SCUDs would be eliminated in five years' time, by 2003, with the remainder to be eliminated by 2013. (In April 2011, the Department of State announced the completion of the elimination of Ukraine's SCUD missiles and their associated launchers, with U.S. assistance.)

One last question concerned modernization of the SCUDs. Washington saw no reason for Ukraine to upgrade them. Horbulin and Hryshchenko, however, insisted on retaining some freedom to modernize, in particular, the missiles' front ends, which had been designed to carry nuclear warheads. Absent some modernization, the missiles would have no warheads. We agreed that a rule of reason could prevail on modernization.

The Secretary's Visit

As the loose ends on proliferation questions came together, the sides translated their understandings into language for a joint statement to be signed by Secretary Albright and Ukrainian foreign minister Hennadiy Udovenko. One question remained on the eve of the secretary's visit: How explicit would the sides be in explaining in public their common understanding on no nuclear cooperation with Iran?

Albright and her party landed at Borispil Airport at 7:30 a.m. on March 6. She proceeded immediately to the Kyiv-Mohyla Academy for a town meeting with undergraduate students. This event was almost scrubbed by the secretary's office. At the end of February, Albright had joined Secretary of Defense William Cohen and National Security Adviser Sandy Berger at a town meeting at Ohio State University. The session went badly, with the president's three most senior foreign and security policy advisers nearly getting hooted off the stage by an audience hostile to the idea of a possible military clash with Iraq.[1]

Not surprisingly, another "town meeting" held little appeal to the secretary's staff. They had nothing to fear. If anything, the embassy worried that the television cameras would make the young audience too nervous to speak up. As it turned out, the students overcame any shyness and posed good questions. Albright slipped back into her Georgetown professor persona, and she ran twenty minutes overtime on an already tight schedule.[2]

Albright and Udovenko held a one-on-one discussion on the question of publicly mentioning Iran. Udovenko did not want to single out Iran in the joint statement. Albright could accept that, but they agreed that, at the press conference, Udovenko would say Kyiv would refrain from nuclear cooperation with Iran, including the Bushehr nuclear power plant project.

Albright's subsequent meeting with Kuchma and Udovenko began with a recap of the understandings on proliferation issues. Albright and Kuchma also discussed the state of economic reform and the U.S. business dispute cases. The secretary noted the importance of continued democratic reform, including a free press. The two touched on developments in Russia and relations between Ukraine and the European Union.

With the meeting concluded, Albright and Udovenko appeared before the press to sign the joint statement. It noted that the sides "agreed on the need for responsible policies regarding nuclear cooperation." Based on those understandings, the sides had "reached a bilateral agreement for peaceful nuclear cooperation." The statement expressed U.S. support for "immediate Ukrainian membership in the MTCR." It also announced that the United States would provide assistance to qualify an alternative supplier of nuclear fuel rods for Ukraine, send a mission to Kharkiv to explore investment and business opportunities there, and boost funding for the Science and Technology Center of Ukraine.[3] In his comments, Udovenko made the key point for American ears: "In this [nonproliferation] connection, Ukraine has decided to refrain from nuclear cooperation with Iran, including the supply of turbines to the 'Bushehr project.'" Kuchma downplayed the Bushehr contract, noting that it dated from Soviet times and amounted to only $45 million.[4]

By all appearances, the Ukrainian government abided by its commitment to end nuclear cooperation with Iran. Turboatom terminated the turbine sale. Several months after the secretary's visit, the State

Department sent the embassy information suggesting that a different Ukrainian company had begun to explore nuclear cooperation with Tehran. I shared that with Buteyko, who doubted its veracity but agreed to check. A week later, he advised that the information had been correct. He said that the authorities had ordered the company to drop the contacts and threatened it with severe punishment if it proceeded—just the kind of action that Washington had sought.

The Kharkiv initiative unfortunately got off to a rocky start. In June, I accompanied the assistance coordinator for the New Independent States, Richard Morningstar, to the city to explore possible U.S. assistance. National Agency for Reform director Roman Shpek and Kharkiv governor Oleh Dyomin made clear that they wanted new contracts for Turboatom. We found that dealing with a large industrial concern that was still more comfortable with the Soviet command-style system would not be easy. Turboatom's leadership claimed to face a loss of $260 million, a sum they arrived at by calculating the price of turbines for four reactors, when only one was under construction. Turboatom suggested the U.S. government persuade General Electric or Westinghouse to cede one of their contracts to Turboatom, something plainly beyond the U.S. government's authority. Morningstar asked Turboatom's general director for his "elevator speech" to sell a potential partner on working with Turboatom. The response: "Why, we're Turboatom."

The U.S. government could not help Turboatom build better turbines, but it could provide advice on marketing. That was a new game for Turboatom, which normally simply fulfilled orders for turbines placed from Moscow. Still, it took many months to persuade Turboatom's leadership to accept the services of two businessmen with international marketing experience, whose salaries and costs would be covered by the U.S. government, to provide advice on how best to compete and succeed in the global market.

Morningstar and I also visited the Antonov aircraft factory. Antonov built the An-140 turboprop and An-74 jet, both to serve as regional passenger aircraft. No U.S. producer built such short-range commuter planes, so we suggested that Antonov consider the American market. The first step required securing Federal Aviation Administration certification for the aircraft, a complex process that could take considerable time. The embassy gave Antonov the contact information for the Federal Aviation Agency's Europe representative in Brussels and offered to facilitate a meeting to start that process—but never heard back.

In November, William (Bill) Taylor, who had succeeded Morningstar as assistance coordinator for the New Independent States, traveled to Kharkiv. He pressed the idea of creating an office whose purpose would be to help potential investors navigate the labyrinth of tax, customs, and registration rules. That could make Kharkiv more competitive with other cities for American and other international investment. The idea received a lukewarm reception. The U.S. Agency for International Development (USAID) provided funding for the office, but it did not become the dynamic, business-friendly "go to" facilitator that we had envisaged. (A *New York Times* article two years later captured the frustration in Kharkiv.)[5]

Business Disputes and Certification

Before departing Kyiv, the secretary met with representatives of U.S. companies to hear their views on the business climate and the business dispute cases. American and other Western companies faced a difficult, confusing, and corrupt business climate. For example, a large U.S. company had endured weeks of a tax inspection—with State Tax Administration auditors going through all of the company's financial records in painstaking detail. At the end, the chief of the inspection team came to the company director and essentially asked, "Where are you violating Ukrainian tax law?" The director explained that his company's policy was to abide by local tax codes, and he had instructed his accountants to meticulously observe Ukrainian tax regulations. The inspection team leader returned a week later. He informed the director that his supervisor believed the company had bribed the inspection team, since Ukrainian tax law was so complex that no large company could possibly be in full compliance.

The business dispute cases in which American investors said former Ukrainian partners or, in some instances, government agencies had acted illegally to seize or tie up their investments numbered sixteen in February 1998. One American complained that a former partner had manipulated the law to take over a hotel in Lviv. Another had had a profitable radio station stripped away, and a third fought the Security

Service of Ukraine, which blocked development of a commercial property in downtown Kyiv on which the investor held a long-term lease. The embassy did not have full information on the particulars, and its efforts to assist were sometimes hindered by unhelpful surprise revelations from U.S. investors. But certain cases stood out as real problems that the Ukrainian government could and should fix. The business disputes, some of which were reported by papers such as the *Wall Street Journal,* contributed to Ukraine's poor investment image.

The dispute cases took on added urgency in early 1998. Congress had leveled a requirement that the secretary of state certify that Ukraine had made "significant progress toward resolving complaints made by United States investors" by April 30, 1998. Absent such a certification, Congress directed a 50 percent reduction in that year's FREEDOM Support Act funding. Congress was unhappy that American investors were not being treated fairly, but the certification requirement provided nowhere near the leverage that its authors had hoped. Cutting assistance would not affect the Ukrainian businessmen or officials on the other side of the dispute cases, and most U.S. aid did not go to the government. A 50 percent cut, however, would significantly set back U.S. efforts to push reform.

Many of my early discussions in Kyiv focused on business cases. For example, a February 4 meeting with Minister for Foreign Economic Relations and Trade Serhiy Osyka followed up on exchanges in the Gore-Kuchma Commission's committee on trade and investment meeting the week before. While the big issues for the Ukrainian side were most-favored-nation trading status and entry into the World Trade Organization, the discussion devoted equal time to individual business cases. Other meetings followed with Osyka's deputies, Shpek, Deputy Prime Minister Sergey Tihipko, and State Tax Administration head Mykola Azarov.

Part of the challenge for the embassy lay in figuring out which official might be the most helpful in solving which case. The government had identified Osyka as the principal point of contact, but he lacked the authority to direct other parts of the government to act.

In a March meeting with Tihipko, Morningstar noted that the secretary wanted to certify Ukraine's progress, but she needed a basis on which to do so. Meetings included marathon sessions with Osyka that covered in detail each of the major disputes. One senior Ukrainian trade official conceded privately that some U.S. cases had merit, but he could not bring Ukrainian officials into line to resolve them. Morningstar, accompanied by the NSC director for Ukraine, Carlos Pascual, returned to Kyiv on April 6 for a last push. The three of us had lengthy meetings with Osyka and Tihipko, as well as with Horbulin given the political importance of the certification decision.

The Ukrainian side made halting progress, and the State Department delayed the decision. The Chamber of Commerce wrote the secretary on April 15 to express its view that the Ukrainian government had not made sufficient progress to warrant certification, though at the same time it endorsed continued U.S. assistance to Ukraine.[6] In the end, the department recommended that the secretary certify.

Albright approved the recommendation. She wrote Kuchma on April 29 to inform him, noting that the U.S. government had seen little progress on many cases and expressing concern about "the retaliation that has been taken by agencies of your government against certain U.S. companies that have openly—at the invitation of our governments—spoken out concerning problems."[7] Ukraine got a pass, but not a complete pass. The State Department spokesman said, "The secretary has directed the withholding of certain assistance funds to the government of Ukraine in areas where reforms have stalled and such assistance cannot be used effectively. If there is not significant progress in the next few months, these funds would be redirected to other areas in the private and non-governmental sectors."[8]

The secretary's certification allowed U.S. assistance programs to continue. Although it was often difficult to gauge the effectiveness of the programs, there were anecdotal successes. In fall 1998, I attended a land-titling ceremony in western Ukraine. USAID assistance had helped divide up a collective farm into roughly equal parcels in the belief that, if farmers owned their own land, they would work harder and more effectively than if they were part of a collective. Each member of the collective was awarded a parcel as his or her own land, to work or rent out as he or she chose. As the title documents were handed out, a large elderly farmer surprised me with a bear hug and declared to the audience: "Sixty years ago, the communists took my grandfather's farmland. Today, the Americans gave it back to me."

March Rada Elections

The secretary's visit, work on nonproliferation questions, and business disputes played out against the backdrop of the Rada election campaign, with the vote scheduled for March 29. The U.S. government took no position on particular parties but stressed the importance of a free and fair ballot. The embassy did not expect a problem-free process. In January, the Ukrainian government shut down *Pravda Ukrayiny* (Truth of Ukraine), a newspaper close to former prime minister Pavlo Lazarenko's Hromada Party. The U.S. government had no interest in supporting Lazarenko, but shutting down a paper in the middle of an election campaign hardly looked democratic.

At the end of a January 30 meeting with Prime Minister Valeriy Pustovoytenko, I privately raised *Pravda Ukrayiny's* closure. The next morning, the foreign ministry invited me to meet with Minister of Information Zynoviy Kulyk. He offered a confused and unpersuasive defense. Two weeks later, he told me that *Pravda Ukrayiny* had been "suspended," not "closed"—a distinction that made little difference in the near term. I reiterated U.S. concern about the selective closure of a newspaper in the run-up to an election and made the point publicly.

At about the same time, British ambassador Roy Reeve and I paid a call on Kuchma to discuss joint EU-U.S. positions (the British held the EU presidency for the first half of 1998). We reiterated U.S. and EU support for Ukraine and economic reform, described the coming Rada election as an opportunity to demonstrate democratic progress, and noted in particular the importance of respect for the freedom of the press and for the constitutional role of the Rada. Our comments touched a nerve. Kuchma launched into a sharp attack on Lazarenko and complained of the election's "dirty campaign." He dismissed the *Pravda Ukrayiny* closure and expressed disappointment that Kyiv had not received greater Western support. Reeve and I were taken aback by the vehemence of the complaint.

On March 12–13, I traveled to Dnipropetrovsk for calls on local officials, politicians, and businesspeople plus a visit to the Pivdenmash rocket factory. I had my first meeting with Yuliya Tymoshenko, then a member of Lazarenko's Hromada Party. An intelligent and very focused woman, she had served as president of United Energy Systems, a company that acted as a middleman for importing gas from Russia into Ukraine. Sometimes called the "gas princess," she was reputed to be one of the richest individuals in the country, allegedly having used her connection to Lazarenko when he was prime minister to increase her business. Tymoshenko had served just over a year in the Rada. As in subsequent meetings, she offered an interesting perspective on the country's politics. It was also evident that her comments sought to influence as well as to inform.

I also met with Viktor Pinchuk at his Interpipe company headquarters. Pinchuk was the first "oligarch" that I called on in Ukraine. The embassy had vetted him and concluded that, while he might have bent some rules, his past contained no ugly bombshells. (That was not something that could be said about other oligarchs.) An engineer by training, Pinchuk had developed a new process for producing large pipes just as the Cold War came to an end. He founded Interpipe, quickly secured customers in Russia for oil and natural gas pipes, and became one of the wealthiest businessmen in Ukraine. Pinchuk was running for the Rada and invited me to stop by his campaign office that evening. It did not seem appropriate for the U.S. ambassador to visit just one candidate's campaign headquarters, but Julie Fischer, a smart young political officer who had accompanied me to Dnipropetrovsk, could go. She reported the next morning that Pinchuk's headquarters looked much like a congressional campaign office, with people working phones, planning get-out-the-vote efforts, and so forth—with one additional interesting feature. The television was airing an Interpipe-sponsored debate on the local candidates that had been taped earlier in the day. Fischer watched three men on the show discuss the merits of Pinchuk and his competitors, and then turned to see the same three men at a table stuffing campaign literature for Pinchuk.

I joined other embassy officers on election day, March 29, as Organization for Security and Cooperation in Europe (OSCE) observers and visited polling stations in and around Kyiv. The observation visits ran short, fifteen or twenty minutes at most, given the need to cover several polling stations. Because polling officials likely would play by the rules when foreign observers were present, we made sure to talk to domestic observers at each one.

At a dozen polling places I saw no major irregularities, and the local observers had nothing striking to report. Husbands and wives sometimes entered the voting booth together or had the discussion about whom to vote for that they should have had at home. Local polling officials appeared to take their duties seriously and tried to enforce the rules. They often looked to us for validation, but OSCE rules prohibited any on-the-spot assessment.

We found one polling station that broke the rules, but it was hard to fault the local election commission. Regulations allowed for a "mobile ballot box" to travel to the home of eligible voters who were ill or infirm, but such voters had to be registered several days before the election. At this station, the typed list of mobile ballot box voters had three handwritten names at the bottom. The head of the electoral commission explained that three voters had taken ill the day before the election, and their relatives had asked that they be added to the mobile list. He had convened a meeting of the commission and, after a lengthy discussion, it decided to add the names. The commission had prepared a several-page-long handwritten protocol explaining the rationale for its decision, and all of the commission members had duly signed it. Technically, they broke the rules, but with the right intentions.

Election returns began coming in late on March 29, with the count continuing into the next day. In the party-list vote, the Communists came out ahead, polling nearly 25 percent, while no other party scored more than single digits. Eight parties won more than 4 percent, which entitled them to a share of the 225 seats to be distributed on the basis of the party-list vote. Other parties did well in the 225 races for individual constituency seats, so the new Rada promised to be a fractionated body, as its predecessor had been.

As the Central Electoral Commission tallied votes, the OSCE election observation mission began preparing its preliminary assessment of the election. The assessment cited shortcomings but reported "a generally adequate legal and administrative framework" and a process that was "carried out in a generally peaceful and orderly manner." It noted "a very great effort in polling stations to complete the polling process."[9]

Although not the epitome of a democratic election, the vote generally met the free-and-fair standard. Political counselor Bob Patterson coined an apt descriptor in the embassy's reporting cable: "Free, Fair, and Ugly." Concerns about possible manipulation of votes proved unfounded. The two strongest bits of evidence: the Hromada Party, despised by the Presidential Administration, received 4.67 percent of the vote, just clearing the 4 percent threshold needed to win seats on the party-list vote, while the Agrarian Party, a strong supporter of Kuchma, won only 3.68 percent, falling just short.[10] It would have required no major act of vote-rigging to bring the Agrarians above and push Hromada below the necessary 4 percent.

Ukraine and Europe

A key element of the U.S.-Ukraine dialogue continued to concern Ukraine's relations with the European Union and NATO. I joined an April meeting with Deputy Foreign Minister Anatoliy Orel and the EU representative plus the British and Austrian ambassadors. Orel stressed the importance of deepening EU-Ukraine relations and expressed concern that the looming addition of states such as Poland and the Czech Republic to the European Union ranks could disrupt Ukraine's trade and visa relationships with those countries.

Orel made a pitch, which other Ukrainian officials, including Kuchma, often made, for the European Union to offer a "membership perspective" (the prospect of EU membership). I sympathized on this point. A membership perspective could provide additional motivation for Kyiv to make needed but painful reforms. EU states would always have the right to decide whether Ukraine had done enough to meet the EU's standards. Not providing a perspective meant giving up valuable leverage. The European Union, unfortunately, held to its position. (Indeed, the EU-Ukraine association agreement that was finally signed in 2014 contained no membership perspective.)

In July, NATO secretary general Javier Solana visited Kyiv. He told NATO member ambassadors that the first year of the distinctive partnership had gone well but that Ukraine needed to work harder on promoting interoperability between NATO and Ukrainian forces, defense reform, and strengthening civilian control. Solana saw Foreign Minister Borys Tarasyuk, who had just replaced Udovenko, as a driving force for a deeper relationship with the alliance.

Tarasyuk was about to make his first visit as foreign minister to Washington. The relationship between Albright and Udovenko had not been the best, so the embassy suggested that Tarasyuk's meeting with the secretary focus on the broad picture—Ukraine's overall foreign policy and how it related to Europe—in hopes of not getting bogged down on specific issues. We hoped that approach would lead to a good start.

Tarasyuk's visit raised an issue that often came up when Ukrainian officials traveled to Washington, one faced by most U.S. embassies around the world. An American ambassador normally could get meetings with very senior host country officials, but foreign ambassadors and foreign ministers often could not get equivalent access in the U.S. capital. Tarasyuk expressed frustration that he could not meet with the vice president. We urged him nevertheless to see Leon Fuerth, Gore's national security adviser and close confidant who also had a strong interest in Ukraine. Tarasyuk's frustration reflected a broader exasperation that we sensed in Kyiv. Many in the Ukrainian government did not feel that Washington treated the "special" relationship as all that special. The embassy in August sent the State Department ideas for upgrading relations, including policy planning talks and sharing more background material about U.S. thinking on global issues. For example, Russian president Boris Yeltsin received a presidential message explaining the rationale for the American cruise missile strikes that summer against al Qaeda targets in Afghanistan and Sudan, and the embassy in Kyiv received talking points to use with Ukrainian officials; perhaps Kyiv could be added to the list for presidential messages in future cases? We made some progress but still fell short of Ukrainian desires.

In November, Tarasyuk convened a meeting with NATO member ambassadors, including the Polish, Czech, and Hungarian representatives, whose countries had been invited to join the alliance and would do so formally at NATO's April 1999 summit. Tarasyuk described an ambitious program that envisaged cooperative links between NATO and as many as twenty-four ministries and agencies in Kyiv. He proposed a NATO-Ukraine summit to review progress in the distinctive partnership. The embassy worried, however, that Kyiv needed to focus more on implementing existing programs.

Gore-Kuchma

In spring 1998, the American embassy began conversations with the Ukrainian Presidential Administration about a July visit by the vice president. Gore planned to spend two days in Ukraine before traveling to Moscow. I made the rounds in Kyiv, including a short meeting with Kuchma, to firm up the agenda. The embassy considered the economic message so important that we advised Gore to focus on that, even at the expense of discussing democracy matters. The vice president would have later opportunities to raise democracy concerns, and the Ukrainian presidential election was still fifteen months away.

Air Force Two touched down early on July 22. The vice president first met with American business representatives. They vented their frustration about the troubled business climate. By their calculation, Ukraine had recorded a cumulative total of only $2.2 billion in foreign direct investment; in comparison, $20 billion had gone to Poland and $15 billion to Hungary. Those numbers showed the real cost of Ukraine's poor investment reputation.

The vice president held six hours of discussions with Kuchma and the heads of the four Gore-Kuchma committees in the Mariinskyy Palace. The first plenary discussion focused on the need for economic reform and bilateral trade and investment. Tihipko and National Bank of Ukraine governor Viktor Yushchenko asked that Washington weigh in with the International Monetary Fund and World Bank to get their programs on track. Gore said the U.S. government was prepared to do so but needed to understand precisely what reforms Ukraine was pursuing, since they would be key to any IMF or World Bank decisions.

The leaders also reviewed steps that the U.S. government would take in light of Kyiv's March agreement to terminate its participation in the Bushehr reactor project. First, Washington would provide a minimum of $40 million in assistance to qualify a U.S. company to provide nuclear fuel rods for Ukraine (Westinghouse later won the bid). Even if Kyiv never purchased fuel rods from Westinghouse, it would have greater leverage to negotiate more favorable prices with its Russian supplier. Second, a bilateral 123 agreement had come into force, which enabled this project and other civil nuclear cooperation. Third, the U.S. government would direct an additional $6 million to the Science and Technology Center of Ukraine. Fourth, U.S. officials had begun to examine what assistance they might provide as part of the Kharkiv initiative and would send medical equipment and supplies valued at more than $5 million. (In 1999 nearly 200 containers of new or barely used hospital beds, operating tables, X-ray machines, hospital-sized washers and dryers, and tons of medical supplies were delivered from U.S. Army stockpiles to medical facilities in Kharkiv.)

The second plenary focused on foreign policy and security issues. Gore and Kuchma discussed the developing NATO-Ukraine relationship. Deputy Defense Minister Vasyl Sobkov and Assistant Secretary of Defense Ted Warner outlined a robust bilateral military-to-military relationship, which included an expanding Cooperative Threat Reduction program, assistance on defense planning and resource management (including on downsizing the Ukrainian military), and support for a joint Ukrainian-Polish peacekeeping battalion. Kuchma expressed pleasure that the Gore-Kuchma Commission was supporting the bilateral relationship with "real cooperation." He returned at the end, however, to the importance of U.S. support with the IMF and World Bank to resume loan programs.

On the second day, U.S. Army Chinook helicopters ferried the vice president's party to Chornobyl. Gore, who had declined a safety belt, spent much of the flight looking out a large open window at the countryside below. This clearly dismayed the crew chief, especially when we hit bumpy air. The helicopters overflew the "equipment graveyard," where Soviet emergency personnel had parked thousands of fire trucks, armored personnel carriers, helicopters, and other vehicles that had been employed during the Chornobyl fire until they had become too radioactive for further use, and then circled the plant itself.

Chornobyl officials gave Gore a quick orientation before taking the party to view the sarcophagus covering destroyed reactor four and then to Pripyat, a town that had housed 40,000 people and much of the Chornobyl workforce before being evacuated. Twelve years later, Pripyat had the eerie appearance of a ghost town. The visit fascinated Gore, who returned to Kyiv and gave a short speech on nuclear matters in the city's museum on Chornobyl, before departing for Moscow.

Economic Reform, the IMF, and Financial Crisis

By 1998, Ukraine had built a troubled history with the international financial institutions. IMF disbursements were often delayed when Ukraine failed to meet the agreed performance targets or conditionalities. Kuchma sought a new longer-term agreement, an extended fund facility (EFF), to provide additional credits. To secure an EFF, the Ukrainian government had to work with the Rada to complete ninety actions.

Doing so could open $2.2 billion in IMF lending over three years and enable an additional $700 million–$1 billion from the World Bank. But IMF officials saw no plan for completing the required actions; in the spring, an IMF official briefing Western ambassadors called Ukraine's performance "absolutely horrendous."

In early May, the British, Dutch, Austrian, and EU ambassadors, representing the European Union and EU member states, and I met with Kuchma. The joint EU-U.S. message stressed the need for Kyiv to work closely with the IMF to implement the EFF conditionalities. Kuchma voiced his unhappiness with the conditionalities, asserting that he could not control the pace of reform when it depended on actions that needed Rada approval. There was some truth to Kuchma's statement, but unresolved differences with the parliament would delay the EFF.

Several days later Kuchma used his address to the opening session of the new Rada to press for pension, tax, and other economic reforms, announce that the cabinet of ministers would lay out a program of draft reform laws, and ask for cooperation from the Rada. The government, however, had little immediate success in securing support from a divided parliament. Finance Minister Ihor Mityukov warned in early June that Ukraine faced the prospect of a financial crisis.

I had a chance to discuss these questions one week later with Yushchenko at the National Bank of Ukraine. Yushchenko, an ardent Ukrainian nationalist, was born and raised in Sumy in the northeastern part of the country, not the west. His country dacha looked like a museum of Ukrainian culture and history, incorporating in the living room a large oven of the kind typical of traditional peasant houses as well as a stone that Yushchenko had brought back from Kazakhstan, because Taras Shevchenko, considered Ukraine's national poet, allegedly had once sat on it. His hobbies ranged from beekeeping to painting. The son of an English teacher, and married (his second time) to a Ukrainian American from Chicago, he was slightly embarrassed by his own lack of English. A banker by training and experience, Yushchenko became governor of the National Bank in 1993 and was widely credited with helping to bring the country's hyperinflation under control. Many saw him as a rising reform star. He readily drew graphs to illustrate key economic points, and meetings often ran far longer than planned because he went into such detail, sometimes excessively so. Indeed, he

was not the most organized individual, but he had a vision for a reformed Ukraine.

Yushchenko reiterated to me Kyiv's interest in securing an EFF but
conceded that the Rada would not pass the necessary reforms. The
government lacked a strategy to gain parliamentary support. Yushchenko admitted that the government had no point person in charge of
reform.

IMF deputy director Stanley Fischer visited Kyiv later in June. He
had good meetings with Kuchma and Pustovoytenko, and most Rada
faction leaders expressed a readiness to cooperate. The Ukrainian government implemented enough prior actions, largely through executive
branch decree, to reach a preliminary agreement on an EFF at the end
of July. Kyiv-based IMF officials, however, showed less confidence in
the government's commitment to implement the reforms.

Few foresaw the calamity that struck in August. A financial crisis
that began in East Asia spread to Russia and then quickly swept over
the border into Ukraine. The country's currency, the hryvnya, came
under extreme pressure, and foreign reserves plunged. On August 21,
Tarasyuk and Mityukov convened an urgent meeting of ambassadors
from the G-7 states to request assistance in securing IMF board approval of the EFF. Kyiv was having trouble restructuring its international private debt. Mityukov faced a tough situation: private debt
holders knew that the restructuring of their debt was a requirement for
the EFF, which gave them leverage to press for more favorable terms.

On August 22, Horbulin called Deputy Secretary of State Strobe
Talbott for help. Without the first EFF tranche, Kyiv's foreign reserves
would fall to dangerously low levels. Talbott said the U.S. government
wanted to help but stressed the need for a credible reform program.
Officials in the Treasury Department held to a harder line. They continued to harbor doubts about Ukraine's willingness to meet the IMF
requirements, even though the German, French, and British finance
ministries had begun to come around.

The crisis continued into September, and Kuchma called Gore on September 2 to discuss the situation. Kyiv received good news on September 4. The IMF announced that it had approved a three-year EFF worth
$2.2 billion, with some $260 million available for immediate disbursement. The announcement made clear the IMF's intention to closely monitor Ukraine's progress in meeting the program's reform conditionalities.

On September 16, Deputy Coordinator for the New Independent States Ross Wilson phoned to advise me that Washington had become alarmed about Rada votes to overturn cabinet decrees that were essential for IMF approval of the EFF. Washington also worried that the level of Ukraine's foreign reserves had fallen so low—perhaps to just $100 million–$300 million—that the IMF and World Bank might well decline to lend anything. I wrote the prime minister to warn of the possibility that the IMF could suspend the just-approved program.

I saw Yushchenko and Mityukov separately the next day. Yushchenko said the National Bank had almost $900 million in reserves in mid-September, though liquid reserves amounted to only $320 million by IMF calculations. Mityukov confirmed the numbers. That development posed a big problem, as the EFF required foreign reserves of $1.3 billion.

Pustovoytenko led a team to Washington in mid-October for meetings with the IMF and the World Bank. They returned to Kyiv in an optimistic mood. Pustovoytenko, Yushchenko, and Mityukov all told me that they were close to meeting the IMF's requirements. Close perhaps, but they fell short. IMF officials indicated there would be no further lending for the remainder of the year.

Military-to-Military Relations

In contrast to difficulties over business disputes and economic reform, U.S.-Ukraine military-to-military relations continued to provide a bright spot. The Cooperative Threat Reduction program focused on eliminating SS-19 and SS-24 intercontinental ballistic missiles as well as their silos plus Bear-H and Blackjack strategic bombers. Eliminating the SS-19 was relatively straightforward. The liquid fuel was removed and the missile shipped to Pivdenmash, where fuel residue was purged and the missile body cut up for scrap. In August 1998, I traveled with Senator Richard Lugar (the author, with Senator Sam Nunn, of the Cooperative Threat Program) to witness the destruction of the last SS-19 ICBM, well ahead of the 2001 deadline by which Ukraine was to eliminate all of the strategic systems on its territory.

The SS-24, a solid-fuel missile, posed a more difficult elimination challenge. U.S. officials proposed a controlled burn, essentially bolting down the missile and igniting the engine to burn out the rubber-like fuel, after which the missile body could be scrapped. The ministry of defense wanted instead to remove the fuel and convert it to explosives for use in commercial mining operations.

Conversion seemed to be a fixation for the ministry of defense. The Ukrainians hoped to find ways to convert the Blackjack bomber rather than destroy it. They suggested ocean surveillance or fast air freight delivery, but the plane really had only one function: to deliver nuclear weapons. Defense Department officials worked out procedures so that as much as possible could be salvaged, such as wiring, but the bombers were broken up, in accordance with agreed treaty procedures, turning them into expensive scrap metal.

The U.S. military had a variety of other programs. U.S. European Command had a military liaison team working directly with the ministry of defense on cooperative projects. American assistance funded radios and Humvees for the Ukrainian elements of a joint Ukrainian-Polish battalion, so that they would have common communications and transport with their Polish counterparts, who received like equipment organized by the U.S. embassy in Warsaw.

At the end of August, the commander of the U.S. Sixth Fleet, Admiral Dan Murphy, arrived in Sevastopol on his flagship for a visit hosted by the Ukrainian navy commander, Admiral Mykhaylo Yezhel. The largely ceremonial visit gave the two a chance to discuss practical cooperation between the U.S. and Ukrainian navies. Murphy also had the chance to meet the commander of the Russian Black Sea Fleet, who had his headquarters in Sevastopol as well. During a meeting with Sevastopol's mayor, I asked whether hosting the two navies in his harbor caused problems. He replied that issues occasionally arose, but he met with Ukrainian and Russian naval officers on a monthly basis, and they worked things out in practical ways. The only difficult problems, he added wryly, were ones created in Moscow or Kyiv.

Before he left Ukraine, Murphy and I flew to Kyiv for a meeting with Defense Minister Oleksandr Kuzmuk. A career military officer from western Ukraine, Kuzmuk had served nearly twenty years in the Soviet army before taking the oath to Ukraine. After two years as commander of the National Guard, Kuchma promoted him to minister of defense. Kuzmuk and Kuchma had a personal link: they were married to sisters. Kuzmuk expressed appreciation for the military-to-military program, which by the end of 1998 included ninety-four activities. (The U.S.-Ukrainian military-to-military program had overtaken the level of U.S.-Russian military contacts. Both countries received similar menus, and the Ukrainians chose more.) The two military leaders closed with a discussion of Kosovo, where Serbian oppression of ethnic Albanians was provoking a crisis between NATO and Belgrade.

As the Kosovo situation deteriorated in October, Tarasyuk convened a meeting with several ambassadors from NATO member states. We told him that NATO would likely approve military action against Serbia. Tarasyuk said Kyiv could not support such action without an explicit UN Security Council authorization. He expressed concern that NATO air strikes on Serbia would complicate Kyiv's efforts to deepen its relations with the alliance. As it turned out, U.S. diplomat Richard Holbrooke was able to broker an agreement with Belgrade. That put off the crisis, until it boiled over five months later.

At the end of October, three U.S. Navy ships and a Marine amphibious landing unit visited Odesa for the annual Sea Breeze exercise. U.S. Marines and Ukrainian naval infantry were joined by naval infantry units from Georgia and Romania for land exercises, while warships and planes from other countries—including Russia—took part in the at-sea portion of the exercise. As with most joint activities, the professional military personnel had little trouble working with colleagues from other militaries. Not all in Kyiv were pleased with the exercise, however. Communist Party Rada deputy Heorhiy Kryuchkov complained to a visiting U.S. senator that Sea Breeze had taken place without formal authorization from the Rada. He left no doubt that he, as well as a number of his Rada colleagues, took a dim view of military cooperation with NATO and the United States.

Economics and Business Disputes—Round II

At the embassy's request, Washington sent a senior team to Kyiv in January 1999 to discuss economic reforms and the need to meet EFF conditions, as well as to review the status of business disputes. Congress had again imposed a certification requirement. The team consisted of Sestanovich, Pascual, Taylor, Assistant Secretary of the Treasury Ted Truman, and Deputy Assistant Secretary of the Treasury Mark Medish.

Their jammed two-day schedule included meetings with Tarasyuk, Orel, Tihipko, Horbulin, Pustovoytenko, Yushchenko, and Mityukov.

The U.S. team starkly warned of a "double whammy." First, if the government did not perform better on economic reform, it could not resume drawing credits from the EFF. Second, the lack of economic reform and absence of progress on the business cases would mean that Albright could not certify that it had met the requirements for certification. Without certification, U.S. assistance would be cut and give Ukraine's investment reputation another blemish. Absent IMF credits, government wage and pension arrears could grow, and inflation could spike—all in the run-up to the fall presidential election.

That U.S. team feared that, without additional IMF credits, Ukraine could run out of foreign reserves in June or July. Yushchenko shared the grim assessment. Tihipko thought that, if anything, the projection was optimistic; Ukraine could face an economic crisis as early as March. Mityukov cautioned that the absence of IMF credits would require Kyiv to rethink its entire economic policy. He hoped the IMF would show flexibility.

The U.S. message regarding the business dispute cases was bleaker. Sestanovich said Albright at that point could not make the required certification. Not a single dispute was in better shape than when the secretary had certified the previous April. Some were in worse shape. In one case, the company had given up. It had had a contract with the ministry of defense to demilitarize tens of thousands of old artillery shells and convert the explosives from the shells to commercially useful explosives for the ministry to sell. The company paid for the process by selling brass and other metal recovered from the shells. The company, however, had been blocked from exporting the metal, so it had no revenues to cover its costs. The embassy secured a meeting in September 1998 with Pustovoytenko to discuss this problem. He began the meeting by expressing pleasure that all problems had been resolved, only to be told by the American manager that the company had not operated for six weeks. Pustovoytenko ordered the ministry of defense officials present to resolve the situation within four days. The situation instead deteriorated when the ministry denied the company access to the work site and effectively seized all of its equipment.

I later wrote the prime minister and asked his assistance in facilitating the company's access to the site so that it could remove its equipment, noting that the company planned to file an expropriation claim with the Overseas Private Insurance Corporation (OPIC). Nothing happened, and shortly thereafter the company left Ukraine. It filed a claim for some $20 million with OPIC and quickly received a settlement. OPIC promptly sent the Ukrainian government a bill for the amount and took Ukraine "off cover," meaning that OPIC would insure no U.S. investment projects there until the debt was paid off. (It would take ten years to restore OPIC insurance.)

Orel asked Sestanovich and his colleagues for a "political" decision on certification. Sestanovich responded that Ukraine had to create a basis for the decision. If the secretary again certified but had no progress to cite, Congress might simply cut assistance on its own. I followed up with Osyka in a four-hour Saturday meeting, in which we reviewed the status of each case. I confided that the word from Washington in early 1998 was that we needed to find a way to certify Ukraine, but now, in January 1999, no one was saying that. At the end of the meeting, Osyka advised that he was resigning; his deputy, Andriy Honcharuk, would take his place.

Five days later, Honcharuk hosted Jan Kalicki, counselor at the Department of Commerce. Kalicki stressed that time had almost run out. Honcharuk commented that the disputes involved less than 1 percent of U.S. business in Ukraine, a point echoed by the prime minister to Kalicki. Kalicki did not argue—the point may well have been correct—but the cases had major visibility in Congress, and there was no progress to report. Tihipko told Kalicki that not all of the cases could be resolved, but he expected settlements on some.

I discussed the disputes with Volodymyr Ohryzko, Kuchma's foreign policy adviser, the day that Kalicki left. He said Washington had a choice: it could either support Kuchma, which meant certification, or it could see the left—in the person of Communist Party leader Petro Symonenko or Socialist Party leader Oleksandr Moroz—win the presidency, in which case Ukraine could well turn back to Russia and Belarus. I replied that the Presidential Administration at the Bankova building (which also housed Kuchma's working office) needed to instruct those responsible to resolve the disputes, so that the secretary would have grounds to certify.

Gore saw Kuchma at the end of January on the margins of the World Economic Summit in Davos, Switzerland. The vice president urged action on specific IMF points of concern and on the business disputes. Kuchma hoped to resolve half of the nine principal dispute cases in the near future. Washington thought the vice president's messages had resonated. The embassy heard from senior Ukrainian officials that Kuchma also was pleased, though one said Kuchma appreciated the "vice president's commitment to work on certification," a comment that suggested not all had understood Gore's message. He was ready to help, but the Ukrainian government needed to help itself.

Discussions on the dispute cases continued during the first half of February. No one on the American side felt optimistic. The USAID mission submitted a proposed budget reflecting a 50 percent cut in funding should the secretary not certify. Pascual sent a note to President Bill Clinton advising that certification might not be possible (the president's reaction: be careful to protect the credibility of the decision).

Some good news came on the reform front. A Ukrainian team's visit to Washington had produced a draft letter laying out specific actions that Kyiv would take so that the IMF board in early March could consider resuming the EFF program. That action appeared sufficient to meet the part of the certification requirement related to economic reform. On the disputes, however, the embassy could report that only one case had been definitively resolved. I called Wilson in Sestanovich's office and asked that the State Department not request an embassy recommendation. Washington clearly wanted to find a way to certify, but any report that the embassy filed would not support such a decision.

On February 18 the secretary issued the certification. Even more so than in 1998, it was a tenuous call. The State Department released a statement the next day noting, "This Administration and Congress remain very concerned about the uneven pace of reform and difficult investment climate in Ukraine. We continue to urge the Government of Ukraine to accelerate the market reform process and improve the climate for foreign investors by resolving remaining disputes."[11] Albright made the right decision, even if Kyiv had given her very weak grounds on which to do so. I conveyed the news to senior Ukrainian officials, stressing that Albright had gone out on a limb, and gave a press conference to explain the certification decision. (The English-language *Kyiv Post* took a dim view, headlining its next edition, "Pifer Fudges the Numbers" and charging that the embassy had overstated the number of disputes that had been resolved.[12] The paper did not bother to ask the embassy for a comment before running the story, though there was little we could have said.)

After 1999, Congress no longer imposed the certification requirement. It also stopped ear-marking FREEDOM Support Act funding for Ukraine, which meant that in future fiscal years the funding for Ukraine would almost certainly decline. Faced with declining budgets, USAID and the embassy looked at ways to refocus assistance on key reform priorities.

Pavlo Lazarenko

I returned to the embassy from the press conference on the certification decision to an urgent call from Washington. After being sacked as prime minister, Pavlo Lazarenko had remained a Rada deputy. But the Rada had just lifted his parliamentary immunity, and the State Department phoned to advise that he was on an airliner bound for New York. I suggested that he be turned away under a provision of the Immigration and Nationality Act that requires foreign nationals seeking to enter the United States for a temporary visit to demonstrate that their visit will indeed be temporary. Lazarenko owned a large house in northern California, had two children studying in American schools, and would likely be arrested if he returned to Ukraine. There was no reason to think that he would leave the United States any time soon.

Immediately on landing, however, Lazarenko requested political asylum. Immigration officers took him into custody pending a resolution of his request.[13] This became big news overnight in Kyiv. Although Lazarenko's attorneys announced that he had sought asylum, U.S. officials were barred from confirming or denying the status of a particular asylum request. The Ukrainians quickly issued an extradition request, despite the fact that they had no extradition treaty with the United States. I described how the U.S. asylum process worked and privately cautioned Ukrainian officials not to politicize the case, as that would only bolster Lazarenko's asylum claim.

The case took several twists. In April the Swiss government presented an extradition request for Lazarenko, whom the Swiss sought

to bring to trial on money-laundering charges. The Swiss case trumped
the asylum request, but Lazarenko's team fought extradition. While they
did so, he remained in the custody of U.S. federal marshals. In the fall
Lazarenko was arrested on U.S. money-laundering charges, which
trumped both the extradition and asylum requests and potentially carried far more severe penalties than the charges he would have faced in
Switzerland. (The case eventually went to trial and, in June 2004, he
was convicted by a court in California on twenty-nine counts that included wire fraud, money laundering, transportation of stolen property, and extortion.[14] Until his sentencing to nine years in prison and
fines in August 2006, Lazarenko was kept under house arrest guaranteed by an $86 million bail.[15] After serving years in pretrial custody
and jail, Lazarenko was released from prison in November 2012.[16] In
2014 an attorney for Lazarenko asked if I would testify on Lazarenko's behalf in his effort to recover the money seized by the U.S. government. I declined.)

Ukraine, NATO, and Serbia

Kyiv continued to wrestle with how to handle its relationship with
NATO in early 1999. Washington was set to host the alliance's fiftieth
anniversary summit on April 22 and 23. Alliance leaders planned to
hold a NATO-Ukraine meeting with Kuchma on the margins. Horbulin met with NATO ambassadors in mid-January and suggested that
the NATO-Ukraine meeting produce a declaration expressing strong
support for Ukraine's westward course. He also hoped that NATO
would reaffirm its "open-door" policy for aspiring members. A week
later, Ohryzko described a more nuanced position. At a time when
Kuchma pursued a multi-vector foreign policy—the three vectors being
Europe, Russia, and the United States—Kyiv did not want to confront
a decision in 1999 about whether to seek NATO membership. Ohryzko
hoped that the April summit would not group countries into aspirants
and others, as Ukraine did not want to be left in what might be seen as
a "bottom" grouping. (It was too late, however, as NATO intended at
the summit to give other countries membership action plans.)

Two months later, on March 18, the embassy organized a day-long
conference on NATO-Ukraine relations. Horbulin delivered the key-

note, a very well argued speech in which he expressed appreciation for NATO's open-door policy and said any decision about Ukraine's relationship with NATO should be between Kyiv and the alliance, not subject to influence by a third party (read Russia). At the same time, Horbulin conceded that a decision to seek membership could only be taken once a societal consensus had formed in favor of such a course, which did not exist in Ukraine. (Most polls at the time showed that 20 to 30 percent of Ukrainians favored NATO membership, with the remainder split between opposed and undecided.)

Unfortunately, Kyiv's practical engagement with NATO was falling short. Alexander Vershbow, the U.S. permanent representative to NATO, came to Kyiv in February to discuss Ukraine's interaction with the alliance and how it might be improved. Vershbow saw Deputy Foreign Minister Yevhen Bersheda, Tarasyuk, and Kuzmuk. Vershbow explained that Ukraine had difficulty executing programs; as a result, it did not have a good corridor reputation at NATO headquarters. For example, in 1997–98, Ukraine had implemented only half of the activities on its agreed individual partnership program, and it had not used 60 percent of the slots reserved for Ukrainian personnel at NATO schools, slots that then could not be offered to other partner countries.

Vershbow told Tarasyuk that the U.S. mission at NATO was prepared to assist, as was the Polish mission. He suggested that Kyiv test ideas—for example, draft language for a joint NATO-Ukraine summit statement—with the Americans or the Poles (or both) first. They could advise on what would and would not fly with the rest of the alliance.

Kuzmuk made a PowerPoint presentation showing 130 partnership activities for 1999. Vershbow cautioned that the ministry might better aim for fewer activities but do them well and with qualified participants. Kuzmuk advised that Ukraine did not want to hold the annual Sea Breeze exercise that fall, given the presidential election. That preference presumably reflected concern at Bankova that military cooperation with NATO or the United States might become a campaign issue against Kuchma.

The NATO-Ukraine relationship faced a far bigger test in late March. Serbian paramilitary units in Kosovo launched a campaign aimed at ethnic cleansing of the Kosovar Albanian population, and NATO edged closer to military action. Few in the Ukrainian government showed sympathy for Serbian president Slobodan Milošević.

Kyiv, however, did not support NATO military action, in part out of concern that political opponents would use it to condemn Kuchma's cooperative relationship with the alliance.

The embassy lacked useful guidance for briefing Ukrainian officials on NATO thinking, so I took to calling Vershbow to get suggestions on points to make. In a March 23 meeting, Bersheda asked for no surprises on Kosovo. I responded that the embassy would try to keep the ministry informed, but matters at NATO headquarters in Brussels were moving very quickly.

The next day, I visited Zaporizhzhya for a full program—meetings with the governor and mayor, a lecture at Zaporizhzhya State University, and visits to a small and medium-sized enterprise development agency and the Institute of Economic and Information Technology. I had a moment before joining local Peace Corps volunteers for dinner so turned on CNN. Cameras near Aviano Air Base in Italy showed F-16s taking off with full bomb loads and turning southeast toward Serbia. NATO's long-threatened air campaign had begun.

That evening the embassy passed a letter from Clinton to Kuchma outlining the rationale for NATO's action: Milošević had refused a possible agreement, specifically rejecting the provision for deployment of a NATO-led peacekeeping force in Kosovo, and a humanitarian catastrophe loomed; more than 250,000 people had already been displaced. The letter asked Kuchma to use any influence that Kyiv had with Milošević to get him to accept NATO's terms. I returned to Kyiv early the next morning to an immediate request to come to the foreign ministry. Bersheda urged NATO member ambassadors to provide as much information publicly as possible and proactively explain why the alliance had acted. He expected a strong negative reaction in the Rada. At Bankova, Horbulin also stressed the need for as much information as possible on NATO activities, as the Ukrainian government shifted to damage control. In public, Ukrainian officials tried to strike a balance, calling for negotiations and criticizing NATO's resort to force, but saying that Kyiv could not support the Serbian government's actions against its own people in Kosovo.

Tarasyuk spoke to Albright late the afternoon of March 25 and offered to travel to Belgrade. Albright told him that there might be a role for Ukraine to play, but now was not the time. Orel called me into the foreign ministry about midnight to follow up, reiterating Tarasyuk's desire to go to Belgrade. He argued that, if Tarasyuk went and Serbian officials were recalcitrant, the world would see that Belgrade was the problem. But a positive response from the Serbians might open a new round of negotiations. I expressed concern that Tarasyuk could get caught between Belgrade and NATO. Orel indicated that Tarasyuk would go in any case, but he did not offer any reason to believe the visit would succeed. I urged that, if Tarasyuk planned to fly to Belgrade, the Ukrainians notify the NATO military authorities who were running the air operations over Serbia.

Tarasyuk traveled to Belgrade on March 26. NATO denied flight clearance to Belgrade, so he had to fly to Budapest and drive from there. Unsurprisingly, the Serbian government portrayed the visit as indicating Ukrainian support. The alliance was not happy about the visit. Tarasyuk's executive assistant that evening conveyed to me Tarasyuk's frustration that NATO ambassadors in Brussels had declined to meet with him for a debrief of his talk with the Serbian president.

Two days later, Tarasyuk told Western ambassadors that the Ukrainian government did not believe NATO air strikes would resolve the crisis and wanted to facilitate a return to negotiations. A foreign ministry official subsequently told me that Tarasyuk had made specific proposals in Belgrade, but the Serbians had not yet responded. I urged him to share those ideas with NATO, so that there would be no surprises. In one sense, Tarasyuk's activism was understandable, given the heavy pressure on him to do something and to try to minimize the growing anti-NATO sentiment at home, but he ran the risk of operating at cross-purposes with the alliance.

The Ukrainian government feared a backlash from public opinion. Ukrainians did not seem reflexively pro-Serbian, but they questioned why NATO had initiated military action when Serbia posed no threat to the alliance. The government also worried about the Rada. A member of the Green Party privately told me, however, that most deputies who had taken an anti-NATO position had done so for domestic political reasons. While the Green Party opposed NATO air strikes, he said it was quietly working with the foreign ministry to avoid a Rada resolution that might call for damaging actions. The gentlemanly Rada deputy who represented the district housing my residence, a member of the Communist Party but a regular attendee at embassy receptions, boycotted us for a while in protest, but decently passed on a message that it was nothing personal.

Part of the problem was that the Ukrainian media had missed the Serbian ethnic cleansing in Kosovo. NATO member ambassadors engaged the media more actively to explain what had triggered the alliance actions. The embassy's press section began organizing travel for journalists to Macedonia, where refugee camps struggled to accommodate the tens of thousands of ethnic Albanians who had fled Kosovo. That coverage seemed to help, but it was too little too late, and NATO's image in Ukraine suffered.

Kuchma critics began to suggest that he cancel the NATO-Ukraine summit. Officials gave conflicting signals. Ohryzko expressed concern that it would be impossible for Kuchma to travel to Washington. Others seemed confident that he would go. I had a brief meeting with the president on April 14. He confirmed that he would attend the summit but added that he would face considerable criticism for doing so.

Kuchma did go to Washington. According to a State Department official's readout on Kuchma's meeting with NATO leaders, Kuchma said little about the NATO-Ukraine relationship or Kosovo but instead launched into a "tirade"—the State official's description—on the West's lack of support for Ukraine as it faced challenges such as economic crisis. NATO leaders were taken aback, and only two spoke in response. Rather than endorsing the progress made in nearly two years of NATO-Ukraine relations, Clinton and the other leaders sat on their interventions, and the summit concluded early.

Oddly, the embassy heard a positive assessment from Ukrainian officials. Ohryzko called the meeting very useful, though he said Kuchma had been surprised by the lack of response from his NATO counterparts. He observed that the challenge for Kyiv now was how to maintain domestic support for its relationship with NATO if the conflict over Kosovo continued for long. Kyiv remained interested in facilitating a settlement, and Kuchma was prepared to engage Milošević.

In early June, after enduring more than two months of air strikes, Milošević accepted an agreement brokered with the help of Finnish president Martti Ahtisaari and Russian prime minister Viktor Chernomyrdin that, among other things, permitted deployment in Kosovo of a NATO-led peacekeeping force, including a Russian contingent. Officials in Kyiv welcomed the end of the conflict with evident relief, though they showed their frustration that NATO had not taken up their offers to mediate.

The Ukrainian government, however, found itself almost immediately caught in the middle again, this time between NATO and Russia. Moscow raced to fly troops into Kosovo without consulting with NATO. I called the foreign ministry late the evening of June 11 to ask that the Ukrainians deny Russian military aircraft overflight clearance until such time as the troop movements could be coordinated. Ukraine had granted clearance, believing that Hungary had done so. In fact, Hungary, Romania, and Bulgaria had all denied overflight permission.

Although the Ukrainians granted clearance, they informed the embassy of specific Russian flight plans. Bersheda explained to me that the Ukrainians had no good reason to deny the clearances and, in any case, saw no problem: if Hungary, Romania, and Bulgaria continued to deny permission, Russian transports overflying Ukraine still could not get to Kosovo or Serbia. The Ukrainians later amended their position and began giving the Russians flight clearances contingent on the planes also having clearance for onward flight over Hungary, Romania or Bulgaria.

As force planning for the Kosovo peacekeeping force (KFOR) proceeded, Kyiv offered to contribute troops. NATO welcomed soldiers from a Slavic country in addition to Russia. The ministry of defense, however, lacked funds to cover the deployment, in part because Ukrainian soldiers deployed on peacekeeping missions received substantial salary boosts. The U.S. military could not pay salaries but, given the interest in having Ukrainian troops on the ground, worked out ways to provide in-kind goods and services, such as fuel, that cut the costs for Kyiv.

At the end of July the embassy assessed the consequences for Ukraine of NATO's campaign against Serbia. Kyiv had had no dog in the fight. It saw Milošević as responsible for ethnic cleansing but opposed the use of force without a UN Security Council mandate. The negative public and Rada reaction would complicate Ukraine's effort to deepen relations with NATO and Europe. Kyiv also felt unappreciated because the alliance never took up its mediation offer. Kosovo turned out to be a public relations disaster for NATO's image; one July poll showed 82 percent of the population opposing NATO's action and only 6 percent supporting.

During a late July visit by the secretary of defense, NATO-Ukraine cooperation and Ukraine's participation in KFOR topped the agenda. The visit, which went well in substance, showed a real culture clash. The ministry of defense wanted to host Secretary of Defense Cohen for an overnight visit, but the secretary's party had been distinctly unimpressed by Kyiv's hotel accommodations during his 1997 visit; the Pentagon early on sent the message, "No overnight." When a day visit was set for July 31, we decided to hold it in Crimea. The embassy suggested that, after Cohen landed at the Ukrainian naval air base at Belbek, he travel to Foros to pay a courtesy call on Kuchma and then return for a longer meeting with Kuzmuk at Belbek, which had a perfectly fine meeting room. The ministry of defense, however, insisted that Cohen travel on to Kuzmuk's dacha for a meeting—even farther away from Belbek than Foros. As a result, of the time that the secretary had on the ground in Crimea, he spent two-and-a-half hours in meetings and nearly five hours in a motorcade racing at speeds that appalled the Americans.

The Serbia crisis deepened Kyiv's interest in securing a nonpermanent seat on the UN Security Council for 2000–2001. Foreign ministry officials made clear their hopes for U.S. support. They saw Slovakia as the primary competition. The UN General Assembly was scheduled to vote on nonpermanent members for the Security Council in October.

I had a chance to meet with Tarasyuk in mid-September, just before he departed for New York to take part in the General Assembly meeting. Tarasyuk reiterated his hope, if not expectation, that Kyiv would have U.S. support for the Security Council seat. I noted that he would meet with Secretary of State Albright in New York, while his Slovakian counterpart would not, and suggested that, instead of basing his pitch on the U.S.-Ukraine strategic partnership, he talk about issues that the Security Council would deal with in the coming two years and how Ukraine would work closely with the United States—in other words, make the secretary, a former representative to the United Nations, want to have Ukraine on the Security Council because it would be a supportive voice. Tarasyuk liked the idea and on the spot dictated instructions as to how his talking points should be rewritten for the Albright meeting. It was not clear what happened between our talk and the meeting in New York, but the read-out that the embassy received afterwards said the foreign minister had pressed Albright to support Ukraine on the basis of the strategic partnership. Who the United

States votes for in the secret ballot is decided by the secretary and national security adviser and closely held. Ukraine won the seat on the fourth ballot after Slovakia withdrew, but I have doubts whether Ukraine won the U.S. vote.

Assistance Bumps

Although the U.S. assistance program survived the certification challenge for a second year, it encountered other problems in 1999. The embassy began hearing complaints about the Kharkiv initiative. Part of the problem was the mismatch between expectations and what the U.S. government could provide. USAID could help the city set up an office to assist potential investors, and the embassy's commercial section could flag investment opportunities in Kharkiv for U.S. companies. The U.S. government had no way, however, to direct American investment to the city. I am not sure this was ever fully understood in Kharkiv.

Yet another initiative got off to a slow start in 1999. Washington, Kyiv, and Warsaw had agreed to establish the Polish-American-Ukrainian Cooperation Initiative (PAUCI) on the belief that Ukrainians might learn more appropriate reform lessons from Poland, which had energetically been adapting its economy for the previous ten years, than from America. The U.S. government accordingly decided to direct assistance to fund exchanges between Ukraine and Poland. Unfortunately, just as the project was ready to launch, the American nongovernmental organization chosen to run it had to withdraw. A new problem arose when the PAUCI office in Warsaw wanted to vet all Polish-origin proposals before they were submitted to the full secretariat, despite the agreed principle that the full secretariat should review all proposals. "Initiative" became an unpopular word around the embassy.

Better news came on the international assistance front. The IMF in May approved an EFF disbursement of $180 million. Moreover, the IMF board approved an augmentation of the EFF, increasing the total possible credits from $2.2 billion to almost $2.6 billion—provided that Ukraine continued to implement the reform program it had agreed to. (In the end, Kyiv's regular failure to meet the conditionalities meant that Ukraine received less than it might have. The three-year EFF was originally planned to run until July 2001, but its term was extended.

As of September 2001, Ukraine was able to access only $1.6 billion of the $2.6 billion on offer.)

The Presidential Election

Kuchma's attention increasingly shifted to the 1999 presidential election, with the first round scheduled for October 31 and a runoff, if necessary, on November 14. During his January visit, Ambassador Sestanovich raised the election with Horbulin, noting that Kuchma's four years as president had been largely positive from the viewpoint of democracy, but actions such as curtailing press freedom in an election run-up could change the tenor of U.S.-Ukraine relations. He cited the negative experience of Kazakhstan, where President Nursultan Nazarbayev had just won reelection in a vote that fell far short of democratic standards. Horbulin replied that they could not permit an election loss, given its importance for the future of Ukraine. Sestanovich cautioned that Kuchma not act like Nazarbayev. Horbulin responded that the Ukrainians would not repeat the Nazarbayev election; theirs would have "democratic clothing." He reiterated that Ukraine could not afford a loss. Sestanovich, Pascual, and I left the meeting, unhappy with Horbulin's message but acknowledging his candor.

Ohryzko conveyed a similar message. He argued that the United States had to choose between supporting Kuchma and seeing the left come to power. Roman Bezsmertnyy, Kuchma's representative to the Rada, said the Presidential Administration needed to pull out all the stops to win the election but that there would be "no visible violations" of democratic rules. I replied that it would be better if there were no invisible violations as well.

Few expected anyone to win outright in the first round. Most believed Kuchma would make it to the runoff. Vyacheslav Chornovil, a member of the Rada and leader of the Rukh faction, thought Kuchma wanted to run against Symonenko, the Communist Party head. Some speculated that Kuchma's model was the 1996 Russian presidential ballot, in which Boris Yeltsin had won reelection in a runoff against the Communist Party leader. Although some mentioned Chornovil as a candidate, he expressed no interest. (Five weeks after our meeting, Chornovil died in a car accident on a highway outside of Kyiv.[17] Some suspected foul play, but Ukrainian roads were notoriously dangerous after dark. The embassy discouraged its staff from driving outside of major cities at night.)

Symonenko in a spring meeting opined that a single candidate from the left might be possible and asserted that, if there were honest elections, there would be a new president. He charged that Progressive Socialist Party leader Nataliya Vitrenko had covert support from Bankova, which hoped that she would draw votes away from Symonenko and Moroz. The embassy heard this from others as well.

Former president Leonid Kravchuk described an uphill battle confronting Kuchma. Pensioners would constitute about half of those who turned out to vote, and they tended to support the left. Symonenko could be defeated easily, but Moroz or Rada speaker Oleksandr Tkachenko (a former Communist Party member) could challenge Kuchma. Kravchuk expected Kuchma's team to stretch democratic practices; they had put out the word to state organs about the need to ensure an election success. Kravchuk nevertheless regarded Kuchma as the only choice, adding that another five years would fully deplete the Communist base in the country.

Other candidates expected campaign problems. Yevhen Marchuk anticipated that the Presidential Administration would make it difficult to secure sites for campaign events. Oleksandr Moroz complained that he could not get access to the media. People's Movement of Ukraine head Yuriy Kostenko planned to work on local media, where he believed access would be easier than with the national broadcasters.

The embassy over the summer grew increasingly alarmed by the campaign problems, particularly media access and abuse of administrative resources. For example, several sources told the embassy that those who contributed money to candidates other than Kuchma could expect a tax audit. STB, the national television network that seemed to provide balanced election coverage, had come under pressure from the State Tax Administration.

In comparison with election processes in other post-Soviet states, Ukraine's presidential election process did not look so bad. But it fell short of U.S. and EU expectations, and it did not meet the democratic standards that the Ukrainian government had set for itself as part of its drive to integrate with Europe. The embassy consulted with the State Department about how to proceed. On the one hand, Kuchma was "the best of an uninspiring lot," as one U.S. official observed. On the other hand, democracy was a key value and central element of the U.S. vision for Ukraine.

In the first half of September, I began pointing out problems such as media access, selective audits by the State Tax Administration, reports that the Security Service of Ukraine (SBU) kept opposition candidates under surveillance, and other misuses of administrative resources with officials, including Orel (who had become Kuchma's foreign policy adviser), Deputy Foreign Minister Oleksandr Chalyy, and Horbulin.

The election campaign swung into high gear in September. Thirty-two candidates registered for the election, and the Central Electoral Commission accepted nineteen, though a number of them dropped out before election day. Kuchma's campaign stressed stability and continuity. "Vote for me, things could be worse" was the slogan coined by one of the embassy's political officers. Actually, that had resonance with the electorate. Some Ukrainians explained to me they would vote for Kuchma, since, even though things were not going particularly well, they had more goods in the stores than Belarus did, and there was no war, which the Russians faced in Chechnya.

As election problems mounted, the embassy and Washington agreed that it was time to voice our concerns publicly. We had little expectation that public criticism would increase our impact. It came down to making clear that the United States supported democratic principles.

I noted U.S. concerns about the election process in a September 15 press conference. The following week, Mark Taplin and Kathy Kavalec, who respectively headed the embassy's press and political sections, suggested that I visit STB and meet with the network's management on the pressure it faced from the State Tax Administration. I did so on September 24. That evening, STB ran a lengthy story on my visit and the tax pressure.

Late in September the Canadian ambassador and I worked with the Finnish ambassador (Finland held the EU presidency) on a coordinated démarche on the importance of a free, fair, and democratic election, including media freedom, media access for all candidates, and transparent and unbiased election procedures. The three of us met with Kuchma on October 3. The Finnish ambassador highlighted the main points of the EU's position, and the Canadian ambassador and I associated our governments with his comments. I mentioned STB's travails, adding that the State Tax Administration had declined to meet with embassy officers to discuss the case. Kuchma responded defensively. I noted that Kuchma had a special burden: he was a candidate, but as the incumbent he also bore a responsibility to ensure that his opponents had the chance to compete fairly. He voiced wider unhappiness with the slowness of EU engagement and with the way that the U.S. government had handled Lazarenko's case. It was not a happy meeting.

The joint démarche usefully complemented the concerns that the embassy had raised bilaterally. Kuchma, however, saw everything on the line politically and likely assumed that, for the West, his reelection was preferable to a win by a leftist candidate. We thus saw little prospect of an improvement in campaign practices in the four weeks remaining before the election.

Washington officials began to speak publicly. John Tedstrom, the director for Ukraine on the National Security Council, arrived in Kyiv on October 19. In addition to reiterating U.S. election concerns with officials, he voiced them in an interview with the newspaper *Fakty* (Facts). Tedstrom's comments echoed those expressed by Talbott in an interview with *Dzerkalo Tyzhnya* (Weekly Mirror) published on October 23. In an October 23 meeting Tarasyuk noted the remarks, saying that they were not appreciated in Kyiv. I replied that they offered a balanced critique. Tedstrom added that the U.S. government could not remain silent on the democracy question. In a separate meeting Orel asked me to go through the U.S. criticisms. I reviewed the problems the embassy had seen, noting that they would taint a Kuchma victory and provide a poor setup for his planned December visit to Washington.

Tarasyuk called in several ambassadors on October 26 for a meeting that included Azarov plus senior officials from the National Security and Defense Council, the State Committee on Information Policy, the SBU, the ministry of justice, and the ministry of internal affairs. They complained that the European Union, OSCE (which had an election observer mission operating in Ukraine), and foreign governments had publicly criticized the election process. The Finnish, Norwegian, and EU ambassadors and I, as well as the head of the OSCE observer mission, reviewed specific problems. The Ukrainian officials attempted a not particularly convincing rebuttal. One pointed out that each presidential candidate had two ten-minute evening blocs on the state-run UT-1 television channel to present his or her platform, but he neglected to mention that a pro-Kuchma commentator usually appeared after each segment to mock the opposition candidates. It was a long, painful meeting. Tarasyuk seemed a bit embarrassed at having to host it. As we left, my Norwegian colleague asked, "Why organize such a meeting simply to mislead us?"

The next day, I was called in to a follow-up meeting at the State Tax Administration with Azarov, who gave a long explanation of the case against STB, asserting that the network had underreported its revenues by 2.3 million hryvnyas. The previous day at the foreign ministry, however, he had handed out a paper showing that Inter, a much larger broadcaster that had adopted a decidedly friendly approach toward Kuchma, had underreported revenues by 15 million hryvnyas. Azarov could not offer a convincing explanation for why the tax authorities had targeted STB but not Inter.

The election campaign came to an end on October 29, as electoral rules prohibited campaigning on October 30, the day before the voting. The One-Plus-One television network, which had made a belated effort to put some balance in its political reporting, had organized a series of debates among interested presidential candidates, to run for ninety minutes each night from October 25 to October 29 (USAID provided funding for the debates). Ten candidates showed up on October 25 for a freewheeling exchange; Kuchma did not come, though he made a brief appearance by video. At the end of a lively session, the moderator, Vyacheslav Pikhovshek, slumped over on his stool. One-Plus-One reported that he had taken ill and canceled the debates scheduled for the subsequent evenings. Then, on October 29, One-Plus-One announced a final debate that evening, running from 10:00 p.m. to midnight.

I decided to go and watch from the audience, and arrived at the studio to find six candidates, including Moroz, Vitrenko, and Kostenko, milling with a crowd outside a locked studio door. The candidates, having just been told that Pikhovshek had again taken ill and that there would be no debate, were furious, since they had canceled final campaign rallies to take part in the television debate. Several gained entry to the building (I tagged along behind) and confronted One-Plus-One's general director, Oleksandr Rodnyanskyy, peppering him with demands that the debate proceed. Rodnyanskyy told me that he had no time to find a replacement, at which point another One-Plus-One correspondent offered on the spot to moderate, an offer Rodnyanskyy plainly was not thrilled to hear; he ignored it. The candidates angrily departed the studio. An embassy political officer subsequently heard that the Presidential Administration had ordered the debate off the air, which sounded entirely plausible.

On October 31, Kuchma received 36 percent of the vote, and Symonenko came in second with 22 percent, so they would face off in a second vote on November 14. The OSCE observation mission criticized the campaign, stating that "the coverage of the campaign by the media and the widespread involvement of public officials in the campaign breached both the legal framework governing these elections and the relevant OSCE commitments. Although the laws showed improvement, implementation and enforcement was often selective and did not provide a level-playing field for all candidates in the pre-election period." It gave the voting day procedures a more positive grade: "Observers reported that election day procedures were carried out in a peaceful and orderly manner, despite minor irregularities in very few polling stations. . . . The [OSCE's Office of Democratic Institutions and Human Rights] has not been informed of any widespread irregularities at this stage."[18]

I met with Orel two days later at Bankova. In response to his question, I expressed the hope that the problems seen during the campaign would not be repeated in the two weeks before the runoff. Orel commented that a Symonenko victory would mean the end of Ukraine; the West should thus not criticize Kuchma. I agreed that Kuchma was the better choice, but that should not be taken to mean the U.S. government would support nondemocratic practices. In a meeting three days later, Mykola Biloblotskyy, head of the Presidential Administration, also warned of the consequences of a Symonenko victory. He expressed concern about foreign government statements about the campaign and criticized the OSCE's preliminary assessment.

Most expected Kuchma to handily defeat Symonenko, who was not a particularly inspiring campaigner. Support for the Communist Party, moreover, had declined steadily. Kuchma easily won reelection, polling almost 58 percent to just under 39 percent for Symonenko. The OSCE observation mission released its preliminary assessment on November 15. It was critical of the two-week campaign, noting that "the conduct of the campaign for the second round of the presidential election in Ukraine was in breach of the election law and the relevant OSCE commitments on democratic elections and showed no improvement over the first round of the election." The assessment also stated that "voting day procedures according to the law were not followed as closely as they were in the first round." But it did not report any major systemic violations in the balloting process.[19]

After the Election—A Chance for Change?

In anticipation of a Kuchma victory, the embassy had sent Washington its thoughts on what the first postelection messages should convey. The embassy proposed stressing the need to finally get serious on economic reform, develop a more cooperative relationship with the Rada, and deal with corruption.

Tihipko told me the day after Kuchma's reelection that he saw a window of opportunity. With political will, the government could now move quickly on reform. He expected Kuchma to have a new prime minister in place by late December. On November 16, I met with Marchuk, whom Kuchma had appointed the week before to replace Horbulin as secretary of the National Security and Defense Council. (Many saw this as a maneuver to secure Marchuk's support for Kuchma and capture the 8.1 percent of the vote that had gone to Marchuk on October 31.) He also saw a chance for real economic reform.

I paid a call on Andriy Fialko, the deputy foreign policy adviser to Kuchma, to pass over the vice president's congratulatory message for Kuchma. Fialko raised the State Department's statement on the election. That was a bit of a surprise; although the statement echoed OSCE criticisms of the election process, it was relatively upbeat and congratulated the Ukrainians on "the expression of their commitment to democracy." Later that afternoon at the foreign ministry, Chalyy also brought up the statement and asked if the U.S. government regarded Kuchma's election as legitimate. The question surprised me. I replied that Washington regarded the election as legitimate but that the campaign problems had caused concern.

Sestanovich and Pascual visited Kyiv for a November 22 meeting of the Gore-Kuchma foreign policy committee. In a private meeting with Tarasyuk they noted that the West felt Ukraine was doing too little on reform, that the Ukrainian government appeared to believe that the

West did not care, and that a resulting downward spiral would be in neither side's interest. Tarasyuk said Ukraine was about to launch a new beginning, which he hoped the United States would support.

Sestanovich and Pascual also discussed Kuchma's upcoming trip to Washington. The Ukrainians had pressed hard for a Clinton visit to Ukraine in 1999, but the president's schedule did not allow it. Gore's office had offered to host a Gore-Kuchma Commission meeting in August. Kyiv asked to delay the meeting until the autumn, perhaps hoping a meeting with Gore and Clinton would prove useful as the election neared. Autumn turned out to be difficult for Gore, who was beginning his campaign travels in preparation for a run for the U.S. presidency. We finally agreed on a short Gore-Kuchma Commission meeting on December 8.

As well as pressing the reform message privately, after consulting with Washington, I decided to give a public speech on U.S. hopes in the aftermath of the election. We chose Taras Shevchenko University as the venue for what would be a "tough love" address. The speech noted that the political calendar was right—Kuchma did not face another presidential campaign because the constitution limited him to two terms, and Rada elections were two years off. The government now had a window of opportunity in which to pursue a serious reform effort. The speech focused on the importance of reform and noted the need to tackle corruption in a serious way, including for senior leaders to distance themselves from those who engaged in corrupt practices.

The Shevchenko speech drew more extensive media coverage than any that I gave in three years in Ukraine; some papers printed lengthy excerpts. As the embassy press officer observed, the media could not say certain things but felt comfortable reporting that the American ambassador had said them.

The speech did not go down well with the government. The next day, Chalyy shared with me a paper that Buteyko, who was then Ukraine's ambassador to the United States, had been instructed to deliver to the State Department. It protested the speech as interference in Ukraine's domestic affairs, noting that this was "not the first instance in a series of unfriendly statements by the senior leadership of the United States and its official representatives." On returning to the embassy I called Wilson to give him a heads-up. He called in Buteyko to protest the protest before the Ukrainian ambassador could even present it. Wilson told Buteyko that the speech had been cleared by both the State Department and National Security Council and represented U.S. policy. He added that the protest did not bode well for Kuchma's visit the following week. This was one of the few times when I had felt the need to clear a speech in advance with Washington, and Wilson could not have provided stronger support. (Buteyko ended up as a diplomatic casualty of the Ukrainian election. He was relieved of his position at the end of 1999, after just one year. Rumors in Kyiv attributed his sacking to the low number of votes for Kuchma among Ukrainian citizens voting at the embassy in Washington.)

I saw Orel and Fialko on December 4 to preview Kuchma's Washington visit. Fialko asked what the U.S. government thought of Kuchma's inauguration speech. I responded that it laid out the right agenda for reform; Kuchma's U.S. interlocutors would want to hear his plans for implementing that agenda. Orel raised my Shevchenko speech and asked what I thought of my meeting the previous day with Chalyy. I said the speech had been balanced and not all that different from what Kuchma had said a few days earlier; as for the formal U.S. reaction to the protest, Wilson had conveyed that to Buteyko. On the way out, Fialko suggested that Bankova had been fine with my speech and that the protest had originated in the foreign ministry (that did not ring entirely true). A press report a couple of days later criticized the foreign ministry for the protest. The embassy assumed that it had been a plant aimed at tarnishing Tarasyuk.

Marchuk arrived in Washington a day before Kuchma for preparatory meetings with Fuerth. He also had a private meeting with CIA director George Tenet, during which Tenet addressed corruption close to Ukraine's Presidential Administration. He noted in particular that three individuals—Ihor Bakay, Vadym Rabynovych, and Oleksandr Volkov (the oligarch, not the former Atlanta Hawks basketball player)—should not bother applying for U.S. visas. Washington had agreed with the embassy that raising specific cases could underscore the U.S. message on corruption. Volkov was already on the visa lookout system to be denied entry into the European Union's Schengen countries. As for Rabynovych, the Ukrainian government had announced in June that he had been banned from entry for five years, yet he had returned in late September. To the embassy's dismay, he had originally been included on the protocol list submitted of those traveling to Washington with Kuchma; he was dropped after I called Bankova to advise that Rabynovych would not be welcome. (Interestingly, within a week after the Marchuk-Tenet conversation, someone in Kyiv leaked the story and the names to the media. That was fine by me, as it strengthened the U.S. message against corruption.)

Kuchma had a packed schedule on December 8. After a breakfast hosted by the U.S.-Ukraine Business Council, Kuchma met with Clinton in the Oval Office. Clinton stressed reform. Putting on his politician's hat, he noted that Kuchma now had a chance to build a legacy and that it was better to make hard political decisions early in a second term. Kuchma responded that he planned radical reforms and a serious anticorruption campaign. While he had found it difficult to work with the Rada, he hoped to build a progovernment majority coalition. Kuchma asked for help with the IMF and World Bank, whose programs remained suspended. Clinton closed the meeting by saying he was glad that Kuchma had won but that Kuchma now had to act.

The vice president continued the reform message, stressing that now was the time to make hard decisions on reform. Kuchma expressed concern about my Shevchenko speech and was defensive about corruption when Gore noted that the U.S. government had concerns about some of the people around the Ukrainian president (one of those was Volkov, who had an office at Bankova).

The Gore-Kuchma plenary session quickly reviewed the work of the four committees. Kuchma said Ukraine's foreign policy priority was entry into the European Union. Ukraine also wanted to develop its strategic partnerships with the United States and Russia, as well as its partnership with NATO, though Kyiv realized that there was no support in the alliance for Ukrainian membership. Gore expressed support for Kuchma's "European choice"—the foreign policy priority that the Ukrainian president increasingly stressed in his public remarks. Kuchma said Ukraine still needed to achieve a critical mass of reforms, but he claimed Kyiv had a plan to do that. Gore and Kuchma issued a joint statement that provided a broad and upbeat assessment of the state of U.S.-Ukraine relations.

Over lunch, the vice president suggested that Kuchma move immediately on administrative reform, even before naming a new cabinet of ministers. Tihipko observed that, under the reform plans, the government might downsize by 200,000–300,000 employees, which would be very welcome news to the IMF and World Bank. Gore told Kuchma of the U.S. intention to increase exchange opportunities for Ukrainians to come to the United States to 2,000–2,400 per year, almost double the number of exchanges in 1999.

There was one nice touch at the plenary for me personally. When the U.S. president travels overseas and meets his counterparts, the ambassador in protocol terms outranks everyone else in the president's party after the president. Wise ambassadors do not overplay that point with the secretary of state or national security adviser, but the ambassador typically is seated next to the president in meetings. Not so in Washington, where the ambassador on his home turf falls lower down in the protocol pecking order. Fuerth and Sestanovich arranged the Gore-Kuchma plenary, however, so that I was at the center at the vice president's side. It was a gesture of support, which I appreciated given the negative official reaction to my Shevchenko speech.

That afternoon, Treasury Secretary Lawrence Summers met with Kuchma at Blair House. Summers was direct, delivering the toughest message of the visit to the Ukrainian president. The IMF and World Bank believed Kyiv had failed to meet past commitments, and things were no better with private capital markets. The first weeks of Kuchma's second term would be key to changing Ukraine's image. That meant a serious fight against corruption, privatization, and a realistic state budget. Kuchma recounted the problem that he faced with the Rada. Summers suggested giving priority to reforms that could be accomplished by executive action. He offered that, if Ukraine reached agreement with the IMF and then stayed on its program, the U.S. government could be very helpful in supporting debt rescheduling. If Ukraine was not on track with the IMF, the United States could do little.

Talbott and Marchuk met later that afternoon. Marchuk said Kuchma was resolved to bring major change. The next day, Tihipko told Pascual that he thought Kuchma had understood the U.S. message. Later, back in Kyiv, Orel offered a very positive assessment of Kuchma's Washington visit and reiterated that the president intended to push forward on reform.

The big news in mid-December was that Kuchma decided to nominate Yushchenko as the next prime minister. U.S. and international financial institution officials had long worked with him at the National Bank and believed he fully understood the needs of a modern economy and the reforms that Ukraine required. On December 22 the Rada approved Yushchenko's nomination by a vote of 296 to 12, a strong endorsement that few had anticipated. At a holiday reception that I hosted that evening, many guests were almost giddy with excitement.

The embassy sent Washington a short assessment the next day, commenting that much had happened in the two weeks since Kuchma had visited Washington. Expectations for change had gone through the roof. In addition to Yushchenko's appointment, the government instituted administrative reforms that exceeded the World Bank's hopes, and a revised budget plus decrees on privatization and deregulation waited in the wings. Embassy contacts in the government, the Rada, and the media credited the Clinton, Gore, and Summers meetings with turning Kuchma toward a more radical reform program. The embassy's message recalled Ukraine's stop-and-go history on reform and past disappointments. No one could rule out another disappointment—Lucy might once again yank the football from Charlie Brown—but the odds for real reform appeared better at the end of 1999 than they had in years.

Y2K—The Great Nonevent

The year concluded with fears of what January 1, 2000, might mean for computers: the Y2K problem. A group of Western ambassadors had met with Pustovoytenko in February 1999 to discuss the Y2K issue. The meeting left a distinct impression that Kyiv had not thought much about it. Of particular concern were the country's fourteen nuclear reactors. The electric power grid was fragile, and some experts feared that if computer problems forced one or more reactors offline the grid might collapse.

In September, USAID brought in a team that had overseen Southern California Edison's Y2K preparations to examine the Ukrainian power grid. Energy Minister Ivan Plachkov very much doubted that any kind of Y2K issue would arise. The Southern California Edison experts reported back in October that they saw no major risks to the power grid, primarily because it made far less use of computers than did electrical grids in the West. The Ukrainians, moreover, had made some smart last-minute preparations. In the worst case, the team predicted that a rural oblast might lose power for a few days, but Kyiv would experience no problems.

The State Department had worried about Y2K's impact on Ukraine and Russia and raised the possibility of evacuating most of the two embassies' American staff. The Southern California Edison report did not justify that action. Moreover, Gary Bagley, the embassy's energetic management officer, had already developed a Plan B in case Y2K plunged Ukraine into darkness. It had the embassy community sheltering in place for several days. He had the U.S. Army ship in 4,000 meals-ready-to-eat and worked out a housing plan to accommodate the staff; some forty Americans would be joining my family at the residence, where we had a generator and a large water supply. If we had to leave, Bagley planned a car convoy to Germany and had arranged for Polish and German visas for all of the embassy's motor pool staff as well as a fuel truck—embassy staff would car caravan out and take along a mobile gas station.

With no expectation of a problem and an excellent Plan B in hand, I recommended to Washington that there be no evacuation. Just a few days later the under secretary for management put Kyiv on "authorized departure," meaning that anyone not designated essential could leave at the end of December. The evening of December 31, we held a New Year's party for the American staff that remained in Kyiv. I went to the embassy around 11:00 p.m. At 11:30 p.m., the embassy disconnected from city power and switched to its generator; we waited for midnight. Nothing happened. About 12:10 a.m., Peace Corps volunteers from various cities began phoning in to report that, other than a big New Year's celebration, nothing untoward had occurred elsewhere in the country.

Early Hopes in 2000

With Yushchenko having taken office as prime minister, many in Ukraine greeted the year 2000 with optimism. His economic team included people with strong reform credentials: Tihipko as minister of economy, Mityukov as minister of finance, and Yuriy Yekhanurov as deputy prime minister. The appointments also included Tymoshenko as first deputy prime minister (a senior official close to Yushchenko told me nothing derogatory had turned up in her background check). Many in the Western diplomatic community regarded her appointment as a major question mark. One senior Ukrainian official disagreed: "Yuliya Tymoshenko is not a question mark; she is an exclamation point!" As it would turn out, she became the cabinet's most effective minister, though not without stepping on a lot of toes.

I made my first call on the new prime minister on January 14. Yushchenko seemed confident, in part because a Rada majority had just been formalized with 237 votes—a thin majority, but a majority nevertheless. He laid out his priorities: optimize the budget process, administrative reform, deregulation, and energy sector reform. That seemed the right agenda. Yushchenko expressed interest in an early March visit to Washington, both for bilateral discussions with senior U.S. officials and meetings with the IMF. He hoped by that time to have a new budget in place and to have met the IMF's conditions for an extended fund facility.

On January 18, I paid my first call on Tymoshenko since her appointment as deputy prime minister. She underscored the new cabinet's commitment to reform and sounded as optimistic as Yushchenko about Kyiv's readiness to do what was needed. That evening, at the president's annual reception for the diplomatic corps, Kuchma credited his December visit to Washington with providing a new dynamism that produced a new government and new reform steps.

IMF assistant director for Europe Mohammad Shadman-Valavi told G-7 ambassadors that Yushchenko was the "dream" choice. He noted Ukraine's good progress on administrative reform and managing its external debt, but said it needed to devote more attention to the budget and privatization of state assets.

Mityukov said his focus was on raising budget revenues and negotiating an agreement that would restructure debts due in 2000 and 2001 to the 2002–10 period. Success on those fronts would create some fiscal breathing room. Minister of Agriculture Ivan Kyrylenko described the government's plan to end its involvement in providing inputs to the agricultural sector and leave the provision of tractor fuel and fertilizers to private firms, something that reform experts had long urged as central to the creation of a genuine market in the country's potentially rich agricultural sector.

Cabinet Secretary Viktor Lytsytskyy told me of his efforts to streamline cabinet operations. He hoped to reduce staffing by 20 percent but noted some practical difficulties, including the fact that the cabinet of ministers had 550 computers but no local area network to link them. Oleh Rybachuk, Yushchenko's chief of staff, saw a major challenge for the cabinet in getting the bureaucracies in the ministries on board with the prime minister's program.

The Yushchenko cabinet faced significant challenges at the start of 2000. Ukraine's economy continued to struggle, with gross domestic product having declined by a cumulative total of 61 percent between 1991 and 1999 (given the size of the shadow economy, this figure likely overstated the decline). Ukraine had not recorded a single year since regaining independence in which the economy had grown.[20] Some reforms had been implemented during Kuchma's first term, but much of the old command-style system remained, and corruption continued to run rampant. The country badly needed a modern tax code and a land code that would allow agricultural land to be freely sold and mortgaged. Yushchenko and the cabinet had to figure out how to outmaneuver the oligarchs. A Yushchenko adviser said some—particularly Hryhoriy Surkis and Viktor Medvedchuk—had already launched an "information war" to undermine the prime minister.

Political Intrigues

Yushchenko's cabinet enjoyed only a brief honeymoon before political intrigues began to swirl. Kuchma had made clear his intention to go forward with a referendum, planned for April 16, that would reduce the authority of the Rada relative to that of the president. Rada chairman Oleksandr Tkachenko and First Deputy Chairman Adam Martynyuk resisted the referendum and efforts by the newly formed Rada majority to change the leadership. They ignored a resolution signed by 238 deputies—more than a majority—calling for the two of them to step down. That triggered a crisis on January 19, when right and center factions numbering some 240 Rada deputies walked out. Two days later they set up their own meeting in Ukraine House, three blocks down the street from the Rada building.

Kuchma sided with the group in Ukraine House. The foreign ministry convened a meeting of foreign ambassadors on January 24 with Medvedchuk, who was introduced as the "acting chairman" of the "new Rada." Medvedchuk asserted that 246 deputies had formed a majority and had decided to remove Tkachenko and Martynyuk but that Tkachenko had refused to put the question of his dismissal on the agenda. The deputies had therefore left the Rada and were consulting on how to "normalize" the Rada's work. Medvedchuk asserted that the ministry of justice confirmed the legality of the new majority's unorthodox action. He called Tkachenko's effort to convene the diplomatic corps—Tkachenko's office had faxed embassies a letter proposing a meeting just minutes before the meeting at the foreign ministry—illegitimate.

Kyiv endured a brief period of two competing Radas, which caused a great deal of political heat and pulled attention away from the needed reform effort. In early February, Tkachenko and Martynyuk threw in the towel, and the new majority returned to the main Rada building. The reunited Rada elected Ivan Plyushch as Rada chairman. Medvedchuk became first deputy chairman.

Late January brought a separate crisis for Yushchenko. The *Financial Times* ran a story alleging that IMF funds had been diverted from the National Bank of Ukraine (NBU) in 1997, when Yushchenko was governor, and used to invest in speculative bonds issued by the Ukrainian government, with some monies deposited in bank accounts in Switzerland and Belgium. The accounts reportedly were connected to people in Kuchma's inner circle. The source of these allegations was Pavlo Lazarenko, who was then sitting in custody in the United States.[21] (I heard several weeks later from the State Department that in the summer of 1999 Lazarenko's lawyers had approached U.S. legal officials with an offer that Lazarenko would "spill the beans" on Kuchma if the charges against him were dropped. Since Lazarenko had shared nothing like this to date, the Department of Justice wondered if he had anything.)

The story broke at the worst possible time for Kyiv, which was in the process of finalizing an agreement with the IMF to resume credits. Yushchenko flatly denied the allegations.[22] On January 31, Yushchenko, NBU governor Volodymyr Stelmakh, and Tarasyuk convened a meeting of G-7 ambassadors plus the EU, IMF, and World Bank representatives to refute the *Financial Times* claims. Yushchenko noted that the NBU had gone through an international audit and had shared all the information with the IMF. Stelmakh added that he had engaged the accounting firm PriceWaterhouseCoopers to perform a special audit of NBU accounts. The *Financial Times* story had the Ukrainians rattled. Indeed, IMF officials announced that they would investigate the allegations and examine whether the NBU had overreported the level of its usable reserves in 1998.

Sestanovich and National Security Council senior director Mark Medish arrived at the beginning of February for consultations. They urged key Ukrainian interlocutors to offer full transparency regarding the NBU's activities. They also talked about the importance of political cooperation between Kuchma and Yushchenko. Yushchenko could not carry out his reform program without the president's help in the Rada and in keeping the oligarchs in line; while Washington had confidence in the Ukrainian economic team, it was not clear that the executive branch—particularly the president—had fully committed to the reform program.

One week later, Volodymyr Lytvyn, head of the Presidential Administration at Bankova, called in the G-7 ambassadors to discuss Ukraine's reform plans. He asserted that Kuchma saw his number one task as supporting Yushchenko. With the Rada situation stabilizing, the president, prime minister, and new Rada speaker would soon meet to coordinate securing approval for needed reforms. He defended the planned April referendum, claiming that petitions supporting the referendum had gained 4 million signatures (a number that did not sound plausible to any of the Western diplomats).

The *Financial Times* allegations, however, continued to resonate as the paper published additional stories with increasing detail and questioned the IMF's practice of extending such loans. Those allegations now overshadowed the progress that Kyiv was making on reforms. The IMF's Shadman-Valavi told Western ambassadors on February 21 that the IMF was still seeking to establish the truth about the NBU's earlier actions. Some actions seemed to violate the spirit of the IMF's memorandum with Kyiv, though perhaps did not constitute technical violations. IMF officials had found no substance to Lazarenko's charge that IMF funds had been diverted, but they had launched two audits to put the allegations to rest. The IMF board would only consider a resumption of credits in the second half of April, at the earliest—a big disappointment for Kyiv.

On the positive side, IMF officials praised the new budget being prepared as "the best that Ukraine has had." They also gave good marks to reforms in the agricultural and energy sectors. All in all, the IMF officials described a largely positive picture except for the *Financial Times* allegations, but those remained very damaging.

Rybachuk told me on March 3 that Kyiv was increasingly worried that the IMF was dragging out the audits. He added that Yushchenko still planned to visit Washington later in March. Rybachuk, who had worked with Yushchenko at the NBU, denied that IMF funds had been misused. He said the bank had played by the rules, but that the rules had changed in September 1998. He noted the urgency of the current situation: NBU foreign reserves had fallen to $1.2 billion; absent IMF disbursements and an agreement on restructuring Ukraine's debt to private creditors, they would be exhausted in the summer.

Although U.S. officials had earlier agreed to a mid-March Yushchenko visit, Washington now concluded that that would not be a good time. On March 11, I paid a Saturday call on Tarasyuk to tell him that the U.S. government urged postponing the trip. Tarasyuk expressed dismay, saying that a postponement would undercut the Yushchenko government. I sympathized with his point, but it was also clear that, were Yushchenko to proceed with his travel plans, the allegations of mishandling IMF monies would overshadow everything. Yushchenko reluctantly canceled his trip. A few days later a senior U.S. official explained the rationale for waving off the prime minister's visit: "There was the sense that they should go fix this and then talk about a visit. . . . They clearly have some business to do at home to clean up this problem."[23]

At the same time, the IMF informed the Ukrainians that it would shortly issue a statement regarding the NBU allegations. The statement, publicly released on March 14, noted that a number of NBU transactions in the period 1996–98 appeared designed to convey an impression that NBU reserves were greater than they were. As a result, three IMF disbursements in late 1997 and early 1998 had been made that would not have been made had the IMF had an accurate picture. The statement concluded by noting certain remedial actions that the IMF and NBU were taking, including detailed audits.[24]

The statement stunned Kyiv, which saw another setback to its hopes of resuming the extended fund facility. Ukraine's situation with the IMF topped the agenda ten days later when Bill Taylor and USAID's assistant administrator for Europe and Eurasia, Don Pressley, came to discuss economic reforms. Yekhanurov expressed concern that it might take the IMF three months to reach a decision on the EFF, leaving Kyiv with a significant financing gap. Yushchenko noted that the new Rada majority had passed a budget and the economy was growing. But he thought a political game was being played against him. Kyiv could not afford endless audits. It badly needed the EFF and a disbursement by late May; if not, "the game [for reform] would be over."

Tedstrom, who accompanied Taylor and Pressley, stayed over. We met Orel and his deputy, Leonid Kozhara, on March 25. Orel stressed Kuchma's support for Yushchenko but launched into a long complaint about the prime minister's actions. Kuchma wanted speedier reforms, and Orel did not understand why the cabinet had taken no action. He claimed that the administrative and agricultural reforms already in place had been implemented by the president, not the cabinet. We found the complaint disquieting. It seemed to confirm rumors of tensions between the president and prime minister. We stressed the need for the Presidential Administration and the cabinet to work together.

A senior cabinet official told me at the end of March that Yushchenko wanted to get his reform program passed and make April a "month of implementation." Yushchenko expected Kuchma to endorse the program. If the Rada did not approve it, Yushchenko intended to resign.

Meanwhile, the *Financial Times* stories continued. Summers told Congress in late March that the U.S. government was "deeply concerned" about the reports that the NBU had overstated its reserves.[25] In Kyiv, Chalyy worried that Summers's remarks might trigger additional IMF conditions. A senior Presidential Administration official said ten *Financial Times* articles had come out in one month, which he saw as a campaign to undermine both Yushchenko and Kuchma, a view shared by other analysts, including some in the embassy.

Under Secretary of State for Economics Alan Larson visited Kyiv on April 4 and 5 to talk about reform and Ukraine's relationship with the IMF. I had just flown back from Donetsk, where I had joined Kuchma for the opening of a Cargill sunflower seed processing plant (the launch of such a large U.S. investment in Ukraine was a welcome if rare event). Larson credited Ukraine's positive cooperation with the IMF on the audits but flagged a new bilateral problem related to intellectual property rights (IPR): Ukraine had become a major source of pirated compact discs for the European market, as a result of which the U.S. recording industry was petitioning to remove the Generalized System of Preferences trade benefits for Ukrainian exports to the United States. He asked the Ukrainian government to close the pirate plants. Larson commented that Yushchenko's visit to Washington, now rescheduled for early May, could be successful if the prime minister arrived with Ukraine having met the conditions for the extended fund facility, a date for closure of the last operating reactor at Chornobyl, a resolution of the IPR issue, and progress on the still-lingering business dispute cases. Achieving all that would be a tall order.

Albright Returns

The Larson visit helped set the stage for Secretary of State Albright's April 14 visit for meetings with Tarasyuk, Yushchenko, and Kuchma. We and the Ukrainians had agreed on an agenda: overall U.S.-Ukraine relations, Kyiv's reform efforts, Ukraine-Europe relations, Russia, and the rescheduled Yushchenko visit to Washington. However, an SBU decision to block Jed Sunden, publisher of the *Kyiv Post*, from reentering Ukraine threatened to derail the plan. I was not a big fan of the *Kyiv Post*, believing it had not treated the embassy fairly on several occasions. But the SBU had no valid reason for keeping Sunden out of the country. With the secretary's arrival two days out, I called Chalyy at the foreign ministry, Yushchenko's chief of staff, and officials in the Presidential Administration to warn that, if they did not resolve Sunden's case quickly, it would be the first item the secretary would raise in each of her meetings. The SBU allowed Sunden back in.

Albright and Tarasyuk discussed Ukraine's European aspiration, in particular its desire to integrate with the European Union. Albright said Washington wanted to see closer relations between Ukraine and Europe. She recommended that Kyiv focus on practical steps to implement agreements already concluded with the European Union.

Yushchenko expressed concern to Albright that the IMF did not believe Ukraine had done enough to secure an EFF. He hoped to receive a disbursement from the IMF in May or June. That would help Ukraine's foreign reserves balance and also send a positive signal to the World Bank, from which Kyiv hoped to receive additional funding, and the Paris Club, where the Ukrainians sought a more generous restructuring of their sovereign debt. Albright assured the prime minister that the U.S. government would support IMF disbursements if Ukraine met the EFF conditions and the ongoing audits produced no surprises. The Yushchenko meeting left the secretary impressed; she expected that he would hit it off well with Clinton.

The secretary's main message to Kuchma was the importance of moving on economic reform. She stated that Yushchenko had been an excellent choice and stressed the importance that Kuchma support him. The president seemed restrained in his response, noting that the prime minister needed to have more than just the "aura of reform."

Albright and Kuchma also discussed Russia; the Ukrainian leader expressed concern about Vladimir Putin. He had become acting president of Russia on December 31, 1999, when Yeltsin unexpectedly stepped down, and won the early presidential election three weeks before Albright's arrival in Kyiv. Kuchma worried that Putin would seek to rebuild greater Russia. Things already were not going well between Kyiv and Moscow. Russia had stopped some oil flows, and bilateral trade had fallen.

The secretary concluded her day with a strong performance in a live interview on the national One-plus-One channel.[26] Despite some unease that Kuchma and Yushchenko were not in sync, she departed Kyiv the next morning in a good mood. Later that day, I got a call from the White House and informed Tarasyuk that Clinton would like to visit Kyiv in early June. Tarasyuk confirmed that the Ukrainians would welcome the visit, which they had long sought.

More Politics

Ukraine held its referendum on constitutional questions on April 16, the day after the secretary's departure. According to the Central Electoral Commission, the questions all passed by large majorities, with more than 80 percent turnout. The numbers struck many in the diplomatic corps as exaggerated. Anecdotally, one of the embassy's local employees reported that someone had come to her door to urge her to vote, claiming that everyone else in the apartment building had already done so. "Everyone?" she asked. "Yes, everyone." "Including the person in that apartment across the hall?" "Yes." She found that more than a little curious, since the resident across the hall was a foreigner. Western diplomats suspected that the referendum was just a starting point for a lengthy political process.

Rada members, who had shown little enthusiasm for the referendum from the beginning, weighed how to deal with it. Symonenko charged that Kuchma, Medvedchuk, and Volkov had engineered the referendum and hoped to lay a path for a third presidential term for Kuchma, even though the constitution specified a two-term limit.

The embassy began to hear that support for Yushchenko in the Rada was fraying. One deputy observed that Volkov and Surkis wanted Yushchenko to secure the IMF extended fund facility, or at least the initial disbursement of funds, but that they would then move against him. Another Rada deputy noted that Kuchma stood between Yushchenko and the oligarchs (and their deputies in the Rada); the prime minister needed to engage the oligarchic factions in parliament and get them to buy into his reforms. Others attributed a weakening relationship between Kuchma and Yushchenko to the president's sensitivity about the prime minister's high popularity. Later in April we heard that Yushchenko had almost resigned after a difficult meeting with Kuchma.

Yushchenko Goes to Washington

With the *Financial Times* stories fading and the Ukrainians appearing to make progress with the IMF, Yushchenko's visit to Washington was rescheduled for May 8 and 9. The embassy's scene-setter cable noted that the unmet conditions for the EFF meant that the prime minister would be presenting more plans than accomplishments. Yushchenko seemed to lack the clout to overcome special interests. Kuchma had mobilized support in the Rada to approve the cabinet's budget proposal but had not pressed the oligarchs into line on other issues, such as elimination of tax breaks or reform of the energy sector. The main question was whether Yushchenko and his cabinet could get their act together and secure consistent support from Kuchma.

The embassy had worked with Chalyy on a full bilateral schedule, in addition to Yushchenko's meetings at the IMF and the World Bank: Albright, Summers, Berger, U.S. Trade Representative Charlene Barshevskiy, and the U.S.-Ukraine Business Council. The Ukrainians were unhappy that no meetings were scheduled with the president or vice president. I urged them not to worry, as the embassy had been in touch with the National Security Council to propose "drop-bys" by Clinton and Gore during the Berger meeting. (One trick that I had learned from my time at the White House was that a drop-by was much easier to get on the president's schedule than a meeting in the Oval Office; if Clinton clicked with the foreign visitor, as would likely be the case with Yushchenko, a five-minute drop-by could stretch to twenty or even thirty minutes.)

Yushchenko's schedule began with a call on Albright. The prime minister expressed concern that, because the IMF extended fund facility program was a prerequisite for Ukraine to reschedule its official debt in the Paris Club, a failure to get the program would mean no IMF money and no debt relief. Albright replied, "I know it must sound like we are never satisfied," but Ukraine still had more to do on its budget, privatization, and energy sector reforms. She advised that, as soon as Kyiv publicly announced a closure date for Chornobyl, the U.S. government would announce an additional $78 million for building the new sarcophagus.

Summers was characteristically blunt in a meeting that did not go well. He said Kyiv had a serious problem of integrity. There had to be strict and scrupulous reporting of NBU reserves; another deception would be a disaster. He urged total transparency to put to rest allegations about the NBU misreporting. Yushchenko denied that the NBU had deceived the IMF. It had provided the required information, though some was reported in a different format than the IMF used. The answer did not satisfy Summers, and the meeting ended on a cool note.

Barshevskiy expressed concerns about compact disc piracy. U.S. industry claimed a loss of $200 million per year, and it had identified five pirate plants in Ukraine, which she wanted the authorities to shut down. The Ukrainians voiced frustration that U.S. companies did not use the Ukrainian legal system to go after the pirate plants and noted that Israel, which also had an issue with pirate compact disc plants, had been treated differently. (I later heard that the latter point went down badly with Barshevskiy's team, who interpreted it as an anti-Semitic remark. That had not been the Ukrainians' intent.)

The Berger-Yushchenko meeting went far better. They met in the national security adviser's office in the West Wing, down the hall from the vice president's office and the Oval Office. Just after the beginning of the meeting, there was a knock on the door and Clinton walked in. Yushchenko obviously interested him, and the president took a seat. Yushchenko expressed gratitude for U.S. support and described the changes taking place in Ukraine. Clinton acknowledged that reform was difficult—but it could open the door to billions of dollars in investments. He hoped the pirate compact disc factories could be shuttered quickly. Yushchenko said Ukraine intended to shut down the last Chornobyl reactor on December 15 and could announce that publicly when the president visited Kyiv. After an upbeat back-and-forth (much longer than the five minutes the schedulers had hoped for), Clinton departed.

A few moments later there was another knock on the door, and Gore came in for a short exchange about developments in Ukraine. Berger suggested that the sides use Clinton's June visit to draw attention to Ukraine and to try to spark some investment interest. He closed out the discussion by returning to the need for full transparency with the IMF.

The last official event on the prime minister's calendar was a wreath-laying in Arlington National Cemetery at the Tomb of the Unknown Soldier. A troop of the Old Guard stood in review as Yushchenko placed a wreath before a small crowd. Interestingly, the U.S. Army rendered Yushchenko the full honors normally accorded to a head of state but not to a head of government.

Preparing for the President's Visit

The day following Yushchenko's departure, Sestanovich hosted Chalyy for a meeting of the Gore-Kuchma foreign policy committee. It focused on Clinton's June 5 visit to Kyiv. Sestanovich hoped that Clinton would be able to congratulate rather than hector. The U.S. government looked forward to a full list of deliverables, including an announcement of the date for closing Chornobyl, expanded commercial space cooperation with the removal of quotas on Ukrainian launches, and progress on IPR questions, including closure of some pirate compact disc plants. Chalyy suggested a declaration on the bilateral strategic partnership, but Sestanovich said a joint statement reflecting practical achievements would be preferable.

Back in Kyiv, I saw Orel at the Presidential Administration on May 15. He said the Ukrainian side was happy with the Yushchenko trip and looked forward to hosting Clinton. I handed over a letter from Clinton to Kuchma expressing the president's desire to use his upcoming visit to help bolster Ukraine's reforms and its integration into the Euro-Atlantic community. We agreed that there would be a joint statement if the deliverables merited one. As for the schedule, we envisaged that Clinton and Kuchma would meet first in a small group and then in a plenary session, followed by a reception hosted by Kuchma with a larger group of Ukrainians, from both the government and the Rada. The visit would conclude with a public speech by Clinton.

The pre-advance team had visited Kyiv in late April and advised that the White House was interested in a speech, which the embassy readily endorsed. The embassy had suggested two indoor venues: the Rada and the House of Teachers (home to the Central Rada in 1917–18 during Ukraine's brief period of independence as World War I concluded). The embassy also suggested an outdoor venue while cautioning that late afternoon weather in June could be unpredictable: the square directly in front of St. Mykhaylo's monastery, whose restoration had just been completed. The pre-advance team arrived in the square on a warm spring day with blue skies and the golden domes of St. Mykhaylo's brightly reflecting the sun. It won hands down, even if it meant running the risk of a downpour.

Chalyy and I regularly touched based on the preparations. The meeting could drive completion of bilateral agreements: a civil aviation agreement, a memorandum of understanding regarding cooperation in the event of disasters, a science and technology agreement, an agreement on limiting double taxation, and an agreement terminating the commercial space launch agreement and allowing Ukrainian entities to compete without limit to launch U.S.-manufactured satellites. These were the practical steps that built the substance of a broad relationship.

We worked on an action plan for addressing the IPR problem as well. In the second half of May, Jay Berman, chairman of the International Federation of the Phonographic Industry (IFPI), came to Kyiv. We set up a session with Deputy Prime Minister Mykola Zhulynskyy, where Berman described the problem: Ukraine's five pirate plants produced 70 million compact discs per year, when the IFPI estimated that domestic demand in Ukraine ran to no more than 1 million. The cost to American filmmakers came to hundreds of millions of dollars. I separately urged Ukrainian officials to take the issue seriously and close at least some plants; the IFPI had political clout and had begun to lobby for suspension of Ukraine's trade benefits. Zhulynskyy told me on June 2 that the Ukrainians had suspended operations at four of the five pirate plants.

The president arrived the afternoon of June 5, on what was the fifth and last stop on a seven-day Europe trip. The advance team had warned that, after a week on the road, Clinton was tired and had not had a good night's rest. I greeted the president on board Air Force One, briefly previewed the schedule, and reminded him not to take too large a piece of bread at the bread-and-salt welcoming ceremony at the foot of the stairs (having left several of these ceremonies with an uneaten chunk of bread stuffed in my jacket pocket).

From the airport, the president's party proceeded to Mariinskyy Palace, where Kuchma hosted the working meetings and a reception. In the small-group session, Kuchma and Yushchenko reviewed progress on economic reform, again noting the importance of IMF agreement to an EFF. Clinton agreed that Ukraine had made progress but still needed to complete its reform agenda. In particular, progress on strengthening the rule of law and containing corruption would send a positive signal to private investors.

Kuchma and Yushchenko noted the difficulties that Ukraine faced in its economic relations with Moscow. Ukrainian exports to Russia faced tariffs, since Russian customs authorities had exempted 300 Ukrainian goods from the free trade agreement. Moreover, Russia, the source of almost all of Ukraine's oil, charged high prices. In light of this, Kuchma hoped that Kyiv could move closer to European structures. He expressed concern that, once Poland gained EU membership, expected in 2004, Ukraine could have more difficulty getting its goods into the Polish market. Kuchma also sought graduation from the Jackson-Vanik amendment, which would allow Ukraine to get permanent normal trade relations status with the United States. (The 1974 Jackson-Vanik amendment blocked the Soviet Union and later its successor states from attaining permanent normal trade relations status until they permitted free emigration for religious minorities, particularly Jews. Upon regaining independence, Ukraine allowed open emigration, and tens of thousands of Jews left in the early 1990s. Still, Congress did not graduate Ukraine from the provisions of Jackson-Vanik and grant it permanent normal trade relations status until 2006.)

In the plenary session, Clinton expressed appreciation for the contribution that the joint Polish-Ukrainian battalion was making to the peacekeeping operation in Kosovo. Secretary of Energy Bill Richardson praised Ukraine for setting a date for closing Chornobyl and noted that Washington was moving forward on helping Ukraine qualify Westinghouse to provide fuel rods for Ukraine's nuclear reactors.

The plenary concluded with another discussion on Russia. Clinton, who had just arrived from Moscow, thought his meeting with Putin had gone well. He observed that the Russians seemed to have a difficult time imagining a future for themselves that was different from their past as part of the Soviet and Russian empires; Putin was smart and tough, and wished to succeed, but one should not assume that his intentions were necessarily malign.

The two presidents signed a joint statement reaffirming their commitment to the bilateral strategic partnership and recording specific agreements. The statement made public Kuchma's decision to shut down the last operating reactor at Chornobyl by December 2000 and announced the U.S. commitment of an additional $78 million for the Chornobyl Shelter Fund. The statement announced the termination of the 1996 U.S.-Ukraine Commercial Space Launch Agreement, leaving Ukraine free to provide launch services for U.S. commercial satellites without any quotas. The statement also noted the sides' intention to implement the Joint Action Plan to Combat Optical Media Piracy in Ukraine and welcomed the fact that Kyiv had suspended the operation of some pirate production plants.[27]

Following the discussions, Kuchma led Clinton to a large hall where the Ukrainians had laid out a typical official reception, where guests stood around tables piled high with all manner of food and drink. I took the opportunity to introduce the president to several Ukrainian guests, including members of the Rada and government officials. As was his style, Clinton showed that he could engage just about anyone in conversation. He then bade farewell to Kuchma and headed to St. Mykhaylo's, where the advance team advised that the crowd numbered somewhere between 70,000 and 90,000.

On arrival at St. Mykhaylo's, the president greeted members of the American Chamber of Commerce, who had pitched in to help make the speech happen (the White House travel budget had funding for the sound equipment but not for the stage, seating, security checkpoints, and large television screen; the city of Kyiv and local business community provided those). The president took a moment to lay a wreath at the memorial commemorating the millions who perished in the artificial famine of the 1930s and proceeded to the stage. Before climbing to the top, Clinton met the two high school students selected to introduce him (the embassy and advance team originally had planned on selecting one, but the two finalists had both shown incredible poise and presence and spoke nearly flawless English in addition to their native Ukrainian). Having two young people introduce the president set the tone for his speech, which focused on a bright potential future for Ukraine. Clinton had looked tired during the meetings and reception; when he stepped on the stage, the roaring welcome seemed to give him a shot of adrenaline.

The president's short, upbeat speech noted the tribulations that Ukraine had endured, most recently Stalin, the Nazi occupation, and the Soviet dictatorship, and outlined the future that the country could realize. He urged Ukrainians not to give up but to "keep on fighting" for a free and prosperous country; Ukrainians should seize the moment.[28] The crowd loved it. Following the speech Clinton worked the rope line, greeting hundreds of Ukrainians and Ukrainian and American members of the embassy staff. It was then off to Borispil Airport, Air Force One, and a long flight back to Washington. Fortunately, the feared thunderstorm did not show up. The June 6 edition of the *New York Times* on page one, above the fold, carried the picture that the pre-advance team had so eagerly envisaged six weeks earlier: a smiling Clinton against the backdrop of St. Mykhaylo's gleaming golden domes and a bright blue sky.[29]

From the embassy's point of view, Clinton's visit was a resounding success. He had given the right reform message to Kuchma. While the Ukrainians may have grown tired of the "do more" refrain, they saw the chance to host Clinton as a political plus. The summit served to affirm Kyiv's links with the West. It had driven the bureaucracies to complete agreements that otherwise might have taken months more to finish. Over and above the private discussions and specific agreements, the president's speech had sent a strong public message of U.S. support.

Back to Reform and Assistance

In the aftermath of Clinton's visit, the embassy continued to closely follow Kyiv's reform program and progress with the IMF. The Ukrainian government offered periodic high-level briefings, sometimes with the prime minister himself, to report progress on the EFF conditionalities and to say it was answering all IMF questions about past NBU actions.

Unfortunately, Western embassies received less optimistic briefings from IMF officials. I had raised this disconnect between what diplomats heard from Ukrainian authorities and what they heard from the IMF with the finance minister in late May. Mityukov conceded that Kyiv could not meet all of the conditionalities. Yekhanurov told me in September that the IMF had finally closed the audits, but there was still no decision on resuming disbursements. At that point, Ukraine had gone one year without IMF credits. Yushchenko made a similar point in an early October meeting, noting that the EFF remained a prerequisite for further credits from the World Bank and the European Bank for Reconstruction and Development (EBRD).

The embassy, USAID, and the assistance coordinator had decided to restructure U.S. assistance by reducing the number of programs and targeting more funds at priority areas. Over the course of the summer the embassy became intensely involved in several reform and assistance issues that showed the varying degrees of difficulty of effecting genuine change, even when the U.S. and Ukrainian governments agreed on the objective.

One example of success involved the electric power sector. A senior cabinet official had told me that Yushchenko wanted Tymoshenko to tackle the energy sector because she knew it and was prepared to take on the oligarchs, particularly Surkis and Bakay. She also appeared to want to build a reputation as a reformer. She had earlier raised with U.S. officials the issue of privatized *oblenerhos* (regional energy distributing companies) collecting electricity tariffs but not remitting monies to the generating or long-line transmission companies. She said this was the case with ten of the twenty-seven oblenerhos, and some of the ten were collecting 90 percent of the electricity tariffs and remitting as little 4 percent to the generating companies, even though generating the electricity amounted to roughly 75 percent of the overall cost of providing electricity. Her initial recommendation was that the government "reprivatize," which in effect meant nationalize, the oblenerhos. Her enthusiasm for the project was likely enhanced by the fact that several of the oblenerhos were owned by her political opponents.

The embassy worked with the EBRD and Tymoshenko directly on this problem. Neither EBRD officials nor the U.S. government favored nationalization. We proposed instead that, in each of the oblasts where a privatized oblenerho operated, a special account be established at a local bank and all electricity tariffs be paid into that account. Each week, the bank should distribute the collected monies to the local oblenerhos, the long-line transmission company, and a fund for the generating companies according to a transparent algorithm, based on a cost breakdown between the three. We discussed this proposal in a June 16 meeting with Tymoshenko and EBRD first vice president Charles Frank. After a lengthy exchange, she agreed to pursue it. It took several weeks to finalize details, but we had a fully agreed plan in early July, and it soon went into effect.

At the end of July, Mityukov told me that the new procedure would benefit the budget; as more money flowed to the electricity-generating companies, instead of being siphoned off by the oblenerhos and their owners, he could reduce budget subsidies. At the end of September, Tymoshenko told me that cash collections had increased by 77 percent, an important achievement. Others agreed that the situation with the electric power sector had improved dramatically. (Subsequent U.S. assistance went toward privatizing some oblenerhos through international tenders, though the process took years.)

Reform of the electricity tariff showed what was possible. We attributed much of the success to Tymoshenko, who had gained a reputation as the most effective minister in the cabinet or, as one Yushchenko aide put it more colorfully, "the only one in the cabinet with any balls." The electric power reform also got into the murky question of insider infighting: several oligarchs, reportedly including Surkis, Bakay, and Volkov, owned the privatized oblenerhos and took a major financial hit when the new payment plan went into effect. Western diplomats heard that all three opposed Tymoshenko politically, and all had ties to the Presidential Administration.

A second issue centered on the possible construction of a 675-kilometer pipeline to bring oil from Odesa, on the Black Sea coast, to Brody, in the Lviv region of western Ukraine, where it would feed into an existing pipeline system carrying oil to Central Europe. Ukrainian officials had begun discussing this idea in 1998. It offered a shorter path from the Caspian region to refineries in Germany and Slovenia than transporting oil by tanker out of the Black Sea and via a circuitous route to ports in the northern Adriatic Sea, where the oil was offloaded and piped north. Ukrainian officials believed an Odesa-Brody pipeline would yield significant transit revenues.

Moscow, however, sought to keep as much Caspian oil and gas flowing through Russian pipelines as possible and did not like the Odesa-Brody project. BP Amoco had expressed interest in 1999 in bringing Caspian oil from the port of Supsa, Georgia, to Odesa as a test run, but the company could not send an 80,000-ton tanker to Odesa because it was not clear that the Odesa port had the capacity to offload and store 80,000 tons of oil. The embassy had received a report that a Russian company stored oil at Odesa purposely to reduce the port's offloading capacity. I shared this information with Ukrainian officials, including some in the Presidential Administration, since they would have to sort the question out.

The U.S. Trade Development Agency funded a grant for a study of the economic feasibility of an Odesa-Brody pipeline, which the Ukrainians by 2000 had already started building on their own. The agency completed the study in the spring of 2000. It indicated that, if Ukraine could line up suppliers for oil and refineries in Central Europe to buy it, an Odesa-Brody pipeline would make commercial sense. Oddly, having received a report that could attract investor interest, the Ukrainian government did not seem eager to release it. I ended up lobbying the foreign ministry and the National Security and Defense Council to make the report public. The foreign ministry wanted to get the report out—and Chalyy worked hard to do so—but other parts of the government opposed the release, for no apparent good reason (the embassy wondered about possible Russian influence).

The Ukrainians finally did release the report but, in the end, completed the pipeline themselves without seeking foreign investment. They finished the project by early 2002, without having signed up a supplier or oil refineries to which the oil could be shipped. The newly completed pipeline sat empty until mid-2004, when the Russians and Ukrainians agreed to use the pipeline to ship oil in the reverse direction, from Brody to Odesa. Those shipments yielded transit revenues, but the pipeline lost its potential as a means to integrate Ukraine into Europe's energy network (at least until 2011, when the pipeline began moving Caspian oil from Odesa to Brody, as had been the original intent.)

One area where reform seemed to go completely wrong was agriculture, when the Presidential Administration issued Presidential Decree 832, entitled "On Immediate Measures to Stimulate Production and to Develop the Grain Market."[30] The decree reinstituted state grain orders and restricted grain movements, including grain for export, just a couple of months after the government had announced that it would not intervene in the grain market. Bankova released the decree without normal consultations with the cabinet. Rybachuk told me in early July that the cabinet was unaware of the decree until it had become public.

The Presidential Administration also had not consulted with the IMF, World Bank, or international providers of agricultural reform assistance, and they were angry. The IMF believed Decree 832 directly contradicted the conditions for the EFF. I joined IMF senior resident representative Henri Ghesquiere and World Bank country chief Gregory Jedrzejczak in a July 12 call on Presidential Administration deputy head Pavlo Haydutskyy. We raised concerns about both the process by which the decree had been adopted and the substance, which set back the introduction of market principles in the agricultural sector. Ghesquiere and Jedrzejczak said the decree contradicted specific guarantees Kyiv had given to their institutions.

The weak harvest shaping up for the summer of 2000—less than 25 million tons of grain—had unnerved the government, which now sought to purchase grain and hold down exports so as to keep domestic bread prices low. Haydutskyy defended the decree and claimed that it had been agreed with the ministry of agriculture, contradicting what the embassy and international financial institutions had been told by the cabinet of ministers. He said the decree's goal was to "slow down" grain exports given the weak harvest.

The decree suppressed prices that farmers could earn for their grain, which would continue to hold back development of the agriculture sector. Ghesquiere warned that the decree could endanger the EFF, and Jedrzejczak said it could block several World Bank projects. In addition, the decree endangered all U.S. government technical assistance in the agricultural sector.

Ghesquiere, Jedrzejczak, and I met with Yekhanurov, Haydutskyy, and Deputy Prime Minister Mykhaylo Hladiy on July 25 to again discuss Decree 832. The Ukrainian officials wanted to avoid the 1999 experience, when grain was exported but then had to be bought back at a higher price. We replied that the decree would prevent the development of normal market mechanisms, while also suppressing prices for grain producers. Yushchenko joined the meeting toward the end and said Ukraine did not intend to dismantle market mechanisms, but the meeting concluded with no resolution.

USAID experts reported on August 1 on the decree's negative impact. The state-owned Khlib Ukrayiny (Bread of Ukraine) company appeared to be the only entity authorized to buy grain in those oblasts with surplus production. The absence of competing grain buyers meant farmers received lower prices. The decree continued to be a problem into September and for years thereafter. USAID responded by reprogramming funds to directly assist private farmers and other private actors in the agricultural sector.

Another U.S. assistance project ran into difficulty that summer, the program to help Ukraine qualify an alternative supplier of nuclear fuel for the country's reactors. Westinghouse had shipped a trailer full of diagnostic equipment to Ukraine to run a fuel flow test on a working reactor. That would give Westinghouse the data it needed to produce nuclear fuel rods compatible with Ukraine's reactors. But the test program had run into multiple problems. Customs officials had not cleared the test equipment, and others told Westinghouse that they needed Russian permission to use a fresh fuel rod assembly for the flow test. The Russians had no incentive to provide such permission; why would they want to help Westinghouse end their monopoly?

In August the customs question was resolved, but only after Tymoshenko intervened. The Ukrainians still had to secure permission from the Russians to use a fresh (Russian-provided) fuel assembly for the test, and a new problem arose. Westinghouse had concluded a confidentiality agreement with its designated Ukrainian counterpart, the Center for Reactor Core Design. Westinghouse considered the test results proprietary information, which it would share only with the center. But the fuel and energy ministry and Enerhoatom, the state company responsible for operating Ukraine's nuclear plants, wanted access to the test results, which Westinghouse declined to provide. If the Ukrainian government sought to force Westinghouse to share the results with Enerhoatom, it would delay the project. The matter acquired urgency, as the embassy learned that Westinghouse was considering pulling the test equipment to use elsewhere. (Westinghouse finally secured a contract to supply fuel rods years later in 2008, with a major extension of the contract in 2014 following the Maydan Revolution.)

The President and the Prime Minister

Western embassies continued to receive reports of discord between the Presidential Administration and the cabinet of ministers. By the second half of June, a close adviser to Yushchenko described the relationship between the two institutions as "open war," asserting that the state-owned UT-1 television channel and people close to Kuchma were leading the public charge to undermine the prime minister. New irritants had arisen: Bankova had begun telling Yushchenko that he had to attend meetings and other events on an hour's notice. The adviser held Surkis, Medvedchuk, and Volkov responsible; they feared Yushchenko would run for president in 2004 and sought to damage his public popularity.

In a mid-July meeting I asked Moroz about rumors that Yushchenko was about to be fired. He thought Yushchenko was trying to make the economy more transparent by disregarding the interests of various oligarchs. But the prime minister had to depend on a majority in the Rada that was pro-Kuchma, not pro-cabinet. Moroz believed Kuchma saw Yushchenko as a potential political rival; he added that people close to the president—including Surkis, Medvedchuk, and Volkov—strongly opposed the prime minister.

At about the same time, a senior cabinet official said Yushchenko had directly asked Kuchma to order the Presidential Administration to stop undercutting the cabinet, saying he was prepared to resign. That seemed to have some effect. And Yushchenko, who at first had refused to meet with most oligarchs, sat down with Volkov and Bakay in an effort to smooth things over with Kuchma's people, though he refused to meet with Surkis. The official added that the Presidential Administration now had it in for Tymoshenko, who had burnt a lot of bridges within the government, to say nothing of oligarchs with ties to the president.

Other officials downplayed the differences. Chalyy dismissed the reports as simply a public relations spat. Presidential Administration deputy head Vasyl Rohovyy claimed that Bankova sought ways to work better with the cabinet and support its program. Yet Presidential Administration sniping at the cabinet only seemed to increase, and Western embassies began hearing rumors about Tymoshenko's future status and Yushchenko's readiness to resign. Bankova officials asserted that Kuchma's criticism of the cabinet was aimed at accelerating reform and did not signal an intention to change the cabinet. From the outside, however, there was little evidence that the president supported his prime minister.

Yushchenko told me in early August that he had spoken to Kuchma several times about the Presidential Administration's criticism and expressed frustration that it continued. He did not hold Kuchma responsible for this, blaming instead Medvedchuk and Surkis. Tensions only seemed to escalate. In August, *Kiyevskiye Vedomosti* (Kyiv News), a paper close to Kuchma's inner circle, ran an article charging that Yushchenko worked under the influence of the U.S. and German governments and verbally attacked his wife, an American citizen. A cabinet official noted that the general prosecutor—who reported to the president—wanted to question Tymoshenko after arresting her husband. He complained that Kuchma's chief of staff constantly overruled cabinet proposals for administrative reform, while the Presidential Administration gave the cabinet no credit and downplayed its accomplishments. Sadly, this report of internal infighting tracked with what the embassy heard elsewhere.

One Rada deputy seemed to capture accurately Yushchenko's pluses and minuses, as seen in the parliament. On the plus side, the prime minister was reform-minded and analytical, understood finance, and had the public's confidence. On the negative side, the cabinet was disorganized, the prime minister did not understand industry, and he did not have his own team. Moreover, Tymoshenko was a minus in the parliament because of her link to Lazarenko (who was then awaiting trial in the United States). The clash between the Presidential Administration and cabinet stemmed partly from concern about Yushchenko's popularity, partly from the circle around Kuchma that disliked the prime minister and his reforms.

Tihipko was back in the private sector after having resigned as minister of economy in July, reportedly owing to clashes with Tymoshenko. He apportioned a large share of the blame to Yushchenko, who he said had to work more actively with the Rada majority and do a better job at playing the political game. Tihipko felt the Presidential Administration was right to criticize. He nevertheless believed Yushchenko had a bit more time—Kuchma had never initiated dismissal of a prime minister in less than one year—but expected that the Rada would turn Yushchenko out in March 2001. Still, he urged that the United States support him.

Against this backdrop of unsettled relations between Kuchma and Yushchenko, Dan Fried, Sestanovich's principal deputy, arrived on September 20 with one central message: the reform process had stalled, there was uncertainty whether Kuchma supported his prime minister, and the U.S. government had become concerned over differences between the Presidential Administration and the cabinet. Kuchma had the political power, and he needed to use it to back Yushchenko and his reforms. Fried hammered that message home in meetings with Marchuk, Yekhanurov, Chalyy, Tymoshenko, Rohovyy, Lytvyn, and others.

Fried's message was clear, but the responses provided little encouragement. Presidential Administration officials denied that internal differences posed a serious problem, dismissed rumors that Kuchma would fire Yushchenko, and suggested that the influence of the oligarchs on Kuchma was overstated. After two days of talks, Fried left Kyiv with a less-than-optimistic sense of where Ukraine's internal politics and reform were headed. Ten days after Fried's departure, Yushchenko played down any differences with the Presidential Administration and said he regarded Kuchma as an ally. His assertions did not sound true.

Ukraine, the West, and Growing Anxiety about Russia

As the memory of the previous year's NATO air campaign against Serbia faded in 2000, Kyiv pressed forward with the European vector of its foreign policy. In January, Tarasyuk told me that he wanted to deepen NATO-Ukraine relations but that Kyiv had to move carefully in view of Russian sensitivities. NATO secretary general George Robertson paid a visit to Kyiv in late January. He found Ukrainian officials keen on developing relations with the alliance but not focused on specific goals; the Ukrainians seemed content to let NATO drive the process. He noted that Tarasyuk had raised the prospect of ultimate membership but thought the foreign minister was on the leading edge within the government.

During an early February meeting with Sestanovich, Tarasyuk gave a positive assessment of NATO-Ukraine relations. As Vershbow had done the year before, Sestanovich stressed the need for more work on practical developments. When NATO ambassadors came from Brussels to Kyiv in March for a meeting of the NATO-Ukraine Commission, they also noted the need to implement the programs that had been agreed to and to emphasize quality rather than quantity.

In February 2000, I hosted Richard Morningstar, who had left his position as assistance coordinator to become the U.S. ambassador to the European Union. Morningstar was well known in Ukraine, and I thought he might give the Ukrainians useful advice on how to engage the European Union more effectively. Morningstar had meetings throughout the government. He urged the Ukrainians not to expect a change in the EU's reluctance to state that Kyiv had a prospect of membership. Ukraine needed to take practical steps, including full implementation of its 1994 partnership and cooperation agreement, to change skeptical views in Brussels. Tarasyuk expressed concern that the Europeans lacked a strategic vision for Ukraine. He was correct, but he took Morningstar's point about the importance of Kyiv doing its homework.

Given Morningstar's past work with Yushchenko, the embassy requested a brief courtesy call. We ended up spending more than an hour-and-a-half there, as the prime minister reviewed in great detail the state of reform. We were grateful for the meeting but wondered whether such a long session was the best use of his time, particularly since his staff kept coming in to remind him that he was late for a press conference.

As for Russia, the Ukrainian government took a less benign view of the change in leadership in the Kremlin than did Washington. Putin's surprise ascent to the Russian presidency left the Ukrainians with a sense of unease. Yeltsin had been a known quantity. Whatever his foibles, Kyiv could count on him when it came to what the Ukrainians regarded as the most important issue in their relations with Moscow: recognition of Ukraine's sovereignty and territorial integrity. Yeltsin had regularly said the right thing on these questions when Russian Duma members challenged the status of Sevastopol and Crimea.

The Ukrainians were more wary of Putin. In February, Tarasyuk complained to me about the tough positions Moscow had taken on issues with Kyiv. He expressed concern about an information campaign to make the Russian language a political issue. Moscow, moreover, was dragging its heels on delimiting the state border in the Azov Sea and the Kerch Strait as well as on the question of a Commonwealth of Independent States (CIS) free trade zone. He found Putin more dynamic and shrewder than Yeltsin and predicted that Putin would not be an easy partner.

Putin paid a visit to Kyiv on April 17. Kuchma and Putin praised the state of Ukraine-Russia relations, though they noted some problem issues, including Kyiv's outstanding gas debt. Kuchma even acknowledged that Ukraine had siphoned off gas from transit pipelines that had been bound for Central Europe. Putin traveled with Kuchma to Sevastopol on April 18. In Sevastopol harbor, the two presidents met on board the flagships of the Ukrainian navy and the Russian Black Sea Fleet, which had moored side-by-side for the occasion. Putin acknowledged Ukraine's sovereignty over the harbor city and the Crimean Peninsula (something about which he would change his mind fourteen years later).

Chalyy provided a read-out after Putin had departed. The Ukrainians thought that the new Russian president showed a mix of "old think" and some readiness to change positions. Kuchma had pressed Putin not to exclude so many Ukrainian goods from the free trade regime, but the Russian had responded that Moscow needed the customs duties. Putin wanted to resolve Ukraine's outstanding debts to Russia and proposed that Kyiv either pay up or transfer physical assets of equivalent value to Russian control. The sides agreed there were no major problems regarding the Black Sea Fleet's presence in Crimea, though the Ukrainians had proposed procedures that would give them a say over modernization of the fleet's weapons and had suggested a mechanism to "coordinate" when Russian ships deployed from Crimea in a crisis. Interestingly, the Ukrainians heard no complaints from Putin about their relationship with NATO or the Euro-Atlantic vector of Kuchma's foreign policy.

Irritants continued to dog the Ukraine-Russia relationship. Tarasyuk told me in mid-July that Kyiv had protested Russian charges that ethnic Russians and Russian-speakers were being discriminated against in Ukraine. He felt that Moscow sought to create an artificial issue and wondered if such allegations would be part of a tougher Putin line toward Ukraine.

Kyiv remained leery of the CIS as an institution. Kuchma hosted an informal CIS summit in Yalta in mid-August, where the workings of the CIS free trade zone were discussed. Kyiv remained dissatisfied that so many of its exports to Russia could not enter duty-free. Orel told me that Kyiv had hoped to make the CIS—which he referred to as a "virtual" organization—something real based on a genuine free trade zone, but the Ukrainians did not get far. In their bilateral meeting, Kuchma had complained about the trade problems. Kyiv believed Putin's main goal was to draw Ukraine closer to Russia.

Natural gas sales and gas transit remained key issues in the Ukraine-Russia relationship. Ukraine imported about 75 percent of its gas from Russia or from Central Asian states through Russia. Kyiv balanced this, however, by transporting most of the gas that Russia's Gazprom sold to Germany, Austria, Italy, and other European countries—making up well over half of Gazprom's revenues—through Ukrainian pipelines. Big money was involved, and Ukrainian officials regularly complained that Gazprom charged Kyiv European prices, or even more, for the gas that Ukraine consumed but paid considerably less than European tariff rates for transiting gas through Ukraine. In 2000, officials in Kyiv began to worry that Russia might build new pipelines circumventing Ukraine. Chalyy told me in August that the Poles had informed Kyiv that they were blocking a Russian proposal to build a new pipeline through Belarus and Poland.

Moscow scored a victory at the end of September when Kuchma dismissed Tarasyuk as foreign minister. Tarasyuk's contribution to shaping Ukraine's initial engagement with NATO and the European Union had won him no fans in Moscow. The embassy heard rumors that Tarasyuk had been forced out by Russian pressure, though foreign ministry officials denied that. Other rumors attributed his ouster to Kuchma's frustration over the slow pace of Euro-Atlantic integration—though that depended far more on democratic and economic reform than it did on the foreign ministry's actions—and the president's anger over a letter that the heads of the IMF and the EBRD plus the Canadian ambassador and I had signed expressing concern about budget reform, as if Tarasyuk was somehow supposed to stop it. When I met Tarasyuk a week later, he ruefully noted that he had not been a favorite in Russia but also suggested that Bankova had been unhappy with his inability to "restrain" foreign ambassadors from criticizing the government (I was fairly sure he included me in that group). He gently chided me for my comments regarding problems in the 1999 presidential election process and criticized the West for not being more supportive of the Yushchenko government.

Anatoliy Zlenko, who had served as independent Ukraine's first foreign minister, returned to the position. He and others said there would be no change in Ukraine's foreign policy approach, but he intended to give greater emphasis to the economic aspects and promote integration into the global economy. I encouraged that and, looking toward the U.S. presidential election, ventured that Kyiv's performance on its internal reforms would play a big part in shaping the new administration's view of Ukraine.

Heorhiy Gongadze Disappears

I was first interviewed by Heorhiy Gongadze in 1999, when he was with Radio Kontynent and found him to be an independent-minded and inquisitive journalist. He had written tough articles, including one that skewered Oleksandr Volkov, an associate of the president. On September 7, I saw Gongadze for an hour-long Internet dialogue at

Ukrayinska Pravda (Ukrainian Truth), Ukraine's first web-based news outlet. *Ukrayinska Pravda* had a modest launch; Gongadze said the website received about 4,000 hits per day, half of which came from outside the country.

The news of Gongadze's disappearance the night of September 16 shocked Kyiv.[31] His abduction (which it appeared to be) was much worse than the previous kinds of harassment that media critical of the government had faced. I took advantage of a September 18 meeting with Chalyy to urge that the authorities do everything that they could to locate the missing journalist. Later that week, Fried and I raised Gongadze at the Presidential Administration. Fried stressed the damage that the journalist's disappearance would do to Ukraine's image.

Western embassies discussed how they might press the Ukrainian government to make a genuine investigation, as the effort spearheaded by the ministry of internal affairs inspired little confidence. They also exchanged theories about who might be behind the disappearance. One held that an oligarch who had been a target of an unfavorable Gongadze story was responsible. Within the embassy, that was my initial view. Given the relatively limited reach of *Ukrayinska Pravda* at the time, it was hard to see why the Presidential Administration would move against him. That said, another rumor pointed directly at Bankova, alleging that Gongadze had come into possession of incriminating material on Kuchma. I used several departure interviews—my tour in Kyiv was coming to a close—to publicly urge the government to locate Gongadze, though hopes of a good outcome faded with each passing day. The embassy had Democracy Commission funds, from which it could make grants of up to $25,000 on its own authority. Just before completing my assignment and departing Kyiv, I signed off on approval of a $25,000 grant to *Ukrayinska Pravda*.

Carlos Pascual arrived in mid-October to take up his position as the fourth U.S. ambassador to Ukraine. He brought deep expertise on the country, having spent four years at the center of U.S. policy toward Ukraine at the National Security Council, first as director for Ukraine, then as senior director for Russia, Ukraine, and Eurasia. Before that he had served with USAID, which gave him a detailed understanding of reform requirements and how U.S. programs might assist.

Pascual arrived while the Gongadze disappearance was still dominating the news. He underscored that the U.S. government would closely follow the case, urged that the investigation be conducted with full transparency, and suggested that U.S. agencies could assist. Unfortunately, the ministry of internal affairs, SBU, and other officials seemed more intent on denying any government connection to the disappearance than on finding the missing journalist. The sad news broke in early November that Gongadze's decapitated corpse had been found in a forest south of Kyiv.

Later that month, Moroz charged Kuchma with responsibility for Gongadze's abduction and murder, releasing audio recordings that appeared to implicate the president or, at the least, senior members of his staff. Kuchma denied any responsibility and called the recordings fake, but the revelations touched off a firestorm. Rada members demanded explanations and held a special session on Gongadze on December 14. Internal Affairs Minister Yuriy Kravchenko, General Prosecutor Mykhaylo Potebenko, and SBU head Leonid Derkach again denied any government involvement, challenged the veracity of the recordings, and generally aimed at obfuscation. The Rada failed to pass a motion to begin an impeachment process against Kuchma, but demonstrations began several days later and continued into 2001 as the "Ukraine without Kuchma" protests.

Reflections

I concluded my assignment in Kyiv at the beginning of October. In line with tradition, I sent Washington an end-of-tour cable, summarizing my expectations for Ukraine and U.S.-Ukraine relations. The message noted that the key foreign policy challenges facing Kyiv were its uncertain relationship with Moscow—many Russians had still not come to terms with the fact that Ukraine was an independent state—and a European Union that was reluctant to fully embrace Ukraine. Kuchma's ambitions for his "multi-vector" policy with the United States, the European Union, and Russia were based in part on unrealistic expectations of support from Europe and the United States. But Kyiv saw the United States as the primary counterweight to an overbearing Russia, which should give Washington leverage.

The message identified the primary question, however, as how fast Ukraine would move on reform. Yushchenko understood the need and had a vision. But he lacked strong managerial skills and struggled to control the cabinet bureaucracy. Moreover, he had yet to show the political skills needed to deal with a Rada that was fractious and contained influential deputies who hoped to see him fail. Kuchma, however, posed the biggest question mark. He did not seem to be a reformer by nature, and the Presidential Administration had constantly undercut Yushchenko. Many in Kuchma's inner circle saw the prime minister as a threat and used their access to the president to turn him against Yushchenko. When Kuchma backed Yushchenko, he could deliver the Rada and get serious legislation passed. When Kuchma did not back Yushchenko, reform foundered. The trick for the U.S. government's effort to promote reform was to get Kuchma and Yushchenko to work together.

The message concluded that democratic development had had its ups and downs and predicted that democratic reform was unlikely to advance during the remaining years of Kuchma's presidency. The U.S. goal thus should strive to prevent the erosion of democratic norms, so that Ukrainians would have the opportunity in 2004 to vote in a free and fair election for their next leader. I expressed hope that he or she would prove to be a stronger agent for change than Ukraine's first two presidents had been.

U.S. diplomacy in the late 1990s succeeded in its primary foreign policy goal, to align U.S. and Ukrainian nonproliferation policies. As far as Washington could tell, Ukraine abided by its commitment to refrain from nuclear cooperation with Iran. U.S. diplomacy managed enough engagement with Kyiv regarding NATO's military action against Serbia to contain the damage that that action might otherwise have inflicted on the bilateral relationship. Kuchma remained interested in deepening Ukraine's links with the West, though it rankled in Kyiv that Washington and NATO did not find a more creative way to use Ukraine as a mediator with Serbia—and it rankled even more that Washington turned to the Russians to play such a role. It is not readily evident how Kyiv could have been engaged in the effort to resolve the Serbia conflict. But had we found a way to do so, Washington and NATO would have received credit from the Ukrainian leadership, and the Ukrainian government could have fended off public criticism of its closeness to the alliance when NATO was at war with Belgrade.

The United States probably could have done more to help make the bilateral relationship strategic and special to Kyiv, or at least to make it feel that way. While we had a fairly good record in the 1990s of high-level visits—by the president, the vice president, and Cabinet secretaries—Ukrainians had hoped for more. The problem, of course, was limited time on busy calendars. Gore did a lot; one of his foreign policy advisers once half-jokingly, half-seriously told me that it was important to keep the vice president's scheduling office from focusing on how much time he devoted to working on relations with countries such as Ukraine. At lower levels, the embassy tried to come up with other ways to fill out the relationship. For example, it suggested—but did not succeed in achieving—a set of regular talks between the policy planning staffs at the State Department and the ministry of foreign affairs. Such talks would not have had to address the burning issues of the moment, which often were problems, but could instead have taken a wider perspective and look forward.

More broadly, Kyiv still had not decided how far it wished to go with the West, with Kuchma's multi-vector foreign policy suggesting that the president continued to favor a balance between the West (Europe and the United States) and Russia. While giving weight to Kyiv's relationship with Moscow, Ukrainian officials saw more quickly than their American counterparts that Putin's ascent to the presidency boded problems for the future, though no one in 2000 in a serious position in Kyiv foresaw what would happen in 2014.

The U.S. government was far less successful at getting Ukraine to move on internal change. Questions had begun to arise about Kuchma's readiness to embrace democratic norms. The 1998 Rada elections had shown some problems, but the 1999 presidential election featured significantly worse abuses of administrative resources and resort to nondemocratic means to boost Kuchma's candidacy. U.S. interventions, both private and later public, had little visible impact, other than possibly dissuading the government from even more egregious electoral violations. To those of us in the embassy, the Kuchma government's electoral misdeeds seemed unnecessary, as Kuchma appeared to have the greatest amount of popular support. Once it became clear that the center-left would not unite behind a single candidate, the embassy expected Kuchma to handily win in a second-round runoff.

Following the 1999 election, the *Financial Times* revelations in early 2000 wrong-footed Yushchenko's prime ministership from the beginning. When he later recovered, however, differences with Bankova began to emerge. By late spring, Yushchenko and Kuchma were not working on the same page. Lacking the president's political support, particularly in the Rada, Yushchenko faced an uphill fight in most of his reform battles. The situation grew so alarming over the summer that Fried came out from Washington solely to reiterate the embassy's urgings that the Presidential Administration should support the prime minister and cabinet.

U.S. officials had begun to appreciate more fully just how hard getting Ukraine on a real reform path would be, and that it would require pressing Ukraine's senior leadership to do things that it did not want to do. Too many oligarchs had close ties to Bankova and were positioned to impede changes that would negatively affect their personal economic interests. While a FREEDOM Support Act appropriation of $225 million was serious assistance money, it flowed to a diffuse set of recipients, many of whom were American consultants and contractors, and much of the money spent inside Ukraine went to civil society rather than the government. The oligarchs, on the other hand, had hundreds of millions of dollars at stake and mobilized accordingly to protect their interests.

Could Washington have weighed in more heavily with Kuchma on the democracy issue or the need to work with Yushchenko on reform? A string of assistant secretary and deputy assistant secretary–level officials from Washington reinforced the embassy's messages on these points, but the level was not the right one. Clinton and Gore met with and spoke by phone to Kuchma, but it would have been unrealistic to find time for them to hammer the democracy and reform messages home on a continuing basis.

Likewise, could we have weighed in more successfully with Kuchma on the need to fight corruption? Although senior U.S. officials raised the issue, we never seemed to find a message that had resonance at Bankova and among the elite connected to the president. Moreover, while the split between Kuchma and Yushchenko was easy to discern, the U.S. government had less information on the specifics of corruption than many Ukrainians assumed. Lazarenko moved tens of millions of dollars through American banks and left behind a paper trail, acts that landed him in a U.S. federal prison. But American officials rarely had such clarity about other corruption schemes. For example, it was clear that Kuchma tolerated people around him who were corrupt, but the embassy had no clear picture as to how personally corrupt the president himself might be.

Clinton and Gore had significant face-to-face time with Kuchma, but corruption, democracy, and reform were only three topics on a long list of issues. And when it came to tough problems, the Americans often spoke with a subtle voice that was intended to convey their message in diplomatic terms; the message might have been too subtle for Ukrainian ears, especially when delivered by interpreters. In any case, interactions at the highest level, even in the best of times, numbered only three or four meetings per year. Looking back, I wonder if I could have developed a closer connection to Kuchma or his inner circle at Bankova, but it was not easy to see how to forge a relationship that would allow open discussion of such sensitive issues as corruption. After my late 1999 Shevchenko University speech, there was no chance.

One thing that contributed to the difficulty in engaging Bankova was that the Presidential Administration's inner workings fed Kuchma strange information at times. In the spring of 1999, Horbulin asked me if the U.S. energy secretary planned to snub Kuchma during an upcoming visit. Nothing was further from the truth, and I was glad that Horbulin could set the record straight, but the embassy wondered where Bankova got such an idea. Kuchma likewise was badly misinformed about U.S. policy during the 1999 presidential election campaign. He believed Washington supported Moroz. The U.S. government supported Moroz's right to run and to expect an even playing field, but few if any U.S. officials thought that Moroz's socialist policies would benefit Ukraine. A Ukrainian paper reported in May 2001 that, according to one of the recordings made in the president's office in the summer of 2000, Dmytro Tabachnyk gave Kuchma a detailed account of his meeting in Washington with the U.S. deputy secretary of state. That was odd, since Talbott had not met with Tabachnyk in more than five years.

One card that the U.S. government could have played more aggressively was visa denials to the oligarchs and others known to be corrupt. CIA director Tenet's private message to Marchuk that Bakay, Rabynovych, and Volkov should not bother to apply for visas was promptly leaked to the media by a Ukrainian source and generated a lot of attention. The embassy felt that greater use of visa sanctions would have a noticeable impact. I explored the possibility with my British, German, and French counterparts, but they were not ready to pursue a joint approach. There was also a problem with the State Department's Bureau of Consular Affairs, which required a strong evidentiary case for putting an individual on a visa ban list.

The difficulty of preventing someone from getting a visa was illustrated in early 2000. Hryhoriy Surkis applied for a visa in order to attend the National Prayer Breakfast organized by Congress. Given Surkis's reputation, neither the embassy nor the National Security Council wanted to run the risk that he might encounter the president and have a photo snapped on the margins of the breakfast. Consular procedures did not allow us to deny the visa because the evidentiary case had not—yet—been assembled. So, after consulting with Washington, the embassy's consular section informed Surkis that he could receive a visa, but it would only be issued after the date of the prayer breakfast.

The late 1990s revealed the dysfunctional nature of the Ukrainian government in resolving certain problems. The business dispute cases illustrate the point. Many could have been settled at relatively low cost. Not addressing them put at risk hundreds of millions of dollars in U.S. assistance and also did enormous reputational damage to Ukraine's investment climate. Few Ukrainian officials seemed to grasp how costly a businessman's letter of complaint to a member of Congress or a negative story in the *Wall Street Journal* could turn out to be. Likewise, being "off-cover" with OPIC meant not only no insurance for U.S. companies who wished to make investments in Ukraine, but it contributed to the country's poor investment image. Yet, even when the embassy engaged at the deputy prime minister level and higher, the government could not settle more than a small handful of the disputes.

What the embassy heard instead was an expectation from officials close to the president that the United States would make a "political" decision to secure the necessary certification for Ukraine, despite the small number of resolved disputes. The fact that the State Department made the certifications likely contributed to a view in Kyiv that Washington could—and would—make a political decision, even if there was scant real progress to report.

Differing expectations about what the U.S. government could and could not do led to frustration over the Kharkiv initiative. Local Kharkiv officials and Turboatom's management seemed to assume that Washington could order private American businesses to invest in Kharkiv or partner with Turboatom, perhaps because of the close relationships they saw between major Ukrainian companies and the government. But Washington had no such influence with American companies. What U.S. assistance programs could do—place international marketing expertise with Turboatom, help Kharkiv set up an office to assist potential investors, and sponsor a Ukrainian investment mission to the United States—fell far short of local expectations. On the one hand, we wanted to portray measures such as the Kharkiv initiative as large and important, in order to help Kuchma and his government justify their cancellation of the Turboatom contract. On the other hand, perhaps we should have been more explicit at the start about the limitations on what the U.S. government realistically could do, in order to keep expectations in check.

When Kyiv was "off-program" with the International Monetary Fund, IMF officials in Kyiv would lay out the steps necessary to get back on track and resume the flow of IMF credits. They often found, however, that the government was incapable of coordinating the necessary actions. We saw this in bilateral assistance programs as well. As part of the Defense Department's effort to help the Ukrainian military, it provided several million dollars each year to buy fuel from local sources for the Ukrainian army and navy to use to prepare for and conduct joint exercises with U.S. forces. But the State Tax Administration insisted on taxing that assistance. The embassy worried that, if Congress learned U.S. assistance was being taxed, it would cut the assistance. This problem seemed beyond the ability of the Ukrainian government to fix. The embassy finally had to threaten to cut off the fuel funding, and the State Department withdrew tax-free benefits for Ukrainian diplomats in Washington. The problem should have been fixed well before that, but the State Tax Administration wanted its piece of the pie, even if that might mean the pie would be taken away. Motivating the Ukrainian government to overrule the tax authorities so that the military could receive badly needed funding required extraordinary steps. And the U.S. record of motivating the government to resolve business disputes was not a positive one.

Looking back, perhaps the U.S. government should have considered a program to help Bankova and the cabinet of ministers come up with a more workable structure, one that would ensure that decisions were taken—and implemented—on the basis of what was good for Ukraine as a whole rather than on what was good for a particular ministry or agency. Designing such a program could have been tricky. Several years later, after I had retired from government, I became involved in a project to recommend to the Ukrainians a National Security Council–like structure, but the recommendation did not acquire any traction. Some recognized the problem, though; early during the Yushchenko presidency following the Orange Revolution, I was in Kyiv and ran into John Podesta and Mike McCurry, White House chief of staff and White House spokesperson, respectively, during the Clinton years. They had been brought to Ukraine to consult with the president's office on ways to make the office function more effectively.

CHAPTER 5

Coping with Downturn

The year 2000 ended on an uncertain note for U.S.-Ukraine relations, with a new administration set to take over in Washington.
The years 2001 and 2002 proved even more difficult for the bilateral
relationship, which went into a steady downturn as new problems
arose and few solutions were found. By the end of 2002, the relationship
had hit its lowest point since Ukraine regained independence in 1991. It
was so difficult that President Leonid Kuchma told a December 2002
press conference in Kyiv that the year's "most difficult thing is the worsening of relations with the United States. The main task for me as president will be to solve this problem."[1]

Initial Contacts with the Bush Administration

On January 20, 2001, George W. Bush took office as the forty-third
president of the United States, following a controversial and drawn-
out fight over the vote count in Florida. The Ukrainian government
probably had hoped for a victory by Al Gore. After all, the outgoing

vice president had taken a keen interest in Ukraine during his eight years in office and had a well-established relationship with Kuchma.

On November 8, 2000, the day after the U.S. election—though the results were in dispute—Ukraine's presidential spokesperson, Oleksandr Martynenko, stated that Kyiv hoped that "the new U.S. presidential administration will continue . . . to deepen the strategic partnership with Ukraine."[2] The previous day, Kuchma had said U.S. policy regarding Ukraine would not change and added, "The policy will not change until we have changed ourselves."[3] He was largely correct. Although Bush had said little specifically about Ukraine or U.S.-Ukraine relations during the campaign, nothing in the Republican's campaign had suggested that the presidential transition would produce a major shift in the American approach to Kyiv.

In Ukraine, the bloom had come off of the prime ministership of Viktor Yushchenko. Divisions between the Presidential Administration at Bankova and the cabinet, which had begun to emerge in 2000, had grown wider. "Ukraine without Kuchma" protests continued during the first three months of 2001. U.S. ambassador Carlos Pascual found the political scene chaotic. There was constant speculation over how long Yushchenko would last. The embassy heard that Kuchma wanted Yushchenko to split with Deputy Prime Minister Yuliya Tymoshenko, which the prime minister refused to do. His support for Tymoshenko and refusal to take on Sergey Tihipko as deputy prime minister reportedly further displeased Kuchma.

However, at the behest of the Presidential Administration, Tymoshenko—widely seen as the most effective of Yushchenko's ministers—was fired on January 19. Her reforms of the energy sector apparently had had too great an impact on the interests of influential oligarchs around Kuchma. She was arrested in early February and briefly detained, in what many regarded as an effort to intimidate the president's political opponents.

Pascual called on the government to strengthen its commitment to the rule of law. He stated, "Ukraine has to make decisions on how it is going to deal with this political instability and uncertainty, and whether it is going to continue to keep itself on the path to an independent, democratic, and market-oriented state."[4] The March 1 dispersal of a demonstration in Kyiv drew public criticism from the State Department. Spokesperson Richard Boucher said Pascual had conveyed an oral message from Bush to Kuchma that called the crisis "a test of [Ukraine's leaders'] commitment to the rule of law, democracy, and human rights" and said "success in reaching that goal [of an independent, democratic, and market-oriented Ukraine] and our ability to provide support towards that goal depend on Ukraine's taking concrete steps towards meaningful reform."[5] The protests faded away during the month of March, but U.S. officials remained wary of Kuchma's political tendencies.

On April 26, Yushchenko himself was gone, fired after a vote of no confidence by the Rada. The vote was spearheaded by the Communists, who were joined by many other Rada deputies in groups beholden to oligarchs and other moneyed interests who did not support Yushchenko's reforms. Bankova did nothing to mobilize votes to block the prime minister's dismissal. Oleh Rybachuk, Yushchenko's chief of staff, said the vote was "not a big surprise" as there has been "a very strange alliance forming up based on the Communists . . . and of the new Ukrainian business elite or business clans group, sometimes called pro-presidential."[6] Many attributed the sacking to concern on the part of the Presidential Administration about Yushchenko's popularity as well as to Kuchma's desire to have someone closer to him in the job, particularly with Rada elections scheduled for early 2002.

Washington took Yushchenko's long-rumored ouster in stride. The State Department's acting spokesperson said the U.S. government had "enjoyed good working relations with the Yushchenko government, and we look forward to similar close cooperation with Ukraine's new government." The spokesperson went on to note U.S. support for "an independent, democratic, and market-oriented Ukraine committed to the rule of law and integrated in the Euro-Atlantic community" and called for continued reform.[7]

As Yushchenko's prime ministership entered its final ten days, Major Mykola Melnychenko, the source of the previous November's recordings from Kuchma's presidential office, was granted political asylum by the U.S. Immigration and Naturalization Service. Melnychenko claimed to have 1,000 hours of recordings and had given some of them, notably some involving Heorhiy Gongadze, to Socialist Party head Oleksandr Moroz, who made them public.[8] (In May 2001, FBI analysis confirmed that the headless body found the previous November was indeed Gongadze's.)

Asylum cases are normally handled on a close-hold basis within the U.S. government. The primary question is whether the applicant has a legitimate fear of political persecution at home. John Beyrle, the acting coordinator for the New Independent States at the State Department, received little notice before the news broke publicly on April 16. The Ukrainian government reacted quickly and angrily and summoned Pascual to the foreign ministry, where Foreign Minister Anatoly Zlenko personally delivered the protest.

Kyiv appeared especially concerned that Melnychenko's recordings might fall into the hands of the U.S. government. Ambassador Kostyantyn Hryshchenko met with Deputy Secretary of State Richard Armitage, who assured Hryshchenko that the U.S. government did not intend to exploit the recordings. Although the recordings suggested that misdeeds had occurred, perhaps even criminal activity by senior Ukrainian officials, Washington took the view that any crimes were violations of Ukrainian law; it therefore was up to the Ukrainians to sort matters out. Kyiv nevertheless remained displeased, and Pascual found himself persona non grata with certain parts of the government; it would be many months before he could meet again with Kuchma. The embassy believed the president took the asylum decision as a personal slap and that it played a role in the Rada's vote of no confidence in Yushchenko. The Trudovaya Ukraina (Working Ukraine) party, which had close connections to the president, pulled its support for the prime minister and sealed his fate in the vote. That action may have been intended as a measure of revenge since Kuchma believed the Americans regarded Yushchenko as "our guy."

Despite the early bump, Bush made clear his administration's interest in Ukraine in a speech in Warsaw on June 15. He stated, "The Europe we are building must include Ukraine, a nation struggling with the trauma of transition. Some in Kyiv speak of their country's European destiny. If this is their aspiration, we should reward it. We must extend our hand to Ukraine, as Poland has already done with such determination." Earlier in the speech the president expressed his view that NATO membership should be open to "all of Europe's democracies that seek it and are ready to share the responsibility that NATO brings. The question of when may still be up for debate within NATO, the question of whether should not be."[9] That sentiment did not go down well with Russian president Vladimir Putin, into whose eyes Bush would look the next day in Ljubljana.

I returned to the State Department as deputy assistant secretary in the Bureau of European and Eurasian Affairs on July 16, where I took up responsibilities for Russia, Ukraine, Moldova, and Belarus. I traveled almost immediately to Kyiv with National Security Adviser Condoleezza Rice and her senior adviser on European questions, Dan Fried, who had moved over from the State Department. Rice's visit was the first to Ukraine by a senior official of the Bush administration. Although the Gongadze murder, Melnychenko recordings, and firing of Yushchenko had caused Washington to worry about Ukraine's direction, especially on democracy questions, it nevertheless remained interested in engagement. U.S. officials hoped to find a way to move the relationship in a more positive direction and encourage Kuchma to adopt a more democratic course. Rice planned to explore the possibilities for doing so.

The national security adviser met with Kuchma on July 25 at Bankova. Her opening points noted that Washington believed democracy was key to Ukraine's ability to draw closer to Europe and thus Kuchma should lead his country down the democratic path, in particular by ensuring free and fair Rada elections in early 2002. Rice raised the Gongadze case. Kuchma replied that Ukrainian law enforcement agencies would solve the journalist's murder, adding that the Ukrainian government had hired Kroll Associates, an American company with expertise in private investigations, to assist.

Kuchma continued that he saw no alternative for Ukraine other than its "European vector." He reiterated his long-standing frustration that the European Union had declined to give Kyiv a signal about the possibility of EU membership, which he described as Ukraine's ultimate goal. Rice raised the question of energy security, noting the importance for Ukraine of the Odesa-Brody oil pipeline, which could tie Ukraine and Europe more closely in their energy relations.

Rice also suggested Ukraine consider assembling an international consortium to run its natural gas pipelines, reinforcing a proposal that Pascual had been pressing for more than half a year. On his arrival, Pascual had pushed for reform of the energy sector, stressing the importance of Ukraine strengthening its energy security situation. Kyiv had made progress in the electric power sector, and Pascual urged that Kyiv focus next on reforming its gas transportation and distribution network, the network of pipelines that moved gas to Ukrainian consumers—industrial, commercial, and residential—as well as transporting more than 100 billion cubic meters of gas each year from Russia to other countries in Europe. Kyiv needed to invest to maintain and upgrade the pipelines, in order to reliably move gas to Central and Western Europe. The proposal pressed by Pascual suggested that an international consortium assume management of the gas transit pipelines. The consortium could involve Naftohaz (the Ukrainian company overseeing the pipelines), the Russian energy giant Gazprom, and a Western European energy company. It could run the pipelines as a long-term concession, with ownership remaining fully in Ukrainian hands. Rice shared a paper prepared by Pascual and the embassy staff on how such an arrangement would work.

Rice raised U.S. and NATO concerns about Ukrainian transfers of tanks and other heavy weapons, including armored personnel carriers and helicopters, to Macedonia. In January 2001 the Albanian National Liberation Army had attacked Macedonian forces in the north of the country, demanding equal rights for the 25 percent of Macedonians who were ethnic Albanians. Subsequent fighting in the spring threatened to extend into a drawn-out conflict. The U.S. government and NATO worried that an influx of major weapons might fuel the internal fighting, just as the alliance was on the verge of deploying a stabilization force. Rice urged Kuchma to suspend the arms transfers, and Kuchma said he was prepared to do so.

The Ukrainians expressed interest in an early Kuchma-Bush meeting, noting that Kuchma could travel to New York in September for the annual United Nations General Assembly session. Rice suggested instead a short meeting between Bush, Kuchma, and Polish president Aleksander Kwasniewski—provided that Kyiv suspend its arms transfers to Macedonia and show progress on the Gongadze investigation. After she departed Kyiv, Pascual discussed with Presidential Administration officials what might constitute progress on Gongadze. He suggested that the general prosecutor could hold a press conference to outline where the investigation stood, and the Ukrainian government could request assistance from the Federal Bureau of Investigation. These steps did not set the bar particularly high, but they could open a more serious approach to the Gongadze case. Pascual pursued these ideas with Bankova officials through the rest of July and into August.

On her return to Washington, Rice wrote to Presidential Administration head Volodymyr Lytvyn, who had sat in on her meeting with Kuchma, to reiterate her understanding that Ukraine would immediately suspend arms transfers to Macedonia. Lytvyn's reply did not dispute that. However, notwithstanding the discussions in Kyiv and Lytvyn's letter—and despite additional assurances on August 24 by Kuchma to visiting Senator Richard Lugar and Assistant Secretary of State for European and Eurasian Affairs Beth Jones, who had traveled to Kyiv for the tenth anniversary of Ukraine's independence—the flow of Ukrainian weapons continued. (NATO had little trouble following the arms transfers, since the Ukrainian arms export agency shipped tanks and other heavy equipment via boat to Greece, a NATO member, where the vehicles were offloaded and transported by rail to Macedonia.) Frustration began to grow in Washington and at NATO that Kyiv had failed to abide by Kuchma's word.

During their visit, Lugar and Jones raised with Kuchma and other senior officials the importance of beginning work already in 2001 to lay the basis for a free and fair presidential election in 2004. Kuchma asked, with some exasperation, "Why are you pushing this now? The election is years from now." Jones responded, "We want to make sure that you know at this early stage how important this issue is for good U.S.-Ukraine relations, and we know that assuring a free and fair election takes a lot of work."

In early September, Pascual reported from Kyiv that there had been no progress on his suggestions regarding the Gongadze investigation. The White House nixed the idea of Bush meeting with Kuchma and Kwasniewski on the margins of the UN General Assembly meeting due to Kyiv's failure to follow up on the Macedonia arms transfer and Gongadze questions. The Ukraine interagency working group was authorized, however, to quietly consider the possibility of a visit by Kuchma to Washington in spring 2002, as long as progress could be made on key issues on the U.S.-Ukraine agenda.

Kroll Associates submitted its report at the end of September. Among other things, the report questioned whether Melnychenko could have made the recordings in the manner that he described. U.S.

officials did not find the report persuasive. Some believed it had been written with a predetermined goal of exonerating Kuchma.

September 11 and the Sibir Shootdown

The tragic September 11 terror attacks on the United States prompted an outpouring of sympathy in Ukraine. Kuchma immediately sent a telegram to Bush expressing his "deep grief and concern" and saying, "We feel this tragedy of the U.S. people together with you."[10] Zlenko led a delegation to the U.S. embassy to convey condolences. As one of the nonpermanent members of the UN Security Council, Ukraine called for an emergency meeting of that body to help coordinate "the efforts of the international community."[11]

Over the following week, the U.S. military began ramping up for operations against Afghanistan. Preparations accelerated as the Taliban government in Kabul ignored demands that it shut down the operations of al Qaeda, which had orchestrated the September 11 attacks. Pascual told Ukrainian officials, and I advised Hryshchenko, that Kyiv should be ready to receive a request, probably for clearance for U.S. Air Force overflights, that would require a rapid answer. On September 22, the State Department formally asked Pascual to transmit requests for over-flight clearances and possible landing and refueling rights. Kyiv promptly granted a blanket clearance for U.S. military aircraft, offering the use of three airfields. The Ukrainian government's rapid response won Kyiv credit in Washington, where smashing al Qaeda and the Taliban had become the number one priority. Soon thereafter, the first overflights took place.

Another tragedy struck the next month. Early on October 4, the State Department received word that Sibir 1812, a Russian Tu-154 air-liner flying from Tel Aviv to Novosibirsk with seventy-eight passengers and crew on board, had disappeared over the Black Sea. Coming so soon on the heels of September 11, many feared another terrorist attack. Shortly after the news came in, Debra Cagan, then director of the European and Eurasian Bureau's regional political-military affairs office, showed me information indicating the Ukrainian military had shot down the Sibir flight with a surface-to-air missile. Although the details could not be shared with the Ukrainians, the evidence was compelling. The assumption was that the Ukrainian military had made a horrible mistake.

I called Pascual and asked him to inform the Ukrainian government that U.S. information indicated the Ukrainian military had shot down the airliner and to urge Kyiv to say it was investigating the matter rather than denying involvement. I conveyed a similar message to Hryshchenko and cautioned that, for its credibility, the Ukrainian government should avoid a repeat of the April 2000 Brovary incident in which an object had struck an apartment building in Brovary, outside of Kyiv, killing three people. Although a military test range was located nearby, the ministry of defense denied any involvement—until firemen recovered from the wrecked building the tailfin and other fragments of a Ukrainian short-range surface-to-surface missile that had gone astray.

Hryshchenko asked that the U.S. government exercise caution in its public commentary. He was furious when, shortly thereafter, Department of Defense officials told the press on background that a Ukrainian missile had downed Sibir 1812. The Pentagon backgrounder aimed to put a halt to fears that a new terrorist attack had brought down the plane. At about the same time, the Ukrainian government in Kyiv denied any involvement.

A joint Russian-Ukrainian-Israeli investigation committee subsequently scoured the Black Sea for clues to the plane's downing. It located the wreckage and concluded that a Ukrainian missile had indeed brought the airliner down. (The U.S. belief was that the Ukrainians had fired a surface-to-air missile at a target drone. Although the Tu-154 airliner was miles farther away, it presented a larger radar target, and the missile ignored the drone, instead going after the Sibir flight.) Defense Minister Oleksandr Kuzmuk acknowledged responsibility on October 13, saying that an S-200 missile had been responsible. Kuchma issued a statement with his condolences and noted that Ukraine would "do everything possible to ease the suffering of the families of the victims."[12]

Establishing a High-Level Dialogue?

Kyiv continued to press for a high-level dialogue with Washington. The Bush White House showed no enthusiasm for continuing the binational commission, which Kuchma had chaired with Gore, though it did not object to continuing individual committees. On Pascual's recommendation, the U.S. government invited Anatoliy Kinakh, who had succeeded Yushchenko as prime minister. Kinakh's visit at the end of October focused on economic questions. It included a short meeting with Secretary of State Colin Powell and a brief videoconference with Vice President Dick Cheney, who spoke from a secure location outside Washington. Although these contacts raised the level of the bilateral dialogue, when I visited Kyiv in early December for a meeting of the foreign policy committee, securing additional high-level visits—in particular at the presidential level—topped the Ukrainian agenda. Lytvyn proposed a Kuchma visit to Washington, and Zlenko suggested that Powell travel to Kyiv.

I agreed to take the suggestions back to Washington but pointed out that continuing arms transfers to Macedonia remained a major problem. Zlenko asserted that there had been some misunderstanding: Kyiv supported the Macedonian government, believed NATO was pleased with what Ukraine was doing (the alliance decidedly was not), and felt that, if Ukraine did not arm the Macedonians, a less responsible actor would do so. He stated that Ukraine would proceed with delivery of some helicopters and armored personnel carriers that were in the pipeline but would not sign further contracts. Pascual and I noted that continuing deliveries to Macedonia remained problematic for the U.S. government and NATO, especially as it was inconsistent with the promise of an immediate halt that Rice thought she had received in July. (In early 2002, Ukraine finally stopped the transfers. Although U.S. and NATO officials welcomed this development, the fact that the transfers had continued for months after Kyiv first promised to end them damaged Ukraine's image in Washington and at NATO headquarters in Brussels.)

Pascual and I discussed the upcoming Rada elections with Zlenko and others, including Lytvyn. We noted that the elections provided an opportunity for Ukraine to demonstrate its commitment to democratic practices and improve its battered image. A good Rada election that met free and fair standards could clear the air between Kyiv and Washington.

As 2002 began, the run-up to the Rada elections was not going well. Kuchma and his government had thrown their support behind the For a United Ukraine Party, seen by many as the "party of power." The embassy reported sinking prospects for a level playing field. Opposition parties encountered problems gaining access to the media; the administration misused government resources for electoral purposes; and the Security Service of Ukraine and the State Tax Administration targeted opposition figures and their supporters. Independent Ukrainian watch groups reported similar disheartening developments. Meanwhile, Radio Liberty advised that it might lose access to its transmitters in Ukraine, and the government had become sensitive about the democracy-promotion efforts of the National Democratic Institute and the International Republican Institute. Pascual, in Washington for consultations in January, noted that Ukrainian officials were feeling unloved and might do some unfortunate things as a result.

In early February, former National Security and Defense Council secretary Volodymyr Horbulin, who continued to serve as a senior adviser in the Presidential Administration, visited Washington to discuss possible cooperation on missile defense, a high priority for the Bush administration. The Ukrainians knew a lot about missile technology. The Missile Defense Agency at the Pentagon saw cooperation as potentially useful; among other things, the Iranian and North Korean ballistic missiles that topped the list of U.S. concerns were based on Soviet SCUD missile technology, which was also familiar to Ukrainian missile experts. Horbulin had good talks, though they ultimately did not lead to the degree of cooperation that the Ukrainians sought.

Horbulin held a less senior position than he had in the 1990s, but Washington continued to regard him as a serious interlocutor. He had direct access to Kuchma. The Bureau of European and Eurasian Affairs arranged a meeting with Deputy Secretary of State Armitage. The two got off to a good start with an exchange over their common interest in basketball. Turning to business, the deputy secretary spoke in his characteristically to-the-point style, something that Horbulin appeared to appreciate. Armitage said the U.S. government wanted a stable, broadening relationship with Ukraine, but difficulties such as the Gongadze case and arms transfers to Macedonia hindered this, and it had been twenty months since the last meeting at the presidential level (when President Clinton visited Kyiv in June 2000). The upcoming Rada elections offered an opportunity to turn the page. If the electoral process met democratic standards, that would enable a Bush-Kuchma meeting in the spring. Armitage expressed hope that, following the March 31 ballot, the State Department and the National Security Council staff could recommend to Bush that he invite Kuchma. A meeting would benefit the U.S.-Ukraine relationship. Horbulin commented that the elections would be difficult, but he hoped they would be open and straightforward. He promised to convey Armitage's message, which he regarded as a hopeful signal, directly to Kuchma.

That evening, Cagan arranged a courtside seat for Horbulin at a Washington Wizards basketball game (Horbulin, an avid basketball fan, also chaired the Ukrainian national basketball association). At half-time, the Wizards front office gave him a basketball signed by all of the Wizards, including his personal favorite, Michael Jordan. Horbulin got into the game with the rest of the crowd in the second half, though his yells of "davay, davay" ("get 'em, get 'em") drew puzzled looks from the referees, Wizards, and opposing players alike.

There was no question that Horbulin would deliver the message on the importance of a good Rada election process. The State Department nevertheless asked Pascual to underscore that Kuchma had a path to an invitation to visit Washington. I reiterated the message with senior foreign ministry officials, Anatoliy Orel and Andriy Fialko at Bankova, and National Security and Defense Council Secretary Yevhen Marchuk during a late February visit. Pascual arranged a meeting with the All Ukrainian Monitoring Committee, an impressive collection of domestic nongovernmental organizations, supported in part by U.S. assistance, that were monitoring the election run-up and the election itself. They reported a series of electoral problems. Pascual and I used a press conference to reemphasize the importance for Ukraine and U.S.-Ukraine relations of a free and fair election.

Subsequent indications offered little encouragement. Media access remained uneven, and reports of the abuse of administrative resources to support the pro-Kuchma For a United Ukraine Party were rampant. Pascual reported that, during a visit to Dnipropetrovsk, he had seen hundreds of banners endorsing For a United Ukraine—even on government buildings—but only one banner for any opposition party. As the weeks passed and reports of electoral abuses piled up, U.S. officials concluded that Kyiv had made no real changes in its problematic behavior. A second opportunity to create the basis for a meeting at the highest level faded.

Ukrainians went to the polls on March 31. Yushchenko's Our Ukraine Party came in first in the party-list vote, which decided half of the Rada's 450 seats, followed by the Communist Party. For a United Ukraine performed rather dismally on the party-list vote, placing third, but it did well in individual constituencies (which analysts feared were more readily manipulated). For a United Ukraine ended up as the largest party in the Rada, before it broke up into various factions later in the year.

The Organization for Security and Cooperation in Europe (OSCE) election monitoring team noted some improvements in the March 31 elections since the 1998 Rada balloting, but it expressed concern about the pervasive distrust that characterized the electoral process. Among the factors that contributed were: "illegal interference by public authorities and abuse of administrative resources, including allegations of pressure on public employees to vote for certain candidates"; "failure by some political forces to distinguish between state and party activities, compounded by the abuse of incumbency to gain undue campaign advantage; unfair distribution of leadership positions on district and lower election commissions"; "inaccurate voter registers, including deceased persons and non-residents on the lists, while omitting entitled citizens; and failure to publish all polling station results aggregated by district in a timely manner." The OSCE mission nevertheless noted, "The 69 percent turnout of voters on election day is an indication of the level of interest voters have in the outcome of the elections despite the low level of confidence in the process. The polling was conducted in a generally calm atmosphere, and observers rated positively the performance of a large majority of polling station commissions."[13] Once again, OSCE scored Ukraine well on the voting process itself but found significant flaws in the election run-up.

An Inquiry Regarding NATO

As Washington hoped—fruitlessly—for a change in behavior regarding the elections, Deputy Foreign Minister Oleksandr Chalyy quietly approached Pascual in February on an entirely different matter. He asked how the U.S. government would react if Ukraine were to announce a goal of joining NATO. Only two months earlier Zlenko had told Pascual and me that Ukraine was "prepared to go as far as NATO was prepared to go," which, he added, could even include an invitation from NATO to join the alliance. His formulation had been strange: NATO would not invite a country to join unless that country first asked to become a member. Now, Kyiv seemed to be asking.

The declaration issued at the July 1997 NATO summit had reaffirmed the open-door policy, stating, "NATO remains open to new members under Article 10 of the North Atlantic Treaty. The Alliance will continue to welcome new members in a position to further the principles of the Treaty and contribute to security in the Euro-Atlantic area. . . . No European democratic country whose admission would fulfill the objectives of the Treaty will be excluded from consideration."[14] That statement applied, at least implicitly, to Ukraine even if the wording had been drafted more with the countries in Central Europe and the Baltic region in mind. Ukraine had military assets that could make a contribution to transatlantic security. The more difficult question turned on Kyiv's readiness to implement democratic reforms to meet NATO standards.

The State Department, National Security Council, and Pentagon carefully weighed the question posed by Chalyy. Some doubted whether Kyiv seriously wanted to join NATO or questioned whether the senior leadership understood what kinds of reform joining NATO would require. Others noted the possibility of a negative Russian reaction, at a time when relations between Washington and Moscow seemed to be developing in a positive direction. The majority view held that Ukraine, like other European countries, should have the opportunity to be considered for membership if it wished to join. Washington asked Pascual to inform Chalyy that the U.S. government would support a Ukrainian goal of joining NATO—provided that Kyiv did all the necessary homework and instituted the reforms needed to meet the alliance's standards. This meant not just military reform, but also democratic and economic reforms, since NATO represented a community of shared values as well as a defense pact. If anything, democratic reforms counted more than modernizing the military. (These conditions were by no means Ukraine-specific. U.S. diplomats in 2001–02 made a series of visits to aspiring states in the Baltic region and Central Europe to discuss each country's progress toward receiving an invitation to join the alliance. In almost every capital the American diplomats spent more time talking about the criticality of locking in political and economic reforms than they spent on the military.)

U.S. officials pondered what had led to this decision by Kyiv. Even if Ukraine in the end proved unready to make the needed reforms, simply making a public declaration of membership as a policy goal could prove controversial among the Ukrainian elite and with the public. It would hardly go down well in Moscow. The most persuasive assessment was that Kyiv had watched the development of NATO-Russia relations, including the intention announced in December 2001 to deepen the link between the alliance and Moscow, and Ukrainian officials did not want to be left behind. Kyiv may also have concluded that the warming trend in the NATO-Russia relationship gave Ukraine greater freedom to advance its own relations with the alliance.

U.S. support for Ukraine's membership, even as conditioned, was not shared widely at NATO. After joining in 1999, Poland had established itself as Ukraine's foremost advocate, with the United States a close second, but many other allies voiced skepticism.

On May 23, when Bush was in Moscow for a summit with Putin, Kuchma publicly announced that Ukraine would seek to join NATO. Kuchma suggested that recent developments in NATO-Russia relations had affected his thinking and that he did not want to lag when he told a journalist, "We can see that Russia today has or will have a totally different format of relations with NATO. . . . I feel glad that neither does NATO see an enemy in Russia, nor does Russia see an enemy in NATO."[15] Ukrainian officials noted that membership in NATO was not a near-term prospect, but they had publicly established the goal. Whether Kyiv was prepared to do its homework remained the key question.

The next day, however, brought troubling news suggesting that some in Kyiv did not understand the importance that NATO attached to democratic reforms. Dovira, the Ukrainian TV and radio company that transmitted Radio Liberty's programming, was advised by the National Council for TV and Radio that its broadcasting license could be revoked if it continued to work with Radio Liberty. Dovira's director traced his company's problems with the government back to its January 2001 airing of a live program on the subject of the Melnychenko recordings. Radio Liberty president Thomas Dine noted the disconnect between Kyiv seeking to close down his radio's operation at the same time that it aspired to join European institutions.[16]

The Kolchuga Question

In the run-up to the March 31 Rada elections, the State Department had received a letter from Scott Horton, Melnychenko's New York attorney. The letter asserted that Melnychenko had a recording of a July 2000 meeting between Kuchma and Ukrspetseksport head Valeriy Malev, a meeting that took place just weeks after Clinton's visit to Kyiv. (Ukrspetseksport, Ukraine's special export company, had almost sole responsibility for major arms exports.) Melnychenko's attorney wrote that, in the conversation, the president had approved Malev's proposal to sell the Kolchuga air defense system to Iraq via a Jordanian middleman. Melnychenko was prepared to share the recording with the U.S. government.

This report posed a dilemma. Armitage had assured Hryshchenko that the U.S. government had no intention of exploiting Melnychenko's recordings. But if such a recording existed, the U.S. government could hardly ignore it. At the time, U.S. and British fighter aircraft, as part of the UN-sanctioned Operations Northern Watch and Southern Watch, flew air missions daily over northern and southern Iraq. The Kolchuga air defense system, if actually deployed in Iraq, posed a threat to those aircraft and their American and British aircrews.

The Kolchuga air defense system, built by the state-owned Topaz Company in Donetsk, raised alarm bells because of its operating characteristics. Radars usually transmit a radio beam to locate and track aircraft. Properly equipped aircraft can detect the radio beam and alert the pilots to the fact that they are being tracked. The pilots can then possibly take evasive action or employ other countermeasures. The Kolchuga system operates differently. It tracks aircraft passively by following their radio and other electronic emissions. It emits no radio beam of its own that might be detected by the aircraft. Pilots thus would have no way of knowing that a Kolchuga was tracking them. A Kolchuga could provide an anti-aircraft missile with a vector toward a target aircraft, and a targeting radar could be turned on at the last moment to guide the missile. At that point the aircraft's pilot might have little or no time to take evasive action.

Given the potential risk to U.S. and British pilots, the recording could not be ignored. U.S. officials were mindful, however, of the timing of the letter, with the Rada elections just weeks away. They worried that the approach might be an attempt to provoke a political scandal that would drag Washington into the middle of the elections. The State Department alerted Defense Department officials to the Kolchuga allegation and the possible threat to aircraft (they informed the British), but the U.S. government decided to take no action until after the March 31 vote.

On April 2, State Department officials decided, with National Security Council concurrence, to invite Melnychenko or his representative to hand over the recording. Melnychenko's representative came to the State Department and did so.

U.S. officials agreed that it would be sensible to be transparent with the Ukrainians. I informed Hryshchenko that the U.S. government had the Kolchuga recording and intended to examine it. As expected, he protested that doing so would contradict what the deputy secretary had told him in 2001. I took his point but explained that, given the risk to pilots, Armitage had personally approved this course of action. The U.S. government made no official public comment, though *Dzerkalo Tyzhnya* reported on April 20 that "U.S. diplomatic sources" had confirmed that the recording in question had been handed over to the State Department. The paper quoted Security Service of Ukraine (SBU) head Volodymyr Radchenko as categorically ruling out the transfer of any Kolchuga systems to Iraq.[17]

The State Department passed the recording to the FBI. The examination took longer than expected, because the forensics laboratory gave priority to domestic criminal cases. At the beginning of August, the FBI informed State Department officials that its experts as well as experts from two other agencies had examined the recording. They had found no technical evidence to suggest the recording was not genuine, and all experts had concluded that the voice approving Malev's suggested sale was Kuchma's.

Fried hosted a meeting on August 2 with Pascual, who was in Washington for consultations, Assistance Coordinator for the New

Independent States Bill Taylor, and me for a preliminary look at response options. One possibility would be to isolate Kuchma, at least partially. Another would be to send a stiff "you need to get things in order" message. At this point, the recording had decimated Kuchma's remaining credibility in Washington. Thought was given to shifting U.S. policy to focus on the goal of strengthening the prospects for Ukrainian voters to have a real voice in their 2004 presidential election.

We also discussed the fact that the Ukrainians had yet again not responded to a U.S. proposal that could put a Bush-Kuchma meeting on the agenda. Earlier in the summer, Kyiv had raised the idea of scheduling a U.S.-Ukrainian-Polish presidential meeting on the margins of the September UN General Assembly session. U.S. officials had responded that this might be possible and had laid out a list of some twenty problematic issues on which progress could help lift the broader relationship out of its malaise and put it on a more positive track (this was before the results of the examination of the Kolchuga recording had become known). Pascual discussed this list in Kyiv, while I reviewed it with Hryshchenko. At the end of the July, however, with work in both capitals slowing for the summer break, no significant progress had been made. The National Security Council ruled out a trilateral presidential meeting. It was the third time in thirteen months that U.S. officials had suggested actions that would enable a Bush-Kuchma meeting, but again Kyiv appeared to do little to make a meeting happen.

The Ukraine interagency working group convened on September 10 to consider the full ramifications of the Kolchuga issue. All agencies agreed on two points. First, Washington had to react to the fact that Kuchma had agreed to the transfer. Second, the United States needed to determine whether the transfer had actually taken place. If the transfer had occurred, it would constitute a violation of UN Security Council sanctions on Iraq. It would also likely be a violation of the Iran-Iraq Nonproliferation Act, which could trigger U.S. sanctions against Ukraine.

The interagency group further agreed that the U.S. government should target its reaction at Kuchma while trying to preserve the broader bilateral relationship with Ukraine. Some questioned whether that would be possible. Others worried that, once Congress learned of the Kolchuga recording, it would enact legislation to cut the assistance program. Official U.S. assistance to Ukraine in fiscal year 2002 came to some $280 million. The two biggest pieces were FREEDOM Support Act funds ($159.9 million) and Department of Defense programs ($57 million). Of the FREEDOM Support Act funds, about $74 million went to USAID programs, mostly to promote economic reform, democracy, and civil society, and $25 million funded public diplomacy programs, including people-to-people exchanges, run by the Department of State.[18] The Ukrainian government might not mind a reduction in these categories. At the interagency group's request, Taylor identified $55 million in U.S. assistance slated for the Ukrainian government that could be suspended to indicate Washington's displeasure while other actions were weighed. The USAID mission in Kyiv thought the reductions were manageable, but some U.S. assistance providers whose programs would be affected voiced their unhappiness.

On September 19, the Bureau of European and Eurasian Affairs learned that Moscow-based *New York Times* correspondent Michael Wines had the Kolchuga story. The State Department asked the *Times* to hold it for a few days, offering a more detailed background briefing in return. That evening, State sent a cable asking the embassy in Kyiv to brief the Ukrainian government on the conclusions regarding the recording and to ask for clarification of what had happened and whether any Kolchuga systems had been shipped to Iraq. Ukrainian officials denied that Kuchma had approved the sale or that any Kolchugas had been transferred to Iraq.

In parallel, an instruction message went to U.S. embassies in NATO capitals to share with allies U.S. concerns about the Kolchuga question. State Department officials briefed staff members of the appropriate Senate and House committees, including the Senate Foreign Relations Committee and the House International Relations Committee, on September 20 and 23 on the finding and on the State Department's decision to suspend $55 million in assistance.

The Kolchuga story broke in the *New York Times* on September 24.[19] It correctly depicted the U.S. government's view that Kuchma had approved the transfer, although U.S. officials did not know whether the transfer had in fact taken place. At the State Department press briefing, Boucher addressed the story in some detail. In Kyiv, the Presidential Administration released a statement saying, "Ukraine has never sold weapons or military material to Iraq" and that the Ukrainian government "was prepared to give any information and is open to verification by the relevant international bodies, including U.S. experts." The foreign ministry likewise rejected the charge.[20]

The State Department's Beth Jones made an urgent trip to Kyiv on October 1 to follow up. In meetings with Kuchma and other senior Ukrainians, she delivered a tough message regarding U.S. concerns about the Kolchuga case and the need for Kyiv to address them in a forthright and serious way. Her message clearly discomfited the president. While the Ukrainians denied that the transfer had taken place or that Kuchma had ever approved a transfer, they offered to host a joint U.S.-British team of experts to discuss the full range of Kolchuga issues, an offer that Washington immediately accepted. The British government agreed as well. The joint team prepared to travel to Ukraine in mid-October.

Chalyy visited Washington in early October and, at a lunch hosted by Hryshchenko, both stressed that the experts team would find there was no truth whatsoever to the Kolchuga story. I cautioned that proving a negative could be difficult; there might be no definitive proof. It thus would be critical for U.S. and British experts to come away from Kyiv with the impression that they had received full cooperation from their Ukrainian counterparts.

Later in October, meetings between the U.S.-British team and a range of Ukrainian officials yielded a mixed picture. On the one hand, the team felt that it had received complete cooperation from the foreign ministry and the ministry of defense. On the other hand, it found the officials from the SBU and the National Security and Defense Council evasive. For example, in response to the team's questions, Ukrainian officials had said the general prosecutor's office, the SBU, and the National Security and Defense Council had each prepared a written report of its own investigation into the matter. When the team asked for copies, the response was less than reassuring. It received the general prosecutor's report with two of five chapters redacted, an uninformative one-and-a-half page summary of the SBU report, and nothing from the National Security and Defense Council. One team member commented that he had gone to Kyiv with an open mind, but the evasiveness left him thinking that the Kolchuga transfer might have taken place after all.

The visit failed to resolve the questions about Kolchuga and Kuchma's original reaction to the proposed transfer to Iraq. It provided some information that seemed to confirm the reported Kuchma-Malev conversation. One U.S. team member received a copy of the relevant page from a logbook of presidential visitors, which showed that Malev indeed was in Kuchma's office at the time the conversation reportedly occurred. (The team could not interview Malev, who had died in a car accident the previous March.)

Following the experts' visit, the U.S. government decided that it could not support a NATO-Ukraine summit on the margins of the Prague NATO summit scheduled to begin on November 18, as had been tentatively planned and as had occurred in 1997 and 1999. Washington proposed, and NATO members agreed on, a NATO-Ukraine foreign ministers' meeting in lieu of a summit. The interagency working group asked Taylor to look at further options for suspending assistance to the Ukrainian government.

I visited Warsaw on November 4 and 5 for meetings with Polish officials, followed by a U.S.-Poland-Ukraine trilateral meeting, before traveling onward to Kyiv. Pascual joined me, and we had excellent conversations, including with Deputy Foreign Minister Adam Rotfeld, who would lead the Polish team in the trilateral meeting. We discussed the U.S. message: the Kolchuga affair had created a situation in which the U.S. government had lost confidence in Ukraine's senior leadership, but it still hoped to maintain the broader bilateral relationship, though that could prove difficult. Washington did not intend to ask others to isolate Kuchma and recognized the importance of Kwasniewski's relationship with Kuchma.

Rotfeld observed that it would be important in Prague not to let Kuchma and Kolchuga overshadow the summit's big news: NATO's decision to invite the Baltic states, Romania, Bulgaria, Slovakia, and Slovenia to join the alliance. It would also be important not to let the Kolchuga question overshadow the broader NATO-Ukraine relationship. We shared the Polish view that NATO should try to make the NATO-Ukraine ministerial a positive event.

The trilateral meeting, in which we were joined by Ukrainian deputy foreign minister Volodymyr Yelchenko and his team, opened with a discussion of the NATO-Ukraine ministerial in Prague. Rotfeld conveyed the Polish-U.S. view that the three countries should work to make the ministerial a successful meeting. Yelchenko responded that the atmospherics would be difficult; Kyiv had not decided whether to attend the NATO-Ukraine meeting, since it would not take place at the summit level. The Ukrainians, moreover, leaned toward having Kuchma attend the Euro-Atlantic Partnership Council summit, which would also take place in Prague. Rotfeld and I argued that Zlenko should go to Prague, or Kyiv would send a very negative signal to NATO. The alliance had developed a very substantive action plan for Ukraine that could help Kyiv draw closer to NATO, if that was the Ukrainians' desire.

At the end of the meeting, I pulled Yelchenko aside and told him that the U.S. government did not intend to mount a full-court press against Kuchma's attending the Euro-Atlantic Partnership Council. Washington felt, however, that the Ukrainian president's presence would cast a cloud over what could be a positive meeting between Zlenko and his NATO counterparts. If Kuchma went, he should not expect to be greeted by Bush.

The trilateral discussion also covered energy security, including the possibility that the Odesa-Brody oil pipeline might be extended into Poland. Ukrainian officials hoped to fill the already constructed Odesa-Brody pipeline with oil for Polish refineries. Polish officials, however, did not consider the project viable unless the private sector financed the extension.

As anticipated, my November 6–8 Kyiv visit proved difficult. In meetings on November 7 at the National Security and Defense Council, Bankova, and the foreign ministry, I reiterated that Washington had lost confidence in Ukraine's senior leadership but still hoped to preserve broad engagement. Marchuk took the point but questioned whether broad cooperation would be possible without confidence at the top, a reasonable question. Pascual and I admitted that we did not have a good answer. Marchuk thought that Zlenko should go to Prague for the NATO-Ukraine ministerial, but Kyiv had not yet made a decision.

The meeting with Presidential Administration head Viktor Medvedchuk ran long, well over two hours. U.S. officials harbored certain suspicions about Medvedchuk and his connections to Russia (his daughter's godfather was Putin). Medvedchuk claimed to be surprised that the U.S. and British experts had not been convinced by their visit; he asserted that there was no proof that Ukraine had been involved in any Kolchuga transfer to Iraq and argued that the recording of the July 2000 Kuchma-Malev conversation had been edited. Pascual recounted at some length the lack of cooperation that the team had experienced, noting that the SBU's information in particular had proven useless. Medvedchuk claimed that he could not force the SBU to cooperate, an implausible statement coming from the head of the Presidential Administration. A lawyer by training, Medvedchuk tried to argue that the U.S. government had provided no evidence that would stand up in a court of law. But the matter was not before a court of law. U.S. experts had found nothing on the recording to suggest that it had been altered or edited.

Medvedchuk said Kyiv had not yet decided who would attend the Prague meetings, but Kuchma might take part in the Euro-Atlantic Partnership Council summit. He opined that the NATO-Ukraine event should take place at the "same level"—that is, it should be a summit. I replied that Washington wanted to keep the door open for developing the U.S.-Ukraine and NATO-Ukraine relationships, but there would be no NATO-Ukraine summit in Prague and no Kuchma-Bush meeting; NATO had offered a meeting at the ministerial level. I told him that although Kuchma might want to be present at the Euro-Atlantic Partnership Council event, the Ukrainians should ask themselves whether his traveling to the Czech capital would be wise.

In conversations at the foreign ministry, Chalyy and Yelchenko asked whether confidence could be restored between Bush and Kuchma. I noted that it was possible but would be difficult. The two of them, and Horbulin in a separate meeting, seemed to grasp a key point of the U.S. message: despite difficulties at the top, the Ukrainian government had a way forward to develop its relations with NATO—that is, a NATO-Ukraine ministerial meeting in Prague that would endorse a substantive action plan.

Pascual and I met separately with Rada members Viktor Pinchuk and Inna Bohoslovskaya, who were personally close to Kuchma (Pinchuk had married Kuchma's daughter). They expressed concern that, absent high-level U.S.-Ukrainian contacts, Kyiv would turn to Russia. We responded that that suggested Ukraine was not seriously committed to its European aspirations; if that were the case, it would be good for the United States and Europe to know sooner rather than later. Pinchuk commented that, assuming the discussion on the recording had happened, Kuchma could have reversed himself. That was possible, but no Ukrainian government official had argued that.

Back in Washington, I went through the U.S. points with Hryshchenko on November 13. Secretary of State Powell called Foreign Minister Zlenko on November 18 to urge that he attend the NATO-Ukraine ministerial, stressing its importance for Ukraine's relationship with the alliance.

Kuchma decided to attend the Euro-Atlantic Partnership Council summit in Prague. His attendance raised an immediate problem for Washington: seating at NATO-hosted meetings is normally arranged by country according to the English-language spellings, which would place Ukraine's Kuchma next to the United States' Bush and the United Kingdom's prime minister Tony Blair. The NATO secretary general came up with a solution at the last minute. NATO has two official languages, English and French. Robertson decided to seat leaders according to the French spellings of their countries (Ukraine, Etats-Unis, and Royaume-Uni), which put distance between Kuchma and his American and British counterparts. As for the NATO-Ukraine meeting, Zlenko came after all but chose to focus on the Kolchuga charges, which he called unjustified. That statement prompted rebuttals from a number of NATO foreign ministers, not a forward-looking discussion of the relationship between Kyiv and the alliance.

Powell had a brief encounter with Zlenko on the margins of the meeting. During my visit to Kyiv earlier that month, embassy security personnel had become alarmed when they noticed cars following Pascual and me as we traveled to our meetings. They learned that the cars belonged to the SBU. In his November 18 phone call with Zlenko, Powell had asked, "Why are you following my guys?" Zlenko was caught wholly unaware, but in Prague he gave Powell a diplomatic note saying that the SBU had been conducting "internal security work." We were not exactly sure what that meant.

The independent press in Ukraine had a field day with the French spellings story, depicting Kuchma as an unwelcome guest. When a Ukrainian official suggested on background that Kuchma had met, or at least run into, Bush in Prague, I asked Fried at the National Security Council about that. Fried replied that, if Bush had encountered Kuchma at the summit, he (Bush) had not realized it. The embassy reported that Horbulin had been the only senior adviser to suggest to Kuchma that he not go to Prague, for fear that it would overshadow the NATO-Ukraine relationship. Horbulin was fired shortly thereafter.

Beginning at the end of November, the interagency working group conducted a further review of U.S. policy toward Ukraine. The working group considered the key challenges: how to maintain broad engagement with Ukraine given concerns about Kuchma; how to manage the Kolchuga question; how to generate progress on other issues on the bilateral agenda; and how to better influence reform within Ukraine. The review assumed that Kuchma would remain in office until the 2004 election. The working group recognized that cutting back contacts with Kuchma could complicate engagement with the rest of the Ukrainian government but decided that engagement remained worthwhile, even if it might not prove easy.

The review concluded in January 2003 and set the goal of trying to resolve individual problems on the agenda and ultimately seeking to change the overall dynamic of the relationship. Everyone recognized that doing so would take time. Much of the burden for turning things around rested with Kyiv, but Washington needed to do its homework on certain questions. Getting Congress to graduate Ukraine from the provisions of the Jackson-Vanik amendment and granting Kyiv permanent normal trade relations status, for example, were long overdue.

As for Kolchuga, the sides likely would never agree on what had happened, but the United States had an interest in working with Kyiv to strengthen its export control system. There was a list of other issues on which the United States and Ukraine might work together, including the NATO-Ukraine relationship. Few in Washington, however, talked about a U.S.-Ukraine strategic partnership, and American officials increasingly worried about the course of democracy in Ukraine. During the review, officials voiced exasperation over the apparent inability to get through to the Ukrainian leadership. The foreign ministry and the Presidential Administration had stressed for more than eighteen months the importance that Kyiv attached to a meeting between Kuchma and Bush, either bilaterally or in a trilateral format with the Polish president. But every time U.S. officials laid out a path to enable such a meeting, Kyiv seemed to ignore the necessary steps. In Washington's view, the Ukrainians had done virtually nothing to create the conditions for the meeting they so eagerly sought.

Pascual shared the results of the review with the Ukrainian government during the second half of January, offering as well an illustrative list of issues for U.S.-Ukrainian dialogue. The relationship was in trouble, but Washington sought to leave the door open for improvement. The initial Ukrainian reaction to the policy review seemed positive, an assessment that Hryshchenko confirmed to me when I ran through the review's conclusions with him. Senior officials in Kyiv got the message that Washington intended to stay engaged.

In February, I gave a talk at the Center for Strategic & International Studies in Washington to lay out the basic conclusions of the policy review, noting at the outset that the review had been completed at what was probably the most difficult point in U.S.-Ukraine relations since 1991. The U.S. government nevertheless understood the importance of Ukraine, and it remained in the U.S. interest to remain engaged. The question was Kyiv's willingness to work with Washington in resolving problem questions. I cited Pascual's energy and creativity; if Kyiv wanted to find solutions, it could have no better interlocutor. As for reform, Washington would devote particular attention to building democratic institutions, with a view to leveling the playing field for the Ukrainian presidential election in fall 2004.

The end of 2002 marked two years of virtually steady decline in the U.S.-Ukraine relationship. With the exception of Condoleezza Rice's stop in July 2001, there had been no senior-level administration visits—by Bush, Cheney, or a Cabinet secretary—to Ukraine. Although Washington had hosted a visit by the prime minister, Kuchma had yet to meet Bush. By contrast, in the period from 1998 to 2000, Ukraine had hosted presidential, vice presidential, and four Cabinet-level visits, and Kuchma and Yushchenko had visited Washington. It was no surprise when, in his end-of-the-year press conference, Kuchma again denied that Ukraine had sent Kolchuga radars to Iraq, but he also decried the worsening of U.S.-Ukraine relations.

Ukraine and the Iraq Conflict

What prevented a near-total collapse in the bilateral relationship in 2003 was Bush's looming decision to go to war with Iraq. In the eighteen months since the September 11 terrorist attacks in the United States, Kyiv had offered political support on the UN Security Council for resolutions to frame and enable a broad response to terrorism, supported eleven of twelve international counterterrorism conventions, and increased intelligence sharing on possible terrorist activities. U.S. Air Force flights regularly transited Ukrainian air space (more than 4,500 in the September 2001–October 2002 period alone), and Ukrainian heavy-lift aircraft had moved humanitarian assistance, as well as German and Turkish troops, to Afghanistan. The Ukrainian military was also helping to reequip the Afghan National Army.

As tensions between the United States and Iraq grew, one of the many concerns facing the Pentagon was the possibility that Saddam Hussein's military might use weapons of mass destruction. Although the concern turned out to be unfounded, in the run-up to the conflict fears arose about the vulnerability of U.S. and coalition military forces massing in Kuwait should Saddam decide to use biological or chemical weapons.

The Ukrainian army was one of the few in the world that had trained and appropriately equipped nuclear/biological/chemical (NBC) defense units, which could, for example, assist in defending against a strike with chemical weapons and cope with the task of securing and decontaminating an area after an attack. Above and beyond securing the commitment of specific military capabilities, the Bush administration sought to assemble as many participating countries as possible in the coalition to build international political legitimacy for a military operation that did not receive sanction from the UN Security Council.

U.S.-Ukrainian discussions at the end of 2002 suggested that the Ukrainian military could provide an NBC defense battalion, and talks moved to a more formal level in early 2003. The Ukrainian government indicated that it would not deploy the unit into Iraq proper, but the battalion could deploy to one of the frontline Gulf states, such as Kuwait. The Pentagon eagerly welcomed this possibility. In late January, however, a letter from Zlenko listed political preconditions for Ukraine's agreement to deploy its battalion. In a January 30 meeting at the White House, Fried complained to visiting presidential foreign policy adviser Leonid Kozhara and sharply rejected Zlenko's preconditions. Washington decided simply to ignore the letter, and Secretary of Defense Donald Rumsfeld did so when he met with Minister of Defense Volodymyr Shkidchenko on the margins of the Munich Security Conference in early February. Zlenko told Pascual on February 13 that Ukraine would deploy the battalion. On February 20, the National

Security and Defense Council approved a decision, subject to confirmation by the Rada, to send a battalion of about 500 soldiers to the Persian Gulf.

The sides quickly reached agreement on specific details, such as the command-and-control arrangements and the kinds of support the U.S. military would provide. On March 6, Kuchma requested formal Rada approval for the deployment. Two weeks later the Rada gave its approval by a vote of 258 to 121—just as U.S., British, Australian, and Polish military forces launched initial operations against Iraq. The Rada subsequently passed a resolution with 229 votes condemning the attack.

U.S. forces took Baghdad on April 9. Fortunately, the Iraqis did not resort to biological or chemical weapons (it turned out that they had possessed only a small number of chemical arms). The Ukrainian battalion in Kuwait had a quiet war. In Washington, attention turned to securing additional ground troops for an Iraq stabilization force to take some of the burden off of the U.S. military. Washington asked Pascual to explore the possibility that Ukraine might withdraw its NBC defense battalion and provide two or three battalions of regular troops to the stabilization force.

The embassy reported the Ukrainian military's interest. The ministry of defense regarded multinational peacekeeping and stabilization operations as the most likely tasks for the army, and participation in the Iraq stabilization force would provide useful experience. Others in Kyiv hoped that participation would give Ukraine an inside track on reconstruction contracts as a new Iraqi government took form, and the Ukrainian embassy in Washington eagerly sought the guidelines for contracts to share with firms at home. Finally, and perhaps most importantly, Bankova saw a troop contribution as a way to help repair the badly frayed bilateral relationship.

When Pascual and I made the rounds during my mid-May visit to Kyiv, our Ukrainian interlocutors, including Kuchma and Marchuk, had a consistent message: Ukraine wanted to improve bilateral relations, understood that this required Kyiv to take action, and would contribute to the Iraq stabilization force. The ministry of defense had ordered two battalions to prepare. The Ukrainian military proposed to deploy as part of a Polish-led division, which made sense, as the two had cooperated in a joint Polish-Ukrainian peacekeeping battalion. The Ukrainians noted that they would need help from the U.S. military in deploying and sustaining their troops. The technical questions all appeared manageable.

Following passage of a UN Security Council resolution that, among other things, provided the basis for an international stabilization force, the Ukrainian government sought Rada approval for deployment of about 1,800 troops. On June 5, the Rada voted 273 to 103 to approve (most of the no votes came from Yushchenko's Our Ukraine bloc and the Tymoshenko bloc). In asking the Rada to approve the deployment, Marchuk stressed the potential for Ukrainian companies to take part in the reconstruction of Iraq as well as gain access to Iraqi oil exports.[21] The first troops left for Iraq in early August.

The deployment flowed smoothly, and the Ukrainians took up positions as part of the Polish-led division operating at Al-Kut, located between Baghdad and the southeastern city of Basra. The U.S. military provided desert kits, fuel, and other supplies. By the end of 2003, the Ukrainian military's troops constituted the fourth largest contributor to the stabilization force after the United States, Britain, and Poland.

Working Other Issues

In May, Kuchma made clear to Pascual and me his desire to turn a page in U.S.-Ukraine relations. We stressed the importance of progress on democracy and on Kyiv's relationship with Europe. Beyond Iraq, Washington and Kyiv had a full agenda. The U.S. government had expressed readiness to support Ukraine's accession to the World Trade Organization (WTO) if Kyiv made the necessary changes to its trade legislation (a process that, as with other WTO aspirants, would take considerable time). We strongly urged that Ukraine place priority on WTO accession and aim to accede before—or at least simultaneously with—Russia. WTO rules gave member states the right to negotiate a bilateral agreement with new acceding states. If Ukraine entered before or at the same time as Russia, Kyiv would not have to negotiate bilateral trade arrangements with Moscow. Given the trade difficulties between Ukraine and Russia, a bilateral negotiation could prove difficult.

Marchuk, Horbulin (who had been reappointed as a presidential adviser on national security questions and was chair of the National Center of Euro-Atlantic Integration), and senior foreign ministry officials stressed Kyiv's desire to further develop relations with NATO, following up on the Ukrainian announcement the year before of its interest in joining the alliance. Pascual and I noted that the next step for Ukraine would be an intensified dialogue, but we underscored the need for Ukraine to fulfill as much as possible of the action plan that had been agreed in Prague. Actions would determine the pace of the NATO-Ukraine relationship. In this regard, progress on democratic reforms, which constituted part of the action plan, was particularly important. Horbulin, who had accompanied Marchuk to a NATO-Ukraine conference the previous week in Washington, had heard that from U.S. government officials and nongovernmental experts during his visit. (Yet another requirement, which Jones and other U.S. officials regularly emphasized to Ukrainian officials, was domestic support in Ukraine for alliance membership. NATO did not want to bring in new members where public support for joining was weak, and most polls at the time showed that NATO membership did not enjoy wide support among the Ukrainian public.)

We also discussed the possibility of high-level visits. Pascual and I noted that Viktor Yanukovych, who had become prime minister in November 2002, would be welcome. But Washington and Kyiv should first solve some of the bilateral agenda's problems, what U.S. officials had come to call the "must-do" questions. These included fixing the difficulties that the National Democratic Institute (NDI) and International Republican Institute (IRI) faced in registering to continue their democracy-promotion operations in Ukraine; certification questions regarding the import of U.S. poultry; and Ukraine's failure to enact and enforce an optical media law that would protect U.S. companies' intellectual property rights (stemming from the pirate compact disc plants issue that first arose in 2000). While none of these problems approached the scale of the Kolchuga question, Kyiv's continuing inability to resolve them contributed to the impression of a bilateral relationship that—except for the Ukrainian troop deployment in Iraq—was misfiring. Progress on some issues could set the stage for a successful visit by the prime minister, perhaps in the summer or autumn.

Pascual and I discussed the must-do questions in our meeting with Yanukovych. The prime minister came from the coal-mining and industrial Donetsk region in Ukraine's east. He lost both of his parents as a child and reportedly had a violent temper. As a young man he was arrested twice and served prison time. Yanukovych later worked as a regional transportation manager before joining the Donetsk oblast administration. Kuchma appointed him governor in 1997, though he had relatively little visibility on the national stage before becoming prime minister (I first met him in early 1998 during a visit to Donetsk and found him not particularly impressive). When Pascual and I met with Yanukovych, he did not seem fully comfortable with the U.S.-Ukraine agenda. He read his talking points, barely looking up and sticking primarily to economic questions. He told us the Ukrainian side was working on the must-do list and believed answers could be found for most of the problems. Other Ukrainian interlocutors seemed to understand that actions would be the key to changing the tenor of the overall relationship. By June the scorecard showed some progress.

During the visit, Pascual and I had to deliver one bit of difficult news. Going back to the early 1990s, the Defense Department's Cooperative Threat Reduction program had proven one of the most successful U.S. programs in Ukraine. Unfortunately, a problem with elimination of the SS-24 intercontinental ballistic missile had now arisen. The SS-24s had been removed from their silos (all of which had been destroyed), and the missiles themselves had been separated into stages, but differences between the Pentagon and the Ukrainian ministry of defense over how to deal with the missiles' solid fuel held up their final elimination.

The Ukrainians wanted to convert the solid fuel into commercial explosives for use in mining operations. Defense Department officials regarded the solid fuel conversion plan as technically risky, had been embarrassed by the failure of a parallel project in Russia, and believed conversion would cost more than simply burning the fuel and buying an equivalent amount of commercial explosives. The Pentagon nevertheless previously had relented and agreed to the Ukrainian proposal. But, with no warning to the Ukrainians—or to others in the U.S. government, for that matter—the Pentagon reversed itself in May 2003 and canceled the conversion program. What made this change particularly awkward was that, just a few months earlier, Kuchma and Pascual had visited the site where the conversion process would take place. The Ukrainians made very clear their unhappiness with the sudden reversal and said they could not accept burning the fuel. So the must-do list added a new problem (it was not resolved until several years later, when the Defense Department again reversed itself and agreed to support a conversion process).

I paid another visit to Ukraine in July, this time as the U.S. observer to the Georgia-Ukraine-Uzbekistan-Azerbaijan-Moldova (GUUAM) summit hosted by Kuchma in Yalta. (GUUAM had originally formed in 1997 as the GUAM group; Uzbekistan joined in 1999.) Ukraine had tried to make GUUAM a real institution. It held regular summits but was slow to develop an organizational structure or cooperative activities. The U.S. government had urged GUUAM to focus on practical projects and had offered assistance to promote a virtual law enforcement center that would improve cooperation among the countries' police forces. It also offered to provide assistance for a trade and transportation project that would facilitate border crossings and trade among the five countries.

Pascual and I saw Kuchma the day before the GUUAM event. We focused our discussion on democracy issues and stressed the positive impact that a free and fair presidential election process in 2004 would have on Kyiv's relations with the West. The Ukrainian constitution limited the president to two terms, which meant that Kuchma could not run again. Rumors had circulated in Kyiv, however, that Kuchma might seek an interpretation from the Constitutional Court that, since he had been elected only once under the current constitution (which had been adopted in 1996), he could run legally for what would be a third term. When we raised the question, Kuchma told us that he had no intention of running. Pascual and I made sure to relate that to the Ukrainian press, who were waiting for us after the meeting.

Later in the summer, Pascual's tour in Kyiv came to an end. He returned to Washington and succeeded Taylor in coordinating the assistance program for the post-Soviet space, a role that ensured his continued close engagement. To replace Pascual, the president selected John Herbst, a career foreign service officer who had served in Moscow during Soviet times and had represented the United States as ambassador to Uzbekistan from 2000 to 2003. At about the same time, Hryshchenko prepared to depart Washington for his next assignment:

foreign minister. On September 4, Powell hosted a small swearing-in ceremony for Herbst, which Hryshchenko attended. Following the swearing-in, Powell had a short, private meeting with Hryshchenko and told him that the U.S. government hoped to find ways to improve bilateral relations.

Russia, the Single Economic Space, and Tuzla Island

Herbst arrived in Kyiv a few days later and almost immediately found himself confronted by two of the stranger episodes in post-1991 Ukraine-Russia relations. First, to the surprise of Washington and European capitals, and to many in Kyiv, Kuchma on September 19 joined with the Russian, Kazakhstani, and Belarusian presidents in signing an agreement to create a Single (or Common) Economic Space among the four countries. Moscow had earlier proposed establishing such an institution, but Kyiv had resisted. Kuchma's agreement sparked protests in the western Ukrainian cities of Lviv and Ivano-Frankivsk. The Our Ukraine bloc circulated an open letter calling for Kuchma's impeachment, and several ministers expressed reservations.

Joining the Single Economic Space threatened to derail Ukraine's bid to accede to the WTO as well as any future economic integration it might seek with the European Union. As Herbst noted in one of his first meetings with Ukrainian journalists, Kyiv could well face a choice between the Single Economic Space and the WTO. The Single Economic Space appeared to be a customs union, and as a member Ukraine would not be able to join the WTO until every other member of the Single Economic Space qualified for WTO membership. Most knowledgeable observers believed Ukraine to be ahead of Russia and significantly ahead of Kazakhstan and Belarus in meeting WTO conditions. The Single Economic Space thus would hold back Kyiv's WTO aspirations.

In late September, Kuchma's deputy chief of staff Serhiy Lyovochkin visited Washington. He confirmed the embassy's report that the Ukrainian government had at last reregistered the National Democratic Institute and International Republican Institute. Lyovochkin said Kuchma's decision on the Single Economic Space could be seen as a victory for Russia—that was how most U.S. officials viewed it—but

Kuchma believed the economic benefits justified the agreement. He added that Kyiv nevertheless wanted to maintain its course toward European integration and WTO accession. In the Ukrainian view, the Single Economic Space amounted only to a free trade agreement. (Virtually every Ukrainian official asserted the same thing, claiming it should not hinder Ukraine's WTO accession. The Russians, however, maintained that the Single Economic Space was a customs union.)

Lyovochkin's visit was handled oddly. The week before he arrived, a private U.S. consulting firm phoned the Ukraine desk at the State Department to request a meeting for Lyovochkin with Jones. The desk replied that U.S. government officials did not work through private firms to schedule meetings with Ukrainian officials, especially when Ukraine had an embassy. The embassy later contacted the desk with the meeting request, and Jones promptly agreed. The consulting firm then called to advise that their representative would accompany Lyovochkin. The desk responded that the representative would not be allowed entry. (This event foreshadowed a trend among senior Ukrainian figures inside and outside of government to get a private lobbyist. But doing so rarely seemed to help their interactions with U.S. officials.)

A new problem in Ukraine-Russia relations quickly overshadowed questions regarding the Single Economic Space. The Tuzla Island crisis sent State Department officials scrambling for maps. Tuzla Island is a small, sandy spit of land that lies in the middle of the Kerch Strait, with Crimea to its west and Russia's Taman Peninsula to its east. Tuzla once was an extended peninsula connected to the Russian mainland, until a storm in 1925 washed out the connecting isthmus, leaving behind an island three miles long about three miles off the Russian coast. Soviet-era administrative boundaries subsequently put the island within Crimea. In late September the Russians, without consulting with Kyiv, began building a causeway from the Taman Peninsula toward Tuzla, with the apparent goal of linking the island to Russia.

The Ukrainians sent a protest to the Russian embassy in Kyiv on September 30. Having received no official response, the foreign ministry went public with the Ukrainian complaint on October 3, noting that the causeway would violate Ukraine's sovereignty by linking the island to Russia. Hryshchenko, less than one month into his job as foreign minister, traveled to Moscow the next day to discuss the problem. The Russians publicly asserted that the causeway was necessary for environmental reasons. Moscow, moreover, denied that it had any foreknowledge, claiming implausibly that regional authorities in Krasnodar had decided on their own to build the causeway.

Rada members began calling on the government to seek U.S. support as well as to raise the question with the NATO secretary general, who paid a short visit to Kyiv on October 20. As Ukrainian officials explained to their U.S. counterparts, Tuzla Island had a clear history. After Tuzla became an island, it had fallen under the jurisdiction of Crimea. Moscow transferred Crimea to the Ukrainian Soviet Socialist Republic in 1954. In Kyiv's view, the administrative record from Soviet times made clear that Tuzla belonged to Crimea, and thus to Ukraine. Kuchma broke off a state visit to Brazil in order to return to Ukraine and visit the island personally on October 23, the day after the Rada passed by an overwhelming majority a resolution reaffirming that Tuzla belonged to Ukraine. The Ukrainians deployed a small detachment of soldiers to the island. They also moved a barge with a dredge on board into the channel between Tuzla and the ever-lengthening Russian causeway. This produced a memorable picture: Russian trucks at the end of the causeway dumped rocks into the water to extend the causeway, while just off shore, a dredge mounted on a Ukrainian barge deepened the channel to make extension of the causeway more difficult.

Although the Ukrainians had not invoked the 1994 Budapest Memorandum on Security Assurances, in which the United States, Britain, and Russia committed to respect the "sovereignty and existing borders of Ukraine," the State Department reviewed the history of Tuzla and concluded that the Ukrainian position was correct: the island was Ukrainian territory. The question then arose, should the United States take a public position on the issue? Some believed Washington should support Ukraine's claim, citing U.S. commitments stemming from the Budapest Memorandum (Herbst and I were in that group). Others pointed out that numerous similar territorial disputes existed around the world, and the U.S. government did not take a position in each case. The National Security Council decided, at least initially, to let the Ukrainians and Russians work out the issue themselves. Herbst so

informed Hryshchenko and reported back that the foreign minister
had expressed deep displeasure. Herbst had to strike a careful public
position. He told a Ukrainian newspaper, "We support the sovereignty
and territorial integrity of Ukraine. However, we have friendly relations with both Russia and Ukraine. We hope that the governments of
these neighbors will be able to resolve the argument in a positive and
responsible manner."[22]

Yanukovych met with Russian prime minister Mikhail Kasyanov
and reportedly defused the crisis on October 24. Kasyanov told the
press that Russia would "not restart construction [of the causeway].
Ukraine will withdraw its border guards from Tuzla, which is a disputed territory."[23] But the settlement did not hold. Three days later, the
border guards remained on Tuzla; Kuchma complained, "Some people
in Russia have strong imperialist impulses" and added that "the closer
the dam [causeway] gets to our coast, the closer we move toward the
West."[24] In Washington, during a lunch with Russian ambassador
Yuriy Ushakov, I raised the Tuzla dispute. Without expressing a policy
view, I noted that the U.S. government had closely examined the history and, if pressed to state a position, would have to say Tuzla belonged to Ukraine. Ushakov apparently relayed that to Moscow, as
Herbst reported shortly thereafter that the Russians had complained to
Hryshchenko about efforts to pull the United States into the dispute.

What surprised many in Washington was that the Ukrainians chose
not to invoke the Budapest Memorandum. The memorandum says that
if a party feels "a situation arises which raises a question concerning
these commitments" it could call for consultations among the signatories. Kyiv never proposed consultations, though Ukrainian officials told
EU diplomats that they were prepared to invoke the Budapest Memorandum and appeal to the UN Security Council. (Years later, when I
asked Hryshchenko, he explained that although the Ukrainians did not
invoke the memorandum formally, they regularly threatened to do so in
their diplomatic exchanges with Moscow.)

On December 24, 2003, Putin and Kuchma signed a framework
agreement on the future use of the Kerch Strait. That seemed to bring
the dispute to an end. (In 2012, Russia and Ukraine were still holding
talks on drawing a border in the strait. Two years later, Russia illegally
seized Tuzla Island along with Crimea.)

The Bilateral Agenda

Although U.S. officials would have liked more progress on the must-do list, enough was accomplished so that they agreed to an autumn visit by Yanukovych. Kyiv's decision to reregister NDI and IRI cinched the decision.

Yanukovych came to Washington on October 6, two weeks before he would get entangled in the Tuzla Island dispute. As with the Lyovochkin visit the previous month, Yanukovych's trip seemed to have been organized more by a private consulting company than by the Ukrainian embassy. During his three-day visit he met with Vice President Cheney as well as several Cabinet secretaries. Although U.S. officials had intended that he take back a clear message on democracy, the agenda focused more on economic questions. Cheney's meeting with Yanukovych also covered Iraq and Ukraine's Euro-Atlantic ambitions (Yanukovych said the NATO action plan defined Kyiv's course toward the alliance). Yanukovych also made a plug to work with the United States on missile defense, noting that Ukraine had extensive experience in designing and building ballistic missiles. Cheney did not press the democracy question.

The vice president and prime minister spent particular time on the Odesa-Brody pipeline issue. Cheney pointed out that a decision by Kyiv to reverse the pipeline to pump Russian oil from the Druzba pipeline at Brody to Odesa would make it impossible for the pipeline to convey Caspian oil from Odesa to Brody and on to refineries in Central Europe. Yanukovych reiterated the Ukrainian desire to extend the pipeline to Poland but conceded that Ukraine had not yet lined up any Caspian oil to put into the pipeline, a critical lack.

Yanukovych underscored Ukraine's objective of joining the WTO and its hope of concluding a bilateral trade protocol with the United States. U.S. officials raised nagging trade problems: despite the action plan agreed in 2000, Ukraine still failed to protect U.S. intellectual property, and import barriers to U.S. poultry continued with little justification.

One of the final meetings of Yanukovych's visit was with Powell. After expressing U.S. appreciation for Ukraine's help in Iraq, the secretary noted the importance of the electoral process in Ukraine. It was essential that the presidential election in 2004 be open, free, and fair. Yanukovych replied that Kyiv had learned from the "intermission" in the U.S.-Ukraine relationship of the previous two years and wanted a new quality in those relations, as part of its strategic course of integration with the European Union and NATO. Powell said the United States wanted a positive relationship, as evidenced by the high-level reception that Yanukovych had received. The prime minister replied that he understood the secretary's message and "our responsibility" regarding a democratic election process. He reiterated Kyiv's desire to take the bilateral relationship to a new stage.

Approaching Ukraine's Election and the Istanbul Summit

As 2004 began, it appeared that two issues would dominate the U.S.-Ukraine relationship: the fall presidential election in Ukraine and Ukraine's relationship with NATO. Washington hoped that Ukrainians would have the chance to make a free and democratic choice in what was shaping up as a contest between the two Viktors: Yanukovych and Yushchenko.

Two events in late December 2003, however, had raised new questions about Ukraine's politics. First, the Rada voted to approve changes to the constitution that would give the Rada more authority, including the right to select the prime minister. Some saw this as a move by the pro-Kuchma "party of power" to improve its relative position if Yushchenko should win the presidential election. Just a few days later, the Constitutional Court ruled that Kuchma, having been elected only once under the current constitution, could run for a third term.

During a consultation trip to Washington, Herbst met with Pascual and me to discuss the U.S. message regarding the election and how U.S. assistance could best be targeted to promote a free and fair ballot. I suggested that the public U.S. message be the same as it had been in 1999: Washington supported a fair and democratic election process that allowed Ukrainians to freely decide their next president and supported those candidates who favored positive relations with the United States and the West. Herbst urged dropping the second part, as that would be heard in Ukraine as code for support for Yushchenko. His proposed deletion made sense.

In a choice between Yushchenko and Yanukovych, there was little doubt who would have won a vote in Washington. Herbst, Pascual, and I talked about whether, apart from the formal public line, the United States should do something to help Yushchenko. We concluded that we should not. First, it was the Ukrainians' choice to make. Second, we doubted that we understood enough about the Ukrainian electorate and how it might react if it believed the United States backed Yushchenko; any action on our part could well backfire and prompt an electoral backlash against him.

We also discussed assistance for the election process, which Pascual was coordinating. By early 2004, the U.S. government had identified some $10 million for five major programs: improving election processes and electoral administration; supporting independent media; monitoring the electoral process and strengthening political entities; supporting election-related civic activism; and promoting voter education and mobilization. These programs might not have always appeared nonpartisan to the Ukrainians, as some American nongovernmental organizations that received U.S. government funds for nonpartisan election-related projects also had other funds that they used to help certain politicians and parties. But we concluded that the programs funded by the U.S. government could withstand challenge by the Ukrainian government or others because they focused on strengthening the process, not on assisting a specific candidate.

Roman Zvarych, a native New Yorker who had given up his American citizenship to become a Ukrainian and who had a close relationship with Yushchenko, came to the State Department in early February. He handed over documents that he said implicated senior Ukrainian officials in certain misdeeds. I told him to keep his expectations modest about what Washington might do with the documents, especially if they contained no evidence of a violation of U.S. law. Two weeks later, Herbst informed Yushchenko that Washington had no intention of publicizing the papers.

The second big question for 2004 concerned Ukraine's relationship with NATO. The alliance's leaders would gather in Istanbul for a summit on June 28–29. In the U.S. government's view, the level at which the NATO-Ukraine meeting would take place would depend in large part on how the Ukrainians managed the election run-up in the first half of the year. Ukrainian officials had expressed interest in a membership action plan in Istanbul. U.S. officials were prepared to leave the door open, with a decision to be taken in May based on how much progress Ukraine had made in implementing the 2002 Prague action plan and, as critically, an assessment as to whether Kyiv was creating a level playing field for the upcoming election.

Zlenko, who had become a presidential adviser after Hryshchenko became foreign minister, and Fialko visited Washington in mid-January. In a meeting with Jones and me, Zlenko said Kyiv sought to do its best on both democracy and its relationship with NATO. Ukraine very much wanted a NATO-Ukraine summit in Istanbul. Jones replied that the U.S. government had taken no decision yet about a summit. Positive actions, such as a good electoral process, fair media access for candidates, and no abuse of administrative resources would help greatly. Fialko commented that Kuchma had no intention of running; the West should not humiliate him. Zlenko and Fialko proposed establishing a "direct channel" to Washington. Jones turned the proposal aside, saying she was happy to meet with visiting Ukrainian officials and that the U.S. embassy in Kyiv had a good channel to the foreign minister and other officials. The interagency group met the next day to discuss relations with Kyiv. The question of a NATO-Ukraine summit would be a White House decision, and Fried reiterated that it was too early to raise the question.

At the end of January, I had a chance to exchange views with Adam Rotfeld, the Polish lead in the trilateral talks with Ukraine. He expressed concern that the West's democracy message had not been well received in Kyiv. If the Ukrainians did not get a membership action plan in Istanbul, Rotfeld suggested that NATO foreign ministers could consider giving Ukraine a plan, or at least conduct an intensified dialogue, when they met in December after the Ukrainian presidential election. As for the election itself, Warsaw saw three serious candidates: Yanukovych, Yushchenko, and Communist Party leader Petro Symonenko. The Poles were not sure whether Yushchenko was electable. Rotfeld said Kuchma had confirmed to the Polish president that he would not run.

A mid-February interagency meeting reaffirmed the U.S. approach toward Ukraine and Istanbul. Kyiv needed to take positive steps on democracy, as had been spelled out in a recent U.S.-EU paper delivered to Ukrainian officials (U.S. and EU officials had worked out an illustrative list of democracy and election reform steps for the paper). Meanwhile, the U.S. government looked at how best to reinforce the democracy message, both via official and nonofficial Americans. Former secretary of state Madeleine Albright, then serving as chairman of the National Democratic Institute, traveled to Kyiv in mid-February to meet with Kuchma. She delivered a strong message on the importance of a democratic presidential election for Ukraine and Kuchma's legacy.

On March 25, Deputy Secretary of State Armitage visited Kyiv; he was the highest ranking U.S. official to travel to the Ukrainian capital in almost three years. Armitage, Jones, and Pascual met with Kuchma, Yanukovych, and Hryshchenko on the government side, and saw opposition leaders Yushchenko and Tymoshenko as well. The deputy secretary's message to Kuchma centered on the democracy question and its link to Kyiv's professed desire to draw closer to the European Union and NATO. He handed over a letter from Bush that thanked Kuchma for the Ukrainian troop contribution in Iraq but also stressed the importance of a free and fair election for U.S.-Ukraine relations.

Wrapping up a busy day, Armitage told a press conference, "Ukraine has committed herself to certain standards as she addresses European Union and North Atlantic integration and the NATO action plan. We would be able to develop a political relationship if there were fair, free, open, and democratic elections. It's a very important milestone for Ukraine." Armitage bluntly noted the lack of a high-level dialogue with the Ukrainian president: "One of the reasons was that we had some real questions about the commitment to democracy." He also noted the opposition's expressed hope that "the international community is watching closely to see that generally recognized European standards for elections are upheld."[25] Not surprisingly, in its public commentary, the Ukrainian government played up U.S. gratitude for Kyiv's troop contribution to Iraq rather than the democracy message.

In late May, former president George H. W. Bush visited Kyiv. In meetings with both Kuchma and Yanukovych he emphasized the need for a free and fair election. Before his trip, his office had sought suggestions from the State Department for what he might say, and Bush worked strong points on democracy into his public remarks at Taras Shevchenko University. (On learning that Bush had not planned a separate meeting with Yushchenko, Ukrainian Americans complained to the White House. Bush agreed on the ground to a short meeting, essentially a pull-aside at the university.)

As a related part of its prodemocracy effort, the State Department in consultation with the embassy reached a decision to bar Hryhoriy Surkis, an oligarch with a questionable political reputation and rumored corruption connections, from getting a U.S. visa. Preparing the case—which was based on Presidential Proclamation 7750 on suspending entry to the United States for those "engaged in or benefitting from corruption"—took several months. We thought that such visa bans might lead others to clean up their act; a December 1999 report in the Ukrainian media that U.S. officials had told Marchuk that Ihor Bakay, Vadym Rabynovych, and Oleksandr Volkov should not bother applying for U.S. visas had generated a lot of attention. But the process with Surkis proved so long and complex that there was little enthusiasm in the bureaucracy for targeting others. (Years later, a presidential executive order issued during the Obama administration significantly streamlined the process for denying visas to foreigners tainted by corruption.)

The Europeans pressed a parallel message on the importance of a democratic election. When I met with EU officials in Brussels in March, they told me that the European Union was working on an action plan of its own with Ukraine. The quality of the action plan would be directly tied to democratic progress. EU officials noted that the Ukrainians had begun trying to play the Russia card with them, saying that, if the West did not accept Ukraine on Ukraine's terms, then Ukraine would turn to Russia. The Ukrainian leadership still apparently did not understand that the United States and Europe were not prepared to embrace Ukraine on its terms if that meant the state was not democratic.

We also briefly discussed U.S.-EU cooperation on the ground in Kyiv. In the spring of 2004, Herbst met regularly with his counterparts from European embassies to discuss the latest developments in the budding election campaign and to ensure that they were in sync on their democracy messages. Cooperation became operational as well. Western diplomats believed Yushchenko was less likely to encounter problems on the campaign trail, such as a last-minute denial of access to a hall for campaign rallies, if an American or European diplomat were present. The embassies coordinated to ensure that, when Yushchenko traveled outside of Kyiv to campaign, a Western diplomat would travel to observe. Herbst also organized regular meetings with domestic nongovernmental organizations that were monitoring the election run-up to discuss their work and election preparations.

After my stop in Brussels, I traveled to Warsaw. Rotfeld said the Poles had learned that Kuchma planned to come to Istanbul in any event for the Euro-Atlantic Partnership Council summit and wanted a NATO-Ukraine summit as well. The Poles did not favor holding Ukraine to a higher standard than the alliance held Russia, though Putin was not expected in Istanbul. Washington still saw democracy as the key test and had taken no decision on a NATO-Ukraine summit. Rotfeld advised that Warsaw had heard, as had Washington, of discussion in Kyiv about a possible agreement between Kuchma and the opposition that would give Kuchma immunity against any charges after he left the presidency; such an arrangement might incline Kuchma not to weigh in against Yushchenko during the campaign. If such an agreement were reached, Poland would not oppose it. (The U.S. government had a similar internal discussion but did not reach any conclusions.)

The trilateral meeting with Deputy Foreign Minister Oleh Shamshur (who later became Ukraine's ambassador to Washington) focused on NATO-Ukraine relations and the link to the presidential election process. Rotfeld cited examples of democratic shortcomings, including treatment of the media. I said such problems posed the biggest impediment to a NATO-Ukraine summit and membership action plan at the Istanbul meeting, while Herbst suggested steps that would help Kyiv reverse the impression that recent democratic developments were largely negative. They included putting Radio Liberty on state radio and implementing steps from the U.S.-EU paper. Shamshur reiterated Ukraine's desire for a summit meeting and membership action plan in Istanbul. He expressed concern that linking the NATO-Ukraine relationship too closely to the election process could cause a loss of momentum in the expansion of ties between Kyiv and the alliance.

I visited Kyiv in late April and led with the democracy message in virtually every meeting. According to embassy reports, problems had continued to mount in the election campaign. Media outlets critical of the government encountered tax and licensing problems. Radio Liberty had been shut down after five years when a new propresidential director took charge at Radio Dovira. When Radio Kontynent offered to carry Radio Liberty, its transmitter was confiscated, ostensibly because of problems with its license. Yushchenko and the opposition had rallies disrupted or could not secure venues. More than 100 businesses had reportedly been subject to harassment by the tax police because of their support for the opposition.

The mayoral election in the western town of Mukacheve on April 18 had provoked an uproar. Groups of thugs had attacked election observers, trashed polling stations, and stolen ballots. The official count inexplicably disqualified 6,000 of 19,000 votes for Viktor Baloha, the candidate of Yushchenko's Our Ukraine Party, and instead awarded the election to the candidate of the propresidential Social Democratic Party of Ukraine (united). Exit polls had shown Baloha winning by a sizable margin.

Washington had developed a list of measures that the Ukrainian government might take to ease Western concerns about the election process. They included implementation of steps that U.S. and EU officials had proposed in January; immediately inviting OSCE to send a long-term observation mission; broadcasting Radio Liberty on a state-run radio station; halting tax audits and inspections of businesses that supported the opposition; ending harassment of opposition political events; and providing a statutory basis for domestic observers from nongovernmental organizations to monitor all aspects of the election.

Herbst and I drew on these points in our meetings. We heard assurances that the government was doing all that it could to ensure a good election process, but the evidence was minimal. Yanukovych said he had had no choice but to accept a "preliminary invitation" to run for president (something that had long been expected). He claimed that he wanted a free and fair election.

Lyovochkin at Bankova asserted that there had been positive follow-up to Armitage's visit the month before, but that was difficult to see. Horbulin expected a tense election campaign and conceded that he was not confident that it would be democratic.

Yushchenko and other opposition leaders saw no prospects for a democratic election. Yushchenko worried that Kuchma's decision to contribute troops to Iraq would win him a pass on democracy problems from Washington. I responded that the U.S. government was pressing hard on those problems. Yushchenko confirmed that the opposition had explored the possibility of granting Kuchma a "stable retirement"—

that is, immunity from any prosecution—in return for a free and fair election process; he added that Kwasniewski might play a role as an international guarantor. As for the documents that Zvarych had handed over in February, Yushchenko asked whether Washington would take action on them, a question that arose in a separate meeting that Herbst and I had with Zvarych and other senior Yushchenko supporters. We explained that the documents had indicated no violation of U.S. law, their origin and veracity were unclear, and it would not be appropriate for Washington to make use of them publicly. Doing so could undercut the U.S. approach that focused on the electoral process, not a particular candidate. The Ukrainians themselves would have to decide whether and how to use the papers.

Tymoshenko leaned toward supporting Yushchenko, in part because her poll standing was not sufficiently strong. As usual, she provided the most textured description of the political field. She said Medvedchuk worked quietly with Moroz and had some contact with Symonenko. She figured that Moroz most probably was "lost" to Yushchenko, but Yushchenko should work to get Moroz back on his side. He had not reached out to Moroz, or to Tymoshenko, for that matter. Yushchenko appeared to believe he could go it alone and let Yanukovych, Moroz, and Symonenko divide the vote in eastern Ukraine. Tymoshenko was dubious about that strategy.

Over dinner, a well plugged in Ukrainian journalist shared a story that she had heard about Yanukovych. Kuchma and Putin had met on April 23 in Yalta. Yanukovych reportedly learned of the meeting, thought a photo-op with Putin could help his political campaign, and flew to Crimea unannounced. Putin refused to meet with him, according to the story, because he was put off by Yanukovych's criminal past. The journalist confirmed for us the wisdom of the U.S. choice to focus on a democratic process, not a particular candidate. She opined that any kind of U.S. endorsement for Yushchenko would not help him.

Things did not go better on the democracy front in Ukraine over the course of May and early June. I was asked to testify before the House International Relations Committee on May 12 and noted the U.S. government's view that the single most important question on the bilateral agenda was the presidential campaign and election, and how they were conducted. Unfortunately, recent signs in that regard had been discouraging.

NATO members decided in May to defer the question of giving Ukraine a membership action plan or intensified dialogue until after the Istanbul summit, but they left open the question of whether the NATO-Ukraine meeting would take place at the summit or the ministerial level—essentially waiting to hear the U.S. position. Powell saw Hryshchenko on June 21 and told him that the big issue continued to be: would the election be free and fair? Hryshchenko hoped the election would go better than past elections and added that many in Kyiv believed the U.S. concern centered on who won, not the process. The secretary replied that it was about process; Ukraine needed to create the right environment for a free and fair election. Herbst met with Kuchma the next day in Kyiv, discussed democracy and the election, and reported that the meeting had been difficult.

With the Istanbul NATO summit less than a week away, the view in the interagency group was that Kuchma had not done enough to secure a NATO-Ukraine summit meeting. Jones conveyed that recommendation to the secretary. Powell agreed that Ukraine had not done enough but said he would support a summit. Given all the other problems on Bush's foreign policy agenda, the secretary believed that a flare-up with Kyiv at this point in time could be problematic for the White House, particularly if it might call into question Ukraine's contribution to Iraq. Although he did not accept the interagency recommendation, the secretary's position was not unreasonable, reflecting the choices between competing foreign policy priorities that sometimes have to be made. The White House did not object to a NATO-Ukraine summit, so a summit was fixed for June 29.

One last question came up. The National Security Council suggested proposing to NATO that, as in Prague, the French spellings of Ukraine and the United States be used to determine the alphabetical (by country) seating for the NATO-Ukraine and Euro-Atlantic Partnership Council summits. Kuchma would thus be separated from Bush. We at the State Department did not think that made sense, as a repeat snub would undercut the whole point of agreeing to a NATO-Ukraine summit. On Air Force One en route to Istanbul, Jones persuaded National Security Council staff to stick with English spellings for the seating plan.

Kuchma got his summit in Istanbul, but he also heard a lot about democracy. The NATO communiqué, issued the day before the NATO-Ukraine summit, had one paragraph devoted to Ukraine. It read in part:

We welcome Ukraine's determination to pursue full Euro-Atlantic integration. In this context, we reaffirm the necessity to achieve consistent and measurable progress in democratic reform. We encourage Ukraine to accelerate the implementation of the objectives outlined in the NATO-Ukraine Action Plan, particularly regarding the conduct of free and fair elections, the guaranteeing of media freedoms, and implementation of the results of the Defense Review. We are determined to support Ukraine in these efforts, while noting that a further strengthening of our relationship will require stronger evidence of Ukraine's commitment to comprehensive reform, in particular with a view to the conduct of presidential elections this autumn.

The leaders instructed NATO ambassadors to assess development in Ukraine and NATO-Ukraine relations "with a view to presenting recommendations to foreign ministers after the presidential elections."[26]

During his June 28 press conference, NATO secretary general Jaap de Hoop Scheffer criticized Ukraine's democracy performance, citing problems in the campaign and issues of media freedom. He reiterated this in his opening comments at the NATO-Ukraine meeting:

In adopting the action plan, Ukraine has undertaken a firm commitment to the common values that underpin the alliance. It is no secret that allies have had serious questions with respect to how this commitment has been implemented. In some cases, as in questions related to export controls, substantial steps have been taken to address these concerns. In others, such as media freedom and the conduct of free and fair elections, important questions remain.[27]

Other Spring Issues

While preparations for the presidential election and the Istanbul summit commanded most U.S. diplomatic attention regarding Ukraine in the first half of 2004, the agenda contained a number of other issues. By spring 2004, Ukrainian forces in Iraq numbered close to 1,800 soldiers, and the army had begun training a new unit to rotate in and relieve troops already in the country. The Ukrainians had found themselves under fire on a number of occasions. It was a far more contested military environment—"virtual combat operations," as one Ukrainian ruefully noted—than the peacekeeping operation that Kyiv had expected. The army wanted to revise its rules of engagement to reflect that.

The presence of troops in Iraq continued to pose a delicate political question within Ukraine. Support in the Rada was soft, polls showed that as much as 70 percent of the populace opposed the deployment, and the issue had become something of a political football. Yushchenko complained to Herbst and me that Kuchma tried to portray the Iraq deployment as an Our Ukraine initiative. Our Ukraine sought to distance itself from Iraq.

While Kuchma could not keep Iraq from becoming a political issue, he ensured that the politics did not undermine the commitment. When Surkis could not get a visa to the United States, a senior foreign ministry official attempted to intercede, warning Herbst that a failure to grant the visa might lead the Social Democrats in the Rada to withdraw their support for the deployment in Iraq. Herbst replied that such a blackmail tactic would not work. He raised it with Lyovochkin, who assured him that the visa question would not affect Kuchma's commitment of troops. The embassy had the impression that Bankova was bemused by Surkis's dilemma.

Although the previous fall's crisis over Tuzla Island seemed under control, we continued to hear that all was not well in Ukraine-Russia relations. The Ukrainians did not like Russia's proposal for dividing control of the Sea of Azov. Shamshur in April made clear that the "weak reaction" from Washington to the Russian causeway construction had not gone unnoticed in Kyiv. Ukrainian officials also said differences persisted between Kyiv and Moscow over the Single Economic Space. Moscow continued to maintain that the agreement entailed a customs union. Yanukovych in April told Herbst and me that Kyiv had signed the agreement "with reservations" and that it did not signal any change in the priority that Ukraine attached to drawing closer to Europe. Chalyy worried that Russia's push for the Single Economic Space could be followed by pressure on Ukraine to join a single security space. Horbulin acknowledged that the Single Economic Space raised a question about Kyiv's direction; Ukraine had to undertake policy actions to erase doubts in Europe and Washington about the government's commitment to a Westward orientation.

The U.S. government tried to figure out where the Ukrainians were headed on the Odesa-Brody pipeline. Kyiv still had not lined up a supplier to deliver oil to the Pivdennyy terminal near Odesa, from which it could be sent by pipeline to Brody and on to Central Europe, and Russia was pushing a proposal to reverse the flow and deliver oil from Brody to Odesa. That was unfortunate, since Chevron-Texaco wanted to negotiate the terms and tariffs for using the pipeline to move Caspian oil to Central Europe. In February, Kyiv reportedly shifted and backed an Odesa-to-Brody flow. At the trilateral meeting in March, Shamshur underscored Ukrainian interest in extending the pipeline from Brody to Plock and on to the Polish refinery in Gdansk. The Poles favored an extension in geopolitical terms, as did Washington, but they reminded the Ukrainians that the project had to be commercially driven. Kyiv needed to make the economic case. The next month, Yanukovych asserted that the Ukrainians needed to fill the pipeline with oil or they would have no choice but to reverse the flow. Herbst pointed out that Chevron-Texaco was interested, but no one on the Ukrainian side had met with firm representatives to negotiate possible terms. He cautioned that acceptance of a Russian proposal to use the pipeline to move oil from Brody to Odesa for six months likely was a "salami tactic" aimed at permanently blocking an Odesa to Brody flow.

Reflections

U.S.-Ukraine relations hit a post–Cold War low at the end of 2002. Six years of regular contact at the highest levels came to an end when George W. Bush took office in January 2001. From the moment Bush moved into the White House, Ukrainian officials began pressing for an invitation for Kuchma to visit Washington. The American president's attention in his first year focused on other questions, particularly after September 11. When National Security Adviser Condoleezza Rice visited earlier that summer, U.S. ambassador Pascual laid out steps on the investigation into journalist Heorhiy Gongadze's disappearance that could permit a Bush-Kuchma meeting, perhaps joined by the Polish president, on the margins of the UN General Assembly session. In light of Gongadze's disappearance and revelations in the Melnychenko recordings, it would have been hard to hold such a meeting without something to show on the Gongadze investigation. The steps suggested by Pascual were not meaningless, but they did not set a particularly high bar. From what Washington could see, Kyiv made no effort to clear it.

That misfire was compounded by the Ukrainian government's failure to end its arms transfers to Macedonia until 2002. Rice left Kyiv believing that she had a commitment from Kuchma. His image in Washington, already damaged, suffered further over the next eight months as heavy weapons continued to flow into Macedonia.

In early 2002, the U.S. government hoped to leverage Kyiv's interest in an invitation for Kuchma to encourage, if not a free and fair Rada election process, then a freer and fairer one than was expected. The election problems continued, however, and the OSCE monitoring mission reported a host of shortfalls in the run-up to the ballot. The troubled conduct of the election process reinforced the growing view in Washington that democratic practices would not be consolidated under Kuchma—and were in danger of slippage. Moreover, Washington had seen no effort whatsoever to respond to Deputy Secretary of State Armitage's appeal. The idea of inviting Kuchma to the United States in the spring of 2002 fell by the wayside.

In retrospect, it was probably not surprising that official Kyiv did not respond to U.S. urgings. To be sure, the carrot of a White House visit provided an attractive lure. However, as Washington had seen before, and would see again in the future, the high stakes of domestic politics within Ukraine outweighed whatever incentives the United States (and Europe) could muster.

In summer 2002, Kyiv proposed a trilateral meeting of the U.S., Ukrainian, and Polish presidents on the margins of the UN General Assembly meeting in September. That format had greater appeal in Washington than a bilateral Bush-Kuchma meeting, and U.S. officials responded that it might be possible if progress were made on at least some of the twenty problematic issues on the U.S.-Ukraine agenda. Nothing was accomplished, however. Some of the problem issues could have been resolved relatively easily. U.S. officials saw no effort by the Ukrainians to find solutions. They wondered if Bankova did not care about a meeting with Bush, or whether the Ukrainian government was so dysfunctional that Bankova could not make ministries deliver. In any case, a third opportunity for a Kuchma meeting with Bush passed.

Conversely, Ukraine did show some progress on economic reform in the early 2000s. The reform of the electric power sector led by Tymoshenko, with assistance from the U.S. government and European Bank for Reconstruction and Development, provided significantly greater cash flows to the electric power generators, thus reducing their requirement for subsidies from the government. During Kinakh's short tenure as prime minister, there was progress on land titling and dividing up the collective farms that had lingered since Soviet times. This was obvious when I flew into Kyiv with Rice in July 2001: the tilling patterns showed much smaller plots than what one had seen in the 1990s. Ukrainian agricultural production began to register substantial growth that year.

Reform did not reach every part of the economy. Most of the energy sector outside the electricity sector—particularly natural gas with its opaque intermediaries—remained little changed. The U.S. government did not fully understand how profound the corruption was in the gas sector, where Ukrainians and Russians collaborated with the apparent connivance of officials in both countries, nor did it fully grasp the connection between corruption in the energy sector and Ukraine's politics. When Pascual received information suggesting that Yuriy Boyko, chairman of Naftohaz Ukraine, could be involved in corrupt activities, he asked Kuchma to whom he should pass that information. Kuchma suggested his deputy chief of staff, Lyovochkin. Pascual learned later that Boyko and Lyovochkin were partners. Why didn't Washington and the embassy have a better fix on corruption? Corruption was an inherently murky process, and the U.S. government only rarely received clear and compelling information that described corruption schemes and named names. U.S. intelligence resources had other more important priorities. When someone violated U.S. law, as former prime minister Pavlo Lazarenko had, the matter received considerable attention, but corruption otherwise fell down on the list of priorities. In retrospect, allowing that to happen was probably a mistake on our part, given how badly corruption has held back Ukraine's development.

What truly brought U.S.-Ukraine relations, as well as NATO-Ukraine relations, to a low point was the Kolchuga case. Following the second Gulf War, the U.S. military found no Kolchuga air defense systems in Iraq. American officials had been careful, however, not to claim that a transfer had taken place, only that they were concerned that one of the Melnychenko recordings indicated that Kuchma had approved the transfer. My own belief is that Kuchma initially agreed to the transfer, as the recording showed, but later reversed his decision and had that communicated somehow to Malev. Washington already knew that Kuchma sometimes said yes but later changed his mind when it became clear that his first decision was wrong. Indeed, a source of regular frustration for U.S. officials was the Ukrainian tendency to say yes when Kyiv had little idea how to deliver on the agreement or little intention of doing so.

If Ukrainian officials in September 2002 had told U.S. officials that Kuchma had agreed to the transfer but then reversed himself, Washington would have been unhappy that Kuchma's initial instinct had been to say yes but, knowing how Kuchma operated, would have found it entirely plausible. The admission would have done little additional damage to the bilateral relationship, and the Kolchuga issue would have amounted to a much smaller problem for the relationship. Instead, Kyiv denied the recording and failed to show transparency with a U.S.-British experts team that the Ukrainians themselves invited to investigate the question. The result was a mini-crisis that helped spin U.S.-Ukraine relations down to their lowest point.

Bankova did not seem to fully appreciate how much damage the Kolchuga case did to Kuchma's credibility and to the bilateral relationship. Officials seemed surprised that NATO on a few weeks' notice would cancel the NATO-Ukraine summit in November 2002 in the aftermath of the Kolchuga experts' visit or that the U.S. government would continue to decline proposals for a Bush-Kuchma meeting. Their surprise may have reflected the high estimation that many in the elite in Kyiv seemed to attach to Ukraine's geopolitical importance between the West and Russia.

Kolchuga also took the wind out of Ukraine's expression earlier in 2002 of its desire to join NATO. U.S. officials believed some in Kyiv genuinely held that view, but they never had the sense that it had become a true priority for the Presidential Administration, where Med-vedchuk was viewed as very much a pro-Russian actor. Kuchma still seemed interested in maintaining balance between the West and Russia. It was telling that the Ukrainian government did not publicly announce its intention to seek membership in the alliance until late May—just before a NATO-Russia summit in Rome that was widely expected to inject new momentum into the alliance's relationship with Russia. That gave Kuchma a degree of political cover for saying that he would move closer to NATO without dramatically upsetting the balance with Russia.

Kuchma's flip back toward Moscow in September 2003, when he agreed to join the Single Economic Space with Russia, Kazakhstan, and Belarus, suggested that his professed interest in joining NATO was more of a tactical decision than the reflection of a major change in Ukraine's strategic course. What puzzled U.S. officials was not just the confusion about Kyiv's overall geopolitical orientation but the fact that joining the Single Economic Space—if it were a customs union—would derail Ukraine's bid to join the World Trade Organization. Ukrainian officials maintained that the Single Economic Space was merely a free trade area, which would not have been a problem for the WTO bid, but Russian officials insisted it was a customs union. (In the end, Kyiv did not pursue the Single Economic Space. It joined the World Trade Organization in 2006.)

What saved the U.S.-Ukraine relationship from virtual collapse was Iraq and Kuchma's willingness to commit Ukrainian forces. Ukrainian officials in late 2002 asked Pascual what Kyiv could do to get back in good favor in Washington. At the time, the Bush White House desperately sought to add members to the Iraq military coalition, both in the run-up to the attack on Iraq and in the international stabilization force that was deployed after Baghdad's fall. No contribution was too small; for example, the administration welcomed one country's commitment of a unit of just fifty soldiers. The more flags of participating states, the greater the operation's international legitimacy. Kuchma recognized this, and Kyiv offered serious contributions: an NBC defense battalion to help protect Kuwait and later almost 2,000 troops for the stabilization force. These offers were unpopular with the Ukrainian public. But they achieved their political goal: Kuchma was able to maintain at least a minimal relationship with Washington. In June 2004 he attended a NATO-Ukraine summit in Istanbul that, given problems in the presidential election campaign, the U.S. government might otherwise have sought to cancel. Interestingly, Kuchma found it easier to put troops in Iraq than to address earlier U.S. suggestions for actions that could improve relations at the top.

CHAPTER 6

Election and Revolution

With the Istanbul NATO summit (and its accompanying NATO-Ukraine meeting) out of the way, Washington's attention for the remainder of 2004 focused squarely on the Ukrainian presidential election. U.S. officials continued to press Kyiv to create conditions for a free, fair, and transparent election. They understood that that would be an uphill battle, which became especially clear when the second round of the election on November 21 was marred by widespread vote manipulation. As crowds gathered in downtown Kyiv and other cities to protest in what became known as the Orange Revolution, Secretary of State Colin Powell bluntly told reporters that the U.S. government "cannot accept this result as legitimate."[1]

The Election Run-Up

The Ukrainian presidential election campaign intensified over summer 2004.[2] The struggle boiled down to a contest between Viktor Yush-chenko, a former prime minister, and Viktor Yanukovych, the current prime minister. Their frontrunner status did not prevent others from tossing their hats into the ring. When the Central Electoral Commission closed the election registration on September 20, twenty-six candidates had declared their intention to run. Socialist Party leader Oleksandr Moroz and Communist Party head Petro Symonenko appeared to be the strongest candidates after Yushchenko and Yanukovych. No one else had a serious prospect of winning.

Yushchenko focused his electoral message on liberal economics, anti-corruption, nationalism, and his background as governor of the National Bank of Ukraine and prime minister. Perhaps his strongest selling point with much of the electorate was that, during his time as prime minister in 2000–01, he had ensured that wages and pensions were usually paid on time. Yanukovych also stressed his experience as prime minister but played on themes that would appeal more to his power base in Ukraine's east, including a rejection of closer relations with NATO, official status for the Russian language, and strong relations with Moscow. Most in Washington privately regarded Yushchenko as the better candidate for Ukraine's future; certainly his campaign message corresponded far more closely with the U.S. vision for Ukraine. That said, the U.S. government held to its earlier decision to support a democratic election process and avoid endorsing—overtly or tacitly—any candidate. The Yanukovych campaign nonetheless attempted to portray Yushchenko as closely connected to Washington, citing among other things his American-born wife.

The electoral problems—including abuse of administrative resources to support Yanukovych, harassment of Yushchenko supporters, denial of flight clearances for Yushchenko's plane on campaign trips, and uneven access to the media—worsened through the summer and into the fall. Things took a particularly vicious turn on September 5, when Yushchenko was poisoned. Medical treatment, first in Kyiv and then at a clinic in Austria, kept him off the campaign trail for most of a month. When he resumed campaigning in October, his face showed the devastating effects of the poison. His stamina was greatly reduced. But those close to Yushchenko reported that he returned to the campaign trail with renewed focus and purpose. It could not have been easy; he reportedly campaigned with a catheter implanted in his spine to deliver pain medicine.

The U.S. government meanwhile continued to make clear to Kyiv its interest in a democratic election. Secretary of Defense Donald Rumsfeld visited Ukraine in mid-August, traveling to Crimea to meet with President Leonid Kuchma and Defense Minister Yevhen Marchuk. Though outside his normal portfolio, urging a free and fair presidential election was high on his agenda. He also met separately with Yushchenko. President George W. Bush's message to Kuchma expressing congratulations on Ukraine's August 24 independence day stressed the importance of "holding a free, fair, and transparent election" and of Kuchma's "turning your high office over to a successor who embodies the democratic choice of the Ukrainian people."[3]

On October 7, Ambassador John Herbst expressed Washington's readiness to work with whomever the Ukrainians elected but added, "What matters is the election process's honesty and transparency."[4] An October 14 statement by State Department spokeperson Richard Boucher summed up U.S. concerns that Ukraine was not meeting the standards of a free, fair, and transparent election process. The statement said the U.S. government was "deeply disappointed that the campaign to date has fallen short of international standards. The disruption of opposition rallies, muzzling of independent media, misuse of 'administrative resources,' and other serious violations cast doubt on the Ukrainian government's commitment to its democratic obligations." The statement urged the Ukrainian authorities to allow a free vote and warned that, if the election failed to meet democratic standards, "we would also need to re-examine our relationship with those engaged in election fraud and manipulation."[5]

In Kyiv, Herbst played the Surkis card, which became more effective when the information about Hryhoriy Surkis's permanent ineligibility for a U.S. visa leaked to the local press. As part of his effort to discourage senior officials from subverting the election campaign or the ballot itself, Herbst pointedly told Presidential Administration head Viktor Medvedchuk and Minister of Internal Affairs Mykola Bilokon, "See what happened to Surkis; it could happen to you." That got the attention of senior officials around Kyiv.

The public U.S. criticism paralleled messages coming from Europe. The Polish Sejm (parliament) passed a resolution on October 22 calling on the Ukrainian government to ensure that the election met democratic standards. On October 27, ambassadors from EU member states in Kyiv issued an appeal that noted campaign irregularities and called on the government to observe democratic standards. The next day, the

European Parliament passed a resolution expressing its concern about problems with the election campaign.[6]

While Washington took care to avoid steps that would be seen as supporting Yushchenko, Moscow showed no such hesitation in backing Yanukovych. President Vladimir Putin effectively endorsed Yanukovych following a July 26, 2004, meeting with Kuchma. Shortly thereafter, Gleb Pavlovskiy, a Moscow "political technologist" who had worked on Russian political campaigns, established a "Russian club" in Kyiv that aimed its efforts at supporting Yanukovych and criticizing Yushchenko. Gazprom and other Russian sources reportedly contributed $300 million to Yanukovych's campaign war chest, while Russian electronic media, relatively available in eastern Ukraine, broadcast a steady stream of pro-Yanukovych and anti-Yushchenko messages.[7]

Billboards endorsing Yanukovych festooned Moscow, and Russian political consultant Sergey Markov said their goal was to "underline that Russia backs Yanukovych."[8] Polls showed that Ukrainians held Putin in high regard, and Yanukovych tried to exploit that. In September, Putin agreed to change the value-added tax system between the two countries in a way that benefited Ukraine. On October 9, Kuchma and Yanukovych traveled to meet with Putin in Moscow, where Putin praised the course of Ukraine-Russia relations under Kuchma's presidency and Yanukovych's prime ministership. The Russian president visited Ukraine on October 26–28, ostensibly to attend a military parade marking the sixtieth anniversary of the city's liberation in World War II. The visit instead looked like a thinly disguised campaign stop on Yanukovych's behalf. Putin delivered a lengthy speech, widely broadcast on Ukrainian television, praising bilateral cooperation and the work that Yanukovych had done as prime minister.

The First Round

Ukrainians went to the polls on October 31. As expected, it was a battle between the two Viktors. The Central Electoral Commission initially reported that Yanukovych edged out Yushchenko for the top spot, winning by 40.1 percent to 39.2 percent. Nine days later the Central Electoral Commission released the official count, which showed that Yushchenko had won by 100,000 votes, garnering 39.9 percent of the vote to Yanukovych's 39.3 percent. Moroz placed third with almost 6 percent, and Symonenko came in fourth with 5 percent. Other than Progressive Socialist Party leader Natalia Vitrenko, no other candidate polled more than 1 percent. A runoff election between Yushchenko and Yanukovych was set for November 21.

The International Election Observation Mission, which consisted of the OSCE's Office for Democratic Institutions and Human Rights, the OSCE Parliamentary Assembly, the Parliamentary Assembly of the Council of Europe, the European Parliament, and the NATO Parliamentary Assembly, had operated in Ukraine for some time before the election in order to monitor the campaign and the preparations for the vote. On November 1, it issued its preliminary conclusions, noting that the previous day's election

> did not meet a considerable number of OSCE, Council of Europe, and other European standards for democratic elections. During the preelection period, the governmental, electoral, and other authorities did not create conditions that ensure in practice the free expression of the opinion of electors in their choice of representatives. Consequently, this election process constitutes a step backward from the 2002 elections.... There existed widespread allegations, some of which were verified by long-term observers, that pressure to support the government candidate [Yanukovych] was exerted on certain groups of voters, including those whose livelihood depends upon the state, and students. Such pressures were also exerted on citizens to cease their political activity for opposition candidates. Fundamental freedoms necessary for a meaningful election process were at times infringed upon during the course of the pre-election period. The free movement of opposition candidates or their supporters to campaign events and citizens' rights to peaceful assembly were not always respected, and freedom of association was challenged on occasions.[9]

Yushchenko and Yanukovych had less than three weeks to campaign for the runoff. Yushchenko received endorsements from Moroz and Anatoliy Kinakh (who had placed sixth in the first-round ballot).

These came on top of an earlier endorsement from Yuliya Tymosh-enko. Yanukovych picked up an endorsement from Vitrenko. After the first round, television journalists asserted greater independence and provided more balanced coverage of the two candidates. Yanukovych on November 12 joined Kuchma and Putin in a meeting at Kerch in Crimea. The meeting did not appear to be substantive. Rather, it gave Yanukovych yet another opportunity for a photo op with the Russian president. The main event of the three-week mini-campaign was the November 15 debate between Yushchenko and Yanukovych; most analysts gave the win to Yushchenko.

The U.S. embassy closely followed the short inter-round campaign. Herbst had come to the conclusion that Rada speaker Volodymyr Lytvyn might be a positive political force, since he seemed to recognize that the old ways likely would lose out and did not want to find himself on the wrong side—a recognition based more on his pragmatism than on respect for democracy. Herbst arranged for a quick visit by Lytvyn to Washington, where he met with National Security Adviser Condoleezza Rice, Senator Richard Lugar, and other senior congressional figures. They underscored the importance of a free and fair runoff election, reinforcing with Lytvyn the message that Herbst and the embassy stressed in Kyiv.

The Runoff and the Orange Revolution

The second round of balloting took place on November 21. Foreign and domestic election monitors reported massive irregularities, including abuse of the absentee ballot system, ballot stuffing, and falsified voting counts. Some observers were blocked from entering polling stations, while others reported buses taking voters from one station to another to cast multiple ballots. The Central Electoral Commission experienced a pause that evening in reporting the returns from polling commissions in eastern Ukraine, seen as the pro-Yanukovych stronghold. That raised concerns that the numbers were being manipulated.

On November 22, the Central Electoral Commission's chair issued an unofficial count showing that Yanukovych had won the runoff, polling 49.7 percent compared to Yushchenko's 46.7 percent. These results contradicted an exit poll released the night before by three respected

Ukrainian institutes, which gave Yushchenko 54 percent of the vote to Yanukovych's 43 percent.[10] Moreover, analysts began to question the Central Electoral Commission's reports of voter turnout, which showed significantly larger numbers taking part in the second round than in the first in pro-Yanukovych areas, with turnout in some areas exceeding 100 percent. Shortly after the Central Electoral Commission released the turnout figures, a chart began circulating that showed the difference in voter turnout between November 21 and October 31. In the southern and eastern voting districts that voted largely for Yanukovych, turnout jumped at least 5 to 10 percent on November 21, whereas turnout in the rest of the country ranged from 5 percent less to 5 percent more than turnout on October 31. Most strikingly, some areas in Donetsk and Luhansk—the heart of Yanukovych's power base—reported turnout up by more than 40 percent.[11] The chart convinced many that the Central Electoral Commission had manipulated both the reported turnout and the vote totals.

The International Election Observation Mission coordinated by OSCE delivered a scathing assessment of the election process on November 22, noting that the "authorities failed to take remedial action between the two rounds of voting to redress biased coverage on state media, misuse of state resources, and pressure on certain categories of voters to support the candidacy of Mr. Yanukovych. Overall, state executive authorities and the Central Electoral Commission (CEC) displayed a lack of will to conduct a genuine democratic election process." The report went on to cite "a higher incidence of serious violations" than on October 31, "the suspiciously high turnout in some regions," and the number of voters, mainly absentee voters, added to voting lists on the day of the election. The report stated, "In Donetsk Oblast, preliminary turnout figures announced by the CEC are so improbable as to cast doubt on whether that [the voters'] choice was always safeguarded."[12]

The Bush administration had asked Lugar to observe the second round of the election. The Indiana senator was a logical choice; he had first traveled to Ukraine in the early 1990s and thereafter had visited the country almost every year. He had an established relationship with Kuchma and other senior Ukrainians. He had carried a letter from Bush stressing the importance of a good election process. Lugar and Herbst had shuttled between meetings with Kuchma, Yushchenko,

Yanukovych, and the head of the Central Electoral Commission on the eve of the second-round vote to promote a clean process. Within a couple of hours after the OSCE released its statement on November 22, Lugar delivered his own harsh critique, noting that it was "now apparent that a concerted and forceful program of election-day fraud and abuse was enacted with either the leadership or cooperation of governmental authorities."[13] Lugar made clear that responsibility to fix the problem lay with the Ukrainian leadership.

As OSCE issued its pronouncement, pro-Yushchenko demonstrators were taking to the streets of Kyiv and western Ukrainian cities to protest the stolen election, and the Orange Revolution began. Herbst urged the government to avoid a violent crackdown. He also urged officials in the Presidential Administration at Bankova and the Central Electoral Commission not to officially declare Yanukovych the winner, because that would leave the U.S. government little choice but to slam the election publicly. In Washington, the White House released a measured statement on November 23 expressing concern over the "extensive and credible indications of fraud" and urging the Ukrainian government "not to certify the results until investigations of organized fraud are resolved."[14]

That evening in Kyiv, however, Yushchenko appeared before the Rada and preemptively took the presidential oath, angering Yanukovych and his supporters as well as officials at Bankova. Herbst continued to urge the government not to certify Yanukovych's election while the fraud charges were investigated, but Yushchenko's ploy undercut Herbst's message. The evening of November 24, the Central Electoral Commission officially declared Yanukovych the winner of the runoff. The State Department had prepared language for the press spokesperson's use in such an event, but Secretary of State Powell had a press opportunity almost immediately following the Central Electoral Commission's announcement. He drew on the prepared language himself, saying that the United States could not regard the election result as legitimate, and that he had contacted Kuchma to suggest ways to settle the crisis and to urge him not to use force against the demonstrators.[15] Coming so quickly, and coming from the secretary directly instead of the State Department's spokesperson, the message had strong resonance in Kyiv. Warsaw, Berlin, London, and other European capitals weighed in with their criticism of the election.

As the demonstrations grew in size, particularly in Kyiv, Kuchma began talking to senior European officials, particularly Polish president Alexander Kwasniewski and EU high representative for common foreign and security policy Javier Solana. While Kwasniewski and Solana considered how the Europeans might help resolve the situation, Washington began talking to Europe. Assistant Secretary of State Beth Jones and National Security Council Senior Director for Europe Dan Fried agreed to a forward-leaning U.S. government approach. Bush called Kwasniewski, and Powell spoke to European Commission president Jose Manuel Barroso. Jones and Deputy Assistant Secretary of State John Tefft began what would become a continuing phone dialogue with EU, Polish, and Dutch officials (the Dutch held the EU presidency).[16]

These communications constituted a very intense period of collaboration between Herbst and Jones, between their teams, and between them and their EU and Canadian colleagues. Jones followed up daily with Herbst and her European and Canadian counterparts to calibrate the content, tone, and level of public statements being made in capitals and in phone calls to senior Ukrainians. Fried worked in parallel with his European contacts, including Kwasniewski, whom he had known from his previous service in Warsaw. The goals were to advocate for a fair outcome that respected the will of the voters, to encourage the protest leaders to work through legal and established processes, to warn the Ukrainian government against taking physical action against the demonstrators in the capital, and to encourage the demonstrators not to engage in provocative acts. At times a strong statement from Powell or even the White House was proposed and released. At other times it seemed more prudent for a statement from Warsaw or Brussels to lead the way. The statements and phone calls sought to influence fast-moving events to produce the most constructive results possible and, above all, to avoid bloodshed.

The embassy's stream of reporting developed a loyal following in Washington and in relevant U.S. embassies around Europe. Its constant flow allowed, for example, Jones to insert up-to-the minute details into a NATO intervention that Powell was about to make in Brussels, adding credibility and urgency to his advocacy for support for the Ukrainians demonstrating for their right to a fair election.

As the demonstrations grew, and Yushchenko and Yanukovych dug in, key security services declared their neutrality. Defense Minister

Oleksandr Kuzmuk, a Kuchma appointee in his second stint in the job whose wife was the sister of Kuchma's wife, said the military would not deploy during the crisis. Former Security Service of Ukraine (SBU) officials stated that the service would protect the people.

Kwasniewski and Solana traveled to Kyiv for a roundtable discussion on the situation and possible ways out of the crisis with Kuchma, Yushchenko, and Yanukovych on November 26. Lithuanian president Valdas Adamkus, Bulgarian foreign minister (and OSCE chairman-in-office) Solomon Passy, and Russian Duma (parliament) speaker Boris Gryzlov joined the discussion, as did Lytvyn, former Rada speaker Ivan Plyushch, and former president Leonid Kravchuk. The first roundtable launched a process with an expectation of further roundtable meetings with European mediation.

U.S. diplomats did not take part directly in the roundtable but nevertheless kept close tabs on the discussions and did what they could to support the European effort to resolve the crisis. They also monitored the demonstrations and stayed in regular touch with Yushchenko's camp. Backed by strong public messages coming out of Washington and other capitals, Herbst and the embassy saw their job as twofold: to do everything they could to prevent violence and to push toward a fair outcome of the crisis.

The next day, the Rada under Lytvyn's guidance effectively censured the Central Electoral Commission when it passed a resolution calling into question the election runoff and the preliminary election results reported by the CEC. It had no legal effect, but Yushchenko's team and the demonstrators in the street nevertheless saw it as validating their demands.

The crisis passed through its most dangerous stage on the weekend of November 27–28. On November 27, Yanukovych pressed Kuchma for a declaration of a state of emergency and asked that force be used to clear the crowds blocking access to government buildings in downtown Kyiv. Kuchma refused to do so, in part because of a warning from SBU chairman Ihor Smeshko that security forces might not prove reliable if told to act against the protestors.[17] Still, former foreign minister Borys Tarasyuk, who had become the Yushchenko camp's primary interlocutor with embassies in Kyiv, phoned Herbst to warn that a crackdown was coming. Herbst asked embassy officers to check with their contacts, including those at SBU headquarters, who reported that they saw no evidence of preparations for use of force against the demonstrators.

Despite Kuchma's refusal to authorize the use of force, SBU officials received reports on November 28 that a ministry of interior unit had been alerted to move into Kyiv and clear away the demonstrators. Those officials warned Yushchenko's camp and also alerted the U.S. and British embassies. Tarasyuk called Herbst again to report that he had heard reports of an imminent crackdown. This time, when embassy officers checked with their SBU counterparts, they got a more worrisome answer. Herbst worked the phones, calling Ukrainian officials to caution against use of force. He reached out to Serhiy Lyovochkin in the Presidential Administration, who was not available, then to Victor Pinchuk, Kuchma's son-in-law, to get the message to Kuchma. Herbst called Jones and asked her to have Powell call Kuchma directly, noting that the indications of a crackdown were more ominous than the previous day. The secretary tried to call Kuchma, but he would not take the call. Herbst called Pinchuk again, telling him that no one in Washington believed Kuchma truly was unavailable to talk to Powell; he reiterated the importance of the government not using force.

Pinchuk phoned back and said Medvedchuk had told him that nothing would happen. Shortly thereafter, the embassy heard that the ministry of interior troops assembled for the crackdown had returned to their barracks. The embassy learned sometime later that, when the crackdown appeared imminent, Tymoshenko had contacted the head of the army, as had SBU officials. Senior SBU and army officials then contacted the ministry of interior to warn against any effort to enter Kyiv, threatening that they would use armed force to protect the protestors. The ministry of interior unit did not approach the capital.[18]

European mediators conducted a second roundtable in Kyiv on December 1. They encouraged a settlement that drew largely on ideas put forward by Lytvyn envisaging a rerun of the runoff vote if ordered by the Supreme Court, constitutional amendments that would shift some authority from the presidency to the Rada, and formation of a new cabinet based on the constitutional amendments. Kuchma made a surprise December 2 trip to see Putin, but the idea of rerunning the runoff vote gained momentum, winning endorsements from key European officials. On December 3, the Supreme Court ruled the runoff results invalid and determined that a new runoff election should be held on

December 26, a decision that was swiftly welcomed by Washington and the European Union. The final roundtable took place December 6–7. Although it did not produce agreement among the Ukrainians on every point, it endorsed the Supreme Court's ruling for a new runoff election and called for appointment of a new Central Electoral Commission to oversee the process. On December 8, the Rada voted to dismiss the current commission members, amended the constitution, and adopted changes to the law governing presidential elections.

The Rada votes effectively ended the crisis, and Yushchenko and Yanukovych took to the campaign trail once again. Under heavy foreign and domestic observation—including more than 13,000 foreign observers, many funded by the U.S. government—the rerun of the runoff election took place on December 26. Yushchenko won handily, outpolling Yanukovych 52 percent to 44.2 percent. On December 27, the International Election Observation Mission gave the process good marks for being free, fair, and transparent. After the report, Powell told a press briefing at the State Department, "This is an historic moment for democracy in Ukraine. . . . The Ukrainian people finally had an opportunity to choose freely their next president. . . . Throughout the Ukrainian presidential campaign, the United States has supported a democratic process, not a particular candidate. We congratulate Ukrainians for the courage they displayed in standing up for their democratic rights."[19]

On January 23, 2005, Yushchenko took the oath of office as Ukraine's third president.

Reflections

By 2002, the U.S. government had concluded that political reform was unlikely to progress during the remainder of Kuchma's tenure and began to look toward the post-Kuchma era for democratic reforms. Washington took the lead in 2003 and the first half of 2004 in crafting a message to the Ukrainian leadership on the importance of a democratic election. U.S. officials worked closely with their European Union counterparts to ensure that Washington and Europe sent reinforcing messages. When the November 21 runoff election produced massive fraud, followed by the Orange Revolution, European officials took the lead in helping the Ukrainians resolve the crisis. But the United States did not sit on the sidelines; it took on a role that aimed primarily to support the efforts of Kwasniewski and Solana. There were several reasons for this approach.

First, American officials had for some time hoped to see Europe and the European Union play a stronger role in the region, particularly in the post-Soviet space that bordered EU member countries. Managing the crisis triggered by the Orange Revolution constituted an appropriate task for the European Union. Poland and the Polish president, moreover, had taken a particularly strong interest in developments in Ukraine, and Kwasniewski had a personal relationship with Kuchma, which proved an asset in managing the roundtable process. Likewise, Solana's relationship with Kuchma went back to his time as NATO secretary general in the mid-1990s, when he had concluded the agreement establishing the distinctive partnership between the alliance and Ukraine. Kuchma had confidence in the two, and Yushchenko's confidence in their efforts grew as the roundtables proceeded.

Second, U.S. officials understood that Europeans such as Kwasniewski and Solana likely would have greater influence with Kuchma than an American interlocutor would. Bilateral relations between Washington and Kyiv had plummeted during the course of 2002. The relationship had recovered somewhat during 2003, particularly given Kyiv's contribution to the Iraq stabilization force, but it was worse than relations between the European Union and Ukraine. Bush had had only a couple of brief encounters with Kuchma, and Vice President Dick Cheney had no relationship with the Ukrainian president. Likewise, Powell had not visited Kyiv. The administration simply had no one with the gravitas and relationship with Kuchma to match Kwasniewski's and Solana's. That argued for a European lead.

Third, American and European Union officials had long consulted on developments in Ukraine. They had first discussed the 2004 presidential election in early 2003 in Brussels. That conversation set in motion an ongoing dialogue in which they exchanged views on developments in Ukraine and coordinated the messages and assistance that the West would send to increase the prospects for a free and fair election. That process was mirrored by on-the-ground contacts in Kyiv between the American and European embassies. These exchanges gave Washington confidence that American and European Union goals aligned squarely on promoting a democratic election process. U.S. officials were comfortable letting the European Union take the lead. Continuing contacts throughout the Orange Revolution ensured that Washington stayed fully in the loop on EU thinking and could shape messages supportive of what the European mediators sought to achieve in the roundtable discussions.

Finally, having Europeans take the lead avoided the possibility of a competitive dynamic between Washington and Moscow intruding on the effort to peacefully resolve the Orange Revolution. By 2004, the U.S.-Russia relationship had begun to encounter problems after the honeymoon period during Bush's first two years in office came to an end. U.S. officials believed European mediators at the table would be less likely to raise concern in the Kremlin.

This is not to say that the United States was an idle spectator. Herbst was extremely active during the period, reporting developments back to Washington, urging senior Ukrainian officials not to resort to force, and reinforcing the European mediators' messages on how to resolve the dispute. Likewise, U.S. officials in Washington coordinated with their European counterparts on a daily basis to ensure that the two sides of the Atlantic stayed on the same page in what they said to Ukrainians. Washington regarded the effort as a true success for transatlantic collaboration.

One last word on Kuchma. I have been critical of him and his actions (or inaction). I fully credit him, however, for rejecting Yanukovych's pleas to use force against the mass of demonstrators in downtown Kyiv. Had he agreed to Yanukovych's request, there would have been bloodshed, not just between the ministry of interior forces and the demonstrators, but also between the ministry of interior forces and elements of the army and the SBU that would have rallied to the defense of the protestors. The violence likely would have been far worse than the violence that marred the Maydan Revolution in early 2014. Rejecting the use of force and, in the end, accepting Yushchenko's election in the rerun of the runoff ballot, were among Kuchma's greatest services to his country.

CHAPTER 7

History Didn't End with the Orange Revolution

History, of course, did not end with the Orange Revolution, either for Ukraine or for U.S.-Ukraine relations. Much transpired in the succeeding years. Many of the problems that affected the bilateral relationship in the period 1991–2004 continued or appeared again to burden the relationship at different points after 2005. At the end of 2004, I retired from government service. A detailed account of U.S.-Ukraine relations from 2005 on will be a topic for another author, but this chapter briefly describes how the U.S.-Ukraine relationship developed in that period. As I noted in the introduction, the tone and detail of the narrative will now change, as my perspective shifts from policy participant to an interested, but outside, observer.

Orange Failure

On January 23, 2005, Viktor Yushchenko took the oath of office as Ukraine's third president and moved into the Presidential Administration offices at Bankova. Secretary of State Colin Powell led the U.S. delegation to his inauguration. Yushchenko from the beginning signaled his intention to make a distinct shift away from former president Leonid Kuchma's "multi-vector" foreign policy of roughly equal engagement with Russia, Europe, and the United States. Yushchenko indicated a desire for a stable relationship with Russia—and he made Moscow his first foreign destination as president—but the focus of his foreign policy would be to bring Ukraine closer to the West, including integration with institutions such as NATO and the European Union.

Yushchenko sought to anchor Ukraine fully in Europe, which he believed would put his country on the path to prosperity and, with an eye toward Moscow, help shield its independence. In Brussels on February 21–22, Yushchenko signed a "European Neighborhood Policy" action plan with the European Union and joined alliance leaders for a NATO-Ukraine summit. The next day, he addressed the European Parliament.

Yushchenko also attached high importance to relations with the United States. He traveled to Washington in early April, ending a gap of more than five years in visits by a Ukrainian president to the U.S. capital. He received a warm, even boisterous, reception. After their meeting, Yushchenko and President George W. Bush issued a joint statement entitled "A New Century Agenda for the Ukrainian-American Strategic Partnership." That statement listed a series of issues for bilateral cooperation, committed the two to work toward Ukraine's accession to the World Trade Organization, said the U.S. government would recognize Ukraine as a market economy, and expressed U.S. support for Ukraine's NATO aspirations and for an intensified dialogue with the alliance. The statement did not offer any dramatic increase in U.S. assistance for reform but did note an additional $45 million for the Chornobyl shelter project.[1] Yushchenko had the honor of addressing a joint session of Congress.

In the months thereafter, U.S. and Ukrainian officials made progress on resolving long-standing bilateral problems, including on protection of intellectual property rights and a U.S.-Ukraine agreement on Ukraine's accession to the WTO. In March 2006, approval by the House of a resolution graduating Ukraine from the provisions of the Jackson-Vanik amendment, following Senate passage of a similar resolution in late 2005, enabled Ukraine to receive permanent normal trade relations status with the United States. There was disappointment for the White House on one key issue: as Yushchenko had promised during his 2004 election campaign, he withdrew Ukrainian forces from Iraq by the end of 2005. That act did not, however, spoil the overall positive atmospherics in the bilateral relationship.

Yushchenko's desire to draw closer to NATO was rewarded in April 2005. In the still warm afterglow of the Orange Revolution, the alliance offered Kyiv an intensified dialogue. In substance, that largely meant a continuation of the annual plans for NATO-Ukraine cooperation of the previous few years. Of particular importance to Yushchenko, however, an intensified dialogue typically served as the precursor to a membership action plan (MAP). Discussions on a MAP began in 2006, with the possibility that Kyiv might receive one by the end of the year. The U.S. government was supportive, and Borys Tarasyuk, serving his second stint as foreign minister, saw the question as one of when, rather than if. Interestingly, while Moscow never hid its dislike for a MAP for Ukraine, in 2006 it was not nearly as outspoken in its opposition as it would be in 2008.

Internal political discord got in the way of a MAP. Yushchenko had appointed Yuliya Tymoshenko as prime minister after taking office. Their partnership had the potential to be an interesting combination, if Yushchenko could provide the vision and Tymoshenko the implementation, as they had on several issues when they were prime minister and deputy prime minister in 2000. But Yushchenko failed to set clear priorities for Tymoshenko and the cabinet of ministers. He often appeared detached from the cabinet's day-to-day operations. The two fell into disagreement over economic reform issues. The National Security and Defense Council, headed by Secretary Petro Poroshenko and subservient to the president, ended up in conflict with the cabinet as well. Journalists' stories of Bankova feuding with Tymoshenko and the cabinet portrayed a government in disarray.

Tensions between Tymoshenko and Poroshenko boiled over in September 2005. Yushchenko could not find a way to forge a reconciliation, and he asked both to resign. When Yushchenko lacked the support in the Rada to secure confirmation of Yuriy Yekhanurov as prime minister, he turned to his 2004 opponent, Viktor Yanukovych, and the Party of Regions for the needed votes. The Yekhanurov cabinet aligned itself more closely with Yushchenko's policy desires, but it had little time to achieve anything before preparations for the March 2006 Rada elections came to dominate the political scene. The political crisis and long run-up to the Rada elections created a difficult atmosphere for U.S. government efforts to encourage reform.

In January 2006, a new problem arose in relations between Kyiv and Moscow. The failure to agree on the price that Ukraine would pay for natural gas imported from Russia led Russia's Gazprom to reduce gas supplies for Ukraine. Gazprom charged Kyiv with stealing transit gas bound for countries to Ukraine's west and further reduced gas supplies. Fortunately, the mini–gas war was quickly settled, with the Ukrainians accepting a price increase. As seen by the U.S. embassy in Kyiv, Moscow had hoped that the Europeans would understand and accept the gas cutoff to Ukraine when Kyiv refused to pay the higher market prices that the Russians sought. To the surprise of the Russians, however, the Europeans, like the Americans, understood that Moscow's intention was to put pressure on Yushchenko and the government in Kyiv. The European position encouraged the Kremlin to accept something less than a full jump to market prices, though the price increase from $50 to $95 per thousand cubic meters was still significant. As part of the deal, Yushchenko agreed to use RosUkrEnergo, a shadowy middleman company. RosUkrEnergo had replaced EuralTransGas as the gas intermediary not long before the Orange Revolution. Like its predecessor, RosUkrEnergo was regarded by some analysts as having corrupt connections in both Russia and Ukraine. The brief gas dispute had one political casualty: just two months before the Rada elections, the parliament voted no confidence in Yekhanurov.

The March 2006 elections produced a stunning comeback for Yanukovych. Just fifteen months after his loss to Yushchenko in the December 2004 rerun of the presidential runoff vote, Yanukovych led his party to victory, capturing 189 of the Rada's 450 seats. Tymoshenko's party placed second, siphoning off many votes from Yushchenko's Our Ukraine Party. Our Ukraine and the Tymoshenko bloc, in combination with the Socialist Party, nevertheless had the votes to form a majority coalition. But several months of vacillation on Yushchenko's part ensued, and the Socialists jumped over to join with the Party of Regions and the Communist Party to form a majority, which promptly proposed Yanukovych as prime minister.

With the 2006 Rada elections, the full constitutional changes adopted in December 2004 kicked in. In effect, they required that the president nominate as prime minister the candidate selected by the majority coalition in the Rada. This requirement gave the prime minister and the cabinet of ministers a significant degree of independence from the president that previous prime ministers had not enjoyed. It made it even more difficult for the executive branch to function effectively when the president and prime minister had different positions. The president could no longer fire the prime minister if he or she continued to command a majority in the Rada.

The months of internal political indecision and Yanukovych's appointment had a high cost for Yushchenko's foreign policy ambitions. Bush had planned to visit Kyiv in June. The White House, however, did not want the president caught in the middle of a political fight in the absence of a confirmed prime minister. It pulled the plug on the trip (Bush would not make it to the Ukrainian capital for another two years).

An Uneasy Cohabitation

In early August, Yushchenko, Yekhanurov, Rada chairman Oleksandr Moroz, Yanukovych, and several other party leaders held a roundtable discussion. It resulted in signature of a declaration of national unity containing a list of principles for both domestic and foreign policy. Yushchenko tacitly accepted Yanukovych's nomination to become prime minister (though only thirty of the eighty-one Our Ukraine deputies voted for him).

Many Ukrainians hoped for a period of political stability. Yushchenko and Yanukovych had incentives to cooperate because they needed each other to succeed. Aside from the status of the Russian language and Ukraine's relationship with NATO, there seemed to be relatively few disagreements on issues of principle between the two, in part because neither seemed to have a grand strategy in mind. One big question was whether Yanukovych had changed since 2004. Some Ukrainians felt that he had. Others, particularly in the Yushchenko camp, had doubts and wondered if Yanukovych would live up to what the president believed was an agreement to seek a MAP (the language on NATO in the declaration of national unity was ambiguous). Another question concerned Tymoshenko, the sole major party leader who declined to sign the declaration of national unity. Did she have the temperament to play the role of leader of the opposition, for example, by holding the government's feet to the fire on corruption?

Yushchenko and his foreign and defense ministers remained focused on a MAP, hoping that Ukraine could receive one when NATO leaders gathered in Vilnius at the end of November 2006. In mid-September, however, Yanukovych, newly confirmed as prime minister, traveled to Brussels. He had a meeting at NATO headquarters, where he expressed support for cooperation with the alliance but said the Ukrainian government would suspend its effort to secure a MAP: "Because of the political situation in Ukraine, we will have to take a pause."[2] Yushchenko promptly and sharply rebuked Yanukovych, while the cabinet backed the prime minister's position. Yanukovych allies maintained that a MAP would antagonize Moscow and lacked public support (opinion polls showed support for joining NATO at about 20 percent). The split between Yushchenko and Yanukovych derailed Kyiv's MAP bid, which a few months earlier had seemed close to a sure thing. NATO could accept that public support was low—though it would have to rise before an invitation to join could be considered—but the alliance had no interest in giving a MAP to a country over the objections of the prime minister and cabinet.

Yushchenko and Yanukovych ended up differing on more than just NATO. Their lack of a common plan for long-term reform hindered any real headway in that area. That was unfortunate, because the sixth U.S. ambassador to Ukraine, Bill Taylor, had in-depth knowledge of reform requirements and how the West might assist based on his years of service as deputy assistance coordinator and then assistance coordinator.

Yanukovych traveled to Washington in early December (the trip was opposed by Tarasyuk, who was dismissed on December 1 by the pro-Yanukovych majority in the Rada, a dismissal that he and Yushchenko would fight for almost two months). The prime minister came seeking to establish credibility with the U.S. government, where memories of his actions in late 2004 were not pleasant. In meetings with Vice President Dick Cheney and Secretary of State Condoleezza Rice, Yanukovych stressed Kyiv's interest in good relations with the United States and his commitment to reform. He played down reported differences with Yushchenko. He asserted that his goal regarding Europe was the same as Yushchenko's and that Ukraine would join NATO;

the difference was timing and tactics. These themes, which he stressed in public remarks at the Center for Strategic & International Studies, seemed carefully tailored to resonate with his American audiences— probably shaped by political consultant Paul Manafort, a member of the prime minister's entourage.

In reality, the cohabitation was not working. Yushchenko and Yanukovych met only sporadically, and agreements between the two seemed to fall apart quickly. Yanukovych had the backing of a majority coalition in the Rada; Yushchenko's main power on domestic issues was his ability to veto Rada actions. The president was not always successful. In January 2007, the Rada—with the Tymoshenko bloc joining the pro-Yanukovych majority—overruled Yushchenko's veto to pass a law on the cabinet that further strengthened the authority of the prime minister.

Matters erupted into a full-blown political fight in spring 2007. The defection of formerly pro-Yushchenko Rada deputies to the pro-Yanukovych coalition raised the prospect that the coalition might reach 300 deputies, enough to override presidential vetoes. Yushchenko issued a constitutionally dubious decree on April 2 dismissing the Rada. The parliamentary majority essentially ignored it, and a political crisis ensued.

U.S. officials reacted cautiously. They largely shared Yushchenko's vision for Ukraine but had to deal with the prime minister and cabinet that had been voted in. Yanukovych and Yushchenko each had confidence in Taylor and approached him with a request to help mediate a settlement between them. Washington reacted coolly to the idea but deferred to Taylor's judgment. He brought in his German counterpart, as Germany held the EU presidency at the time. The four met privately over the course of a month, trying to find a solution. Taylor urged Yanukovych and Yushchenko to find a compromise, but the situation appeared to deteriorate in late May (Taylor also occasionally met with Manafort to try to influence Yanukovych's thinking). The differences between Yushchenko and Yanukovych were not resolved until May 27, when they agreed, along with Moroz, to hold early Rada elections in September.

Although a total political breakdown in Kyiv was avoided, the dispute had a very negative impact on Ukraine's international image. At the height of the crisis in late May, Yushchenko had to cancel his participation in a summit with Central European leaders, and Yanu-kovych pulled out of a Commonwealth of Independent States meeting that he was supposed to host in Yalta. In Washington, U.S. officials worried that Ukraine's politicians were again focused on maneuvering for position rather than on actually governing the country. Talk of a Bush visit, or even a Rice visit, to Kyiv was placed on hold.

The compromise decision on an election survived through the summer, though not without almost coming apart. The election campaign formerly kicked off at the end of August. The parties led by Tymosh-enko and Yushchenko placed second (with 31 percent of the vote) and third (with 14 percent), respectively, and together won 228 seats, which would constitute a slender majority, but a majority nonetheless. Yush-chenko took two months to consider possible coalitions. He was plainly not happy with the prospective return of Tymoshenko but finally agreed to a coalition with her party. It was announced on November 29, and Yushchenko proposed the appointment of Tymoshenko as prime minister.

The Yushchenko-Tymoshenko Tandem Fails Again

It did not take long for feuding to resume between Bankova and the cabinet. Viktor Baloha, head of the Presidential Administration, launched an early series of public critiques of Tymoshenko and her pol-icies, motivated in part by Bankova's concern that Tymoshenko might challenge Yushchenko for the presidency in the next election. Despite weekly coordination meetings (a mechanism that had not been in place in 2005), the two leaders spent much of their time mired in political games rather than governing, again making it difficult for the United States and the European Union to help Ukraine accomplish much in the reform area.

As 2008 began, Yushchenko and his defense minister continued to attach high priority to securing a MAP from NATO at the Bucharest summit scheduled for April. They urged Tymoshenko to support a MAP request. She initially resisted, concerned that a MAP request could cre-ate problems for her new cabinet and that Germany and France would oppose the request. Eventually, however, she agreed. Yushchenko and Tymoshenko in January issued a "joint address to the NATO secretary general," also signed by Rada speaker Arseniy Yatsenyuk, asking that a MAP be approved at the summit. The rollout of the request was not handled well. It was announced at a press conference with visiting U.S. senator Richard Lugar before the letter had been delivered to NATO. Ukrainian officials privately observed that, although they hoped to get a MAP in Bucharest, it would also be good just to get the issue on the agenda. Others noted that even a lesser outcome—such as agreement for NATO foreign ministers to discuss a MAP with their Ukrainian counterpart—could be considered a victory.

The White House and Bush personally supported Ukraine's bid, though Rice and Secretary of Defense Robert Gates were less enthusiastic. The administration curiously did little lobbying with NATO allies in the run-up to the summit. The White House instead planned for Bush to appeal directly to allied leaders at the summit itself. That turned out to be a tactical mistake. Positions in NATO capitals such as Berlin and Paris hardened against the idea of MAPs for Ukraine and Georgia in the ten weeks between the announcement of the Ukrainian request and the Bucharest summit, in part because of the absence of an American voice arguing for a positive response. (German officials privately expressed surprise at the late push by the president; they had taken the earlier U.S. silence to mean that Washington was not enthusiastic about MAPs for Ukraine and Georgia.)

Objectively, Ukraine at the beginning of 2008 had a strong case for a MAP. It had made as much progress on issues of interest to NATO— particularly on democratic reform—as the Baltic states and others had when they received MAPs in 1999. Moreover, it had shown in Iraq that it had deployable military capability and was prepared to use it. The major gap in Ukraine's argument was the absence of public support; polls typically showed only 20–25 percent of the population in favor of joining NATO. Other countries, however, had received MAPs despite weak public support, with the expectation that they would build that support before receiving an invitation to join the alliance.

In contrast to 2006, Russia this time reacted publicly and negatively to the prospect that Ukraine might obtain a MAP. During a press availability following a February 2008 meeting with Yushchenko in Moscow, Putin expressed concern that Ukraine might host NATO missile defenses and said, "I am not only terrified to utter this, it is scary even to think that Russia . . . would have to target its offensive rocket systems at Ukraine."[3] The Russians also lobbied individual allies. The linking of Ukraine's request for a MAP with Georgia's MAP request may have hurt Kyiv's cause, since Georgian president Mikhail Saakashvili was not a popular figure in key European capitals.

On April 1, on the eve of the Bucharest meeting, Bush paid a quick visit to Kyiv. He had a good meeting with Yushchenko in which Ukraine's relationship with NATO was the focus. In the concluding press conference, Yushchenko stressed the importance that he attached to a MAP and said, "There are no alternatives against the idea of collective security." In turn, Bush stated, "In Bucharest this week, I will continue to make America's position clear: We support MAP for Ukraine and Georgia." In response to a question, Bush ruled out any trade-offs of Ukraine's MAP aspirations for Russian acceptance of U.S. missile defense plans for Europe: "I strongly believe that Ukraine and Georgia should be given MAP, and there's no trade-offs, period."[4]

Bush traveled from Kyiv to Bucharest and made his personal pitch for MAPs for Ukraine and Georgia at the informal NATO leaders' dinner the night before the formal summit. He failed, however, to win a consensus. German chancellor Angela Merkel and French president Nicolas Sarkozy led the opposition composed of a minority of NATO members, but MAPs were a decision that required consensus. Those opposed were apprehensive about overly provoking Russia, worried about the low level of public support for NATO within Ukraine, and questioned the longevity of the already fraying Yushchenko-Tymoshenko relationship.

When MAP failed to win consensus, NATO leaders grappled with how to describe the alliance's relationship with Ukraine and Georgia, at one point reportedly drafting language themselves. The Bucharest summit declaration stated: "NATO welcomes Ukraine's and Georgia's Euro-Atlantic aspirations for membership in NATO. We agreed today that these countries will become members of NATO." But the declaration only noted that allied leaders "support these countries' applications for MAP" and gave NATO foreign ministers the mandate to decide the question, with their first review to take place in December.[5] The summit language was unusual in that NATO had not previously promised membership to a country before it had received and implemented its MAP.[6] Some regarded it as a green light for Ukraine's membership in NATO;

others saw it as kicking the question into the future. The August 2008 Georgia-Russia conflict put the idea of a MAP for Georgia or Ukraine on hold for the indefinite future.

Taylor and the embassy in Kyiv put a positive spin on the summit outcome. They also urged the government to get on with specific actions that would strengthen Ukraine's case. These included further governance reform and an effort to build broader public support for membership in the alliance.

Relations between Yushchenko and Tymoshenko grew even more rocky later in the spring. The weekly coordination meetings broke down, Baloha continued to direct a stream of criticism at the prime minister and her cabinet, and rumors circulated of an imminent collapse of the Rada coalition. Taylor pressed both sides to compromise and stick together. While he did not get involved in the kind of mediation effort that he had undertaken the year before between Yushchenko and Yanukovych (neither side asked for such mediation this time), the sides did use him to reinforce messages to each other. Yushchenko's desire to deepen links with NATO indirectly helped keep the coalition going, as several European officials warned that its collapse would doom any near-term prospects for a MAP.

NATO presented just one problem on the increasingly troubled Ukraine-Russia agenda. Moscow had reacted badly to Yushchenko's policies to encourage use of the Ukrainian language as well as his campaign to win international recognition of the 1930s Holodomor, the artificial famine that killed millions of Ukrainians, as genocide. Things became more difficult after the Bucharest summit, when Moscow seemed to read the NATO declaration more as a green light than an indefinite delay. Yushchenko proposed to begin preparatory talks for the Black Sea Fleet's withdrawal from Crimea, arguing that, although the basing agreement lasted until 2017, early preparations would ensure a smooth transition. That proposal further poisoned relations with Moscow, as did Yushchenko's open sympathy for Tbilisi during the Georgia-Russia conflict. The Russians angrily dismissed the Ukrainian president's suggestion that Ukraine might block Black Sea Fleet warships that had taken part in the conflict from returning to their homeport of Sevastopol. For its part, Kyiv expressed unhappiness with continuing Russian tariffs on Ukrainian goods and Russia's foot-dragging on fully demarcating the land and sea borders between the two countries.

Vice President Cheney traveled to Kyiv, and Yushchenko visited Washington in September in an exchange of visits intended to demonstrate U.S. support for Ukraine in the aftermath of the Georgia-Russia conflict. Yushchenko had a cordial meeting with Bush. The U.S. president noted, however, that the political infighting in Kyiv made it difficult to help Ukraine, and that European skepticism about Ukraine was growing as the political crisis continued. He stressed the importance that Kyiv do what it could to maintain unified European support. The two also discussed domestic politics in Ukraine. The public message of the visit, like Cheney's on his earlier trip to Ukraine, focused on American support. In the fall, U.S. officials in Kyiv continued to urge Yushchenko to end the dispute with Tymoshenko and get about producing coherent reform policies. U.S. exhortations seemed to have little impact. Dealing with a divided government remained a challenge.

As its term came to an end, the Bush administration in late December 2008 concluded the "United States-Ukraine Charter on Strategic Partnership," signed by Rice and Foreign Minister Volodymyr Ohryzko. The document laid out principles for cooperation in the defense and security sectors, on economics, trade, and energy, on strengthening democracy, and on increasing people-to-people contacts.[7] It would have been more appropriate earlier in the Bush term, when the administration still had time to work to implement it. The Bush administration saw the charter as something of a consolation prize for the failure to get Ukraine a MAP; the December NATO foreign ministers' meeting simply kept the question under review. It served as another affirmation of U.S. support for Ukraine in light of the Georgia-Russia conflict.

In Kyiv, many saw the NATO ministerial outcome as positive, or at least as the best that could have been achieved without getting a MAP. Ukrainian officials commented that they could complete all of the actions of a MAP in the form of Ukraine's annual national plan of cooperation with NATO without calling it a MAP. One pollster observed that NATO suffered from a "bad brand" with the Ukrainian public. When he had asked people about joining NATO or joining something called the "North Atlantic Alliance," they opposed the first and favored the second.

A dispute over a new natural gas contract at the start of 2009 led to a second gas war with Russia. Moscow reduced gas flows into Ukraine, then cut off all gas, including the transit supplies for consumers in Central and Western Europe. In a bitterly cold winter, the disruption left Romania, Bulgaria, and Greece in difficult straits, and the European Union sought to facilitate a quick settlement. The Russians largely ignored Yushchenko, and Putin personally concluded an agreement with Tymoshenko. The three-week dispute raised concerns in the European Union about Russia's reliability as an energy provider and Ukraine's reliability as an energy transit country. Moscow moved forward with plans to circumvent Ukraine, including construction of the Nordstream pipeline to transport gas from Russia directly to Germany under the Baltic Sea. The settlement also provoked further division between Yushchenko and Tymoshenko when the president and Presidential Administration questioned the terms of the agreement and whether Tymoshenko had followed proper cabinet procedures in agreeing to it.

Barack Obama became president in January 2009, and his administration reaffirmed the just-concluded charter, but it was not a propitious time to accomplish much in the bilateral relationship. Yushchenko and Tymoshenko's feuding had only deepened. In late 2008 and early 2009, many in Kyiv speculated about a looming breakdown in the Yushchenko-Tymoshenko coalition in the Rada, suggesting that it would be replaced by a coalition between the Tymoshenko bloc and Yanukovych's Party of Regions. Such a grouping would control well over the 300 deputies needed to vote through changes to the constitution. Pro-Yushchenko Rada deputies complained that the president lacked any kind of strategy for managing the contentious politics. In early June, Tymoshenko and Yanukovych reportedly came close to an agreement on joining forces and on a constitutional amendment that would have the Rada elect the president, but Yanukovych pulled back at the last minute. Thereafter, the attention of Yushchenko, Tymoshenko, and Yanukovych, along with Yatsenyuk, turned increasingly to posturing for the January 2010 presidential election. As the months went by, that race became a fight between Tymoshenko and Yanukovych, with Yushchenko's poll numbers falling into the low single digits.

With Ukraine's leaders absorbed by domestic politics and the Obama administration just settling in, U.S.-Ukraine relations went through a pause in the first half of 2009. Taylor concluded his assignment in May, and John Tefft, his successor, did not arrive until late November. Ukrainians worried that the gap between ambassadors suggested that Ukraine was not a priority for the new administration, particularly as Washington announced its effort to "reset" relations with Russia. The problem was partially rectified in July, when Vice President Joe Biden visited Kyiv. It was the first of a series of visits by Biden, though his office decided against the establishment of a bilateral commission along the lines of the Gore-Kuchma commission during the Clinton administration. Biden's first visit came just after Obama's visit to Moscow to meet with President Dmitry Medvedev (Putin had become prime minister in 2008) and was intended in part to balance the Moscow visit. Biden had three main messages for his Ukrainian interlocutors: (1) the need to proceed with reform and fulfill the promise of the Orange Revolution; (2) reassurance that the U.S. effort to reset relations with Moscow did not mean that Washington accepted the notion of spheres of influence; sovereign states had the right to their own course; and (3) the need to put meat on the bones of the bilateral partnership. In November, Tefft arrived just as the Ukrainian presidential campaign entered its final weeks.

Yanukovych's Return

The election took place on January 17, 2010. Yanukovych at 32 percent and Tymoshenko at 25 percent polled the most votes. Yushchenko placed fifth, with less than 6 percent. In the February 7 runoff, Yanukovych outpolled Tymoshenko 48.9 percent to 45.5 percent, and the remainder voted against both candidates. Three factors helped explain Tymoshenko's loss. First, as prime minister, she had presided over the economy when it went into deep recession after the 2008 global financial crisis and contracted by 14 percent in 2009. Second, the infighting with Yushchenko hurt; he told his supporters to stay home and not vote in the runoff election. Third, some voters may have opted for Yanukovych, seeing him as more of a known quantity, while Tymoshenko seemed less predictable.

Organization for Security and Cooperation in Europe monitors pronounced the election process largely free and fair, though Tymoshenko asserted that there had been irregularities. The U.S. and European governments, however, moved quickly to congratulate Yanukovych on his victory, in part to prevent Tymoshenko from making a challenge to the results, for which they saw no basis. Despite serious questions about Yanukovych's character, Washington, like most Western governments, was prepared to give him a chance. His election in an OSCE-approved process gave him a degree of democratic legitimacy. Tefft and other Western diplomats in Kyiv suggested a wait-and-see approach to test Yanukovych's actual policies. They urged engagement to try to shape his actions, noting that the alignment of Yanukovych, the cabinet (under Prime Minister Mykola Azarov), and the Rada could bode well for policies aimed at European integration.

On foreign policy, Yanukovych made clear that his first priority would be to normalize relations with Russia after five years of problems. But Yanukovych also talked about seeking a balance between Russia and the West. He indicated that Kyiv would continue the negotiation with the European Union on an association agreement, including a deep and comprehensive free trade agreement, which had begun in 2008. He said he would not turn back toward the customs union comprising Russia, Kazakhstan, and Belarus. EU diplomats soon began reporting that the Ukrainian government was doing its homework to conclude the association agreement in a more serious manner than it had during the Yushchenko presidency.

As for NATO, Yanukovych's government indicated that it intended to cooperate with the alliance but would not pursue membership. Yanukovych and other Ukrainian officials hoped to build on the strategic charter with the United States concluded in December 2008. They carefully described their policy as "non-bloc" but not "nonaligned," the difference being that such a policy ruled out a MAP with NATO but would allow Kyiv to go as far as it could with the European Union.

In spring 2010, the Obama administration was entering the second year of its reset policy with Russia. Obama and Medvedev had hit it off, and the relationship was showing success on strategic nuclear arms reductions and cooperation regarding Iran and Afghanistan. The administration hoped to build on this. Yanukovych's approach toward the European Union and NATO thus was not unwelcome. An association agreement with the European Union offered a path to deepen Ukraine's integration with Europe. Kyiv's decision not to pursue a

MAP removed from the U.S.-Russia agenda a potentially major problem.

In early 2010, the Obama administration launched its nuclear security summit process, designed to promote enhanced security for highly enriched uranium and plutonium, the fissile materials for nuclear weapons. One element of the administration's approach aimed at removing highly enriched uranium from countries and consolidating it at storage sites in the United States and Russia. Yanukovych saw the first nuclear summit as an early opportunity to engage Obama, and he brought a major deliverable to the summit, held in April in Washington: removal of highly enriched uranium from Ukraine. That commitment earned him a brief bilateral meeting with Obama. However, given U.S. uncertainty about Yanukovych, the meeting took place at the summit site at the Washington Convention Center, not in the Oval Office, despite intense Ukrainian lobbying for a White House meeting.

The first months of Yanukovych's foreign policy fixed on Russia. He dropped many Yushchenko policies that had angered Moscow, such as the Holodomor-as-genocide campaign and Ukrainian language emphasis. In April, less than two months after taking his office in Bankova, Yanukovych met with Medvedev in Kharkiv and struck an agreement extending basing rights for the Black Sea Fleet in Crimea by twenty-five years, from 2017 to 2042, in return for a ten-year cut in the price of gas from Russia, with an immediate reduction of 30 percent. They also agreed to joint Ukrainian-Russian projects in the areas of nuclear power, aerospace, electricity, and ports. Some analysts saw Yanukovych as motivated by a desire to reduce expenditures on gas, which had positive short-term implications for Ukraine's economy.[8]

Yanukovych quickly forced a Rada vote to approve the Black Sea Fleet basing agreement, in violation of the Rada's procedural rules. Still, some Ukrainian officials saw the Kremlin overplaying its hand and began to express unhappiness that Moscow took little account of Kyiv's interests. In particular, the Russians continued to press ahead with their plans for the South Stream gas pipeline project under the Black Sea which, if built, would divert transit gas—and transit gas revenues—from Ukrainian pipelines.

Secretary of State Hillary Clinton traveled to Kyiv in July. In meetings with Yanukovych, Tymoshenko, and Kostyantyn Hryshchenko (now in his second term as foreign minister), Clinton expressed interest in a good bilateral relationship and U.S. support for closer Ukraine-Europe relations. She encouraged Kyiv to work with the European Union on the association agreement. While NATO's open door policy remained in place, she suggested that Kyiv focus on practical cooperation with the alliance. In private meetings with Yanukovych and other senior Ukrainians, she cautioned against democratic backsliding, citing freedom of the press in particular. Acknowledging the Yanukovych government's interest in improving its relations with Russia, the secretary noted the importance of balance in Kyiv's foreign policy (by one Ukrainian analyst's count, in the first months of his presidency Yanukovych had met as many times with Medvedev and Putin as he had with all other foreign leaders combined).

U.S. officials subsequently described a policy of "engagement without endorsement" of Yanukovych. Washington would focus on the European Union rather than NATO as the vehicle to deepen Kyiv's links with Europe and would press the Ukrainians to do more to conclude the association agreement. U.S.-EU contacts had agreed on the importance of a coordinated Western message to Ukraine. U.S. officials felt that Yanukovych did not want to go one-on-one with Russia, which gave the West some leverage with him. They also planned to keep a close eye on internal developments and "stay in Yanukovych's face" on backsliding on democracy issues. If things went well, Obama might travel to Ukraine in 2011.

Things did not go well. Concern about Yanukovych's commitment to democracy grew in the second half of 2010.[9] Reports began to circulate that the Security Service of Ukraine had asked university officials to report on students who participated in antigovernment protests. The October local elections, the first on Yanukovych's watch, evinced many problems and were a major step back from elections conducted the previous four years. After the government replaced four of its judges, the Constitutional Court invalidated constitutional changes approved by the Rada in 2004, reversing five years of constitutional practice and strengthening the president's authority. In early 2011, Freedom House ranked Ukraine as only "partly free," following four years of "free" rankings.

Moreover, reports of corruption under Yanukovych's presidency began to roll in. For example, Dmytro Firtash, a powerful and wealthy oligarch with murky involvement in the Ukrainian gas industry and a part owner of RosUkrEnergo, profited greatly when Ukraine's lawyers essentially abandoned their previous position in a multi-billion-dollar case before the Stockholm Arbitration Court. As a result, the Ukrainian state gas company was required to compensate RosUkrEnergo with 12.1 billion cubic meters of gas, valued at close to $3 billion.[10] Yanukovych's older son, Oleksandr, a dentist by training, became involved in banking, construction, and other activities and began climbing the ranks of Ukraine's richest individuals.

Hryshchenko and Clinton met in February 2011 to chair a meeting of the U.S.-Ukraine Strategic Partnership Commission and reached a number of practical agreements. They agreed on the removal of highly enriched uranium from Ukraine in 2012, in return for which U.S. assistance would help Ukraine build a state-of-the-art neutron source facility. They announced several cooperative steps aimed at enhancing Ukraine's energy security. Privately, Clinton raised growing U.S. concerns over democracy.

Progress on issues such as the removal of the highly enriched uranium and practical military-to-military cooperation took place against the backdrop of worries about domestic trends in Ukraine. One year into the Yanukovych presidency, twenty-two members of the former Tymoshenko government had been arrested or were under investigation. American analysts believed that Yanukovych wanted to replicate some elements of Putin's vertical power structure, in which all real authority rested at the top in the Kremlin, but the Ukrainian president lacked the money and still had to balance among different oligarchic interests.

Things went from bad to worse. By summer 2011, virtually everyone saw Yanukovych moving in the wrong direction on democracy, and reports of government corruption increased. In July, Tymoshenko was arrested and jailed. After previous charges seemed implausible, prosecutors took her to trial for abuse of power in the gas agreement that she had reached with Putin to end the January 2009 gas cutoff. The trial rapidly degenerated into farce and was broadly condemned in the West, where no one regarded the agreement as a criminal matter, as flawed as it might have been. Clinton joined with EU high representative for common foreign and security policy Catherine Ashton in writing Yanukovych to drop the case. Yanukovych in September suggested a possible way out: the Rada could amend the criminal code to remove the provision that provided the basis for the charge against Tymoshenko. Yanukovych's own party, however, refused to support the amendment. When the court found Tymoshenko guilty in October, Yanukovych's government scored the unusual distinction of being sharply condemned in Washington, EU capitals, and Moscow. EU officials canceled a planned Yanukovych visit to Brussels, even though the sides were close to concluding the association agreement. (The Ukrainian leadership went to absurd lengths to justify its treatment of Tymoshenko. When I was in Kyiv for a conference in the fall of 2012, the prime minister invited me to meet and spent forty-five minutes trying to convince me of Tymoshenko's guilt.)

At the beginning of 2012, the Yanukovych policy of maintaining balance between Russia and the West was foundering. Tymoshenko's treatment had a chilling effect on EU-Ukraine relations, which had come to a standstill, even though the technical negotiation of the association agreement had been completed. A growing number of European officials voiced the view that the agreement could not be signed until political circumstances in Ukraine improved, and they called specifically for Tymoshenko's release. In the United States, any thought of an Obama visit had evaporated. Ukraine slipped off the radar in the face of other foreign policy challenges and the 2012 U.S. presidential election. Meanwhile, Yanukovych's relations with Moscow had become strained, as Ukrainian officials increasingly felt that Kyiv had received little in return for the concessions that they had made to Russian interests.

Kyiv continued to seek high-level meetings for Yanukovych and portrayed a presidential handshake at Obama's reception at the annual UN General Assembly session as a "meeting." Neither Obama nor Biden had any incentive to meet except in the occasional pull-aside. Ukrainian officials began to complain that the West had forgotten about their country's geopolitical importance. What Yanukovych did not appear to understand was that values did affect Western policy; the United States and the European Union would not turn a blind eye to his increasing authoritarianism. Backsliding on democratic principles had badly tarnished his image in the West, made good relations with the United States and Europe more difficult to achieve, and left him in a weaker position in relation to Moscow.

In March 2012, a senior U.S. official described Yanukovych as one who believed he knew what he was doing but who had made major miscalculations. First, Yanukovych thought that, after the Black Sea Fleet deal, he would get a better price from the Russians on natural gas. But Moscow sought control of Ukraine's gas transit system in return for a lower price. Second, he assumed he could use his Party of Regions management style to run the government, but it was not producing coherent policy. Third, he believed that he could stimulate economic growth while maintaining a crony capitalism model, which was not working. (One result: Tefft had to spend as much as 30 or 40 percent of his time working on U.S. business problems.) Finally, Yanukovych had miscalculated that the West would react passively to democratic regression.

Despite the problems, Ukraine did record a success with the European Union: it completed and initialed the association agreement. The last issue—Kyiv's demand for a membership perspective—had been resolved when Ukrainian officials accepted that the European Union was not prepared to include such language in the agreement. EU officials, however, conditioned signing on two requirements: a democratic process for the fall Rada elections and changes regarding criminal prosecutions, with Tymoshenko topping the list.

Yanukovych traveled to Chicago in May for a NATO-Ukraine summit meeting. Reflecting Washington's concern over developments within Ukraine, the Obama administration refused to organize a bilateral meeting on the margins of the summit. European leaders at the short summit meeting likewise took a cool attitude toward the Ukrainian president. One EU official noted in June that Kyiv's line increasingly boiled down to "You have to take us or the Russians will." The European response was that Ukraine's leadership needed to decide and then take actions to move toward EU values and standards; the country's geostrategic position was not going to win it special treatment.

The run-up to the Rada elections dominated the fall. For these elections, the Rada had passed a law returning to the previous system: 225 seats would be awarded on the basis of the party-list vote, and the other 225 would be decided on the basis of votes in individual constituencies. On the eve of the elections, Clinton and Ashton published a joint op-ed in the *New York Times*. They noted "worrying trends in the run-up to the election," including "reports of the use of administrative resources to favor ruling party candidates and the difficulties that several media outlets face." They cited concern about selective prosecutions, especially of Tymoshenko, and concluded that the European Union could only move forward with its ambitious association agreement if "the democratic rights of the Ukrainian people, including freedoms of expression, political participation, association, and media, are respected."[11]

Their plea seemed to have little impact. In the elections, Yanukovych's Party of Regions narrowly edged Tymoshenko's party (now led by Yatsenyuk, since Tymoshenko remained in jail), polling 30 percent to 26 percent, but Regions did well in the individual constituencies. As to process, Yatsenyuk and others cried foul, and both European and U.S. officials termed the election process a step backward from the previous Rada elections. The Party of Regions ended up with sufficient seats to form situational majorities, in particular with the Communist Party. The Rada reappointed Mykola Azarov as prime minister.

In early 2013, EU leaders and Yanukovych agreed to make the November EU Eastern Partnership summit in Vilnius the target for signing the association agreement. However, views were divided within the European Union on what Ukraine had to do in order to sign the agreement. Some EU member states began to argue for dropping conditions, while a majority, led by Germany and France, maintained that Kyiv had to make progress on democracy issues. By this time the Tymoshenko case had become a domestic question within Germany. Chancellor Merkel warned that the association agreement could not be signed if Tymoshenko remained in prison. Other EU member states were less enthusiastic about the association agreement and seized on the lack of progress on democracy as a pretext for holding up signature. At an April conference in Kyiv, the vice chairman of the European People's Party stated that Kyiv faced a "now or never" choice: it could address EU concerns and sign the association agreement in November, or Ukraine's near-term prospects for a deeper relationship with the European Union would be finished.

Over the summer, Yanukovych made a push to get legislation enacted that was necessary for the association agreement. But what he would do about Tymoshenko was unclear. Tefft's message in Kyiv was that this was the moment of truth: Ukraine had to take the necessary actions to secure the association agreement. The U.S. embassy heard that many around Yanukovych were telling him that the association agreement would be key to his campaign for reelection in 2015. If he secured the agreement, he could run as the leader who brought Ukraine into Europe. That was potentially important; with a stagnant economy and growing public unhappiness with massive corruption, Yanukovych would have little other basis for a reelection campaign. Tefft was very active and did what he could to keep the focus on the importance of Ukraine drawing closer to Europe—and of taking the steps necessary to sign the association agreement. However, some EU diplomats complained that Washington did not seem particularly engaged (perhaps owing to the demands of other crises, such as Syria).

Moscow had not been particularly vocal about its views on the association agreement earlier but in 2013 appeared to realize that the agreement was a real possibility—and that EU ties could anchor Ukraine in institutional Europe just as much as a relationship with NATO could. The Kremlin launched a belated attempt to scupper it. Russia imposed trade sanctions on selected imports from Ukraine and promised further measures. These acts generated greater sympathy for Kyiv in Brussels, as well as sentiment for softening the Tymoshenko condition. Other Russian actions seemed rather ham-handed. Visiting Kyiv in the summer, Putin (who was again the Russian president) talked about Ukrainians and Russians as a single people, offending many ethnic Ukrainians who saw Putin's words as a denial of their culture and history. On another occasion he stressed the Russian contribution to the victory over Nazi Germany, ignoring the fact that, as a percentage of its population, the Ukrainian Soviet Socialist Republic had suffered heavier losses than the Russian Soviet Federative Socialist Republic. Sergey Glazyev, Putin's point man on Ukraine, predicted dire consequences for the country's economy if it signed the association agreement.

Putin offered Yanukovych both inducements and threats in his effort to persuade the Ukrainian to abort the association agreement. Viktor Medvedchuk, long seen by U.S. officials as a pro-Russian agent, funded an anti-EU campaign in Ukraine, including billboards asserting that the association agreement would bring inflation and higher unemployment.

Yanukovych seemed prepared to resist Russian pressure and confirmed his intention to sign the association agreement. By mid-November, just days before the Ukraine-EU summit in Vilnius, it appeared that the European Union would drop its insistence on Tymoshenko's release as a precondition for signature. Then, on November 21, the Ukrainian cabinet announced a bombshell: it would "suspend" preparations for signing the association agreement. (Presidential Administration head Sergey Lyovochkin gave U.S. ambassador Geoffrey Pyatt a heads-up a few days before the public announcement that Kyiv would not sign the association agreement. Pyatt asked what plan the government had to sell the sudden change of course to the Ukrainian public; Lyovochkin said he had no idea.)

The Maydan Revolution

The cabinet's announcement triggered the first pro-Europe demonstration within hours.[12] On November 24, a Sunday, an estimated 100,000 protestors rallied in downtown Kyiv in what was the largest demonstration in the capital since the Orange Revolution; 30,000 more marched in L'viv, all in support of bringing Ukraine closer to Europe. Several days later Yanukovych traveled to Vilnius to meet with EU leaders at the Eastern Partnership summit. He received a cold reception; video showing an angry Chancellor Merkel dressing him down for Kyiv's reversal. Lithuanian president Dalia Grybauskaite said the Ukrainian president's decision left his country stuck between Europe and Russia, on a "way going nowhere."

Demonstrations continued in Kyiv, with students vowing to maintain a round-the-clock vigil on Maydan Nezalezhnosti (Independence Square) in the center of the capital. Early on the morning of Saturday, November 30, special police attacked the student protestors, causing dozens to seek medical care. The next day, the people of Kyiv answered in the form of a huge protest; estimates of the crowd ranged from 200,000 to 750,000.

Putin backed Yanukovych, providing Kyiv a $3 billion credit and promising many billions more, perhaps as much as $15 billion in loans, as well as a significant cut in the price of natural gas. As the protests continued into December, Ukraine moved back onto the U.S. government's radar, but Washington largely left the European Union in the lead. That approach seemed to make sense. The fight in Kyiv had begun over the EU association agreement, though it quickly evolved into something broader—a protest against the growing authoritarianism and corruption of the Yanukovych regime. The association agreement offered Ukraine its best path for integrating with Europe. The Obama administration had nothing better to offer.

Pyatt and other U.S. officials seconded the message being sent by the European Union: the government had to refrain from using force and find a political solution to the crisis. As had happened during the Orange Revolution nine years earlier, Washington and Brussels maintained constant communications. Assistant Secretary of State Victoria Nuland traveled to Kyiv on December 5 for an OSCE ministerial after Secretary of State John Kerry canceled his participation; she urged the government and demonstrators to work together to resolve the crisis. (This would be the first of many trips to Ukraine for Nuland; she returned six days later with the EU's Ashton to again urge a peaceful resolution.) Senators John McCain and Chris Murphy traveled to Kyiv, pointedly showing their support for the demonstrators on the Maydan.

U.S. officials expressed the hope that Yanukovych would deescalate the crisis, but they did not know what he would do. Opposition leaders told them that they were prepared to meet with Yanukovych in a roundtable format with EU officials present, as long as the goal was to put Ukraine on course to sign the association agreement. That seemed difficult to achieve. Yanukovych asserted to Nuland that, if he signed the association agreement without Western financial support, Russia would crash the Ukrainian economy.

Demonstrations continued in Kyiv, centered on the Maydan. The crisis deepened in mid-January 2014, when the Rada rammed through a host of antiprotest laws. That move prompted a small minority among the protestors to resort to tossing rocks and Molotov cocktails at police lines, just two blocks away from the largely peaceful Maydan demonstrations. Yanukovych seemed to step back just days later, firing his prime minister and arranging for the progovernment majority in the Rada vote to repeal the newly passed laws.

Reinforcing Pyatt and Nuland, Vice President Biden made several calls directly to Yanukovych to express U.S. concerns and urge compromise. Washington began to impose sanctions, revoking the visas of officials connected to violent actions against the demonstrators, and considered broader visa and financial sanctions as a mechanism that might peel away Yanukovych's inner circle. U.S. officials in January felt that the path to resolving the underlying tensions was to get to the presidential election in 2015, but they were unsure how to get there and had doubts as to whether a free and fair election would be possible. The alternative, they feared, was that Yanukovych might use force and impose martial law, which could provoke a major public backlash, especially in Kyiv, where most people were now hostile to Yanukovych.

EU and U.S. officials continued to encourage tentative contacts between Bankova and opposition leaders. The embassy maintained contact with a range of opposition leaders, including the Svoboda (Freedom) Party, a right-wing group. U.S. officials were skeptical of Svoboda and had warned the party that continued contacts depended on its behavior. But they judged that Svoboda seemed to be playing a responsible role (Svoboda members had disarmed and removed the more radical Praviy Sektor (Right Sector) group from a government building that it had occupied.)

Wide-scale fighting broke out in Kyiv on February 18. A protest march on the Rada turned violent, and the riot police responded with clubs, stun grenades, rubber bullets, and some real bullets. That evening, security forces launched an assault on the Maydan, which for most of the protest period had been tacitly recognized as a safe area. The succeeding two days produced continuing clashes between security forces and protestors, grim images, more than 100 dead and hundreds wounded—many as a result of sniper fire targeted at people on the Maydan.

The German, French, and Polish foreign ministers arrived in Kyiv late on February 20 to try to broker a settlement between Yanukovych and the three principal opposition leaders: Yatsenyuk, former heavyweight boxer and Udar (Punch) Party leader Vitaliy Klychko, and Svoboda leader Oleh Tyahnybok. Moscow dispatched former diplomat Vladimir Lukin to take part. Negotiations ran through the night and by morning of February 21 had produced a tentative agreement providing for a national unity government, constitutional changes, and moving the presidential election from 2015 to no later than December 2014. The agreement was signed by Yanukovych and the three opposition leaders, as well as by the German, French, and Polish representatives as witnesses (Lukin did not sign, reportedly after consulting with Moscow).

The initial reaction on the Maydan to the terms of the agreement was negative. Yatsenyuk, Klychko, and Tyahnybok likely could not have persuaded the crowd to accept it. After the violence of the three previous days, the demonstrators wanted to see Yanukovych gone immediately. But the three opposition leaders did not have a serious chance to sell the agreement. After the signing ceremony, Yanukovych left Bankova, traveled to his opulent estate outside of Kyiv, packed up some last belongings, and left. (Videotapes at his residence later revealed that the packing of belongings had begun several days earlier.) Other than appearing in a taped statement to the media the next day, the president was not seen again until February 28, when he turned up in southern Russia.

On February 22, the Rada met in extraordinary session and appointed Oleksandr Turchynov interim president and Yatsenyuk as acting prime minister. The acting cabinet featured mostly pro-West opposition figures. The Regions Party—which had largely denounced Yanukovych—declined offers of several ministerial positions. Turchynov and Yatsenyuk made clear that their number one foreign policy priority was to sign the association agreement and draw closer to Europe.

Conflict with Russia

Within a few days, "little green men," as Ukrainians called them, appeared in Crimea and began seizing key installations and checkpoints. Although they were clearly professional soldiers and wore Russian army-style combat fatigues, Putin in early March denied they were Russian soldiers, calling them local defense militia. Putin's claim was belied by video showing helicopters ferrying in additional troops from the Taman Peninsula in Russia. (Weeks later, Putin would tell a telethon that the little green men had in fact been Russian troops.) Ukrainian forces on Crimea remained in garrison and did not challenge the Russians. Kyiv's decision not to resist was influenced in part by the fact that Washington—recalling the difficult experience of the 2008 Georgia-Russia conflict—quietly urged the Ukrainians to take no military action that might provoke a Russian escalation. The Russian military soon controlled the peninsula.

With the crisis deepening, U.S. officials concluded that it was time to take a more active role, though in close coordination with the European Union. Kerry visited Kyiv on March 4, while Washington announced a $1 billion loan guarantee. Ukrainian political leaders told him that they agreed on holding a presidential election on May 25. U.S. officials began consulting with their Ukrainian counterparts on the additional financial assistance the country needed, including from international financial institutions such as the International Monetary Fund. A joint FBI–Department of Justice–Department of Treasury team traveled to Ukraine to try to help track down the large sums of money that Yanukovych and his inner circle were believed to have stolen and moved offshore.

On March 6, the Crimean parliament voted to join Russia and to hold a referendum on March 16. Deputies who might have opposed the votes were reportedly blocked from taking part. The referendum, illegal under Ukrainian law, offered two choices: restore Crimea's 1992 constitution, which would provide substantially greater autonomy; or join Russia. Those who might have preferred Crimea to remain in Ukraine under the then-existing constitutional arrangements found no box to check on the ballot. The conduct of the referendum was a mockery, producing the expected vote to join Russia; there were numerous reports of irregularities, and turnout was much lower than Moscow claimed. Five days later, the Russian parliament voted to annex Crimea in violation of numerous bilateral and multilateral agreements. (Only a small handful of countries have since recognized Crimea as part of Russia.)

Washington rejected the referendum and consulted with other Western countries on appropriate ways to respond. The United States and European Union began applying visa and financial sanctions against individuals connected with the seizure of Crimea and on selected Russian banks. Obama on March 20 announced a new executive order to enable broader sanctions against the financial, energy, and defense sectors of the Russian economy. U.S. and other Western officials began pressing France to cancel its planned sale of two helicopter assault ships to Russia. Leaders of the G-8 countries (the United States, Britain, Canada, France, Germany, Italy, Japan, and Russia) were scheduled to meet in Sochi in June. On March 24, leaders of all the countries except Putin agreed to exclude Russia from the group and revert to being the G-7.

In April, little green men appeared along with armed separatists in eastern Ukraine, particularly in Donetsk and Luhansk, the two oblasts often referred to as the Donbas. This time, Ukrainian security forces resisted, and fighting broke out in a number of places. On April 17, the U.S., Ukrainian, and Russian foreign ministers, plus the EU high representative for common foreign and security policy, met in Geneva to try to resolve the conflict. (This meeting took place after Russian foreign minister Sergey Lavrov declined to join a meeting of the U.S., Ukrainian, and British foreign ministers, which had been called by Kyiv under the terms of the 1994 Budapest Memorandum.) The Geneva meeting produced an agreement on steps to deescalate the crisis in the Donbas. It called for all sides to eschew violence, the disarming of all illegal armed groups, the evacuation of occupied buildings and other public places, and amnesty for those who left occupied buildings and gave up their weapons, provided that they had not committed capital crimes. The agreement also called on the OSCE to monitor the agreed measures and for Kyiv to reform its constitution so that it reached out to "all of Ukraine's regions and political constituencies." After the meeting, Kerry stressed the need for implementation. In Washington, Obama sounded skeptical about the agreement's prospects, and separatist leaders in the Donbas indicated that they would not observe it.[13]

Little came of the Geneva meeting. The Russians did nothing to get the armed "separatist" groups to lay down their weapons or evacuate the sites that they had occupied in the Donbas. The Russian-led and -supported separatist forces spread in the Donbas. The fighting, including with heavy weapons, intensified. Over the next several months, Russia poured leadership, fighters, funding, ammunition, heavy arms, and other aid across the border to support the separatists. The self-described separatists at first claimed that their heavy weapons had been "liberated" from the Ukrainian army, but they soon began operating tanks and other equipment of types that Ukrainian inventories had never held.

U.S. and European officials began discussions about additional sanctions against Russia, sanctions that would go beyond those targeted at individuals. The United States levied sanctions on a few financial institutions that were seen as connected to the Kremlin. In general, Washington inclined toward tougher sanctions but saw value in working with the European Union to apply roughly consistent sanctions in order to project a common U.S.-EU stance. Because Europe's trade with Russia was many times larger than U.S.-Russian trade, the European Union had additional ways to pressure Moscow but also had more at stake economically.

While the fighting escalated in eastern Ukraine, Ukraine conducted a presidential election on May 25. Following a meeting of Firtash, Klychko, and Petro Poroshenko in Vienna, Klychko decided not to run for the presidency (the meeting was held in Vienna because Firtash was stuck in Austria pending resolution of a U.S. extradition request on bribery charges).[14] Klychko ran for and won the position of mayor of Kyiv, and Poroshenko handily won the presidential election, securing some 55 percent of the vote. The margin of victory meant there was no need for a runoff, the first time no runoff had been necessary in a presidential election since December 1991. The voting also belied exaggerated Kremlin claims about the influence of neofascists in Ukraine; the two candidates from far-right parties together polled less than 2 percent of the vote. The election was conducted in all parts of the country except Crimea and those parts of the Donbas occupied by pro-Russian separatist forces. The OSCE monitoring mission found that the election was largely consistent with international norms and Ukraine's commitments. The election gave Ukraine a president with a new democratic mandate.

To demonstrate U.S. support, Biden attended Poroshenko's June 7 inauguration. Washington began new assistance programs aimed at helping Ukraine improve its energy security. American officials worked in coordination with their EU counterparts to develop an International Monetary Fund program for Ukraine that was frontloaded to provide significant funding once Kyiv met certain conditionalities. The Pentagon began providing military assistance, though it was limited to nonlethal equipment.

On June 27, Poroshenko visited Brussels and signed the EU-Ukraine association agreement. Many analysts saw that as a game-changer, as long as Kyiv implemented its provisions. They entailed both a deep and comprehensive free trade area and a revision of many Ukrainian internal regulations to meet EU standards. (As one Central European foreign minister put it in 2013, if Ukraine fully implemented the association agreement, it would be more ready to join the European Union than his country was when it joined in 2004.)

Fighting intensified in the east, with a tragic occurrence on July 17, when a Buk (SA-11) surface-to-air missile shot down Malaysian Air Flight 17, a Boeing 777 with nearly 300 passengers on board. A separatist leader quickly claimed credit for downing a Ukrainian military transport, but there was no loss of a Ukrainian plane, and the time and location exactly matched the Malaysian airliner's downing. The American embassy in Kyiv released a statement on July 19 citing the U.S. government's assessment that "Flight MH 17 was likely downed by an SA-11 surface-to-air missile fired from separatist-controlled territory in eastern Ukraine." The statement said that a surface-to-air missile launch had been detected in the area when contact was lost with MH 17, noted intercepts by the Ukrainian government showing that separatist forces had possession of an SA-11 system, and cited social media postings that showed an SA-11 system in the area.[15]

Initial U.S. and European sanctions, though relatively modest, had an early impact. Capital flight from Russia accelerated after March, and Russian companies found that they were unable to sell foreign currency bonds. The MH 17 shootdown seemed to galvanize opinion in Europe. The United States and European Union coordinated on a far broader set of sanctions targeting the Russian financial, energy, high-tech, and defense sectors, with the goal of effecting a change in Kremlin policy toward Ukraine. U.S. officials described their objective as working in concert with the European Union to raise pressure on Moscow while leaving Putin a way out. Although lethal military assistance was not on the table at the moment, the U.S. military planned to ramp up training and advisory programs, beginning a training program in the fall for national guard and later army units at the Yavoriv facility in western Ukraine. Making reference to the 1994 Budapest Memorandum on Security Assurances and Ukraine's agreement to give up nuclear arms, a number of Ukrainians argued that the United States owed Ukraine more, including lethal military assistance.

By mid-August, Ukrainian military and security forces, in conjunction with volunteer battalions (some of which showed worrisome neofascist leanings), had significantly compressed the territory occupied by the pro-Russian separatists and appeared in sight of regaining control of all of the Donbas. On or about August 23, however, regular units of the Russian army crossed the border and dealt a heavy blow to Ukrainian forces, reportedly destroying between 50 and 70 percent of the armor that Ukraine had deployed in the Donbas and regaining much of the territory that the separatists had occupied. A ceasefire was hastily agreed in Minsk on September 5 by former president Leonid Kuchma and representatives from the so-called Donetsk and Luhansk "people's republics," with Russian and OSCE officials present. The ceasefire never really took hold, however. Fighting continued along the line of contact, particularly around the Donetsk airport.

Poroshenko traveled to the United States on September 17 for two days of meetings with Obama, Biden, and Kerry to discuss the situation in Ukraine and conflict with Russia. The visit served to underscore U.S. political support for Ukraine and went well for the most part. However, although U.S. officials had tried to dissuade Kyiv, Poroshenko asked for major non-NATO ally status, something the U.S. government was not prepared to consider. Washington was also not prepared to grant Poroshenko's request for lethal military assistance. Addressing a joint session of Congress, he raised the lethal assistance request, stating, "Blankets and night-vision goggles are important. But one cannot win a war with blankets." That irritated White House officials, but senior Ukrainian officials felt that the visit largely achieved their objectives, believing they had a clear U.S. commitment to keep the pressure on Russia.

Ukrainians went to the polls again on October 27, this time for early Rada elections. The ballot revalidated the parliament's democratic legitimacy. The Party of Poroshenko and the People's Front (headed by Yatsenyuk, the prime minister), each secured about 22 percent of the party-list vote and, with individual constituencies, won 214 seats. The election left twenty-seven seats vacant, for constituencies in Crimea and the occupied part of the Donbas, where elections could not be held. The following month, three other parties—Samopomich (Self-Help), the Radical Party, and Tymoshenko's Batkivshchyna (Fatherland)—joined the Party of Poroshenko and the People's Front to form a broad coalition that endorsed reform and a pro-Western course, including the goal of joining NATO. Shortly thereafter, Biden—now the face of Washington's policy toward Ukraine—paid a brief visit to Kyiv.

In December, the newly formed coalition overturned the 2010 law on non-bloc status for Ukraine by a vote of 303 to 8. That opened the possibility for Kyiv to again pursue a membership path with NATO. Individual politicians endorsed seeking membership and polls showed rising public support, but Poroshenko did not formally embrace the idea, noting that it would be years before Ukraine was in a position to make a serious membership bid. That made sense, as there was little sentiment within the alliance for putting Kyiv on a membership track.

December saw something of a lull in fighting in the Donbas, but it picked up again in early 2015. In February, Congress weighed providing lethal military assistance to Ukraine as the idea gained traction in Washington. The Ukrainians focused their request on man-portable anti-armor weapons, in view of the heavy equipment that Russia was sending into the Donbas. In private meetings, many senior U.S. government officials appeared supportive of arming Ukraine, while noting it would be a presidential decision. Merkel came to the U.S. capital to meet with Obama on February 9. She was prepared to try to broker a new ceasefire and settlement, in the context of the "Normandy format" (begun when French president François Hollande held a meeting with Merkel, Putin, and Poroshenko in Normandy in June 2014). Obama supported Merkel's effort. Merkel's opposition to providing weapons reinforced Obama's own cautious view. The U.S. government continued to limit its military aid to nonlethal assistance, though it began to provide more useful equipment, such as counterbattery radars.

Merkel, Hollande, Poroshenko, and Putin held a lengthy overnight meeting in Minsk on February 11 and 12, producing an agreement later referred to as "Minsk II." Minsk II called for a ceasefire and withdrawal of heavy weapons from the line of contact by March 1, with OSCE observers to monitor and verify the ceasefire and heavy weapons withdrawal. Minsk II also called for withdrawal of foreign forces and equipment from Ukraine; laid out the elements of a political settlement, such as amnesty, constitutional reform to provide for decentralization of government authority, and special status for the Donbas region; and provided for ultimate restoration of Ukrainian sovereignty over all of the Donbas, including full control over the Ukrainian-Russian border.[16] The terms were problematic for Kyiv, but Poroshenko agreed in the face of a difficult military situation and an urgent requirement for some breathing space in order to focus on a looming financial crisis.

With the ceasefire not kicking in for three days, separatist and Russian forces launched a major assault on a Ukrainian-held salient at Debaltseve, a key transport junction between the occupied cities of Donetsk and Luhansk. With the salient closed, the level of fighting dropped, but it never really stopped. The front began to settle into a pattern of alternating periods of relative quiet and heavier fighting. Areas near the cities of Donetsk and Mariupol (the first in Russian and separatist hands, the second not) saw regular clashes. Some analysts wondered whether the Russians and separatists might try to seize a land bridge to Crimea. (Few in Moscow, however, mentioned the "Novorossiya" [New Russia] concept that had been briefly popular among many Russians in summer 2014—the idea that much of eastern and southern Ukraine would rise up against Kyiv. From the fall of 2014 on, it was clear that there would be no such large-scale uprising, as opinion polls showed a deepening sense of Ukrainian identity across the country.)

The U.S. government threw its support behind the Minsk II agreement and the mediation effort led by Merkel. While some in Kyiv and Europe decried the absence of a U.S. seat at the table, Washington seemed comfortable with the supporting role. Nuland and other U.S. officials, such as Dan Fried, who oversaw U.S. sanctions efforts, maintained close contacts with Brussels, the Germans, and other key European states. Biden continued to lead the high-level dialogue with Kyiv, including regular phone conversations with Poroshenko and Yatsenyuk.

Kyiv received good news in March, when the International Monetary Fund announced approval of a $17.5 billion four-year program, with distribution of an initial tranche of assistance worth $5 billion. The program included a number of conditionalities that Kyiv would have to meet in the future to receive additional tranches. IMF officials believed that Ukraine needed $40 billion in total and thought that the difference could be covered by other international financial institutions, the United States, the European Union, and a rescheduling of Ukrainian government debts.

Fighting continued in the spring and seemed to escalate during the summer months. The ceasefire appeared to take better hold in September 2015, though brief periods of intense fighting occasionally erupted. That pattern would continue.

Meanwhile, politics in Kyiv became more difficult in September. The Rada took up a constitutional amendment on decentralization. It passed with a simple majority on the first reading but at a cost. The Radical Party quit the coalition in protest, raising big questions as to whether the 300 votes needed could be mustered to pass the amendment on a second reading. The government let the amendment sit. Another key vote dealt with the debt-rescheduling deal that Finance Minister Natalie Jaresko had worked out. It was not clear that the Rada would approve it; if not, Ukraine might go off-program with the International Monetary Fund, meaning no further tranches and a very difficult renegotiation with creditors.

More broadly, relations between Poroshenko and Yatsenyuk had begun to fray. The prime minister had taken most of the heat for the heavy impact of austerity measures and watched his approval rating plummet to the low single digits. Officials close to him vented frustration that the president was not more supportive in public. Meanwhile, Tymoshenko had begun attacking government programs, even though her party was still nominally part of the majority coalition in the Rada. Her party had barely cleared the 5 percent threshold in the October 2014 Rada elections to win party-list seats, but she had climbed in the polls to above 20 percent, where she stood second to Poroshenko.

This was not good news for the U.S. government, which feared that a breakdown in the coalition could set back reform efforts and plunge the country into political crisis at a difficult juncture. Washington, moreover, held Yatsenyuk in high regard in view of the difficult decisions he had taken over nearly two years to keep the economy going, in particular by stabilizing the government's financial situation. Pyatt urged the coalition to hang together, a message conveyed as well by Biden in phone calls and when he visited Kyiv in December. Biden also used a speech to the Rada to deliver a blunt message on the need for action against corruption:

> The Office of the General Prosecutor desperately needs reform. The judiciary should be overhauled. The energy sector needs to be competitive, ruled by market principles—not sweetheart deals. It's not enough to push through laws to increase transparency with regard to official sources of income. Senior elected officials have to remove all conflicts between their business interest and their government responsibilities. . . . Oligarchs and non-oligarchs must play by the same rules.[17]

Biden also delivered a tough anticorruption message in private. He told Poroshenko that Viktor Shokin—head of the Office of the General Prosecutor, who appeared to have done next to nothing in the effort to combat corruption—had to go. The vice president added that Washington would withhold a $1 billion loan guarantee until Shokin was fired (Shokin resigned several months later).[18] Biden's message reinforced Pyatt's urgings to the government to get more active in the fight against corruption. Pyatt expressed concern that no one had been jailed for the deaths on the Maydan in February 2014 or for the massive theft that had taken place during the Yanukovych era. The ambassador made these points publicly as well, prompting Ihor Kononenko, a senior member of the Party of Poroshenko, to charge that he was interfering in Ukraine's internal affairs.

With frustration growing in Ukraine about the failure to implement Minsk II, all of whose terms were supposed to be met by the end of 2015, U.S. officials pressed Kyiv to stay with the agreement. At the same time, Washington publicly took the position that, as long as the security conditions such as a ceasefire and withdrawal of heavy weapons had not been met, it was unrealistic to ask Kyiv to move far on implementing Minsk II's political elements. It seemed, however, that Moscow had little interest in implementing the Minsk agreement. No evidence suggested that it had pressured the so-called separatist forces in any serious way to implement the Minsk terms. Russian military personnel remained in the Donbas, providing leadership and training in particular.

The growing strains between Poroshenko and Yatsenyuk became more evident in early 2016. In mid-February, the Rada, with strong support from the Party of Poroshenko, passed a resolution expressing disapproval of the work done by Yatsenyuk and his cabinet. It did not, however, pass a resolution of no-confidence, which would have led to Yatsenyuk's ouster. Western diplomats puzzled over how Ukraine—with conflict continuing in the Donbas, a full reform agenda, and IMF disbursements now suspended—could afford the political fight. Pyatt and his European counterparts urged cooperation but to little effect. Yatsenyuk resigned on April 10, and Rada chairman Volodymyr Hroysman, a close ally of Poroshenko, became the new prime minister. The People's Front remained in the government coalition. Indeed, neither it nor the Party of Poroshenko had an incentive to break away; polls indicated that early parliamentary elections would devastate the People's Front and significantly reduce the number of Party of Poroshenko deputies.

U.S. policy continued to support Merkel's efforts in the Minsk process—even if it appeared to have few prospects for success. No alternative path to a settlement had emerged. Nuland began a side dialogue with Kremlin insider Vladislav Surkov, billed as an effort to support the Minsk process, but little visible progress was made in that channel. A number of Ukrainians worried that the U.S. government would sacrifice Ukraine for a deal with Russia over Syria. U.S. officials adamantly denied that they would consider such a trade, and there was nothing to suggest that they did. Nuland kept close contact with Kyiv in order to calm fears that a deal might be done over the heads of the Ukrainians. Washington continued to support sanctions and coordinate closely with the European Union, including on possible new sanctions if Russia were to significantly increase its aggression against Ukraine. However, with some EU countries beginning to question sanctions, keeping the European Union on board with existing measures appeared to be enough of a challenge.

Biden continued to work the phones with Poroshenko and now Hroysman. Ukrainian officials expressed disappointment, however, that, almost three years after the Maydan Revolution began, Obama had not visited their country. The U.S. government increased its assistance to Ukraine, including providing several loan guarantees, each worth $1 billion. Much of the U.S. interaction with Kyiv continued to focus on trying to promote faster reform and a more vigorous anticorruption effort in order to build a more resilient Ukrainian state. The resolution of the spring political crisis and the Ukrainian government's adoption of several reforms allowed it to get back on track with its IMF program in the fall and to begin receiving disbursements again.

More broadly, at the end of 2016 it appeared that the Ukrainian economy had begun to stabilize after several years of decline, with the prospect of at least slow growth in 2017. One remarkable achievement was Kyiv's weaning itself off of Russian natural gas. Progress in energy conservation, domestic gas production, the loss of gas-hungry industries in the Donbas, and a successful effort to import gas from countries to its west greatly reduced Ukraine's need to buy gas directly from Russia. In 2015, Ukraine purchased a little over 6 billion cubic meters of gas from Gazprom; in comparison, in the late 1990s it had received more than 50 billion cubic meters per year from Russia or from transit lines passing through Russia.

In the Donbas, although the fighting during many periods in 2016 was not as bad as in the first half of 2015, more Ukrainian soldiers died in July 2016 than in any month since summer 2015. In the fall of 2016, the total number of dead climbed toward 10,000. Merkel hosted a meeting with Hollande, Poroshenko, and Putin in Berlin in late October, the first among the four leaders in a year. It called for a roadmap for implementation of Minsk II, but expectations on all sides seemed modest.

As 2017 approached, Poroshenko and Hroysman, and the Ukrainian nation, continued to face two stiff challenges. First, they needed to resist the hybrid Russian aggression in the Donbas and ultimately find a settlement to that conflict. (Crimea remained an open issue—for Kyiv and most of the international community, as well as for the indigenous Crimean Tatar people—despite Moscow's efforts to declare its illegal annexation a closed chapter.) Second, Ukraine needed to complete the process of reforming its economic and political institutions so that it could shape a modern democratic state with a market economy fully compatible with EU standards and values, as well as come to grips with the problem of corruption.

The Ukrainians learned early on November 9 that they would face these challenges with Donald Trump assuming the American presidency in January 2017. Trump on the campaign trail had said that he would build a better relationship with Russia, without indicating that he would first seek a change in Moscow's problematic foreign behavior. He had also suggested that Europe should handle the Ukraine-Russia crisis, that he would consider recognizing Russia's illegal annexation of Crimea, and that he might lift economic sanctions on Russia. In contrast, mainstream Republican thinking in Congress continued to support Ukraine and maintained a wary skepticism about Putin and Russian policy, particularly in view of the interference by Russian intelligence agencies in the U.S. presidential election. As Trump moved into the Oval Office and in his first weeks as president, it was unclear whether his Ukraine policy would be based more on his earlier pronouncements on the campaign trail or follow mainstream Republican thinking, including views expressed by Vice President Mike Pence and Secretary of Defense James Mattis. In Kyiv, the Ukrainians anxiously waited to see what a Trump presidency would mean for the U.S.-Ukraine relationship.

CHAPTER 8

Lessons and Policy Recommendations

L ooking back at the first fourteen years of American engagement with independent Ukraine, we can see that some U.S. policies worked and others proved less effective. The lessons that emerged have been reinforced by the experience of U.S.-Ukraine relations in the period after 2005. This chapter looks at those lessons and concludes with recommendations for how American policy might more effectively help Ukraine develop into a modern and more resilient state with stable democratic institutions, a robust and productive market economy, and a growing prospect of realizing its aspirations and those of its people.

Lessons Learned

For most of the twenty-five years since Ukraine regained its independence in 1991, the U.S.-Ukraine relationship has been strong and positive—as good as any that Washington has had with a post-Soviet state. U.S. policy largely succeeded in mobilizing correct combinations of diplomacy, carrots and sticks to secure Ukrainian agreement to and support for key American foreign policy goals. Washington's number one objective in the aftermath of the Soviet Union's collapse was ensuring that only one nuclear weapons state remained in the post-Soviet space. That meant persuading the Ukrainian government to adhere to its declared objective to be a non-nuclear weapons state and to proceed with the elimination of the nuclear warheads and strategic delivery systems on its territory. The process took time, required hands-on involvement by President Bill Clinton and Vice President Al Gore, and caused a degree of exasperation on all sides, but Washington ultimately found the right mix of policy tools to satisfy the Ukrainian government's conditions for denuclearization. Following the Russian aggression that began in 2014, Ukrainians understandably question the wisdom of giving up nuclear arms, though as explained at the end of chapter 2, an effort to retain them would have had severe political and economic costs for Kyiv.

Likewise, U.S. policy succeeded in getting Kyiv to synchronize its approach to nonproliferation with that of the United States, with the immediate effect in 1998 that the Ukrainian government ordered Turboatom to cancel its contract to provide a turbine generator for the nuclear reactor that the Russians were building at Bushehr, Iran. That nonproliferation success story was replicated in 2012, when the last highly enriched uranium was removed from Ukraine. (Breaking the Turboatom contract helped delay completion of the reactor at Bushehr, though the Russians were able to produce their own turbine and eventually finish the project.)

President Leonid Kuchma's agreement in 2003 to commit troops to the Iraq stabilization mission also was a major win for American policy, at a time when the U.S. military intently recruited other countries' armed forces in order to reduce its own burden in the Middle East. The fact that Kuchma desperately sought a way to maintain some connection to the White House at a time when the bilateral relationship had crashed to its lowest point since 1991 helped secure the desired troop contribution.

What caused more intractable difficulties for the relationship were problems internal to Ukraine: the slow pace of reform, bad election processes, a questionable commitment to democracy, and continuing corruption. The U.S. record of addressing these challenges—and of persuading the government in Kyiv to address them—shows fewer positive results.

Ukraine has made progress to be sure, particularly in the time after the Maydan Revolution in 2014. The post-Maydan elections, like those held in the period from the Orange Revolution until 2010, were among the best and most democratic conducted in the post-Soviet space. While Ukrainian democracy remained imperfect and often messy, it was pluralistic, reflecting a real clash of competing views. A robust, diverse, and motivated civil society has developed, strong enough to overturn a stolen election in 2004 and bring down an authoritarian government in 2014. But civil society, as well as ordinary Ukrainians, still lack established means to influence the political decisions made by the government and the Rada between elections. Likewise, the economy has made some progress, though the global economic recession of 2008 and the conflict with Russia that followed the Maydan Revolution wiped out many of the gains that ordinary Ukrainians realized between 2000 and 2008. Much more needs to be done to make Ukraine a modern market economy and to tackle the scourge of corruption.

Ukraine has seen less reform than U.S. policymakers wished to see. Many of the measures still to be implemented at the end of 2016—including privatization of state-owned enterprises, development of a dynamic small and medium-sized enterprise sector that operates in the open, judicial reform, anticorruption measures, and curbs on the political influence of oligarchs—were recognized as necessary actions for more than twenty years. They remained reform measures still to be taken as 2016 drew to a close, despite advice, cajoling, and many billions of dollars in reform assistance and low-interest credits from the United States, the European Union, and other Western donors, in particular the International Monetary Fund.

Making reform assistance work has faced several challenges. One was the difficulty of measuring success. It is relatively simple to count outputs, such as the number of seminars conducted with Ukrainian officials on how best to rationalize regulatory structures. It is much more difficult to measure impact: How much did the seminars contribute to more streamlined regulations, greater ease of starting up small business, and growth in local economies?

Moreover, and more important, it is not just a question of delivering assistance programs. There needs to be a readiness, indeed a conscious choice, on the part of the receiving government to put that assistance to good use in implementing real change. That commitment must start at the top.

Ukrainian leaders often lacked the will or the ability to pursue reform. In some cases, they feared the political consequences of needed reform steps. For example, it was only in 2016 that the government raised the tariffs on heat charged to individual households to the point where they came close to covering the cost of producing and distributing the heat. That reform had been high on the list of steps advocated by Western donors dating back to the mid-1990s, as a means of promoting energy conservation. A series of Ukrainian presidents and governments chose not to pursue it, in part because such reform would have meant hitting every household in the country with a higher utility bill, even if targeted subsidies might ease the pain for the least well-off. Ukraine's leadership for too long feared the political consequences of such a step and continually put it off, even though it was critical to rationalization of the energy sector and to removing a large, wasteful subsidy burden on the state budget.

At other times, the dysfunctional nature of the Ukrainian constitution's division of executive power between the president on the one hand, and the prime minister and cabinet on the other, complicated reform efforts—particularly when the agendas of the president and prime minister did not closely align. The burst of optimism in December 1999 that followed the confirmation of Viktor Yushchenko as prime minister died out in 2000, when Kuchma and the Presidential Administration at Bankova did not support Yushchenko and his reform program with the Rada. In 2001, Bankova abandoned Yushchenko completely, letting the Rada vote him out of power. In 2005, and then again in 2008, it was the inability of Yushchenko as president to work with Yuliya Tymoshenko as his prime minister that posed an obstacle to serious reform and created the unfortunate image of a government in disarray. In fall 2015, officials close to Prime Minister Arseniy Yatsenyuk complained that the cabinet's reform agenda received less than wholehearted support from President Petro Poroshenko. Yatsenyuk and his cabinet, which contained a number of technocratic reformers, stepped down in spring 2016.

Even when the president and prime minister worked together, the often fractious Rada could prove a difficult partner. Kuchma in 1997 faced a Rada comprising nearly a dozen parties. The Rada in mid-2016 included eight different blocs and factions. Politics remain complex, and Ukrainian parties still struggle to learn the art of political compromise. It too often seems that the focus is on jockeying for position for the next election rather than governing.

By far the biggest obstacle to genuine reform, however, has been and remains Ukraine's corrupt political culture, particularly in the absence of a functioning legal system and a lack of respect for the rule of law. It is a problem throughout the government, affecting many ministries. The country suffers because too many among the elites, including senior government officials, attach greater importance to accumulating personal political power and wealth rather than embracing real reforms based on best practices. A key reason leaders chose not to reform the energy sector for so long was their deference to the corrupt interests of gas traders. The traders exploited and made large profits from the existing ways in which the energy sector operated—and they often enriched senior officials and provided the financing that they needed to maintain their grip on power.

Viktor Yanukovych proved the epitome of the leader who placed personal financial gain above the interests of the country. By some estimates he stole billions of dollars from the nation's coffers. Others did not match Yanukovych's level of personal corruption, but they showed a distressingly high tolerance for people around them who were corrupt and all too ready to take advantage of their proximity to state power.

Ukrainian leaders have come to know the talk that Western officials want to hear about reform. They also know to adopt some reforms to secure Western support. But Ukraine has not yet had a leadership fully prepared to set aside personal political and economic interests in order to adopt the reforms that would genuinely remake the governing structures and the country.

These structural and corruption problems are not easy to fix. U.S. policymakers need to shape their approach with these constraints in mind. It is also important to understand differences in expectations and that U.S. and Ukrainian officials sometimes simply talk past one another. Ukrainian officials all too often said yes to American requests when they had no idea how to implement their agreement or, in some cases, no intention of doing so. That behavior invariably irritated Washington more than if Kyiv had said no at the outset. For example, the Presidential Administration never grasped how much damage it did to Kuchma's reputation in the White House when he told National Security Adviser Condoleezza Rice in July 2001 that Kyiv would end its arms shipments to Macedonia and then continued the arms flow for months afterwards.

Another lesson is the difficulty of reforming existing institutions, in which old habits (including habits of corruption) are deeply ingrained. By contrast, the U.S. embassy after 2014 appeared to have some success assisting in the development of new police forces in Kyiv and other large cities as well as in the development of a new national guard. The takeaway may be that devoting assistance efforts toward creating new institutions that can replace existing ones or fill gaps has a greater chance of succeeding than trying to reform the older establishments.

Ukraine has long suffered from weak state administration in general and, in particular, the lack of a strong National Security Council–type mechanism to enforce decisions and ensure follow-up on presidential commitments. The National Security and Defense Council carried some weight, particularly when Volodymyr Horbulin served as its secretary in the mid-1990s. Even then, however, it had a surprisingly difficult time getting other parts of the government to take action. Resolving a sufficient number of business dispute cases to provide Secretary of State Madeleine Albright a basis on which she could make a certification decision would have cost Kyiv relatively little, but no one in the Presidential Administration or elsewhere at Bankova seemed to have the authority to make it happen. Ukrainian officials may have assumed that the State Department would in any case find a way to justify certification—or make a "political" decision, as one official put it—and that is in fact what happened. A failure to certify would have done further damage to Ukraine's already battered business reputation, at a time when it struggled to attract foreign investment. Likewise, the Pentagon could assist the Ukrainian military by purchasing fuel for it to use in exercises, but the State Tax Administration's insistence on taxing that assistance endangered the funding—and the broader U.S. assistance program if Congress had gotten wind of it. No one in Kyiv seemed to have the power or the will to tell the State Tax Administration to knock it off.

The Ukrainian government sometimes proved incapable of taking actions that would have advanced its goals. In 2002, Bankova lobbied hard for a meeting between Kuchma and President George W. Bush. Washington's decision to press for a good Rada election process as the price for an invitation for Kuchma to visit the White House was probably an overreach on the U.S. part, given the politics in Kyiv and the importance that Bankova attached to the election outcome. But U.S. officials later that year puzzled over why there was no visible push on the Ukrainian side to address the list of twenty problem issues, some of which could have been resolved relatively easily.

Getting decisions was not just a challenge on U.S.-Ukraine issues. A deputy economy minister told me one time of his frustration in trying to get approval for a new economic policy. He needed concurrence from eighteen officials scattered throughout the cabinet and succeeded in securing the approval of seventeen, but the eighteenth held out. When he submitted the proposed policy to Prime Minister Valeriy Pustovoytenko for approval with just seventeen concurrences, the prime minister refused to approve it and bounced it back with a request for a consensus recommendation.

There were problems on the American side as well. Washington and the embassy did not always fully understand the internal political dynamics in Kyiv. Those dynamics led to Ukrainian decisions that struck U.S. officials as wrong-headed or mistaken. They flowed from a political process in which the Ukrainian president was the strongest actor but still had to deal with—and take account of the interests of— influential oligarchs and other key actors. This process often played out in the shadows, making it difficult for U.S. officials, or Ukrainians for that matter, to follow. A better understanding on the U.S. part might have resulted in a more finely tuned and effective diplomacy.

One question is whether Washington should have been more assertive in pressing a reform and development agenda on the authorities in Kyiv, particularly in the early 1990s. President Leonid Kravchuk and his government seemed to have little idea what to do, not surprising given that they had come up under the Communist command economy model, and Kravchuk was focused far more on building a state than on getting the economy right. Unfortunately, it took time for the U.S.

government to put in place and fund the legal authority—the FREE-DOM Support Act—and mechanisms to promote reform. The programs funded by these monies only really began to flow in 1994, nearly three years after Ukraine regained independence.

Another problem was the difficulty of sustaining high-level engagement with Kyiv. Given the sometimes dysfunctional way in which the Ukrainian government works, to get proper attention to issues one has to talk to Ukrainians at a more senior level than in other countries. I often delivered demarches or requests to ministers or deputy ministers on issues that, in another country, would have been delivered by the American embassy's political counselor or an economic officer to a working-level contact in the host government ministry. We judged the higher-level approach necessary in Kyiv to ensure that issues received proper attention. Too many senior officials seemed reluctant to pass authority down the chain so that their subordinates could make decisions and get things done.

On really major questions U.S. officials needed to engage the Ukrainian president. My predecessors and successors had some access, as did I. But the heavy lifting required Washington's involvement at the highest level. Clinton and Gore were prepared to do this. Gore took a particular interest in Ukraine, gave a generous amount of his time, and had the institutional support of the bilateral commission that he co-chaired with Kuchma. Vice President Joe Biden took on a similar role following the Maydan Revolution, though he did not have a formal structure like Gore's. Even with these efforts, however, Washington lacked a constant and consistent channel through which to mentor, coax, and press the Ukrainian president to take actions, particularly on reform, that would have negative political consequences and require Bankova to sacrifice the interests of its close patrons. Neither Gore nor Biden had the time for what might have been required—regular, perhaps even weekly, contacts to advise, mentor, and sometimes hector. (Part of the problem was distance. It was far easier for Polish president Alexander Kwasniewski to forge a relationship with Kuchma, since Poland bordered Ukraine. Kwasniewski also had the advantage of a less busy foreign policy agenda than his U.S. counterpart.)

Although busy schedules mean that the time of American presidents and vice presidents for engaging on foreign policy issues is limited, Washington might have been more generous in responding to Ukrainian requests. Postponing Yushchenko's visit in early 2000 as the *Financial Times* allegations swirled was an understandable decision, but it also sent the unintended message that Washington was distancing itself from Yushchenko. That perception hurt him domestically in the critical early months of his prime ministership. Bush visited Kyiv once toward the end of his second term, but his administration's high-level engagement with Ukraine was episodic at best. In the aftermath of the Orange Revolution, the White House gave Yushchenko a warm welcome in April 2005, but senior-level interest was not sustained, particularly as differences emerged between Yushchenko and Tymoshenko. More intense high-level involvement in 2005 could have pressed the Yushchenko-Tymoshenko tandem to work together more effectively and reinforced the efforts of the embassy in Kyiv.

One lesson learned from the high-level contacts was that subtlety did not work. In translations from English to Ukrainian, diplomatic nuance often softened the American message, sometimes to the point where Ukrainian ears missed it. It is better to be blunt, to ensure that there is no misunderstanding later on. The challenge is to build relationships with Ukrainian leaders that will allow American interlocutors to feel comfortable being blunt.

At times, the U.S. government should have been tougher when pressing Kyiv and should have used the substantial political leverage that it had. On the one hand, the 1998 decision to certify that Ukraine had made sufficient progress on business dispute cases was the right one, because the punishment—a 50 percent cut in assistance—would have undermined the U.S. ability to promote the kind of Ukraine that Washington wished to see. On the other hand, the certification decision sent the message to Kyiv that Washington in the end would find a way to fix things. One result: Ukrainian officials made weak efforts to address the business dispute cases in 1999, almost certainly expecting the State Department to certify regardless of how little progress Ukraine made.

There were also times when the United States could and should have been more supportive. The odd case of Russia's construction of a levee from the Russian mainland to Tuzla Island in 2003 posed a direct challenge to Ukraine's territorial integrity, which both Moscow and Washington had pledged to respect in the 1994 Budapest Memorandum on Security Assurances. The National Security Council's decision not to adopt a stance supportive of the Ukrainian position was a mistake. It sent a disquieting message to Kyiv, and the Russians certainly noticed the lack of a formal American protest—something that the Kremlin might have remembered in 2014 when it considered and then took action to seize Crimea.

Policy Recommendations: Ukraine's Place in Europe

The November 8, 2016, election of Donald Trump sent a shock wave through Kyiv, where most officials had expected (and hoped) for a victory by Hillary Clinton. Trump's election raised questions about the future U.S. approach toward Ukraine, Russia, and NATO, given the statements Trump had made during his electoral campaign. His views on these issues were often at odds with the foreign policy views of mainstream Republicans in Congress (and of his own vice president and cabinet secretaries). It is unclear how soon the Trump administration's policy toward Ukraine will emerge, but one hopes that the president will come to better understand what is at stake in Ukraine for the United States. The concern is not just about Ukraine's development as a stable state on the border of institutional Europe. It is also about persuading Moscow to return to the rules and principles that served post–Cold War Europe and the transatlantic community well, especially regarding the non-use of force.

U.S. policy toward Ukraine should continue to focus on helping Kyiv address its two principal challenges: resolving the conflict with Russia and implementing the reforms that can make Ukraine a successful state. On the former problem, the United States today has to shape and pursue its policy in a Europe that is very different from the Europe of 1991, when Ukraine regained its independence. In particular, Russia blatantly challenges the existing European security order in a manner that it did not in the 1990s. The Kremlin's responsibility for the conflict should not be understated. Had they been left on their own, Ukrainians either would have avoided the bloody fighting that has taken place in the Donbas, or would have brought it to an earlier close at far less cost in lives and destroyed property.

Fully settling the Ukraine-Russia crisis may well require that the West and Moscow come to terms on Russia's place in Europe. That question is made more problematic by the fact that the Kremlin sees Kyiv's relationships with the West and institutions such as NATO and the European Union in zero-sum terms. To the extent that Ukraine moves closer to those institutions, it undermines Moscow's ability to maintain a sphere of influence in the post-Soviet space. At present, Kremlin policy does not appear to allow for the possibility that Ukraine (or other post-Soviet states) could have deepening ties with NATO and the European Union and also have good relations with Russia. That view and the notion of a sphere of influence pose a problem for Kyiv and for the West.

A U.S. policy to assist Ukraine in resolving its conflict with Russia should aim to maintain pressure on Moscow, in an effort to effect a change in Kremlin policy toward one that would facilitate a settlement that brings peace to Donetsk and Luhansk and a restoration of full Ukrainian sovereignty. Unfortunately, indications to date have been that Moscow is not so inclined. The Kremlin instead appears to prefer that the Donbas remain a "frozen" or "simmering" conflict—to serve as a mechanism to distract and destabilize Kyiv, with the goal of making it more difficult for the Ukrainian government to implement the reforms needed to become a successful state and draw closer to the European Union.

A key element of pressure on Russia is the set of sanctions imposed by the United States, the European Union, and other Western states. A collapse of the sanctions would remove much of the West's leverage with Russia. Although German chancellor Angela Merkel has taken the principled position that full implementation of the February 2015 Minsk agreement is the condition for easing the sanctions, some EU countries favor lifting them with a view to getting back to "business as usual" with Russia. Washington should work closely with Berlin and other like-minded EU members to sustain the sanctions until there is real change in the Kremlin's policy. That will not be an easy task. Britain's decision to withdraw from the European Union makes it more difficult. It will remove a supportive British voice for Kyiv from EU councils. Moreover, Brexit poses one more distraction for Merkel and other EU leaders that will require greater attention at summits to internal EU questions at the expense of EU foreign and security policy.

In order to increase the chances that the European Union will stay the course on sanctions, Washington should be clear with Kyiv about the need for Ukraine to do—and to be seen as doing—its part to achieve a settlement. Moscow and the Russian-backed forces in the Donbas have primary responsibility for the failure to implement the Minsk agreement. Kyiv needs to bear in mind, however, that the Kremlin seeks to create a narrative that attributes part or all of the responsibility for failure to Ukraine. The U.S. government should counsel the Ukrainian government to ensure that its actions belie that narrative, such as by passing an election law—incorporating all of the conditions needed for a free, fair, and competitive election—for the occupied Donbas. Such actions will make it easier for Germany and others to sustain EU unity in favor of maintaining sanctions on Russia.

Some inside and outside of Ukraine have suggested that it is time for Kyiv to let the Donbas go, arguing that the population there is out of sync with the rest of the country and that repairing the damage to industry and infrastructure caused by the conflict would be too big a burden for the economy. That is a decision for the Ukrainians, but it would be a decision fraught with political risk for the leader advocating it. Moreover, it is not clear that letting the Donbas go would solve the problem with Russia. Nothing suggests that Moscow wants the Donbas; it wants a mechanism to pressure Kyiv.

While the Donbas presents the more urgent problem given the ongoing violence, the U.S. government should work to keep Russia's annexation of Crimea from falling off the international radar screen. That should be a second vector of American policy. Crimea matters. Russia's instigation of and support for violent separatism in the Donbas has resulted in many more deaths and far more damage to housing, industry, and infrastructure than resulted from its quick capture of Crimea. That said, the seizure of Crimea has done greater damage to the European security order and its underlying principles, particularly the cardinal tenet of the 1975 Helsinki Final Act: European states should not use military force to change borders or take territory from other states. Russian actions have undermined the Final Act and weakened other key mechanisms of global governance. The Organization for Security and Cooperation in Europe operates on the basis of consensus, which Moscow can readily block, just as Russia has used its veto on the UN Security Council to shut down meaningful steps to address the Ukraine-Russia crisis in that body.

One can see a settlement on the Donbas emerging in the medium to long term (Moscow has shown no interest in annexing that war-ravaged territory). There is no reason, however, to think that the current Russian leadership, or any likely successor, would relinquish control over Crimea. Kyiv has been smart to define Crimea's return as an issue for the longer term. A settlement in the Donbas that is acceptable to Ukraine would and should lead to the lifting of some sanctions on Russia. The United States should, however, work with the European Union to ensure that sanctions related to Russia's illegal occupation of Crimea remain in place until the peninsula is returned to Ukrainian sovereignty or, more likely, until Kyiv reaches a settlement with Moscow in which it accepts the existing reality. No one should expect or ask the Ukrainian government to reach that point quickly. The U.S. government knows how to conduct a nonrecognition policy, having done so for nearly five decades with regard to the incorporation of the Baltic states into the Soviet Union. The challenge as time passes will be keeping the European Union on the same page.

Regarding the European security order more broadly, a third if tangential vector of U.S. policy should be to strengthen NATO. In particular, that means bolstering the alliance's conventional deterrence and defense capabilities on its eastern flank. The 2014 Wales and 2016 Warsaw NATO summits reached important decisions in this regard. They must be implemented, and additional measures may be needed. Although the likelihood of Russian aggression against an alliance member is low, it is not zero, and anxiety in the Baltic states is understandable. U.S. leadership will prove key. A secure NATO will mean a confident transatlantic community that is better prepared to support Ukraine.

This raises the question of Ukraine's relationship with NATO and the European Union. Russian aggression has caused a significant increase in the number of Ukrainians who want to see their country in the alliance, with recent public opinion polls showing a growing plurality in favor of joining NATO. There is, however, no enthusiasm in the alliance to put Ukraine on a membership track, even if Kyiv were to meet NATO's criteria. The reason is obvious: Crimea and the Donbas, if unsettled, would mean an Article 5 contingency from the day that Ukraine joined. NATO members are not prepared to go to war with Russia over Ukraine.

Washington thus should urge Ukraine to focus on practical coop-eration with NATO, including implementation of its annual action plans. Kyiv had a weak record on implementation of cooperative plans with NATO in the late 1990s and early 2000s, and its record does not appear to have improved much since then. Taking real actions will tighten NATO-Ukraine cooperation and contribute to a more effective Ukrainian military. Moscow, moreover, seems to pay more attention to titles, such as a membership action plan (MAP), than it does to the substance of the programs. For now, the U.S. government should dis-courage Kyiv from pursuing a MAP. At most, only a few NATO mem-bers would support it, and a MAP conveys no Article 5 protection. At the same time, Washington should use its influence to make sure NA-TO's open-door policy remains in place. Kyiv may have no realistic chance of entering the alliance at present, but NATO should not fore-close that possibility in the future.

The United States should encourage NATO to continue and expand its programs and trust accounts to help Ukraine modernize its military and defense establishment, including the consolidation of civilian con-trol. Washington should also continue to provide military assistance on a bilateral basis. Political and military leaders in Kyiv understand that there is no military solution in the Donbas, because they could not defeat the Russian army. But U.S. assistance that increases the defen-sive capabilities of the Ukrainian military will allow it to raise the costs to Moscow of further aggression by Russian and separatist forces. That prospect would remove easy Russian/separatist military options and, perhaps deter such an attack. The Obama administration chose to limit its military aid to nonlethal equipment. I and others have argued that the United States should provide some lethal assistance, specifi-cally man-portable anti-armor weapons.[1] This is obviously a sensitive issue, but it is one that Washington should consider in the future, again with the view to bolstering the Ukrainian army's ability to deter fur-ther aggression in the eastern part of the country.

Ukraine's best path for strengthening its links with the West in the near term is to implement its association agreement with the European Union. A Ukraine that accomplishes full implementation would be a radically different country, close to ready for EU membership. Kyiv should do its part on implementation but keep its expectations realis-tic. Prime Minister Volodymyr Hroysman's July 2016 prediction that

Ukraine would be an EU member state in ten years was wildly optimistic, particularly as the European Union heads for a period of deeper uncertainty due to British withdrawal (on top of other issues, such as migration, terrorism, and the future of the euro). Kyiv should implement the association agreement because doing so is in the interest of a stronger, more competitive, and productive Ukrainian state, regardless of whether—or when—EU membership becomes a prospect.

For its part, the U.S. government should counsel Kyiv to focus on implementing the association agreement and not overreach in its rhetoric while quietly urging the European Union not to rule out a membership prospect, particularly if Ukraine makes serious progress in implementation. Merkel appears committed to helping Ukraine resolve its crisis with Russia and is the key EU player, though she faces her own election in the fall of 2017. But keeping other EU member states actively engaged may prove more difficult than in the past. Unfortunately, key drivers of the EU's Eastern Partnership Program and of active outreach to Kyiv—Carl Bildt and Radek Sikorski, former foreign ministers of Sweden and Poland, and Stefan Fuele, former EU commissioner for enlargement and European neighborhood policy—have moved on.

The United States, the European Union, and Ukraine should all understand, moreover, that Russia will oppose Ukraine's drawing closer to the European Union almost as much as it opposes Ukraine's drawing closer to NATO. First, a Ukraine that fully implements the EU association agreement would be a stronger partner for the West and a state out of Moscow's reach. Second, some in Moscow fear that the European Union will develop its own defense and security identity or pave the way for entry into NATO, or both, meaning that a Ukraine bound for the European Union could become part of an opposing military grouping.

These de facto limits on its relations with NATO and the European Union will leave Ukraine in more of a security gray zone than it would like. The U.S. government can try to offset that outcome in part by maintaining strong bilateral links with Kyiv, and urging Germany, Poland, Britain, and other key European states to do so as well. That means engaging in high-level contacts with Ukraine's leaders, for whom meetings at the White House, No. 10 Downing Street, and the Bundeskanzleramt constitute important political support. U.S. and European leaders should use those meetings to convey clear messages regarding their expectations for action by their Ukrainian counterparts, particularly with regard to reform and anticorruption. Implementation of such measures will produce a stronger and more resilient state that is better able to resist Russian pressures.

A successful Western policy toward Ukraine requires close coordination and cooperation between the United States and European Union. Washington historically has had a more coherent vision for Ukraine as well as an operational plan to advance that vision. The European Union has the advantage of proximity, and becoming "fully European" is the goal that attracts many Ukrainians. The United States and the European Union have worked closely together on Ukraine policy and related questions, such as sanctions on Russia. Sustained cooperation will increase the chances for the success of Western policy.

Among EU member states, U.S. officials should maintain particularly close contacts with their counterparts in Germany, Poland, the Baltic states, Sweden, and (while it remains a member) Britain, which think in serious ways about Ukraine. Washington should support Merkel in keeping an open channel to Russian president Vladimir Putin. Ultimately, Kyiv will need the Kremlin's buy-in to any settlement if it wishes to return to something approaching normalcy. Moscow has too many levers to affect developments in Ukraine. As long as the Kremlin is dissatisfied with the situation in Ukraine or with the broader European security order, it is difficult to see how even very close cooperation between the United States and Europe—and between them and Kyiv— by themselves will produce stability and normalcy for Ukraine. Although the Russians have shown no sign of readiness to accept a settlement—at least no settlement remotely reasonable or acceptable to Kyiv—the West should stay alert for any future change in Russian policy.

This prospect is hardly satisfying for Ukraine, but it is the reality that Kyiv faces. As long as Putin's current ambitions shape the Kremlin's foreign policy, a quick resolution of the Donbas conflict, to say nothing of Crimea, appears unlikely. The West needs to work with Kyiv on ways to affect Putin's ambitions and persuade him that Russia's interests would be better served by a change in policy course that would facilitate progress toward a settlement and a move toward restoration of a more normal relationship with the United States and Europe.

Finally, in shaping policy to affect Russian choices regarding Ukraine, U.S. policymakers should bear in mind that the Kremlin does not understand its neighbor very well. In 2008, I asked a retired senior Russian diplomat whether anyone in the Kremlin had a good understanding of Ukraine; he replied that there was one person, but no one listened to him. Putin's policies over the past several years reflect that lack of understanding and have engendered a Ukrainian nationalism unknown previously during the country's regained independence. It is imbued with a palpable anti-Russian sentiment. The worrisome thing for Washington, Ukraine, and the West is that bad analysis in Moscow can lead to bad and unpredictable policies.

Policy Recommendations: Ukraine's Future Development

Ukraine has made considerable progress since the Maydan Revolution. As of the end of 2016, the government had, among other things, reformed its finances, consolidated the banking sector, raised energy tariffs to cover the cost of its provision, initiated more transparent procurement procedures, and introduced an e-declaration system requiring that officials provide online information regarding their wealth. All of that is good news. A reformed, stronger, and more resilient Ukrainian state would be good for Ukrainians; it would also offer a more attractive partner for the West. That said, a glass half full is also a glass half empty. Ukraine still has much ground to cover, including on anticorruption measures, reform of the judiciary, privatization of state-owned enterprises, and agricultural land reform. A critical vector for U.S. policy thus should be to press Kyiv to move more rapidly and seriously on reform and anticorruption measures in order to achieve the critical mass of reforms that the Baltic states, Poland, the Czech Republic, and Slovenia achieved much earlier in their transitions. Those transitions brought real change and growing economies.

U.S. policy will need to be both tougher, by becoming more insistent on reform, and more generous, by providing greater assistance if Kyiv accelerates its reform effort. If Ukraine does not put itself on a path to success in the next few years, where will it be twenty-five years from now? Many of the reform challenges that the West discussed with Ukraine in 2016 were discussed in the 1990s and early 2000s.

My fear is that, if Ukraine does not make a decisive break away from past habits and toward real change now, the United States and the rest of the West will be discussing the need for Ukraine to make the same kinds of reforms twenty-five years down the road. Ukraine has demonstrated that it can muddle through, but endless muddling through is not a happy prospect, either for Ukrainians or for the West's ability to sustain interest in the country.

Western patience with Ukraine is not unlimited, and it sometimes seems that politicians in Kyiv do not recognize that. If Poroshenko, his cabinet, and the Rada bog down on reform and anticorruption measures, they will disappoint not only the Ukrainian public. They will disappoint Ukraine's supporters in the West. It would not be the first time. When Kuchma took office in 1994 and launched an important set of economic reforms, expectations rose that Ukraine would turn the corner, but the reform burst died out in 1995. Kuchma's appointment of Yushchenko as prime minister at the end of 1999 generated another wave of optimism about reform prospects, but that dissipated in mid-2000 as differences arose between Kuchma and Yushchenko. The 2004 Orange Revolution captured the imagination of the West, giving rise to hopes and expectations that real change was in the offing. That also fizzled and went so badly off the rails that the electorate turned back to Yanukovych in 2010.

The Maydan Revolution also raised hopes, but questions remain about whether the country can make a real breakthrough. In a number of European capitals, Ukraine is seen as a source of constant headache—continuing corruption, halfway steps on reform, internal crisis after crisis—at a time when there is sentiment for getting back to business as usual with Russia. What happens to Western support if leaders in Europe and the United States conclude that Ukraine's elites are unwilling or unable to make the necessary reforms and that the country is, for lack of a better word, unfixable?

The phenomenon referred to as "Ukraine fatigue" looms. It has emerged several times in Western capitals over the past twenty-five years. Signs of its emergence in some European capitals appeared in 2016. The risk is that Ukraine fatigue could go viral.

The U.S. government thus should press Poroshenko and the Ukrainian government harder on reform. It should use blunt language. It should condition U.S. assistance and loan guarantees on specific actions. For example, Washington issued a third $1 billion loan guarantee to Kyiv in 2016 following the appointment of Hroysman and his cabinet. Future loan guarantees should be conditioned on the government's adoption of specific reform steps, and the U.S. government should raise the bar for compliance.

Likewise, Washington should maintain full support for the International Monetary Fund's insistence that conditionalities be fully met before credits are disbursed. Any temptation to cut Kyiv slack does Ukraine no favor. If certain conditionalities are for the moment unachievable, they should be relaxed only if they are replaced by other conditionalities that are equally significant. U.S. officials should encourage EU officials and other Western donors to take a similar stance.

This approach is necessary given that important and powerful constituencies within the Ukrainian elites do not want reform. The kinds of changes needed to make a successful market democracy—changes that broaden political space and open up the economy to the benefit of the wider population—will damage the economic and political interests of oligarchic groups and their supporters in government ranks. Overcoming their resistance will require sustained pressure. Such pressure will have support from true reformers in the government, the Rada, and civil society.

The U.S. government should push Kyiv particularly hard on reforms to promote good governance and action to curb corruption and reduce the undue political influence of oligarchs. In his first three years as president, Poroshenko has not moved as he should have on these questions. Washington should seek genuine anticorruption measures and hold out the prospect of sanctions, including denial of visas and freezing of assets in U.S. banks, aimed at those who engage in corrupt activities, both inside and outside of government. As with the economic sanctions on Russia, Washington should seek to coordinate a joint policy with the European Union. The adoption of similar measures by EU states would greatly multiply the impact.

While pressing Kyiv to do more on reform and anticorruption measures, the United States and the European Union should be prepared to offer greater assistance if the Ukrainian government responds positively. In fall 2015, former Treasury secretary Lawrence Summers estimated that Ukraine needed an additional $5–10 billion from the West to have a real prospect of successful reform. That is significant money, at a time when budgets are tight. The alternative, however, may be continuing to provide assistance for decades to prop Ukraine up, as the West has done for twenty-five years now. More money combined with a true commitment to rapid reform in Kyiv would accelerate the arrival of the day when Ukraine no longer needs assistance from Western governments or international financial institutions but instead draws in foreign investment to grow the economy.

Washington will need to encourage the European Union to do its share. Ukraine's fate should matter to EU officials. What would be the cost to the European Union of a failed Ukrainian state on its doorstep? If young Ukrainians en masse conclude that their country offers only a grim future, they do not have to get into boats to travel to EU countries; they can simply walk west.

One bright spot is Ukraine's dynamic civil society. Civil society activists have won seats in the current Rada. Although their numbers have not reached the point where they can drive the Rada's agenda, they have had an impact. U.S. assistance should continue to strengthen civil society, even though it is now self-sustaining. While staying nonpartisan, assistance efforts should help to groom next-generation leaders who can build on the gains that civil society has made. In conjunction with grooming new leaders, Washington should look for ways to encourage Ukrainian political parties to evolve from their current status, in which most are centered on one or two personalities, toward broader political organizations that reflect a set of principles or a particular ideology. Such changes would enhance Ukrainian democracy.

The approach outlined here can be called tough love, or perhaps tougher love than U.S. policy has shown to date. It will be important to get the balance right between toughness and love. Some may argue that there is a risk in pushing too hard. Perhaps, but I believe the greater risk is not pushing the Ukrainian government hard enough. As noted, if Poroshenko and the current government do not succeed and the country just muddles through, Ukraine fatigue, with its very negative consequences, becomes a real possibility.

Others may argue that we should not press reforms when Ukraine is at war. But backing off would push reform into the indefinite future. It is better to push for internal change now, which may be easier for the West to affect than a change in Moscow's policy. A reformed

Ukrainian state will be more resilient and better able to stand up to its difficult neighbor. And a reforming Ukrainian state is more likely to secure sustained European support.

Finally, in trying to persuade Kyiv to do more and to do it faster, U.S. officials should look for ways to undermine the view, which seems to hold sway with many Ukrainian elites, that their country is too geopolitically important to fail—that Ukraine is so critical between the West and Russia that, no matter what the country's leaders do or do not do, the United States and Europe will support Ukraine out of fear that otherwise it might turn back to Russia. That calculation has never held much water, though Western actions sometimes inadvertently reinforced it. Now, after Russia's seizure of Crimea and some 10,000 dead in the Donbas, no serious political leader in Kyiv could advocate a turn away from Europe and back toward Moscow. If the West gives up on Ukraine, Kyiv truly will find itself stuck in a gray zone of insecurity, with no path out. One hopes that it would not be necessary, but the West may need to persuade Ukraine's elites that it is prepared to let go and lose Ukraine in order to get those elites to take the actions needed to save their country.

Twenty-five years after regaining independence, Ukrainians still have a prospect of achieving the kind of European state that motivated hundreds of thousands to take to the streets during the Orange and Maydan Revolutions. Doing so requires overcoming tough internal challenges as well as the challenge posed by Putin's Russia. U.S. policy should not just support Ukraine but should press the government in Kyiv to take the often difficult measures that will help the country overcome those challenges. That outcome is in the interest of Ukrainians and in the interest of the United States and the West.

Acknowledgments

I want to express my gratitude to colleagues in the Brookings Foreign Policy Program for their support on this book project, including Charlotte Baldwin, Fiona Hill, Martin Indyk, Bruce Jones, Andrew Moffatt, Michael O'Hanlon, and in particular Hannah Thoburn, for her research assistance. I would also like to thank William Finan, Valentina Kalk, and Janet Walker at the Brookings Institution Press for their help with this publication, as well as Angela Piliouras for her editorial assistance.

I am grateful for the support provided to the Brookings Foreign Policy Program by the Carnegie Corporation of New York, the governments of Norway and Finland, the Liberty Mutual Foundation, the Victor Pinchuk Foundation, and the Brookings Director's Strategic Initiative Fund, which helped to fund the work on this project.

In writing this book I drew heavily on notes that I kept during my time on the National Security Council staff (1994–97), my ambassadorial records from my time in Kyiv (1998–2000), and notes from my time as deputy assistant secretary of state in the Bureau of European and Eurasian Affairs (2001–04). I wish to express my deep appreciation to Rob Siebert, archivist at the Clinton Presidential Library, for facilitating access to my National Security Council notes, and to Jane Diedrich, Alden Fahy, the Office of Ukraine, Moldova, and Belarus Affairs and David Kramer at the State Department for assisting me in gaining access to records and notes from my time in Kyiv and in the Bureau of European and Eurasian Affairs. Their assistance was invaluable. I would also like to express my gratitude to Behar Godani, Daniel Sanborn, and Alden Fahy for facilitating rapid review of drafts of this book for declassification purposes.

I am very grateful to colleagues who took time to be interviewed for this book and/or who read and provided comments on various draft sections. Many of those people served in the U.S. government in positions directly related to U.S. policy toward Ukraine, and in those cases I have indicated their positions and approximate time of service: Anders Aslund, John Beyrle (acting coordinator, Office of the New Independent States, Department of State, 2001), Coit "Chip" Blacker (senior director for Russia, Ukraine, and Eurasia affairs on the National Security Council staff, 1995–96), Nicholas Burns (director for Soviet affairs on the National Security Council staff, 1990–92; senior director for Russia, Ukraine, and Eurasia affairs on the National Security Council staff, 1993–95), Debra Cagan (senior adviser for nuclear and security policy, Bureau of European Affairs, Department of State, 1997–2000; director, Office of Policy and Regional Affairs, Bureau of European and Eurasian Affairs, 2001–03), Chris Crowley (director, U.S. Agency for International Development mission for Ukraine, Moldova, and Belarus, 1999–2005), Orest Deychakiwsky (professional staff member, Congressional Committee on Security and Cooperation in Europe, 1981–present), Robert Einhorn (deputy assistant secretary of state, Bureau of Political-Military Affairs, Department of State, 1996–99), Eugene Fishel (analyst, Bureau of Intelligence and Research, Department of State, 1991–2000; director for Russia, Ukraine, and Eurasia affairs on the National Security Council staff, 2000–01; senior analyst, Bureau of Intelligence and Research, Department of State, 2001–05), Daniel Fried (deputy coordinator, Office of the New Independent States, Department of State, 2000; senior director for European affairs on the National Security Council staff, 2001–05), Sherman Garnett (deputy assistant secretary of defense, Department of Defense, 1991–94); Eric Green (political officer, U.S. embassy in Kyiv,

1994–96), Jon Gundersen (consul general, U.S. consulate general in Kyiv 1991–92; deputy chief of mission, U.S. embassy in Kyiv, 1992–93), John Herbst (deputy coordinator, Office of the New Independent States, Department of State, 1995–97; U.S. ambassador to Ukraine, 2003–06), Beth Jones (assistant secretary of state, Bureau of European and Eurasian Affairs, Department of State, 2001–05), Kathy Kavalec (political counselor, U.S. embassy in Kyiv, 1999–2002), David Kramer (deputy assistant secretary of state, Bureau of European and Eurasian Affairs, Department of State, 2005–07), Robert McConnell, Richard Morningstar (coordinator, Office of the Coordinator for Assistance to the New Independent States, Department of State, 1995–98; U.S. ambassador to the European Union, 1999–2001), Larry Napper (director, Office of Soviet Union Affairs, later the Office of Independent State and Commonwealth Affairs, Department of State, 1991–94), Bob Nurick, Michael O'Hanlon, Carlos Pascual (director, then senior director for Russia, Ukraine, and Eurasia affairs on the National Security Council staff, 1995–2000; U.S. ambassador to Ukraine, 2000–03; coordinator, Office of the Coordinator for Assistance to the New Independent States, Department of State, 2003–04), Roman Popadiuk (deputy press secretary for foreign affairs, National Security Council staff, 1989–92; U.S. ambassador to Ukraine, 1992–93), Geoffrey Pyatt (U.S. ambassador to Ukraine, 2013–16), Dennis Ross (director, Policy Planning Staff, Department of State, 1989–93), Stephen Sestanovich (ambassador-at-large and coordinator, Office of the New Independent States, Department of State, 1998–2000), Strobe Talbott (ambassador-at-large and coordinator, Office of the New Independent States, Department of State, 1993–94; deputy secretary of state, 1994–2000), William Taylor (deputy coordinator, then coordinator, Office of the Coordinator for Assistance to the New Independent States, Department of State, 1996–2002; U.S. ambassador to Ukraine, 2006–09), John Tefft (deputy assistant secretary of state, Bureau of European and Eurasian Affairs, Department of State, 2004–05; U.S. ambassador to Ukraine, 2009–13), James Timbie (senior adviser to the under secretary of state for international security affairs, Department of State, 1988–2016), Andrew Weiss (member, Policy Planning Staff, Department of State, 1997–99), Bill Wise (deputy national security adviser to the vice president, 1993–97), and Marie Yovanovitch (deputy chief of mission, U.S. embassy in Kyiv, 2001–04;

U.S. ambassador to Ukraine, 2016–present). I am especially grateful to Eugene Fishel, Sherman Garnett, Bob Nurick, Michael O'Hanlon, Angela Stent, and Andrew Weiss, who reviewed the entire draft text.

I also appreciate the participation of Anders Aslund, William Miller (U.S. ambassador to Ukraine, 1993–97), Bob Nurick, Roman Popadiuk, Stephen Sestanovich, and William Taylor in a July 2016 roundtable to discuss my draft conclusions and recommendations, as well as written reactions that I separately received from John Herbst, David Kramer, and Carlos Pascual.

Of course, I bear full responsibility for the content, conclusions, and recommendations. As noted in the introduction, the content, opinions, and characterizations in this book are my own and do not necessarily represent official positions of the U.S. government.

Abbreviations and Acronyms

123 agreement civil nuclear cooperation agreement named after section 123 of the Atomic Energy Act

CEC Central Electoral Commission (Ukraine)

CFE Treaty Conventional Armed Forces in Europe Treaty

CIS Commonwealth of Independent States

CNN Cable News Network

CODEL congressional delegation

CSCE Conference on Security and Cooperation in Europe

EBRD European Bank for Reconstruction and Development

EFF extended fund facility

FBI Federal Bureau of Investigation

FREEDOM Support Act Freedom for Russia and Emerging Eurasian Democracies and Open Markets Support Act

G-7 Group of Seven industrial democracies (United States, Britain, Canada, France, Germany, Italy, and Japan)

G-8 the G-7 countries plus Russia

GUAM	Georgia-Ukraine-Azerbaijan-Moldova organization
GUUAM	Georgia-Ukraine-Uzbekistan-Azerbaijan-Moldova organization
HEU	highly enriched uranium
ICBM	intercontinental ballistic missile
IFPI	International Federation of the Phonographic Industry
IMF	International Monetary Fund
IPR	intellectual property rights
JCS	Joint Chiefs of Staff
KFOR	Kosovo Force, the NATO-led peacekeeping force
LEU	low enriched uranium
MAP	membership action plan
MTCR	Missile Technology Control Regime
NATO	North Atlantic Treaty Organization
NBC	nuclear, biological, and chemical (weapons)
NBU	National Bank of Ukraine
NPT	Nonproliferation Treaty
NSC	National Security Council (U.S.)
OPIC	Overseas Private Investment Corporation
OSCE	Organization for Security and Cooperation in Europe
PAUCI	Polish-American-Ukrainian Cooperation Initiative
SBU	Security Service of Ukraine (Sluzhba Bezopasnosti Ukrainiy)
SFOR	Special Force, NATO-led peacekeeping force in Bosnia
SSR	Soviet Socialist Republic
START	Strategic Arms Reduction Treaty
STB	Ukrainian television channel
UN	United Nations
USAID	U.S. Agency for International Development
UT-1	Ukraine's government-owned television channel
WTO	World Trade Organization
Y2K	Year 2000 (computer date issue)

Notes

Chapter 1

1. Paul Robert Magocsi and Orest Subtelny have written excellent accounts of Ukraine's story up through the late twentieth century. See Paul Robert Magocsi, *A History of Ukraine* (University of Toronto Press, 1996), and Orest Subtelny, *Ukraine: A History* (University of Toronto Press, 1988). Magocsi's history is best read with his accompanying historical atlas to get a sense for how borders constantly shifted over and across Ukraine's current territorial space: Paul Robert Magocsi, *Ukraine: A Historical Atlas* (University of Toronto Press, 1985).

2. Andrew Wilson, *The Ukrainians: Unexpected Nation* (Yale Nota Bene Press, 2002), provides a good account of the influences that shaped modern Ukraine, as well as an account of the country's first ten years of regained independence.

3. See Timothy Snyder, *Bloodlands: Europe between Hitler and Stalin* (New York: Basic Books, 2010), for an account of the tragic 1930s and 1940s.

4. For an excellent discussion of the complexities of the Ukraine-Russia relationship, both immediately before and during the early years after the collapse of the Soviet Union, see Roman Solchanyk, *Ukraine and Russia: The Post-Soviet Transition* (Lanham, Md.: Rowman and Littlefield, 2001).

5. For a fuller discussion, see James M. Goldgeier and Michael McFaul, *Power and Purpose: U.S. Policy toward Russia after the Cold War* (Brookings, 2003), pp. 20–26.

6. "Memorandum of Conversation: Meeting with Ukrainian Supreme Soviet Chairman Leonid Kravchuk," August 1, 1991, Mariinskiy Palace, Kyiv, White House, George Bush Presidential Library and Museum, College Station, Texas.

7. George H. W. Bush, "Remarks to the Supreme Soviet of the Republic of the Ukraine in Kyiv, Soviet Union," August 1, 1991, in *The American Presidency Project*, compiled by Gerhard Peters and John T. Woolley, University of California at Santa Barbara (www.presidency.ucsb.edu/ws/?pid =19864).

8. See Serhii Plokhy, *The Last Empire* (New York: Basic Books, 2014), for an excellent account of the failed coup attempt and the reaction in Kyiv.

9. "Memorandum of Conversation: Meeting with Leonid Kravchuk, Ukrainian Supreme Soviet Chairman," September 25, 1991, Cabinet Room, White House, George Bush Presidential Library and Museum, College Station, Texas.

10. "Memorandum of Conversation: Presidential Meeting with Ukrainian-Americans," November 27, 1991, Roosevelt Room, White House, George Bush Presidential Library and Museum, College Station, Texas.

11. "Fact Sheet: Ukrainian President Visits Washington, D.C., May 5–7, 1992," Department of State, May 11, 1992.

12. "Memorandum of Conversation: Meeting with President Leonid Kravchuk of Ukraine, May 6, 1992," Old Family Dining Room, White House, George Bush Library and Museum, College Station, Texas.

13. George Bush, "Joint Declaration with President Leonid Kravchuk of Ukraine," May 6, 1992, in *The American Presidency Project*, compiled by Gerhard Peters and John T. Woolley, University of California at Santa Barbara (www.presidency.ucsb.edu/ws/?pid=20920).

14. Roman Popadiuk, "American-Ukrainian Nuclear Relations," McNair Paper 55 (National Defense University, October 1996), pp. 25–27.

15. Sherman W. Garnett, *Keystone in the Arch: Ukraine in the Emerging Security Environment of Central and Eastern Europe* (Washington: Carnegie Endowment for International Peace, 1997), pp. 118–19.

16. Popadiuk, "American-Ukrainian Nuclear Relations," pp. 29–30.

17. Bradley Doss, "Senate Subcommittee Discusses U.S. Policy on Ukraine's Security," *Ukrainian Weekly,* July 4, 1993, p. 3.

18. Alan Cooperman, "Russia Claims Home Port of Black Sea Fleet, Angering Ukraine," Associated Press, July 9, 1993.

19. "Yeltsin Lashes Out at Parliament on Sevastopol Vote," Agence France Presse, July 10, 1993.

20. See Anders Aslund, *Ukraine: How Ukraine Became a Market Economy and a Democracy* (Washington: Peterson Institute for International Economics, 2009), for a discussion of the economic connections between Ukraine and Russia in the early 1990s.

Chapter 2

1. U.S. Arms Control and Disarmament Agency, *Arms Control and Disarmament Agreements: START Treaty between the United States of America and Union of Soviet Socialist Republics on the Reduction and Limitation of Strategic Offensive Arms*, 1991.

2. White House, "Fact Sheet: Removal of Nuclear Warheads from Ukraine," Office of the Press Secretary, June 1, 1996.

3. Verkhovna Rada website, "Declaration of State Sovereignty of Ukraine," July 16, 1990 (http://gska2.rada.gov.ua/site/postanova_eng /Declaration_of_State_Sovereignty_of_Ukraine_rev1.htm).

4. This discussion draws on an interview conducted by the author with a Ukrainian official, June 2008, and observations from a December 2008 Carnegie Moscow Center workshop.

5. James M. Goldgeier and Michael McFaul, *Power and Purpose: U.S. Policy toward Russia after the Cold War* (Brookings, 2003), pp. 41–49.

6. Agreement on Strategic Forces concluded between the eleven members of the Commonwealth of Independent States on December 30, 1991 (http://www.operationspaix.net/DATA/DOCUMENT/3825~v~Declaration _d_Alma-Ata.pdf).

7. John Buntin, "The Decision to Denuclearize: How Ukraine Became a Non-Nuclear Weapons State," C14-98-1425.0 (Kennedy School of Government Case Program, 1997).

8. Serge Schmemann, "Ukraine Halting A-Arms Shift to Russia," *New York Times*, March 13, 1992.

9. Thomas Graham, *Disarmament Sketches: Three Decades of Arms Control and International Law* (University of Washington Press, 2002), pp. 135–36.

10. Office of the Under Secretary of Defense for Acquisition, Technology, and Logistics, "Treaty Compliance, START I: Lisbon Protocol" (www.dod .gov/acq/acic/treaties/start1/protocols/lisbon.htm).

11. Roman Popadiuk, "American-Ukrainian Nuclear Relations," McNair Paper 55 (National Defense University, October 1996), pp. 3–7.

12. Popadiuk, "American-Ukrainian Nuclear Relations," pp. 16–17.

13. Yuriy Dubinin, "Ukraine's Nuclear Ambitions: Reminiscences of the Past," *Russia in Global Affairs* (April–June 2004), pp. 2–3 (http://eng .globalaffairs.ru/printver/533.html).

14. John Dunn, "The Ukrainian Nuclear Weapons Debate," *Jane's Intelligence Review* (August 1993), pp. 339–42, as cited in Mark D. Sokootsky, "An Annotated Chronology of Post-Soviet Nuclear Disarmament 1991–94," *Nonproliferation Review* (Spring/Summer 1995), p. 75.

15. Dubinin, "Ukraine's Nuclear Ambitions," pp. 3–5.

16. Popadiuk, "American-Ukrainian Nuclear Relations," describes in detail Rada views from 1992–93 on the nuclear weapons issue.

17. Dubinin, "Ukraine's Nuclear Ambitions," p. 6.

18. Mitchell Reiss, *Bridled Ambition: Why Countries Constrain Their Nuclear Capabilities* (Washington: Woodrow Wilson Center with Johns Hopkins University Press), p. 109.

19. The North Atlantic Treaty, Washington, April 4, 1949 (www.nato.int/cps/en/natolive/official_texts_17120.htm).

20. Popadiuk, "American-Ukrainian Nuclear Relations," p. 19.

21. "Memorandum of Telephone Conversation: Telcon with President Kravchuk of Ukraine, December 24, 1992," White House, George Bush Presidential Library and Museum, College Station, Texas.

22. Strobe Talbott, *The Russia Hand* (New York: Random House, 2002), p. 81.

23. Ibid., p. 80.

24. Discussion at December 2008 Carnegie Moscow Center workshop.

25. Interview by the author with a Ukrainian official, June 2008.

26. Alexander Tkachenko, "Kravchuk Says Ukraine Must Disarm Fully," Reuters, November 19, 1993, as cited in Sokootsky, "An Annotated Chronology of Post-Soviet Nuclear Disarmament 1991–94."

27. Word of these letters eventually became public, though they were sometimes referred to as secret protocols; see, for example, Popadiuk, "American-Ukrainian Nuclear Relations," pp. 42–43.

28. Buntin, "The Decision to Denuclearize," pp. 27–28.

29. White House, "Joint Statement on Development of U.S.-Ukrainian Friendship and Partnership," Office of the Press Secretary, March 4, 1994.

30. Dubinin, "Ukraine's Nuclear Ambitions," p. 8.

31. White House, "Joint Summit Statement by President Clinton and President of Ukraine Leonid D. Kuchma," Office of the Press Secretary, November 22, 1994.

32. Council on Foreign Relations, Primary Sources, "Memorandum on Security Assurances in Connection with Ukraine's Accession to the Treaty on the Non-Proliferation of Nuclear Weapons," Budapest, December 5, 1994 (http://www.cfr.org/nonproliferation-arms-control-and-disarmament/budapest-memorandums-security-assurances-1994/p32484).

Chapter 3

1. Anders Aslund, *Ukraine: How Ukraine Became a Market Economy and a Democracy* (Washington: Peterson Institute for International Economics, 2009), pp. 68–75.

2. "The U.S.-Ukrainian Summit: President Bill Clinton's Visit to Kyiv, Joint Statement by the Presidents of the United States and Ukraine," *Ukrainian Weekly,* June 4, 1995.

3. "Remarks by the President to the People of Ukraine, Volodymyrska Street Plaza, Shevchenko University, Kiev, Ukraine," May 12, 1995, White House, Office of the Press Secretary (Kiev, Ukraine).

4. "Joint Statement on U.S.-Ukraine Binational Commission," September 19, 1996, White House, Office of the Vice President.

5. NATO, "Charter on a Distinctive Partnership between the North Atlantic Treaty Organization and Ukraine," July 9, 1997.

6. See Ashton B. Carter and William J. Perry, *Preventive Defense: A New Security Strategy for America* (Brookings, 1999) for a discussion of Perry's four visits to Pervomaysk.

7. For a more detailed discussion of the flap over Sea Breeze-97 see Global Security.org, "Sea Breeze" (http://www.globalsecurity.org/military /ops/sea-breeze.htm).

8. See Aslund, *Ukraine*, chaps. 2–4, for a fuller discussion of the economic and political challenges facing Ukraine in the 1990s.

9. This figure and the following discussion of assistance programs draws heavily on briefing papers prepared by the Department of State and the U.S. Agency for International Development in fall 1997.

10. See Aslund, *Ukraine*, pp. 68–74, for a more detailed discussion of Kuchma's initial economic reforms.

11. G-7 Summit 1994, Communiqué, July 9, 1994.

12. World Bank, "GDP growth (annual %), Ukraine" (http://data .worldbank.org/indicator/NY.GDP.MKTP.KD.ZG?end=2015&locations =UA&start=1994&year_high_desc=false).

13. NATO, "Charter on a Distinctive Partnership."

14. Acronym Institute, "Allegations of Ukraine-Libya Missile Deal," no. 11, December 1996 (www.acronym.org.uk/old/archive/11uklib.htm).

Chapter 4

1. Barton Gellman, "U.S. Officials Heckled at Iraq Seminar," *Washington Post*, February 19, 1998 (www.washingtonpost.com/wp-srv/inatl /longterm/iraq/stories/policy021998.htm).

2. Madeleine Albright, "Remarks at Roundtable Discussion with University Students at Kiev-Mohyla Academy," Archive Website of the U.S.

Department of State, March 6, 1998 (http://1997-2001.state.gov/www /statements/1998/980306.html).

3. "For the Record: Joint Statement Issued during Kyiv Visit of U.S. Secretary of State Madeleine Albright," *Ukrainian Weekly*, text released by Ukrainian Embassy in Washington, March 10, 1998.

4. Department of State, "Secretary of State Madeleine K. Albright, President of Ukraine Leonid Kuchma, and Foreign Minister Hennadiy Udovenko: Remarks at Signing Ceremony on Several Agreements, Kiev, Ukraine, March 6, 1998," as released by the Office of the Spokesman in Rome, Italy.

5. Patrick Tyler, "Deprived Ukraine City Finds U.S. Help No Help," *New York Times*, June 6, 2000.

6. Letter from Mark D. Kalenak, Executive Director, American Chamber of Commerce in Ukraine, to Secretary of State Madeleine K. Albright, April 15, 1998.

7. Letter from Secretary of State Madeleine Albright to President Leonid Kuchma of Ukraine, April 29, 1998. See also Associated Press, "Albright Releases Nearly $100 Million in U.S. Assistance," April 29, 1998.

8. Department of State, Office of the Spokesman (en route to Beijing), April 29, 1998.

9. OSCE Election Observation Mission, "Preliminary Joint Statement Issued on 30 March 1998 by the OSCE and the Council of Europe Parliamentary Assembly," OSCE Office for Democratic Institutions and Human Rights, OSCE Parliamentary Assembly and Council of Europe Parliamentary Assembly.

10. "Pidsumky holosyvannya po partiyakh (vyborchikh blokakh partiy)" [Election results by party (or electoral blocs of parties)], Tsentral'na Vyborcha Komisiya [Central Electoral Commission], March 29, 1998.

11. "Statement by James B. Foley, Deputy Spokesman, on Certification," Department of State, Office of the Spokesman, February 19, 1999.

12. "Pifer Fudges the Numbers," *Kyiv Post*, February 25, 1999.

13. Michael Wines, "Ukrainian Seeks U.S. Asylum," *New York Times*, February 25, 1999.

14. Askold Krushelnycky, "Ukraine: Why Was Former Prime Minister Lazarenko Tried in The U.S.?," Radio Free Europe/Radio Liberty, June 8, 2004.

15. David Kravets, "Former Ukrainian PM Sentenced for Fraud," *Washington Post*, August 25, 2006.

16. Richard Solash, "Ex-Ukrainian PM Reportedly Freed from U.S. Prison," Radio Free Europe/Radio Liberty, November 1, 2012.

17. "Viacheslav Chornovil, 61; Fought Soviet," *New York Times*, March 30, 1999.

18. Organization for Security and Cooperation in Europe, "Preliminary Statement on 1999 Presidential Election in Ukraine," November 1, 1999.

19. Organization for Security and Cooperation in Europe, "Preliminary Statement on Presidential Elections in Ukraine," November 15, 1999.

20. Anders Aslund, *Ukraine: How Ukraine Became a Market Economy and Democracy* (Washington: Peterson Institute for International Economics, 2009), p. 123.

21. Thomas Catan, "Former Premier Alleges Kiev Misused IMF Loans," *Financial Times*, January 28, 2000.

22. Charles Clover, "Ukraine PM Denies IMF Loans Were Misused," *Financial Times*, February 1, 2000.

23. Joseph Kahn with Timothy L. O'Brien, "Ukraine Leader Cancels U.S. Visit over IMF Complaint," *New York Times*, March 16, 2000.

24. "Allegations about the Use of Ukraine's International Reserves," International Monetary Fund, News Brief 00/15, March 14, 2000.

25. Thomas Catan and Charles Clover, "U.S. 'Deeply Concerned' at Ukraine IMF Strategy," *Financial Times*, March 24, 2000.

26. The full transcript of Secretary Albright's appearance can be found here: "Secretary of State Madeleine K. Albright: Interview on Studio 1+1 Talk Show," Department of State Archive Website, 1997–2001, April 14, 2000.

27. "For the Record: United States-Ukraine Joint Statement Signed in Kyiv," *Ukrainian Weekly*, June 18, 2000.

28. "Weekly Compilation of Presidential Documents, Monday, June 12, 2000," vol. 36, no. 23, pp. 1304–06.

29. Elaine Sciolino and Michael R. Gordon, "Ukraine Consents to Shut Chernobyl before Year's End," *New York Times*, June 6, 2000.

30. Ukaz No. 832: "Pro nevidkladni zakhody shchodo stimulyuvannya vyrobnytstva ta rozvitku rynku zerna" [Decree No. 832: On Immediate Measures to Stimulate Production and to Develop the Grain Market], June 29, 2000 (http://zakon4.rada.gov.ua/laws/show/832/2000).

31. Peter Byrne, "Journalist Goes Missing," *Kyiv Post*, September 21, 2000.

Chapter 5

1. Vladimir Isachenkov, "Ukraine to Work on Better Ties with U.S.," Associated Press, December 25, 2002.

2. "Kiev Hopes New U.S. Administration Will Pursue 'Strategic Partnership,'" Agence France-Presse, November 8, 2000.

3. "Ukrainian President Urges Nation to Stand Tall, Not Beg," BBC Monitoring Kiev Unit, UNIAN, November 7, 2000.

4. Patrick E. Tyler, "In Mid-Crisis, Ukraine President Lashes Out at Opposition," *New York Times*, February 15, 2001, p. 3.

5. "State Department Regular Briefing, Briefer: Richard Boucher, Department Spokesman," Federal News Service, March 1, 2001.

6. Marina Kolbe, "Ukraine: Is It Moving Backwards or Forwards?" CNN International Q &A, April 26, 2001.

7. U.S. Department of State, Daily Press Briefing, April 30, 2001.

8. Yaro Bihun, "Mykola Melnychenko Speaks Out on His Mission and the Dangers Involved," *Ukrainian Weekly*, September 8, 2002, p. 1.

9. "George W. Bush, XLIII President of the United States, 2001–2009, Address at Warsaw University, June 15, 2001," in *The American Presidency Project*, compiled by Gerhard Peters and John T. Woolley, University of California at Santa Barbara (www.presidency.ucsb.edu/ws/index.php?pid=45973).

10. "Ukrainian President Denounces Terrorist Act in the USA," BBC Monitoring Kiev Unit, UNIAN, September 11, 2001.

11. "Ukraine calls for UN Security Council to Meet on U.S. Attacks," Agence France-Presse, September 11, 2001.

12. Philippe Coumarianos, "Ukraine Admits Its Missile Downed Russian Airliner," Agence France-Presse, October 13, 2001.

13. OSCE, Office for Democratic Institutions and Human Rights, "Ukraine Parliamentary Elections, 31 March 2002, Final Report," Warsaw, May 27, 2002.

14. NATO, "Madrid Declaration on Euro-Atlantic Security and Cooperation, Issued by the Heads of State and Government," Madrid, July 8, 1997.

15. "Ukrainian President Views NATO Membership as Guarantee of Peace," BBC Monitoring Kiev Unit, Inter TV, Kiev, May 24, 2002.

16. "Radio Liberty Rebroadcaster in Ukraine Complains of State Pressure," BBC Summary of World Broadcasts, UNIAN, May 24, 2002.

17. "Ukrainian Kolchuga Systems All in Place in Ethiopia, Security Service Chief," BBC Summary of World Broadcasts, *Zerkalo Nedeli*, April 20, 2002.

18. "Country Assessments—Ukraine, U.S. Government Assistance Programs to and Cooperative Programs with Eurasia," Bureau of European and Eurasian Affairs, Department of State, January 2003.

19. Michael Wines, "U.S. Suspects Ukraine of Selling Radar to Iraq," *New York Times,* September 24, 2002.

20. Matthew Lee, "U.S. Sticks by Allegations That Ukraine Planned to Sell Radar to Iraq," Agence France-Presse, September 24, 2002.

21. Roman Woronowycz, "Rada OKs Ukrainian Troops for Iraq," *Ukrainian Weekly*, June 8, 2003.

22. "John Herbst: The Context of American-Ukrainian Relations Has Changed," *Zerkalo Nedeli*, October 17, 2003.

23. Olga Nedbayeva, "Ukraine, Russia Take Steps to Calm Border Row," Agence France-Presse, October 24, 2003.

24. Yana Tomusyak, " 'Imperialist' Russia Is Pushing Ukraine Closer to West, Kuchma," Agence France-Presse, October 27, 2003.

25. Roman Woronowycz, "Armitage to Kuchma: Free and Fair Elections Will Be Benchmark for U.S.-Ukraine Relations," *Ukrainian Weekly*, April 4, 2004.

26. NATO, "Istanbul Summit Communiqué, Issued by the Heads of State and Government participating in the meeting of the North Atlantic Council," Istanbul, Turkey, June 28, 2004.

27. NATO, "Introductory Remarks by NATO Secretary General, Jaap de Hoop Scheffer, at the Meeting of the NATO-Ukraine Commission at the Level of Heads of State and Government," Istanbul, Turkey, June 29, 2004.

Chapter 6

1. William Branigin, "U.S. Rejects Tally, Warns Ukraine," *Washington Post*, November 25, 2004.

2. See Andrew Wilson, *Ukraine's Orange Revolution* (Yale University Press, 2005), for an account of the run-up to the Orange Revolution, its history, and its aftermath.

3. "Letter to President of Ukraine Leonid Kuchma on the Occasion of the 13th Anniversary of Ukraine's Independence," White House, Office of the Press Secretary, August 20, 2004.

4. Oleksandr Sushko and Olena Prystayko, "Western Influence," in *Revolution in Orange: The Origins of Ukraine's Democratic Breakthrough*, edited by Anders Aslund and Michael McFaul (Washington: Carnegie Endowment for International Peace 2006), p. 132.

5. "Statement by Richard Boucher, Spokesman, Ukrainian Elections," Department of State, Office of the Spokesman, October 14, 2004.

6. Wojciech Stanislawski, *The Orange Ribbon: A Calendar of the Political Crisis in Ukraine, Autumn 2004"* (Warsaw: Center for Eastern Studies, 2005).

7. Anders Aslund, *How Ukraine Became a Market Economy and Democracy* (Washington: Peterson Institute for International Economics, 2009), pp. 180–84.

8. Anatoly Medetsky and Francesca Mereu, "Yanukovych Billboards Dot Moscow," *Moscow Times*, October 18, 2004.

9. International Election Observation Mission, Presidential Election, Ukraine—31 October 2004, "Statement of Preliminary Findings and Conclusions," November 1, 2004.

10. "Yushchenko Receives 54%, Yanukovych 43% According to 100% of Exit Poll Inquiries Made by Consortium," Ukrainian News Service, November 21, 2004.

11. Serhiy Vasylchenko, "Change in Voter Turnout Compared to October 31," Europe XXI Foundation (circular).

12. "Statement of Preliminary Findings and Conclusions," International Election Observation Mission, Presidential Election (Second Round), Ukraine—21 November 2004, November 22, 2004.

13. Richard Young and Michael McFaul, "International Actors and Democratic Transitions: Ukraine 2004," CDDRL Working Paper 106 (Stanford University, March 2009), p. 33.

14. "Statement released by the Deputy Secretary: The United States Stands with the Ukrainian People in This Difficult Time," White House, Office of the Press Secretary, Crawford, Texas, November 23, 2004.

15. Branigin, "U.S. Rejects Tally, Warns Ukraine."

16. Steven Pifer, "European Mediators and Ukraine's Orange Revolution," *Problems of Post-Communism* 54, no. 6 (November/December 2007), pp. 28–42. Much of the rest of this section draws from this article.

17. C. J. Chivers, "A Crackdown Averted: How Top Spies in Ukraine Changed the Nation's Path," *New York Times,* January 15, 2005, p. A1.

18. Ibid.

19. "Powell Hails Ukraine Election as 'Historic Moment for Democracy,'" Department of State, IIP Digital, December 27, 2004.

Chapter 7

1. "A New Century Agenda for the Ukrainian-American Strategic Partnership: Joint Statement by President George W. Bush and President Victor Yushchenko," White House, Office of the Press Secretary, April 4, 2005.

2. Peter Finn, "Ukraine's Yanukovych Halts NATO Entry Talks," *Washington Post,* September 15, 2006.

3. "Join NATO and We'll Target Missiles at Kiev, Putin Warns Ukraine," *The Guardian,* February 12, 2008.

4. CQ Transcripts, "Bush and Yushchenko Remark on Ukraine and NATO," *Washington Post,* April 1, 2008 (www.washingtonpost.com/wp-dyn/content/article/2008/04/01/AR2008040101600.html).

5. NATO, "Bucharest Summit Declaration, Issued by the Heads of State and Government participating in the meeting of the North Atlantic Council in Bucharest on 3 April 2008."

6. For an account of the questions raised by the Bucharest summit's declaration regarding Ukraine, see James Sherr, "Ukraine and NATO: Desti-

nation Unknown," *The World Today* 64 (August–September 2008), pp. 30–32 (http://gale.cengage.co.uk/images/upload/ChathamHouse/casestudies/russia -ukraine/sherr-ukraine-and-nato-destination-unknown-2008.pdf).

7. "United States-Ukraine Charter on Strategic Partnership," Bureau of European and Eurasian Affairs, Department of State, December 19, 2008.

8. Andrew Wilson, "What Are the Ukrainians Playing At?" European Council on Foreign Relations, April 30, 2010 (www.ecfr.eu/article/%20 commentary_what_are_the_ukrainians_playing_at).

9. For a fuller account of how quickly things changed within Ukraine and in Kyiv's foreign relations in the first months of the Yanukovych presidency, see James Sherr, "The Mortgaging of Ukraine's Independence," Chatham House Briefing Paper, August 2010 (www.chathamhouse.org/sites /files/chathamhouse/public/Research/Russia and Eurasia/bp0810_sherr .pdf).

10. Will Englund, "Gas Deal Disputed in Ukraine," *Washington Post,* December 11, 2010 (www.washingtonpost.com/wp-dyn/content/article /2010/12/10/AR2010121007029.html).

11. Hillary Rodham Clinton and Catherine Ashton, "Ukraine's Troubling Trends," *New York Times,* October 24, 2012 (www.nytimes.com /2012/10/25/opinion/hillary-clinton-catherine-ashton-ukraines-election .html?_r=0).

12. See Andrew Wilson, *Ukraine Crisis: What It Means for the West* (Yale University Press, 2014), for a fuller account of the Maydan Revolution and how the Ukraine-Russia conflict unfolded in 2014.

13. Michael R. Gordon, "U.S. and Russia Agree on Pact to Defuse Ukraine Crisis," *New York Times,* April 17, 2014, (www.nytimes.com/2014/04/18 /world/europe/ukraine-diplomacy.html?_r=0).

14. David Hershenhorn, "Brash Ukrainian Mogul Prepares to Fight U.S. Bribery Charges," *New York Times,* May 6, 2014 (www.nytimes.com/2014 /05/07/world/europe/brash-ukrainian-mogul-prepares-to-fight-us-bribery -charges.html?_r=0).

15. "United States Assessment of the Downing of MH 17 and Its Aftermath," Embassy of the United States, Kyiv, Ukraine, July 19, 2014 (http:// ukraine.usembassy.gov/statements/asmt-07192014.html).

16. "Minsk Agreement: Full Text in English," UNIAN News, February 12, 2015 (www.unian.info/politics/1043394-minsk-agreement-full-text -in-english.html).

17. "Remarks by Vice President Joe Biden to the Ukrainian Rada," White House, Office of the Press Secretary, December 9, 2015 (www .whitehouse.gov/the-press-office/2015/12/09/remarks-vice-president-joe -biden-ukrainian-rada).

18. Steve Clemons, "The Biden Doctrine: Has the Vice President Made a Lasting Contribution in Foreign Policy?" *The Atlantic*, August 22, 2016 (www.theatlantic.com/international/archive/2016/08/biden-doctrine /496841/).

Chapter 8

1. See Ivo Daalder, Michele Flournoy, John Herbst, and others, "Preserving Ukraine's Independence, Resisting Russian Aggression: What the United States and NATO Must Do," Atlantic Council, Brookings Institution, and Chicago Council on Global Affairs, February 2015.

Index